AN APARTHEID OASIS?
Agriculture and Rural Livelihoods in Venda

THE LIBRARY OF PEASANT STUDIES

An Apartheid Oasis?

AGRICULTURE AND RURAL LIVELIHOODS IN VENDA

EDWARD LAHIFF

Routledge
Taylor & Francis Group

LONDON AND NEW YORK

First published 2000 by Frank Cass Publisher

Published 2019 by Routledge
2 Park Square, Milton Park, Abingdon, Oxon OX14 4RN
52 Vanderbilt Avenue, New York, NY 10017

First issued in paperback 2019

Routledge is an imprint of the Taylor & Francis Group, an informa business

British Library Cataloguing in Publication Data

Lahiff, Edward
   An apartheid oasis? : agriculture and rural livelihoods in
Venda. – (The library of peasant studies; no. 20)
   1. Agriculture – Economic aspects – South Africa – Venda
   2. Agricultural development projects – South Africa – Venda
   3. Venda (South Africa) – Rural conditions   4. Venda (South
Africa) – Economic conditions – 20th century
   I. Title
   338.1'0968257

Library of Congress Cataloging in Publication Data

Lahiff, Edward
   An apartheid oasis? : agriculture and rural livelihoods in Venda /
Edward Lahiff
   p.   cm. – (The library of peasant studies; no. 20)
   Includes bibliographical references and index.
   ISBN 0 7146 5137 0 (cloth)
   1. Agriculture – Economic aspects – South Africa – Venda   2.
Agricultural development projects – South Africa – Venda   3. Venda (South
Africa) – Rural conditions.   I. Title.   II. Series
   HD9017.A33 V465 2000
   338.1'096825'7 – dc21
                                        00-060359

Typeset by Regent Typesetting, London

ISBN 13: 978-1-138-96365-8 (pbk)
ISBN 13: 978-0-7146-5137-8 (hbk)
ISSN 1462–219X

For Peter Ntsako

Contents

List of Tables

List of Figures

Maps

List of Abbreviations

ACB	Agricultural Credit Board
Agriven	Venda Agricultural Corporation Limited
ANC	African National Congress
BENSO	Bureau for Economic Research: Co-operation and Development
CONTRALESA	Congress of Traditional Leaders of South Africa
DB	Division Box
DBSA	Development Bank of Southern Africa
ha	hectare
GDP	Gross Domestic Product
GGP	Gross Geographic Product
GNI	Gross National Income
IDT	Independent Development Trust
ISCW	Institute for Soil, Climate and Water
l	litre
LAPC	Land and Agriculture Policy Centre (Johannesburg)
LSU	Large Stock Unit
M	Million
NGO	Non-Governmental Organisation
NTK	*Noord-Transvaalse Kooperasie* (Northern Transvaal Co-operative)
PAC	Pan-Africanist Congress
PTO	Permission to Occupy
R	Rand (unit of currency)
RAU	Rand Afrikaans University
RDP	Reconstruction and Development Programme
RSA	Republic of South Africa
SA	South Africa/South African
SALDRU	Southern Africa Labour and Development Research Unit
SAIRR	South African Institute of Race Relations
SANCO	South African National Civics Organisation
UDF	United Democratic Front
Univen	University of Venda
VDC	Venda Development Corporation
ZAR	*Zuid-Africkaansche Republiek*

Acknowledgements

This study was made possible by a grant from the Economic and Social Research Council (UK). It is based on a doctoral thesis conducted under the supervision of Professor Henry Bernstein at the School of Oriental Studies, University of London. Thanks are due to Ms Catherine Lawrence of SOAS who prepared the maps. Very special thanks are due to Henry Bernstein for his inspiration and support over many years.

1

Introduction

This study is concerned with the conditions under which small farmers in the former 'homelands'[1] of South Africa obtain their livelihood. It focuses particularly on Venda, one of the smallest and least known of the homelands, and includes a case study of a long-standing irrigation scheme at Tshiombo. The objective of the study is to gain an understanding of how small-scale agriculture contributes to household livelihoods in the homelands during the transition from apartheid to democracy and to identify areas in which the state, or other parties, can intervene to redress the historic neglect of black agriculture and develop the rural economy.

This chapter provides a brief historical introduction to the problematic addressed by the study and an overview of the chapters that follow.

1.1 APARTHEID AND RURAL UNDERDEVELOPMENT: THE PROBLEM OF THE HOMELANDS

The formal ending of apartheid, and the coming to power of the country's first democratically-elected government in April 1994, raised the possibility of fundamental social and economic change in South Africa and promised 'a better life for all'.[2] The nature of the negotiated end to white minority rule has, however, left much of the structure of racial inequality intact, particularly in areas such as income, land-holding, and access to health, education and welfare services, which raises serious questions about the ability of the new government to effect radical social or economic change.

Of all the manifestations of inequality and oppression under apartheid, none was as stark, or potentially as enduring, as the territorial separation of people along racial lines. The establishment of separate rural homelands for the African population was central to the aims of 'grand apartheid' and an essential component of the system of economic exploitation and political repression which sustained the power and wealth of the white minority. Overcoming the legacy of this extreme form of racial oppression is probably the greatest challenge facing the 'new' South Africa.

The roots of territorial segregation lie in the uneven pattern of colonial dispossession and settler occupation of the nineteenth century. Sizeable tracts of land – mainly in the eastern half of what became South Africa – continued to be occupied by native peoples, defeated but not entirely subdued, with much of their pre-existing socio-political and economic system intact [*Welsh*, 1971: 29; *Thompson*, 1995: 109].

With the rise of a vast mining industry in the late nineteenth century, these 'native reserves' took on a new significance as reservoirs of migrant labour. The racial order that had characterised pre-industrial settler society found new expression in highly repressive forms of labour organisation on the mines, particularly the system of male-only compounds which arose first on the diamond mines at Kimberley in the 1880s and spread to the much larger gold-fields on the Witwatersrand [*Turrell*, 1987: 149]. By the late 1890s, this tightly regulated system of oscillating migration by male African workers between the mines and the rural periphery (including adjoining territories such as Mozambique and Basutoland) had become established as what Crush, Jeeves and Yudelman [1991: 2] describe as 'one of the key distinguishing features of South African industrialisation'.

The minerals revolution had a profound effect on the agrarian economy of southern Africa, stimulating an enormous demand for land, labour and agricultural commodities [*Bundy*, 1979: 67]. While this created opportunities for many black peasant producers, it also intensified settler pressure on African lands, and gave rise to long-running attempts by white farmers to restrict competition from independent African producers and to extract additional labour from Africans residing on white farms [*Keegan*, 1986: 12].

The drive by an expanding capitalist economy to coerce African peasants into employment was given legal sanction by all four settler polities – the British colonies of the Cape and Natal and the Afrikaner Republics of the Transvaal and the Orange Free State. As Bundy puts it:

> Both the farmer and the mine-owner perceived in the late nineteenth century the need to apply extra-economic pressure to the African peasantry; to break down the peasant's 'independence', increase his wants, and to induce him to part more abundantly with his labour, but at no increased price [*Bundy*, 1979: 115].

The defeat of the Boer republics by British imperial forces in the Anglo-Boer War (1899–1902) paved the way for more systematic control of African labour on mines and farms and the imposition of a more comprehensive system of racial segregation [*Marks and Trapido*, 1981: 69; *Greenberg*, 1980: 187]. The compromise between Boer and Briton represented in the political sphere by the Act of Union (1910) was mirrored by what Trapido [1971: 311] has called 'the uneasy union of "gold and maize"', which united mining and agrarian capital, buttressed by the power of the colonial state, in the suppression of political freedom and the systematic exploitation of (predominantly black) labour. Under the governments of Botha (1910–19) and Smuts (1919–24), the stratification of mine labour along racial lines was given legal sanction and labour contracts for black workers made subject to the criminal law. The migrant labour system was regulated through an oppressive system of 'pass laws' which controlled the recruitment and movement of workers, particularly between rural and urban areas, while political rights for blacks were systematically suppressed [*Dubow*, 1989: 39]. In the wake of the white workers' 'Rand Revolt' of 1922, and the growing tide of 'poor whites' pouring into the cities, Hertzog's Pact government (1924–33) further enforced the two-tier labour force under the so-called 'job colour bar', or 'civilised labour policy', and banned black trade unions [*Hirson*, 1989: 29]. Lacey [1981: 10] sees this increasingly sophisticated system of racial segregation as an attempt to separate white workers from the mass of the working class and so meet the demand of white capital for cheap, disenfranchised and 'super-exploitable' black labour.

The 'native reserves' were central to the policy of segregation, both as a rural base for migrant workers and as places where the African population could be controlled under a separate legal and administrative system. The importance of the reserves to the development of the industrial economy has been theorised by Wolpe [1972: 432] in terms of the articulation of two modes of production. By providing migrant labourers with a supplementary source of livelihood (through agriculture) and a range of welfare services (through the extended family), Wolpe argues, the 'African redistributive economies' of the reserves made it possible for employers to pay their workers less than the true cost of 'reproduction' and minimised the costs to the state of providing housing and other services to migrants and their dependants:

> the rate of surplus value and hence the rate of capital accumulation depended above all upon the maintenance of the pre-capitalist relations of production in the Reserve economy which provided a portion of the means of reproduction of the migrant labour force.

Central to Wolpe's argument, however, is that the development of capitalism tends to undermine other modes of production over time, leading to ever greater efforts on the part of the South African state to sustain the reserves.

The reserves were defined by two key pieces of legislation, the 'Land Acts' of 1913 and 1936, which between them divided the country into legally designated 'white' and 'black' territories and imposed severe restrictions on the property rights of blacks, especially so-called 'squatters' (tenants and sharecroppers) on white farms. Despite their repeal in 1991, the division of territory along racial lines imposed under these Acts effectively defines the pattern of land-holding in rural South Africa to this day.

Under the terms of the 1913 Natives' Land Act, seven per cent of the national territory was reserved for exclusive black occupation and Africans were prohibited from acquiring land outside these 'scheduled' areas. For Bundy [1979: 213], this 'freezing' of African land-holding was intended to inhibit the process of class differentiation within the reserves and prevent the emergence of either a class of black commercial farmers or a landless proletariat, each of which posed its own threat to the system of racial segregation and migrant labour. The 1913 Act also attempted to abolish the widespread practice of sharecropping by black 'squatters' on white-owned farms, particularly in the Orange Free State, and other forms of tenancy that did not involve at least 90 days of compulsory labour service to the landlord. Keegan [1986: 194] argues that the intention of such measures was not to destroy black tenant farmers, 'but to harness their labour, their skill and their capital resources more fully to the profit of the landlords'.

The 1936 Native Trust and Land Act allowed for the extension of the reserves up to a total of 13 per cent of the national territory and created the South African Native Trust (later Development Trust) with responsibility for acquiring the necessary ('released') land. In a reversal of earlier policy, the Trust was also charged with the economic development of the over-crowded and poverty-stricken reserves and preventing what was seen as an imminent economic and ecological crisis [Bundy, 1979: 222]. This led to the highly authoritarian system of 'betterment', which attempted to prevent soil erosion and control cattle numbers in the reserves and in later years was expanded into a comprehensive system of physical planning and 'villagisation' [de Wet, 1995: 40]. Like its predecessor, the 1936 Act combined the allocation of lands to the reserves with a further legal assault on black tenant farmers on white farms through its prohibition of labour tenancy (in favour of a system of wage labour), although opposition from tenants, and some farmers, meant that this provision was not fully enforced for 30 years [Morris, 1976: 334].

While much of the repression of the African population was driven by the desire to mobilise labour for the mines, the political influence of white farmers in the decades following Union meant that their interests were also advanced. In addition to restricting the rights of black tenants on white farms, white farmers benefited from massive state support, including exclusive access to credit and technical services, extension of the railway network and guaranteed prices for their products [Wilson, 1971: 136]. The rapid expansion of the white agricultural sector in the years prior to the Second World War contrasted with the growing crisis of agriculture in the reserves, where the great majority of African households, short of land, labour and capital, and denied access to the increasingly regulated agricultural markets, struggled to achieve even partial subsistence [*Levin and Weiner*, 1991: 88].

The coming to power of the overtly racist National Party in 1948 under the ideological banner of *apartheid*, or 'separate development', marked the beginning of a decisive new phase in the evolution of South Africa's system of racial segregation and in the function of the reserves. Faced with an influx of black people to the cities, drawn by the expansion of industrial employment during and after the Second World War, a rise in militancy by black workers and a continuing crisis of subsistence in the reserves, the new regime greatly increased the range of controls over the black population. The racial stratification of society and economy was entrenched through laws such as the Population Registration Act of 1950, which classified people as either 'White', 'African' 'Coloured' or 'Indian', and a raft of highly repressive measures to tighten controls over the movement, residence, education and employment rights of the 'non-white' majority [*Beinart*, 1994: 147]. The suppression of political rights for Africans which had been effectively achieved with the abolition of the Cape African franchise in 1936 was extended to the 'Coloured' population with their removal from the common electoral roll in 1956.

For Wolpe, the strengthening of the state's repressive apparatus was driven by the wish to conserve the reserves (and hence the whole edifice of white supremacy in state and society) once the destruction of their 'redistributive' economies reached the point where they could no longer contribute to the reproduction of the labour force:

> That is to say, the practice and policy of Separate Development must be seen as the attempt to retain, in a modified form, the structure of the 'traditional' societies, not, as in the past, for the purposes of ensuring an economic supplement to the wages of the migrant labour force, but for the purposes of reproducing and exercising control over a cheap African industrial labour force in or near the 'homelands', not by means of preserving the pre-capitalist mode of production but by the political, social, economic and ideological enforcement of low levels of subsistence [*Wolpe*, 1972: 450].

Under the system of separate development as it evolved in the years after 1948, and especially under Verwoerd from 1958, Africans were to be denied all political rights in 'white' South Africa, where they would be tolerated only as long as they were deemed to be 'economically useful'. Africans were to be made 'citizens' of eight (later ten) ethnically-based 'nations', situated in the reserves, where they would be encouraged to develop separate political institutions and move towards 'independence'. In 1967, the Department of Bantu Administration and Development stated the government's aims thus:

It is accepted Government policy that the Bantu are only temporarily resident in the European areas of the Republic for as long as they offer their labour there. As soon as they become, for one reason or another, no longer fit for work or superfluous in the labour market, they are expected to return to their country of origin or the territory of the national unit where they fit ethnically if they were not born and bred in their homeland (quoted in Platzky and Walker [1985: 193]).

Political power within the homelands was to rest with revamped 'tribal' structures, composed of headmen and chiefs, under the close control of the Department of Bantu Affairs. The basis of tribal administration in the reserves had been established by the 1927 Native Administration Act, but was greatly extended by the 1951 Bantu Authorities Act and the 1959 Promotion of Bantu Self-Government Act which strengthened the political power of the government-appointed Chiefs and created a multi-tiered system of Tribal, Regional and Territorial authorities [Hill, 1964: 15].

The imposition of tribal rule was accompanied by the extension of a much expanded form of 'betterment' to most of the reserves/homelands, involving forced resettlement of villages, strict limits on land for cultivation, and further attempts to reduce the numbers of livestock [Yawitch, 1981: 23]. This was met with violent opposition in places such as Sekhukhuneland, in the northern Transvaal, in 1958 and in Pondoland, in the eastern Cape, in 1960 [Mbeki, 1984: 111]. The demands of rural people also featured prominently in the ANC-led Defiance Campaign of 1952, and in the Freedom Charter of 1955, which stated that 'the land shall be divided among those who work it' [Lodge, 1983: 71].

In the wake of the 1960 Sharpeville massacre, and the banning of anti-apartheid organisations such as the ANC and the PAC, rural revolt was effectively crushed and the South African state accelerated the process of political separation for the reserves. In 1963, the Transkei was the first homeland to be granted 'self-government' and was followed by nine others over the next 20 years.[3] Four of these – Transkei in 1976, Bophuthatswana in 1977, Venda in 1979 and Ciskei in 1981 – eventually achieved the dubious status of 'independence', but even the trappings of statehood could not disguise the complete dependence of these territories on South Africa or the geographic nonsense of their position. At one point, Bophuthatswana was composed of 19 scattered fragments of territory and KwaZulu of 29 major and 41 minor fragments [Thompson, 1995: 191]. While strongly opposed by the majority of the black population, the homelands policy was supported by an emerging stratum of compliant, and often corrupt, tribal chiefs, government officials and petty capitalists within the reserves.

As the homelands policy began to take effect in the 1960s and 1970s, upwards of 3.5 million 'surplus' people were forcibly removed to the homelands, including tenants evicted from white farms, residents of mission stations and other so-called 'black spots' outside the homelands, and people 'endorsed out' of towns and cities [*Platzky and Walker*, 1985: 9]. Millions more, both in the reserves and in 'white' South Africa, were stripped of their South African citizenship.

Economically, the homelands remained extremely poor and underdeveloped, and heavily dependent on remittances from migrant workers in industrial South Africa and direct transfers from the South African government. The communal system of land tenure, under the control of the Tribal Authorities, meant, at least until the 1970s, that most households in the homelands had some access to arable or grazing land but the small size of plots and herds meant that agriculture contributed a relatively minor proportion of household subsistence requirements in most cases [*Simkins*, 1981: 262]. In the wake of the Tomlinson Commission's Report [*Union of South Africa*, 1955], some efforts were made to develop small-holder agriculture, including an expansion of the area under irrigation, but government policy towards the reserves was still largely concerned with 'betterment'. Efforts were also made to establish a small elite of 'commercial' farmers on 'economic' holdings, mainly on land acquired by the Native Trust, who became the main beneficiaries of homeland agricultural policy in the 1970s and 1980s [*Watkinson*, 1996: 48].

From the mid-1970s, agricultural policy in the homelands began to focus on the development of a range of large-scale agricultural projects, mainly under the control of newly-created parastatal (semi-state) organisations but also in collaboration with private-sector investors. Most were highly inefficient and were in decline by the late 1980s, but they did create some opportunities for 'accumulation from above' by a small elite allied to the homeland governments [*Cooper*, 1991: 253]. Agriculture in the homelands today is commonly perceived as 'subsistence' (or even 'sub-subsistence')-oriented and extremely marginal in terms of the white-dominated agricultural sector. Local studies over many years, however, have shown that agriculture continues to play a significant part in the livelihoods of large numbers of households. Bernstein [1996: 38] argues that far from being homogeneous, the agricultural sector is highly differentiated along lines of class, gender and generation (age), with substantial numbers of farmers producing for the market, both 'formal' and 'informal'.

By the final years of apartheid, the homelands were home to over half the black population of South Africa (or over 40 per cent of the entire South African population) and were characterised by extremely low incomes and high rates of infant mortality, malnutrition and illiteracy relative to the rest of the country [*Wilson and Ramphele*, 1989: 25; *DBSA*, 1993a: 37]. Indeed, the available evidence suggests that South Africa has one of the most unequal distributions of income in the world, and income and material quality of life are strongly correlated with race, location and gender.[4] Whiteford and McGrath [1994: 59] estimate that 67 per cent of black households, heavily concentrated in the former homelands, were living below the official poverty datum line; and, of these, households headed by women were substantially worse off then those headed by men. There is also evidence of an increase in inequality within the black population since the mid-1970s:

> almost all the increased income accruing to the black population has flowed to the richest 20% of black households. Simultaneously, the economic position of the remaining 80% of black households has worsened and in real terms they were poorer in 1991 than in 1975 [*Whiteford and McGrath*, 1994: 74].

Problems of poverty and underdevelopment were greatly compounded by the bankruptcy of many of the homeland governments, and the collapse of many state services, during the political turmoil of the late 1980s and early 1990s [*Murray*, 1994: 66]. Despite the (re)incorporation of the homelands into the new provincial structures in April 1994, many of their institutions, including the Tribal Authorities, the system of communal land tenure and much of the state bureaucracy, remain in place.

Overcoming the legacy of inequality and oppression within the rural areas is one the most pressing challenges facing the new ANC-led government. Demands for a radical redistribution of land and other resources to dispossessed groups were at the heart of the struggle against apartheid, featuring prominently in both the Freedom Charter and the programme of the mass democratic movement during the negotiated transition from apartheid to democracy (1990–94) [*Levin and Weiner*, 1997: 14]. The importance of land reform, especially in terms of economic and social development in rural areas, was reflected in the ANC's blueprint for power, the 1994 *Reconstruction and Development Programme* (RDP):

> A national land reform programme is the central and driving force of a programme of rural development. Such a programme aims to redress effectively the injustices of forced removals and the historical denial of access to land. It aims to ensure security of tenure for rural dwellers. And in implementing the national land reform programme, and through the provision of support services, the democratic government will build the economy by generating large-scale employment, increasing rural incomes and eliminating overcrowding [*ANC*, 1994: 2.4.2].

Land reform is supported, at least at the rhetorical level, by much of the political spectrum, both as a means of achieving economic redistribution and growth and, for some on the left, as an essential feature of the democratisation of post-apartheid society. For Murray and Williams [1994: 315] 'the link between access to land and political freedom in South Africa is a fundamental one', while Levin and Weiner [1996: 93] see reform in this area as a necessary part of the national democratic revolution:

> Transforming existing land and agrarian relations presents the new democratic South African government with one of its major challenges. Colonial land dispossession and apartheid forced removals lie at the heart of the repressive regime which the national liberation movement sought to overthrow. A decisive transformation of land and agrarian relations is thus intimately bound up with the construction of a new democratic order in South Africa.

Even relatively conservative commentators such as the World Bank [1994: 157] view land and agricultural reform as essential to overcoming the 'racially based distortions' of the past, if only to avoid more radical action by the rural population: 'significant changes in the structure, ownership, and operation of the agricultural sector are necessary in order to address the serious problems of efficiency and equity'.

Since coming to power, however, the ANC-led government has adopted a broadly neo-liberal approach to economic policy, and has eschewed many of the demands of its more radical supporters for nationalisation or expropriation of white-owned lands [*Murray*, 1994: 23]. Indeed, Bernstein [1996: 34] speaks of 'the strategic lacuna on the agrarian question in the programme of the South African liberation movement and of its current leadership (inside and outside government) and the apparent absence, or weakness, of a mass democratic politics of agrarian reform'. This has led to what Levin and Weiner [1997: 7] describe as 'a triumph of neo-liberalism in the land debate and the privileging of the market as the central mechanism for land redistribution'.

Overall, the long history of racial oppression and rural deprivation, and the very cautious approach to reform on the part of the new government, suggests that the many social and economic problems associated with the homelands are likely to remain a feature of the 'new' South Africa for a long time to come.

I.2 OUTLINE OF THE STUDY

This study starts from the position that small-scale agriculture in the homelands is important, both as a contemporary source of livelihoods and as a central part of any reform process aimed at alleviating poverty and developing the rural economy. During the apartheid years, black farmers suffered systematic discrimination at the hands of the state and, until very recently, were widely ignored in the academic literature. The resulting lack of detailed knowledge about the activities and aspirations of black farmers has been identified by Levin and Weiner [1994: 19] as a potential obstacle to agrarian transformation in South Africa: 'The underutilisation of existing research, and numerous research gaps that still exist, are problems which challenge the viability of the rural restructuring process.'

The aim of this study is, therefore, to fill part of that gap by investigating the agricultural economy and its contribution to household livelihoods in one small part of the homelands during the transition from apartheid to democracy. The area selected for in-depth study was the Tshiombo irrigation scheme, located in the (former) homeland of Venda, in the north-eastern corner of the Transvaal. Very little has been written in any discipline about Venda and no detailed study has been conducted of the Tshiombo scheme, one of the oldest and largest projects of its type in southern Africa. The lack of reliable information about Tshiombo, and Venda in general, was one reason for selecting this particular site, but also important was what appeared to be the relatively high agricultural potential of the area.

The study is based on an extensive survey of the relevant literature, and a survey of 83 plot-holders on the Tshiombo scheme, focusing on patterns of land-holding, agricultural activities and the various means by which rural livelihoods are obtained. This is contextualised within a wider study of Venda, in terms of its history and current social and economic conditions, with particular emphasis on the range of agricultural activities and institutions. These local and regional aspects are informed by a review of the literature on small-scale agriculture in the homelands, which, taken together, allow for a discussion of the prospects for small-scale agriculture and rural reform in South Africa more generally.

The structure of the study is as follows:

Chapter 2 consists of a broad survey of the literature on small-scale agriculture in the homelands over the last twenty years, focusing on the distribution of arable land, patterns of crop and livestock farming and the composition of rural livelihoods. It attempts to show the range of agricultural conditions existing in different parts of the country but also highlights the many common features that have emerged across the homelands.

Chapter 3 traces the history of Venda from pre-colonial times to the end of apartheid and provides an introduction to the physical geography and contemporary social and economic conditions in the area.

Chapter 4 analyses the agricultural sector, both 'formal' and 'informal', in Venda, using official reports and a range of local studies. Together with Chapter 3, it provides the context for the more detailed discussion of conditions on the Tshiombo irrigation scheme in the chapters that follow.

Chapter 5 provides an introduction to Tshiombo and the irrigation scheme and a discussion of the design and methodology of the household survey.

Chapter 6 contains a detailed analysis of household structure, income sources and agricultural assets at Tshiombo. This includes individual examples of land acquisition and estimates of income from livestock.

Chapter 7 focuses more specifically on crop production at Tshiombo, taking in issues of land use, supply and use of inputs, individual estimates of crop output, marketing and agricultural services (state and non-state). Particular attention is paid to the wide differentials in crop output between households in the survey sample.

Chapter 8 concludes the Tshiombo case study with an analysis of household incomes from all sources. This is followed by a discussion of the prospects for reform of the local agricultural economy.

Chapter 9 summarises the main findings of the study, relating the information gained from the Tshiombo case study to the wider issues of agricultural reform and rural development in South Africa.

NOTES

1. The term 'homeland' is used throughout this study to refer to those rural areas officially designated for occupation by the black (African) population of South Africa under the system of extreme racial segregation known as apartheid. They were formerly referred to as 'native reserves' and later, disparagingly, as 'Bantustans', but the term 'homeland' is preferred as it was found to be the usual term used by people resident within them.
2. ANC election slogan, 1994.
3. The ten homelands were Bophuthatswana, Ciskei, Gazankulu, KaNgwane, KwaNdebele, KwaZulu, Lebowa, QwaQwa, Transkei and Venda (see Map 1).
4. The Gini Coefficient, which measures the distribution of income between the richest and poorest sections of the population, is more extreme for South Africa than for any other country on which data is available [*Whiteford and McGrath*, 1994: 1]. In terms of race, whites receive more than 12 times the per capita income of the black population, with the smaller Asian and coloured population groups occupying intermediate positions.

MAP I: SOUTH AFRICAN HOMELANDS

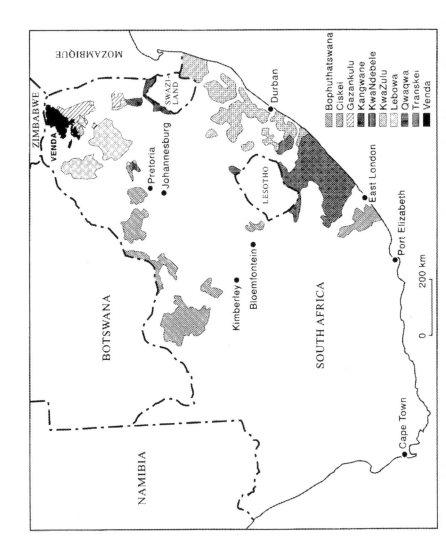

Bophuthatswana
Ciskei
Gazankulu
Kangwane
KwaNdebele
KwaZulu
Lebowa
Qwaqwa
Transkei
Venda

2

Land, Agriculture and Rural Livelihoods in the Homelands

Chapter 1 has traced the broad historical processes which led to the emergence of the homelands and the creation of a racist and highly unequal economic and political order in South Africa. This chapter looks in detail at land-holding and the contribution of small-scale agriculture to livelihoods within the homelands. It draws on a range of literature, including detailed local studies, from the fields of rural sociology, anthropology and agricultural economics to form a picture of the small-holder sector at the end of apartheid.

Conventional approaches to land and agriculture in South Africa emphasise the contrast between 'white' (or 'commercial') and 'black' (or 'subsistence') farming sectors, based on wide differences in land-holding patterns, output and 'efficiency'. Nattrass [1988: 98] is typical of this approach: 'The two sections of South African agriculture are so different from one another that when one moves from a White-owned modern capital using farming sector to a Black subsistence oriented and tribally organised farming area, it is almost like stepping through a time warp.'

At the aggregate level, there is certainly much to distinguish agriculture in the homelands from that found in other parts of the country. In 1988, for example, the agricultural sector contributed 5.3 per cent of South Africa's GDP, and over 90 per cent of this came from 59,000 white-controlled farming units, averaging roughly 1,500 hectares each [*Cooper*, 1988: 48; *van Zyl and van Rooyen*, 1991]. By contrast, somewhere in the order of 1.5 million households in the homelands had access to arable land, averaging around one hectare each, plus a share of communal grazing (see below). Output per worker in white agriculture is estimated to be in the order of twenty times higher than amongst black small-holders, and output per hectare is estimated to be 3.5 times as much [*Nattrass*, 1988: 100].

White agriculture is further distinguished by its institutional strength, and the degree of financial support and protection it has received from the state over many decades. By means of exclusive farmers' unions, large-scale co-operatives and official marketing boards, white farmers have been able to dominate the agricultural economy. State institutions such as the Agricultural Credit Board, the Land Bank and the Department of Agriculture have channelled vast financial and technical assistance to individual white farmers as well as to their organisations and regions [Marcus, 1989: 24]. While large-scale agriculture has been subjected to some reduction in direct state support and the liberalisation of agricultural markets since the mid-1980s, to the detriment of some more marginal producers, it has not significantly weakened the position of white agriculture (or agri-business) as a whole [Bernstein, 1996b]. By contrast, agriculture in the homelands is commonly portrayed as under-developed, unorganised, poorly capitalised, and contributing little in terms of food or cash income to homeland residents [Nattrass, 1988: 112; Bembridge, 1990: 22].

The existence of two separate and distinct forms of agriculture in South Africa has been called into question in recent years, as more critical studies of white and black agriculture, and their histories, have been undertaken. The attack on the conventional view began with the 'new social history' of the 1970s and 1980s, particularly the work of Bundy [1979], Keegan [1986] and Beinart [1982], which convincingly demonstrated the common origins of, and intimate links between, the 'two' agricultures in the late nineteenth and early twentieth centuries. The reappraisal of agriculture in the homelands in the post-1948 period began with the work of Lipton [1977], who challenged the view of African agriculture contained in the report of the official Tomlinson Commission [Union of South Africa, 1955], arguing that productivity in black agriculture was higher than generally believed, and comparable, in many areas, to that of white agriculture. Since the mid-1980s, the work of Cooper [1988], de Klerk [1984] and Marcus [1989], and a group associated with the Development Bank of Southern Africa (DBSA), amongst others, has greatly expanded our knowledge of black and white agriculture, and exposed the wide range of conditions, and many similarities, that exist within them.

Despite this advance, Levin and Weiner [1991: 90] argue that our know-ledge of both white and black agriculture remains very limited and marked by misunderstandings, with major implications for policy-making in the post-apartheid era: 'Current agrarian restructuring debates are proceeding faster than our understanding of the material realities currently evident on white farms and in black rural areas. The consequence is that agricultural develop-ment strategies presented are characterised by a weak empirical base.' Drawing on work by Cooper and others, these authors draw particular atten-tion to what they call 'uneven development between and within white and black agricultural areas'. White agriculture, it is argued, can be divided into a productive core and a large, unproductive periphery, where government subsidies have led to inefficient and inappropriate use of resources, especially land. By the same token, agriculture within the homelands has changed and diversified as a result of government action and the influx of white agricultural capital: 'There is evidence that some agricultural development is taking place in the bantustans with aggregate output increasing, and that agrarian differentiation is in process.' Similarly, Bernstein [1996: 28] draws attention to the emergence of a class of black petty commodity producers and larger capitalist farmers within (and occasionally outside) the former homelands, albeit against a background of growing landlessness.

2.2 LAND AND PEOPLE IN THE HOMELANDS

Of a total South African land area of 122 million hectares (1.2 million square kilometres), approximately 16.7 million hectares, or 13.7 per cent, was allocated to the homelands in 1985 [Nattrass, 1988: 99]. Within this area, the population, for 1991, was estimated at 17.4 million people, or 47 per cent of the South African population [SAIRR, 1994: 83]. Approximately 99.8 per cent of this group were classified as black (African), as compared to 46 per cent of the non-homeland population.

Conventional wisdom for many years held that the homelands, concentrated as they were in the wetter, eastern portion of South Africa, contained a favourable proportion of good quality arable land [Union of South Africa, 1955: 47; Houghton, 1973: 80].[1] This view has been challenged by authors such as Levin and Weiner [1991: 92], and van Zyl and van Rooyen [1991: 184], who suggest that as much as 15.6 per cent of non-homeland land is arable, compared to only 11.8 per cent of the homelands. This would give the homelands just 11.1 per cent of South Africa's arable land once factors such as rainfall, slope and soil are taken into account. Moreover, the quality of land in the two areas may not be comparable: 65 per cent of arable land outside the homelands is considered to be 'of medium to high potential' (mainly concentrated in Natal and the eastern Transvaal), compared to only 50 per cent within the homelands [van Zyl and van Rooyen, 1991: 184]. Levin and Weiner, [1991: 92] put it thus:

> Generalisations about South Africa's agricultural potential are misleading. Approximately half of the country receives less than 400mm of rain annually, and is therefore unsuited for dryland production. A disaggregated analysis of the eastern (well-watered) half of the country shows that designated white farming areas have significantly greater agricultural potential than adjacent bantustans.

In common with most other aspects of life in the homelands, information regarding the distribution of land tends to be incomplete and unreliable. The Tomlinson Commission [*Union of South Africa*, 1955: 85] calculated that the total area of land in the then 'reserves' was equivalent to 32.4 *morgen* (27.9 hectares) per household, including communal grazing, a figure which, the Commission observed, had not changed significantly since the beginning of the century. Amongst households with land, the average cultivated area was found to be 2.2 *morgen* (1.9 hectares) per household in 'high rainfall mixed farming regions', 3.5 *morgen* (3 hectares) in 'low rainfall mixed farming regions', and 4.2 *morgen* (3.6 hectares) in 'pastoral regions' [*Union of South Africa*, 1955: 85]. No estimate was given of the proportion of households without land.

In the decades since the Tomlinson Report, all the available sources point to a dramatic fall in the size of average land-holding, and an increase in the proportion of landless households. Between 1970 and 1985, the population of the homelands at least doubled (from around 7 million to 14 million people), with no more than a marginal increase in land area (under ten per cent) [*Steenkamp*, 1989: 15]. Natural population increase, forced removals from 'white' areas (see below), and the redrawing of homeland boundaries to include a number of densely populated areas (such as KwaMashu and Umlazi in KwaZulu-Natal), meant that the proportion of the black population officially domiciled in the homelands increased from 39.1 per cent in 1960 to 52.7 per cent in 1980 [*Platzky and Walker*, 1985: 18].

Recent estimates suggest that the total arable land in the homelands is only sufficient to provide each household (averaging six persons) with approximately one hectare (*Cobbett*, 1987: 66; *Tapson*, 1990: 566), but, as the following table shows, this figure varies considerably between homelands, ranging from 0.2 hectares per household in QwaQwa to 1.5 hectares in Transkei.

Obviously, these figures represent only the potential distribution, whereas in fact, a substantial proportion of households are known to be landless or near landless. While no precise figures are available for landlessness in the homelands, estimates of 40–50 per cent of households are commonly cited [*Bembridge*, 1990: 18; *Levin and Weiner*, 1991: 92], with major differences within and between the homelands. Cooper [1988: 95] puts the proportion of landless households in the most densely populated homelands, QwaQwa and KwaNdebele, as high as four out of five.

The pattern of land-holding and land use in the homelands has been directly influenced by the policies and actions of the South African state (in its various forms) in pursuit of racial segregation and the promotion of an oppressive migrant labour system (see Chapter 1). State policy on land in the reserves/homelands since 1948 has been based on a number of key elements, described by Hendricks [1990: 162] as the 'three rural pillars of Apartheid' – namely the so-called communal form of tenure, the system of tribal administration ('the chieftaincy'), and various forms of rural planning and development, generally referred to as 'betterment'. To these may be added a fourth – the forced removal of millions of black people from 'white' farms and towns to the reserves/homelands, which began in earnest in the Free State with the Natives Land Act of 1913, and accelerated dramatically throughout the country in the 1960s and 1970s. All of these elements have had a direct impact on the distribution and use of land within the homelands and are worth considering in some detail.

TABLE 2.1
DISTRIBUTION OF ARABLE LAND AND POPULATION
IN THE HOMELANDS, 1985

Homeland	Surface Area ('000s ha)	Arable Land ('000s ha)	Population ('000s)	Number of Households ('000s)	Arable Land per H'hold (ha)
Ciskei	650	75	750	125	0.6
Transkei	4,355	754	3,000	500	1.5
KwaZulu	3,316	565	4,382	730	0.8
Venda	620	65	460	77	0.8
Lebowa	2,454	347	2,157	360	1.0
Gazankulu	773	65	620	103	0.6
Bophuthatswana	4,000	400	1,721	287	1.4
KaNgwane	300	36	448	75	0.5
KwaNdebele	197	24	286	48	0.5
QwaQwa	62	7	209	35	0.2
TOTAL	16,727	2,338	14,034	2,341	1.0

Source: Cobbett [1987: 63].

Tenure

The great majority of land in the homelands is held under some form of communal tenure. Other tenurial forms include freehold land held by individuals and groups, including church missions, and state land, but these account for relatively small areas. For example, in KwaZulu in 1976, 177,000 hectares (5 per cent of the total land area) was held under individual freehold title, 320,000 hectares (10 per cent) was Trust[2] farms, and 2,774,728 hectares (85 per cent) was communal tenure [Bromberger, 1988: 207]. For Lebowa, in 1990, nine per cent of land was held under individual tenure, and 91 per cent owned either by the state or by individual tribes, the great majority of which was occupied under communal tenure [*DBSA*, 1991: 5].

Communal land tenure in South Africa is a hybrid form, specific to the homelands, which combines elements of individual and collective property rights. Although having some basis in African customary law, communal tenure has been greatly modified by successive governments over the course of the twentieth century, and alternative forms of land-holding were effectively denied to black people by law. Authors such as Lacey [1981], Haines and Cross [1988] and Hendricks [1990] argue that communal tenure was an essential component of the migrant labour system, facilitating the concentration of the maximum possible number of Africans in the reserves/homelands, preventing the emergence of a stratum of rich peasants or capitalist farmers, and providing the basis for a high degree of social control through the 'tribal' leaders who controlled access to land.

Communal land is nominally owned by the state, but is held 'in trust' by tribal chiefs, and allocated to people living under their jurisdiction on a usufructuary basis [*Budlender and Latsky*, 1991: 121]. It largely comprises land 'scheduled' for occupation by named tribal groups under the 1913 Natives Land Act, and 'released' land acquired by the South African Native Trust under the terms of the 1936 Native Trust and Land Act. By 1986, control of virtually all communal land had passed to the various homeland governments, as part of the transition towards 'independence' [*Cooper*, 1991: 241]. Apart from the Land Acts, the principal legal instrument governing the ownership and occupation of communal land during apartheid was the Black Areas Land Regulations (Proclamation R188) of 1969, but since the abolition of all 'racially based' land laws in 1991,[3] the legal situation is far from clear [*Cross and Rutsch*, 1995: 23].

Under the system of communal tenure, every household within a communal areas has, in principle, a right to a residential site, an arable plot for subsistence purposes, and access to common property resources, such as grazing, but in practice a large proportion of people in communal areas have little or no access to land (see below). The system is 'communal' in the sense that an individual's entitlement to land flows from membership of a socio-political community (a village or tribal area), rather than from private ownership [*Bennett*, 1995: 168]. Once allocated, residential and arable plots are reserved for the exclusive use of the occupying household. Unallocated lands are generally available to community members as a common pool resource (commonage), providing pasture for livestock and other natural resources such as timber, thatching grass, edible fruits and plants, and materials for use in traditional medicine [*Cousins*, 1996:168].

Land for arable and residential purposes is obtained through the tribal chief or, more commonly, the village headman acting on behalf of the chief, who may allocate plots from whatever land is currently available. Under customary law, the right to land usually applies only to male 'household heads', but in practice is sometimes extended to women [*Bennett*, 1995: 170]. Those who obtain land receive a right to the permanent use and benefits of that land, but have no right to sell it and can only transfer it to another family member with permission of the tribal leaders. Tribal Authorities have, in principle, the power to repossess land if it is abandoned, if it is needed for another purpose such as a road or a public building, if it is deemed surplus to the needs of the holders, or in order to punish a landholder for some offence, but examples of such repossession are rare and the communal system is generally seen as a reasonably secure form of tenure [*Bromberger*, 1988: 208]. Prior to the legislative reforms and the virtual collapse of the homeland administrations in the early 1990s, occupants of communal land could register their residential and arable holdings with the local Tribal Authority and Magistrate's office, where they would be officially granted 'Permission to Occupy' (PTO), either verbally or in writing, but this system was not observed in all cases and in recent years has fallen into disarray in many areas [*Westaway*, 1995: 11].

The communal tenure system is at the heart of current debates around reform and development in the former homelands [*Cross and Haines*, 1988; *Levin and Weiner*, 1997]. While the general thrust of this debate is towards the need for more individually-based forms of land-holding (for example, freehold), Cousins (1996: 173) and the Department of Land Affairs (1996: 50), amongst others, stress the benefits of the communal system, especially communal grazing, in terms of social equity and environmental management.

The Chieftaincy

Control over communal land officially lies in the hands of so-called 'traditional leaders' – chiefs and headmen – and remains central to the power of this largely conservative element within rural black society. Tribal structures, having been virtually destroyed over the course of the nineteenth century by military defeat and loss of land, were revived in new forms by the South African government in the period after 1913 as a form of administration and control within the African reserves [*Lacey*, 1981: 6]. The foundations of the system of administration along tribal lines were laid down by the 1927 Native Administration Act, and much expanded during the apartheid era, despite widespread opposition, as what Lodge [1983: 263] describes as 'a cheap repressive administration for a potentially rebellious population'. Tribal Authorities, composed of chiefs and village headmen appointed and paid by the central government, became (and to a certain extent remain) the principal organs of local governance in the homelands, being responsible for the collection of local revenues, payment of pensions and welfare, the administration of justice (through the Tribal Court) and the allocation of communal land.

Many chiefs have been able to use their position – based on a mixture of modern law and 'traditional' status, backed up in many cases by the threat of physical force – to advance their own material interests and those of their supporters, while denying resources, especially land, to those who opposed them [*Haines and Tapscott*, 1988: 166]. They also played an important part in the moves towards 'self-government' and 'independence' for the homelands, and many were able to strengthen their local power base through participation in the homeland government apparatus.

Despite the formal dissolution of the homeland system in 1994, 'traditional leaders' have been able retain many of their powers, particularly with regard to the control of communal land, and the new democratic government has shown a marked reluctance to challenge their authority in this sensitive area [*Maloka*, 1996: 186]. None the less, there is evidence that the position of the chiefs, both as local leaders and in the specific area of land allocation, is being contested by the new local government representatives, elected since November 1995, and emerging 'civic' organisations[4] at the village level [*Levin and Weiner*, 1996: 102; *Lahiff*, 1997: 106].

Betterment

Various forms of 'betterment', or land use planning, have been a feature of government policy in the African rural areas for much of the twentieth century [*Yawitch*, 1981: 9]. De Wet [1995: 53] argues that, prior to 1945, state policy towards the reserves was largely concerned with the conservation of soil and grazing, which gave rise to cattle-culling and various anti-erosion measures. After this date, however, and especially under the National Party government from 1948, the emphasis switched to the restructuring of land-holding and settlement patterns. Widespread loss of land and culling of livestock, along with the imposition of the system of tribally-based local administration, gave rise to sustained resistance throughout the homelands from the 1940s until the early 1960s, notably in the northern Transvaal (1944 and 1958), Witzieshoek, in the Orange Free State (1950) and Pondoland in the Transkei (1960) [*Mbeki*, 1984: 111; *Lodge*, 1983: 71; *Drew*, 1996: 71]. Despite this opposition, elements of betterment were imposed throughout most of the reserves between 1936 and 1990 [*Cooper*, 1991: 242].

Watkinson [1996: 16] argues that, contrary to popular opinion, the apartheid government did effectively endorse the recommendation of the Tomlinson Commission for the creation of a class of full-time 'commercial' farmers on 'economic units' within the homelands. In the heavily populated 'tribal' areas (that is, the pre-1936 reserves), where the majority of households had land rights, the government adopted a policy of 'stabilisation', which involved restructuring the pattern of land-holding and reinforcing 'tribal' rule. Land was demarcated into arable, grazing and residential areas, and scattered settlements were grouped into new, more compact villages. Those without formal land rights, and especially the growing numbers removed to the homelands from white farms and urban areas, were concentrated in 'closer settlements', with small residential plots but no grazing or arable land, where people were expected to live by wage labour alone [de Wet, 1995: 49].

Away from the tribal areas, particularly on land acquired by the Native Trust, government policy under apartheid was to promote a small elite of 'commercial' farmers, and to development large-scale agricultural projects run by the state and private commercial organisations. Watkinson [1996: 43] argues that the small elite of homeland farmers involved in state-run projects and 'settlement schemes' have remained the focus of state policy from the time of the Tomlinson Report to the present day:

> The concept of projects is important, firstly because it provides a more secure form of tenure in times of great flux, and secondly because they provide a means to modernise a select minority through control and supervision. What initial divisions existed between those that gained access to projects and those that were excluded would be expected to increase dramatically over time. This occurs because of the high level of state assistance directed at those within projects and the virtually absent assistance to the majority of people on 'sub-economic' holdings or even mixed farming 'economic units'.

Betterment is widely seen as having failed in its ostensible goals of protecting the environment and promoting homeland agriculture. Its long-term consequences, however, are profound, and take a number of main forms. In the areas that were subjected to betterment, there has emerged a remarkable uniformity of plot sizes amongst those households with land (0.5–1.5 hectares), and a reasonably strict division of land into the three classes – arable, grazing and residential [Yawitch, 1981: 64; de Wet, 1995: 105]. Through surveying and registering plots, betterment has also formalised the system of land-holding and accelerated the emergence of an entirely landless class of people (the majority of households in many areas), based in overcrowded settlements, which have been the fasting growing areas within the homelands over the last 30 years (see below). Finally, it has created a small class of 'commercial' farmers who have been, and remain, the main recipients of state agricultural support, and are today the most prominent spokesmen (virtually all are men) for the interests of black farmers.

Remarkably, betterment schemes were still being implemented, in one shape or another, in parts of the Ciskei in the late 1980s [*McAllister*, 1989: 362] and form the basis of many of the current (post-apartheid) policies on land reform in areas such as the Northern Province.

Forced Removals and Resettlement

Between the formal demarcation of the reserves in 1913, and the formal ending of apartheid in 1994, the policies of successive South African governments have led to the forced removal of millions of black people from 'white' rural and urban areas to the reserves/homelands. Probably the best known estimate of the number removed is the figure of 3.5 million, given by Platzky and Walker [1985: 9] as the number of people subjected to officially sanctioned removals in the period 1960 to 1983, but this is generally thought to be a considerable underestimate.

The policy of forced removals and 'influx controls' had a profound effect on the distribution of the black population within South Africa, and did much to counteract the underlying flow of people from rural to urban areas. As a result, the biggest shift, over time, has been from 'white' (that is, non-homeland) rural areas to the homelands, as shown in the following table.

TABLE 2.2
DISTRIBUTION OF AFRICAN POPULATION IN SOUTH AFRICA, 1950–80 (%)

Year	Urban Areas	Non-Homeland Rural Areas	Homelands
1950	25.4	34.9	39.7
1960	29.6	31.3	39.1
1970	28.1	24.5	47.4
1980	26.7	20.6	52.7

Source: Platzky and Walker [1985: 18].

Removed people lost their land and other property, and if they obtained land in compensation it was often of much inferior size and quality [*Desmond*, 1971: 8; *Yawitch*, 1981: 57]. Those resettled in the homelands had to compete for scarce resources with existing homeland residents, placing additional stress on land and employment, and on hard-pressed welfare, health and educational services. Murray [1987: 312] speaks of a process of 'displaced urbanisation' whereby people who were effectively part of the economy of the large metropolitan centres were forced to reside in newly created 'rural slums' such as parts of KwaNdebele and Botshabelo (in the Free State), which were 'urban' in respect of their population densities, but 'rural' in respect of the absence of proper urban infrastructure or services. There has also been a process of informal urbanisation within the homelands, as growing landlessness and poverty lead people to abandon the rural areas and squat either around the homeland 'capitals' or in 'border areas' within commuting distance of white farms and towns. Van der Berg [1985: 203] suggests that the combined impact of these processes, together with forced relocation and the redrawing of homeland boundaries, has led to effective urbanisation levels of 30 per cent or more in KwaZulu, and over 40 per cent in Ciskei, but more recent estimates suggest that as much as 56 per cent of the homeland population are 'functionally' urbanised [*Bernstein*, 1996: 29].

Patterns of Land-holding

Detailed information on land-holding within the homelands is extremely limited. Official statistics tend to be compiled from a variety of local studies and from estimates prepared by homeland governments, with considerable variation in quality and reliability. Many people with rights to arable land are not using their land (see below), many people are cultivating land to which they have no formal rights, and substantial amounts of cultivation take place on people's house stands, all of which adds to the difficulty of quantifying land-holding in the homelands with any accuracy.

Agricultural statistics, especially in official and quasi-official sources, tend to focus on 'improving' or 'emergent' farmers, often on government-run schemes, who tend to be atypical of the overall population. Weiner, Chimere-Dan and Levin [1994: 23] speak of 'a tendency to conduct surveys in more rural locations where access to land is greater and peri-urban and squatter populations are underrepresented'. In non-government studies, there is a heavy regional bias towards the homelands of the eastern seaboard – KwaZulu, Transkei and Ciskei. Bophuthatswana, with a relatively large population and land area, is relatively poorly studied, while the homelands of the northern and eastern Transvaal – Venda, Gazankulu, Lebowa, KwaNdebele and KaNgwane – and QwaQwa, in the Free State, have been severely neglected.

The following literature review draws on local studies from throughout the homelands, especially those providing empirical data which can be used for comparative purposes. While the individual studies differ enormously in their aims and in their methods, and their results are not always generalisable, they provide some indication of the range of conditions 'on the ground', revealing the wide differences between areas, and between households in the same area, that may be disguised in more general statistics. This section deliberately focuses on independent small-holders (as opposed to state projects or corporate farms), and on 'rural' as opposed to 'urban' areas (formal or informal) within the homelands.

In one of the largest studies of its kind, covering 1,100 households in five rural districts of KwaZulu, May (1989: 5) found that almost a quarter (23.1 per cent) of households had no arable land and the average holding amongst those with land was 1.4 hectares. Only slightly more than half the households (54 per cent) had both land and livestock, which May describes as 'the minimum factors of production necessary for self-sufficient cultivation'. May also identifies a skewed pattern of land-holding, common to nearly all of the studies cited here: the top five per cent of land-holders in the sample controlled 35 per cent of total land, while the bottom 40 per cent controlled just nine per cent. Slightly more than a quarter (28 per cent) of households with land had only 'garden plots' of 0.5 hectares or less.

Ardington [1984: 70], in a study of the Nkandla district of KwaZulu, found that 99 per cent of households had access to arable land, ranging from 0.5 to 3.0 hectares.[5] Average land per household was 1.5 hectares. In a later study of the same households, Cairns and Lea [1990: 82] found that 87 per cent had access to arable land, and that the average holding amongst those with land was 0.88 hectares (ranging from 0.06 to 4.3 hectares), but it is not clear whether the differences between these findings were due to actual changes in land holding or to differences in research methods. An important issue raised by Cairns and Lea, and neglected in many other studies, is the quality of arable land: only 29 per cent of cultivated land in the study area, they argue, could be classified as arable by conventional standards. Similarly, Levin and Weiner [1991: 93] argue that much unsuitable land in Ciskei and KwaZulu is being cultivated: 'In bantustans with significant numbers of agricultural petty commodity producers, more land has been allocated for small-holder production than is potentially arable'.

In the Umzinto district of southern KwaZulu, Mpanza and Nattrass [1987: 16] found that 90 per cent of households had access to arable land, with an average of 0.4 hectares per household. Again, the distribution of land was far from even, with the top four per cent of households holding 24 per cent of land, and the bottom 21 per cent holding just six per cent. Lyne and Nieuwoudt [1991: 193], in a survey of the literature on KwaZulu, reach the following conclusion: 'it is clear that average farm sizes are extremely small in KwaZulu. Measurements recorded in six separate household surveys between 1980 and 1986 indicate that 80 per cent of rural households have "arable" allotments smaller than two hectares and that these allotments are very uniform in size'.

Somewhat larger land-holdings are found in parts of the KwaZulu sugar belt, which has the largest concentration of so-called 'commercial' farmers in the homelands. In a study of two villages in the Noodsberg area, Cobbett [1982: 132] found average land-holdings of 2.5 and 5.0 hectares, of which 50 per cent and 95 per cent respectively were devoted to sugar cane. Once again, plots varied considerably in size. Approximately 40 per cent of households in the villages studied held less than two hectares each, while a small elite (seven per cent of households) held more than five hectares. The biggest single holding was 36 hectares, more than three times the size of any other plot, and belonged to a local chief. Considerably smaller land-holdings are reported from another sugar growing aica, Ocumisa, where average arable land-holdings per household in two study samples were 1.1 and 0.8 hectares respectively [Stewart and Lyne, 1988: 190]. Absolute landlessness in this area was low, however, at 0.8 per cent and 3.3 per cent of households, and the proportion of households with more than one hectare was 35.6 per cent in one sample, and 21.3 per cent in the other. In a village study from the Umlazi district, Makhanya [1994: 144] found average crop land per household of 3.0 hectares, mainly given over to sugar cane, in an area that had successfully resisted betterment.

Somewhat different conditions are described in studies of the homelands of the Eastern Cape. Drawing on work by Baskin and others for the Second Carnegie Inquiry, Wilson and Ramphele [1989: 40] summarise the position in the Transkei as follows:

> Throughout the Transkei, the degree of landless falls generally within the range of 20 to 30 per cent. But a survey in the south-west Transkei found that 42 per cent of the households had no arable plots. In this sample, 29 per cent had vegetable plots only, 19 had arable land only; 40 had both arable land and vegetable plots; 13 had neither. In another part of the Transkei 41 per cent had no arable fields; and 25 had neither fields nor cattle.

Hendricks [1990: 88] found that 64 per cent of households in the Nyandeni area of Pondoland (Transkei) had access to arable land, and that 46 per cent owned cattle, and draws attention to the close correlation between these two groups: 'it is more likely for land-holders rather than the landless to also own cattle . . . access to [arable] land and ownership of livestock is by and large confined to the same group of people'. McAllister [1989: 351], in a village study from the Willowvale district (also in Transkei), found that only about half of the households had access to arable 'fields', but many more were cultivating garden plots adjacent to their homes. Gardens were often as large or larger than fields, reaching up to 2.4 hectares, and in many cases people were found to be neglecting the cultivation of their fields in favour of their gardens. Also in Transkei, a study of Bizana [cited by Beinart 1992: 186] found that

60 per cent of households had access to some arable land, 21 per cent had fields of two hectares or greater, and just two per cent had more than four hectares. On the basis of this and other studies, Beinart speculates that up to 60,000 land-holders may exist in the Transkei, mainly in the coastal districts, 'who until recently have been making a reasonably successful effort to sustain production in difficult circumstances', combining farming with local employment and small businesses.

Like Transkei, Ciskei has been the subject of considerable research over many years. De Wet and McAllister [1983] draw on the findings of the Keiskammahoek Rural Survey to show a decline in arable land-holdings per household in the Chata valley from an average of 2.4 *morgen* (1.72 hectares) per household in 1949 to 0.5 *morgen* (0.43 hectares) in 1981, largely as a result of 'betterment', while the proportion of households without land jumped from ten per cent to 40 per cent. It is highly likely that similar processes have been taking place throughout much of the homelands, but few areas have the necessary data over time to demonstrate it so convincingly. In another study of the Keiskamma area in 1978/79, Bembridge [1987: 104] found a similar degree of landlessness [45 per cent of households], but considerably larger plot sizes, averaging 1.6 hectares per household. In a study of two villages in the Peddie district (also in Ciskei), Steyn [1988: 243] found that 93 per cent of households had access to arable land, and that average holdings were 1.4 and 1.1 hectares respectively. The majority of plots (61 per cent) were one hectare or less, 38 per cent were between one and two hectares, and less than one per cent of households had more than two hectares of arable land.

Information for the other homelands is much more scarce, but what is available confirms the general pattern of small holdings and widespread landlessness identified above, albeit with considerable regional variation. McCaul [1987: 42] quotes a Human Sciences Research Council study of KwaNdebele which found that only four per cent of households had access to agricultural land in 1980. At the other end of the scale, Watkinson [1996: 60], drawing on data from the files of the DBSA, identifies 225 'private commercial farmers' in KwaNdebele, each with an average of 35.4 hectares of arable land, and another 289 farmers newly settled on state land with holdings (including grazing) that averaged 425 hectares each.

In Lebowa, Vink [1986: 102] found that 45.6 per cent of households in the rural areas surveyed had rights to arable land, and a further 20 per cent had access to grazing land only, but says that only one third of those with grazing rights were actually availing of them. Figures from the Development Bank of Southern Africa [1993a: 105] suggest that more than 50 per cent of rural households in Gazankulu are without land, but the rate varies from 85 per cent in Ritavi Magisterial district to 17 per cent in Giyani. Estimates for landlessness in the neighbouring homelands of Venda and Lebowa were 36 per cent and above 50 per cent respectively. Some years earlier, Moody and Golino [1984: 10] estimated that as many as two-thirds of rural households in Venda were without formal rights to land.

Local-level studies provide more detail of the range of conditions in these areas. In a study from Mhala district of Gazankulu, Fischer [1987: 514] describes a remarkably fluid system of access to land on a former white farm occupied by former tenants and their families. 'Lack of land is not yet an issue in Seville; many households have established rights to more land than they can annually work using current methods', but the exact amounts of land involved are not specified. In Venda, Naledzani [1992: 76] found average dryland holdings of 1.1 hectares in Mashamba area and 0.9 hectares in Khakhu, while Pretorius [1994: 49], in a study of four villages, found average plot sizes ranging from 0.5 to 1.6 hectares, or 1.1 hectares overall. Neither of these studies provides any indication of the extent of landlessness. In Lebowa, Baber [1996: 288] found that 72 per cent of households in the long-established village of Mamone had their own arable land but in the more recent settlement of Rantlekane only 45 per cent of households had land.

Work by Weiner, Chimere-Dan and Levin [1994: 30] in four areas of the Central Lowveld (covering parts of KaNgwane, Gazankulu and Lebowa) provides further information on land-holding in this relatively neglected part of the country. A quarter (24.5 per cent) of households in the study reported having access to 'agricultural land' but, when cultivated land adjacent to homesteads ('gardens') was included, this figure rose to 62.3 per cent. Of the households with land, over 80 per cent cultivated areas greater than 0.1 hectare, and the average area available for cultivation was 0.9 hectares per household. There was, however, considerable variation within the study area, with average holdings ranging from 0.4 hectares in Marite village (Mapulaneng, Lebowa) to 2.8 hectares in Cork village (Mhala, Gazankulu).

Evaluations of the DBSA's Farmer Support Programme (FSP) in a number of homelands provide further information on land-holding in these areas, but generally tend to emphasise farmers with larger holdings who are well-integrated into the state support services. FSP participants in KaNgwane, for example, had an average 3.8 hectares of arable land, including an average of one hectare under irrigation, most of whom were producing cotton [*Singini and van Rooyen*, 1995: 58]. In Lebowa, FSP farmers in Phokoane district possessed an average of 1.38 hectares of dryland crop land per household, and those in Kadishi district had 1.45 hectares.

Despite what appear to be extreme shortages of land (especially arable land) in many areas, there are relatively few reports of any market (formal or informal) in land. Bromberger [1988: 207] (drawing on work by Cross) speaks

of a significant informal market in residential land in peri-urban areas of
KwaZulu, and various forms of leasing arrangements in the sugar belt. Lyne
and Nieuwoudt [1991: 195], however, suggest that rental of agricultural land
in KwaZulu is rare, although 'borrowing' unused land from relatives or close
friends is more common. Land-holders, it is suggested, are reluctant to lease
land to others out of fear of jeopardising their right to land, while the landless
are unwilling to risk paying rent for something that might bring little return. In
a similar vein, Steyn [1988: 305] found that share-cropping, hiring or leasing
of land were virtually unknown in the Peddie district of Ciskei.

While a certain amount can be said about arable land, very little is known
about the system governing formal rights to grazing in the homelands. It
would appear that people with grazing rights are, by and large, those with
arable rights also, although not every household with grazing rights actually
keeps livestock, and many without formal rights do so. Data presented by
Weiner, Chimere-Dan and Levin [1994: 30] for areas as disparate as the
Transvaal Central Lowveld, KwaMakhanya in KwaZulu, and Herschel in
Transkei, suggest that the number of households with access to grazing land is
less than half of the number with access to arable land, although no explanation for this is provided. While pastures are generally used communally,
examples have been found of chiefs and others fencing off land for their
private use. In a study from the Ritavi 2 district of Gazankulu, van der Waal
[1991: 354] speaks of 'an influential relative of the chief whose cattle had
exclusive access to 200 hectares of fenced grazing and an irrigation dam. This
privilege had been given by agricultural officials in order to ensure the co-
operation of the tribal authority in development planning'.

To summarise, the general pattern that emerges from the literature suggests
that arable land in the homelands is distributed between a relatively large proportion of households, perhaps as high as 50 per cent, but average holdings are
extremely small, in the order of 0.5 to1.5 hectares per household. There is,
however, considerable variation in plot sizes, with a substantial proportion of
households having less than half a hectare, and a small elite having plots
greater than five hectares. There is also considerable variation between regions
and districts. In parts of Transkei, KwaZulu and Venda, virtually every household has access to land for agricultural purposes, whereas in many 'closer
settlements' virtually no residents have rights to land other than residential
plots, and in many areas even these rights are not well established. The next
sections will look at how agricultural land in the homelands is actually used,
for both arable and pastoral farming.

2.3 AGRICULTURE IN THE HOMELANDS

Since the creation of the African reserves in the late nineteenth and early twentieth centuries, most of their inhabitants have been able to obtain only a part of their livelihood from agriculture. Awareness of the depressed condition of agriculture in the reserves has been widespread since the 1920s, with numerous official reports – most notably the 1932 Native Economic Commission – identifying trends such as rising landlessness, falling crop yields and a growing dependence on wage income [*Horrell*, 1973; *Bundy*, 1979: 224]. Terence Moll [1988: 5], drawing on data from the Tomlinson Report and other sources, speaks of 'a general economic collapse' in the reserves from about 1930, with a severe decline in maize yields and in numbers of sheep and cattle. Knight and Lenta [1980: 161] argue that overall cereal production actually remained relatively stable in the homelands between 1918 and 1974, but point out that the population more than trebled[6] over the same period: 'Per capita production therefore fell from 2.0 bags[7] in 1918–23 to 0.55 bags in 1971–74'. Simkins [1981: 262] takes a similar position, but argues that the main drop in per capita food output occurred only with the massive influx of population to the homelands after 1955.

Livestock farming in the reserves/homelands has followed a similar pattern. Between 1924 and 1974, per capita livestock numbers fell by almost two-thirds (from 1.82 to 0.66 Large Stock Units per capita)[8] [*Knight and Lenta*, 1980: 161], while the proportion of households without cattle grew considerably [Simkins 1981: 274]. For the Transkei, Beinart [1992: 180] argues that absolute numbers of cattle (as well as sheep and goats) have shown no long-term trend since the 1920s, but that per capita numbers have declined sharply in recent decades: 'cattle stocks remained at around 1.2 per person till 1951 and then declined to one per person in 1960 and 0.5 head per person by the 1980s. The reason for this rapid decline is of course the doubling of the Transkeian population between 1946 and 1985. If . . . cattle owners alone are taken into account, then numbers have remained at about one per person' [*Beinart*, 1992: 180].

Since the mid-1960s, there has been some growth in agricultural production in the homelands, but this has been limited largely to an emerging 'commercial' sector under the control of the state and corporate capital. According to Cobbett [1987: 69], 'The period 1970 to 1985 saw a marked real increase (190 per cent) in the value of commercial agricultural production from R56.2 million to R163 million. This change resulted primarily from investments undertaken by the various parastatal development corporations but included private sector investments as well (particularly in KwaZulu).' Smaller farmers, producing mainly for their own consumption needs, did not fare as well. Cobbett [1987: 69] estimates that the aggregate value of 'sub-subsistence production' declined in real terms by three per cent over the period 1970 to 1985.

Development Policy

Despite improved output in some sub-sectors of the agricultural economy, such as sugar-cane and citrus fruit, attempts by the South African government and the various homeland administrations to develop agriculture in the homelands have met with little success overall. Development policy in the reserves/ homelands has been widely criticised for being costly and inefficient, having a 'top-down' authoritarian approach and promoting the interests of the state and homeland elites at the expense of the mass of small farmers [*Haines and Cross*, 1988: 89; *Cooper*, 1991: 246]. Early interventions in the agricultural economy of the reserves were largely directed towards soil conservation and culling cattle, under the banner of 'betterment' (see above). In the late 1950s, however, the South African government adopted a number of the recommendations of the Tomlinson Commission, such as the creation of small-holder irrigation schemes, aimed at modestly improving the condition of smallholders. Many of these schemes, such as Tshiombo (see below) survive today, but they have tended to be eclipsed by larger and more elaborate initiatives in succeeding years.

With moves towards 'self-government' for the homelands in the 1960s and 1970s, the focus of official development policy shifted towards the creation of a large-scale, commercially-oriented agricultural sector, mainly under the control of the state. Large estate farms growing tea, coffee, sisal, citrus fruit and other crops were established on communal lands, from which the occupants were often forcibly removed, and on former white farms newly incorporated into the homelands [*Cooper*, 1991: 253]. By the late 1970s, many such projects were being developed as joint ventures with (non-homeland) private sector companies, attracted by generous state subsidies, low wages, and repressive labour legislation [*Keenan and Sarakinsky*, 1987: 589]. Few of these projects met with commercial success, however, or contributed much to the homeland economies: 'It appears that substantial losses were the norm with these schemes and the distribution of benefits was very limited in relation to total need and to aggregate resources available for development' [*Bromberger and Antonie*, 1993: 428]. Fischer [1987: 511] argues that the objective of development policy in Gazankulu in the 1980s was to expand the revenues flowing to the state bureaucracy, rather than to individual farmers: 'The national interest of Gazankulu (as seen by the administration) became the chief development priority, the development of the national economy the overriding development goal, and the commercial use of Gazankulu's resources the dominant development trend.'

In addition to the large-scale estate farms, homeland regimes in the 1970s and 1980s attempted to create a class of 'private commercial farmers'. Groups of selected (black) farmers were settled on plots, typically 10 to 30 hectares, on a variety of projects, including irrigation schemes, dairy projects, and schemes producing dryland maize, sugar and sub-tropical fruit, usually managed and controlled by the homeland authorities [*Watkinson*, 1996: 50]. Like the large-scale state farms, many of these settlement schemes have caused dislocation of existing land holders, and have enjoyed very limited success. Evidence from throughout the homelands would suggest that the principal beneficiaries of such schemes have been better-off households and people with close connections to the tribal and homeland authorities. In the Ritavi 2 district of Gazankulu, for example, van der Waal [1991: 347] found that the people who benefited from government-run projects were 'mainly those with access to capital: the chief and his relatives, businessmen and top salary earners'.

Cooper [1991: 246] is highly critical of the state-run projects and the farmer settlement schemes, both for their use of inappropriate technology and for their impact on the environment: 'the model generally followed in bantustans is a high-cost, chemical-input type reliant on fertilisers, pesticides, improved seeds and mechanisation. This is totally unsuitable for the needs of the farmers and is detrimental to the environment.' For Bromberger and Antonie [1993: 429], schemes like the Ncora irrigation project in Transkei were 'expensive, often loss-making, and rarely involved spill-overs or linkages for the surrounding communities'. In Bophuthatswana, Roodt [1988: 241] found that farmer settlement schemes actually resulted in farmers achieving lower per hectare incomes than they had achieved before the government became involved.

Since the mid-1980s, there has been a shift in policy away from large-scale state farms and centrally-controlled farmer settlement schemes. Watkinson [1996: 70], drawing on work by Meth and others, argues that this shift was due to the massive indebtedness and general ineffectiveness of the homeland governments and Agricultural Development Corporations, and the failure of previous policies to benefit more than a tiny elite within the homelands. This policy shift has led to the subdivision of many of the large state-run projects, which are now leased to individual (black) farmers (a process commonly referred to as 'privatisation') [*McIntosh and Vaughan*, 1995: 113]. Having greatly reduced their involvement in direct agricultural production the Agricultural Development Corporations are currently concentrating on providing services such as credit, ploughing and marketing advice to individual farmers on a commercial basis. This approach has been pioneered (and funded) by the Development Bank of Southern Africa, particularly through its Farmer Support Programme (FSP), implemented jointly with Development Corporations in a number of homelands. The FSP approach typically consists of the supply of inputs, mechanical services, marketing support, credit and training (in various combinations) to 'emergent' farmers, with the aim of speeding their transition from 'subsistence' to 'commercial' status [*van Rooyen, Vink and Christodoulou*, 1987: 212]. Watkinson [1996: 75] argues that, far from being a new programme helping previously neglected small-scale farmers, the bulk of FSP spending has gone to the same elite group of 'commercial' farmers that benefited from state assistance since the 1950s and has provided a means for the state to divest itself of many failed projects: 'FSP was intended to target the most wealthy farmers, in the best favoured areas, especially those areas with the best prior support.'

Despite some successes, the small farmer approach, like earlier policies, has experienced many difficulties, including poor management, an inflexible approach, and the supply of what is often an inappropriate 'package' of inputs and services to participating farmers. Klu [1994: 156] is critical of one such programme based on a network of district service centres run by the Agricultural Corporation of Bophuthatswana (Agricor): 'Rich crop and live-stock farmers are the main beneficiaries. The inability of small farmers to afford certified seeds, fertiliser and animal feed from the service centres and the collateral for credit effectively excluded the vast majority of farmers (including potential ones) from the benefits of Agricor's agricultural services.'

Since the late 1980s, a number of non-governmental organisations, such as Operation Hunger and the Independent Development Trust, have become involved in the development of small-scale 'community gardens' and other projects aimed at the poorest sections of rural society, but these have had limited impact, and suffer many of the same technical and financial problems affecting the state-run schemes [*Haines and Cross*, 1988: 88; *Cooper*, 1991: 254].

One other form of agricultural development that has had a substantial impact in the homelands, initiated by the private sector rather than by the state, has been the system of contract farming, or out-grower schemes, mainly of sugar cane, but also of timber. Sugar cane is cultivated by an estimated 30,000 growers in KwaZulu (and much smaller numbers in KaNgwane), but the small scale of plots has meant that it can make only a modest contribution to house-hold incomes in the great majority of cases: 'Cane production does boost household income, but it does not take cane growers households out of poverty' [*Marcus, Eales and Wildschut*, 1996: 65]

Despite these attempts at development, the majority of people attempting to gain some part of their livelihood from the land in the homelands have received little or no assistance from the state. Rudimentary agricultural extension, ploughing, and animal health services are provided by the various homeland (now Provincial) Departments of Agriculture, but these are generally considered inefficient and inappropriate to the needs of small, marginal farmers, and tend to concentrate on well-established farmers on government schemes [Bembridge, 1988: 71; Steyn, 1988: 307]. Poorly developed commercial and co-operative services add to the problems of small farmers attempting to make a livelihood from agriculture. Of particular importance has been the lack of formal credit facilities, poor availability of purchased inputs such as fertiliser and seeds, poorly developed transport services, and a severe shortage of tractor ploughing services. These issues are discussed in more detail below.

Arable Farming

The general impression of homeland agriculture that emerges from the literature is of a sector overwhelmingly composed of very small-scale farmers, producing mainly food crops for direct consumption, under conditions that are relatively underdeveloped in terms of methods, materials and integration into formal markets. These conditions would appear to be similar throughout most of the homeland territory, with the possible exception of the KwaZulu sugar belt, but a number of factors give rise to a degree of differentiation within agriculture. First, the relatively small area of irrigated land tends to be used somewhat (but not entirely) differently from dry (or rain-fed) land. Secondly, there are some regional variations in practices and crop choices, largely related to differences in rainfall. Finally, large-scale ('commercial') farming on government projects, and by some individuals, also diverges from this norm.

Throughout the homelands, the overwhelming majority of cultivated land (excluding large-scale state and commercial projects) is given over to the production of staple cereals, generally maize, but with some sorghum and a little millet in dryer areas of the north and west of the country. The only significant exception is the KwaZulu sugar belt, where the area planted to sugar-cane may equal or surpass that planted to maize (see below). Most small-holder cereal production is intended for direct consumption by the household, although very few households actually achieve self-sufficiency in staple foods.

For KwaZulu as a whole, Lyne and Nieuwoudt [1991: 194] estimated that cereals accounted for 58.9 per cent of total area under crops, followed by legumes (16.4 per cent) and sugar cane (14.7 per cent), with 22.2 per cent of the total arable area lying fallow (over the period 1982/83–1984/85). In the Nkandla district, Ardington (1984: 72) found that 'the vast majority of the land actually in use was planted to maize'. Just over half (54 per cent) of the households surveyed ploughed all their land in a year, and the total proportion of land ploughed was 45 per cent. This limited land use is attributed to shortages of labour, money (for seed and fertiliser) and ploughing oxen, as well as drought. Cairns and Lea [1990: 84] obtained similar results in the same area: 'maize was by far the most dominant crop, occupying over 80 per cent of the total field area'. Beans and *madumbes* (a local variety of tuber), were the only other significant crops in terms of area planted, but cowpeas, calabashes and sorghum were commonly inter-cropped with maize. As with Ardington's study, close to half (41 per cent) of all the households surveyed had left their land fallow for longer than a year, and half of these had done so for more than five years. Cairns and Lea attribute this to a combination of a lack of ploughing capacity (oxen, or money to hire oxen), drought and a shortage of household labour.

Bembridge [1987: 108], in a study of the Ciskei, found that 'maize is grown by almost all farmers who have land rights in a wide range of agro-ecological areas'. Maize accounted for an estimated 88 per cent of the nominal value of all field crops, and 83 per cent of the total value of field crops, gardens and orchards; 'the production of vegetables and fruit makes an insignificant contribution to household consumption'.

A more limited range of crops are found in the homelands of the Transvaal. In Ritavi 2 district of Gazankulu, van der Waal [1991: 353] found that farmers on their half-hectare plots grew 'mainly maize, inter-cropped with many other kinds of cereal and vegetable'. A similar dependence on maize is reported in studies from Mhala district [*Fischer*, 1987: 516], and from districts in Venda and Lebowa that formed part of the DBSA's Farmer Support Scheme [*Singini and van Rooyen*, 1995: 101]. In a study of Manenzhe, in the semi-arid zone of northern Venda, the most common crops were found to be sorghum and millet, with small amounts of vegetables grown on home stands [*Land Research Group*, 1995: 5].

Sugar-cane farmers, of whom there are an estimated 30,000 in KwaZulu, are the main exception to this pattern of staple food production [*Vaughan*, 1991: 172]. Stewart and Lyne [1988: 190] found that in Gcumisa ward (KwaZulu) an average of 36 per cent of the total cultivated area was planted to maize and 37 per cent to sugar. Amongst non-sugar growing households, 86 per cent of cultivated land was planted to maize. Cobbett [1982: 132] found that in two areas of Noodsberg (KwaZulu), sugar-cane accounted for 48 per cent of the area cultivated in one village, and 95 per cent in another. In both cases, the remaining arable land was used for food crops, of which roughly two-thirds was planted to maize. Makhanya [1994: 143], in a study in the Umlazi district of KwaZulu, found that 92 per cent of cultivated land was being used for sugar, with the remainder being given over to vegetables and a little maize.

Although maize is clearly the dominant crop for most households, and is largely intended for home use, the vast majority of rural households fail to produce enough for their own needs. This is due to a combination of small size of holdings and relatively low yields per hectare. The Tomlinson Report [*Union of South Africa*, 1955: 84], writing of the early 1950s, found that average maize yields in the reserves ranged from 3.84 bags per *morgen* (406 kg per hectare) in high rainfall zones to 0.36 bags per *morgen* (38 kg per hectare) in the lower rainfall zones, and suggested an overall average figure of 2.47 bags per *morgen* (262 kg/ha) for the country, compared to an average of 6.98 bags per *morgen* (740 kg/ha) on white farms at the time. These estimates are criticised as 'unbelievably low' by Lipton [1977: 73], who argues that pre-harvest consumption of (green) maize, amounting to approximately one third of total output, was not taken into account.

Subsequent studies from throughout the homelands have found wide variations in yields. Steyn [1988: 298] estimated average maize yields over three years for two villages in the Ciskei at 409.7 kg/ha. Between 18 per cent and 45 per cent of households in one village achieved self-sufficiency in maize over the three years but in another no households came close to achieving this. Bembridge [1987: 115] found average yields of 335 kg/ha in three areas of the Ciskei, but quotes another study by Marais which found an average of 1,045 kg/ha over a five-year period. In KwaZulu, Cairns and Lea [1990: 91] conducted their own harvesting experiments amongst dryland small-holders, and found average yields of 1,200 kg per hectare, of which one-quarter was eaten green, and three-quarters were harvested and stored. Once again, however, the small size of holdings meant that households rarely met their own food requirements.

With the exception of farmers on state-run irrigation schemes, the majority of vegetables, fruit and other non-cereal crops tend to be grown on residential stands or community gardens, some of them started by independent farmers' groups and occasionally funded by NGOs or government nutritional programmes. Many such gardens are irrigated, using water from bore-holes or standpipes, or carried by hand from rivers and streams. In Ardington's [1984: 89] study of Nkandla (KwaZulu) 30% of households had vegetable gardens, and three per cent were members of communal garden schemes which provided irrigation and helped people to buy fencing and seed. These gardens supplied a wide range of root and green vegetables, as well as sorghum and bananas, both for sale and for household consumption. On the government-run Tshifhefhe food plot scheme in Venda, where irrigated plots averaged just 0.13 hectares, Thormeyer [1989: 26] found that over a quarter (27.1 per cent) of households were entirely dependent on them for their livelihood.

In a survey of irrigated food plots in Ciskei, KwaZulu and KwaNdebele, van Vuuren [1988: 41] notes the significant contribution to cash incomes and household food supply of even very small plots, generally no larger than 0.25 ha, but some as small as 110 square meters (0.011 hectares). Van Vuuren argues that that these small schemes, which are mainly targeted at women, are highly appropriate to the users' needs as they keep costs of production low, are of a scale that can be easily managed along with other domestic duties, and require little or no specialist knowledge. A wide range of crops was produced on the schemes surveyed, including cabbage, tomatoes, potatoes, beans, sweet peas, spinach and some indigenous plants, such as 'pigweed' [van Vuuren, 1988: 43].

The generally poor state of agriculture in the homelands is not only due to the small size of holdings. From a conventional economics or agricultural science perspective, the characteristics of small-scale agriculture in the homelands are commonly summarised as a shortage of physical and human capital, resulting in under-utilisation of resources and poor use of purchased inputs, as well as weak integration to produce markets. From a sociological or political economy perspective, however, the distinctiveness of agriculture in the homelands can be explained as an attempt by resource-poor farmers to achieve quite specific consumption-related outcomes under conditions of extreme scarcity of land, labour, capital, support services and markets. As a result, small farmers in the homelands rely upon forms of agricultural activity not generally found in other parts of the country, including cultivation by animal draught or by hand, rather than by tractor, inter-cropping rather than mono-cropping, a heavy dependence on unpaid household labour, and a focus on use values (for example, food) rather than exchange values (for example, cash income).

A useful description of the way in which small farmers adapt to the specific physical, economic and social conditions confronting them is provided by Fischer [1987: 514]. Writing of the extremely marginal lands of Mhala district, in Gazankulu, Fischer argues that the organisation of cultivation centres primarily on the management of risk, through limiting financial input and maximising labour input, and taking full advantage of local soil and climatic conditions:

> By spreading the ploughing season in accordance with the rainfall pattern, cultivating different soil types to obtain the characteristic advantages of each under varied seasonal circumstances, and by inter-cropping maize with various legumes, indigenous melons and different

pumpkin varieties, risk is reduced, output maximised, and a substantial return to labour is virtually guaranteed.

This view contrasts sharply with that of more conservative commentators such as Bembridge [1987: 115], who criticises small, cash-strapped farmers for their lack of modern methods and low yields: 'The extremely low yield levels are a direct reflection of the low rate of adoption of modern technology.' To say that greater use of inputs would improve yields is undoubtedly correct, but it does little to explain the actual choices facing farmers in the homelands, and their behaviour under real conditions.

Shortages of basic tools and implements, especially for ploughing, are amongst the most frequently mentioned limitations to small-holder crop production in the homelands. In Ciskei, Steyn [1988: 306] found the shortage of ploughing equipment, together with an inadequate government tractor service, was 'one of the most serious constraints on crop production'. In a study from Dumisa (southern KwaZulu), Mpanza and Nattrass [1987: 20] found that 30 per cent of households had their own plough, but only half of them had sufficient oxen of their own to plough with. Similarly, May [1989: 7] found that only half the households in his KwaZulu study had all the means (cattle, ploughs and labour) to carry out cultivation on their own.

While cattle are the principal form of draught power in much of Transkei, Ciskei and KwaZulu, the limited evidence available would suggest that donkeys are more commonly used in the homelands of the Transvaal, although tractors are becoming increasingly important in most areas [*van der Waal*, 1991: 353; *Land Research Group*, 1995: 10]. Private ownership of tractors is extremely low, however (certainly less than five per cent of farming households), and government tractor services, where they are available, are widely considered to be inadequate and beyond the means of a large proportion of small farmers [*Bembridge*, 1987 105; *van der Waal*, 1991: 353]. In studies from the eastern Transvaal, KwaZulu and Transkei, Weiner, Chimere-Dan and Levin [1994: 30] found that only 4.1 per cent of households in the survey sample had their own draught animals, and 1.4 per cent their own tractors, and that hoeing by hand was the principal form of cultivation, 'a remarkable reality for the most industrialised nation in Africa, and in which large-scale commercial farms suffer from overcapitalisation'.

In many parts of the homelands, farming households attempt to overcome the shortage of draught animals, and labour, by pooling their resources in a ploughing team or 'company'. The many advantages of this type of co-operation are spelled out by McAllister [1989: 356], in a study of the Willow-vale district of the Transkei:

Ploughing companies partly overcome the problem of shortages of oxen, implements and labour and enable many to plough at what they consider to be the right time and to get the work done quickly once the decision to plough has been made.

In addition to this many people, including the families of absent migrants, would not be able to cultivate at all without the assistance of others due to their lack of some or all of the necessary inputs.

Similar forms of collective ploughing are reported from Gazankulu [*Fischer*, 1987: 515], KwaZulu [*Cousins*, 1996: 176] and the Transkei [*Heron*, 1991: 48].

Alongside the shortage of basic equipment, homeland agriculture is widely believed to suffer from critical shortages of labour. While there appears to be a certain irony in this, given the widespread unemployment (and under-employment) and high population densities found in the homelands, the literature suggests that individual households suffer shortages of labour at key points in the agricultural cycle, particularly ploughing and weeding. Central to this question, of course, is the absence from rural areas of a large proportion of men of working age, but also important are the specific methods of production which, in the absence of tractors, chemical sprays and other modern technology, remain highly labour-intensive.

Agriculture in the homelands is largely a household activity, which in practice means that most of the work is done by women and, to a lesser extent, by children and older men [*Cooper*, 1991: 245]. Collective, inter-household activities tend to be restricted to ploughing, and only a minority of households, usually larger land-holders, would appear to employ non-household labour, for payment either in cash or in kind. Despite the important role of women in agriculture, rural households tend to be dominated by men, often absent for long periods of the year, and women's work is commonly understated in the literature: 'women's work tends to be undervalued and rendered invisible due to the stereotypical understanding that it is reproductive work' [*Levin, Russon and Weiner*, 1994: 245].

In the Nkandla district of KwaZulu, Cairns and Lea [1990: 87] found that the majority of agricultural work was done by women and children. Most ploughing, however, was done by men, either from within the household or neighbours or relatives. Some men, however, did participate in tasks such as hoeing, and in a quarter of households ploughing was done by women and/or schoolboys [*Cairns and Lea*, 1990: 87]. Just one household out of 70 hired labour for weeding, and one other (the village headman's) for planting sweet potatoes [*Cairns and Lea*, 1990: 89]. Elsewhere in KwaZulu (Dumisa), Mpanza and Nattrass [1987: 37] found a high proportion of school-age children (60 per cent of those between six and 15 years) working full-time in the home or the fields. Even in the relatively developed sugar-cane economy of KwaZulu, Vaughan [1991: 177] found that unpaid household labour was the norm: 'Many cane growers do employ wage labour, but family labour seems equally important; there is often a combination of family and wage labour.'

Widespread poverty and poorly developed retail networks in the homelands mean that farmers' use of purchased inputs, such as fertiliser, hybrid seed or pesticides, is generally low. This is commonly held to be a major cause of low yields, but there is evidence to suggest that some farmers in the homelands make use of alternative, and cheaper, methods of maintaining soil fertility and minimising losses from drought and pests. Probably the most important of these is the application of organic material (mainly kraal manure), but this obviously depends on access to livestock. Steyn [1988: 265] found that, in one village in Ciskei, 53 per cent of farmers were using inorganic fertiliser, albeit at less than recommended levels, but in another no households were using it. Cairns and Lea [1990: 86] found only 15 per cent of their sample in KwaZulu using purchased fertiliser, but 55 per cent using kraal manure in one form or another. In village studies from the central Lowveld, Weiner, Chimere-Dan and Levin [1994: 36] found the proportion of households using organic fertiliser on their fields ranged from 29 per cent to 57 per cent, and the proportion using commercial fertiliser ranging from 27 per cent to 62.5 per cent.

Other methods of promoting soil fertility, such as crop rotation or fallowing, would appear to be severely restricted due to the very small size of holdings and the need to produce a supply of staple food every year. One practice that is widely used, however, is inter-cropping, the simultaneous growing of multiple crops, such as maize, melons, pumpkins and sweet sorghum, in the same field, either in alternate rows or, more commonly, by mixing different seed together. This method is widely criticised by agricultural officials and by more conservative commentators as inefficient and having a detrimental impact on yields. Studies by Steyn [1988: 285] and others in Ciskei, however, suggest that the widespread practice of mixing maize with beans improves the nitrogen content of the soil and actually enhances maize yields.

Another characteristic of farming in the homelands is the widespread use of seed retained from the previous harvest. While some farmers use purchased varieties, these work out relatively expensive as they must be purchased every year, frequently offer little resistance to drought or disease and may require levels of fertiliser well above that which poorer farmers can afford. Retaining seed from past harvests allows farmers not only to save money but also to maintain the quality of their crops through selection of varieties which are best suited to local conditions. Estimates of the proportion of farmers using purchased seed varieties vary considerably. In studies from the Ciskei,

Bembridge [1987: 111] found that 31 per cent of farmers used approved seed for maize, while Steyn [1988 : 271] found 51 per cent of farmers using it in one village, and none in another. In KwaZulu, Cairns and Lea [1990: 89] found 24 per cent of households in their sample using purchased seed, and all but one of these did so not through choice but because they had insufficient seed of their own left from the previous year.

In addition to the constraints of land, labour and capital experienced at the level of the household, farmers in the homelands are confronted with major deficiencies in basic commercial and technical services of the kind taken for granted in other parts of the country. The lack of reliable and affordable tractor services has already been mentioned as a major constraint on production. The second most commonly mentioned constraint in the literature is probably the shortage of credit facilities. Attempts were made by the various homeland Development Corporations to provide credit to a minority of 'progressive' or 'emerging' farmers, but such schemes were beset by financial and managerial problems, and did not reach the majority of small holders [Singini and van Rooyen, 1995]. Commercial credit services (for example, banks) are available only to a tiny elite within the homelands and often do not offer the kind of small-scale credit required by small-holders. An unwillingness by lenders to offer loans to farmers on communal land is widely cited as a reason for the scarcity of commercial credit services in the homelands. In the KwaZulu sugar belt, however, farmers obtain materials and services on credit through the milling companies, which are paid for through deductions from payments for sugar-cane delivered to the mills. Vaughan [1991: 177] argues that this close, contractual relationship with the millers works to the disadvantage of growers, as it gives them little involvement or choice in the running of their affairs: 'The administration of the credit system, in particular, inhibits growers from taking effective control of their own farm budgets.'

In a study from Lebowa, Fenyes and Groenewald [1985: 407] found that the majority of farmers borrowing money did so from relatives (68 per cent), or from Tribal Authorities (23 per cent), usually free of interest. Just 6.5 per cent of borrowers obtained loans from formal commercial institutions, such as co-operatives or Development Corporations. None borrowed from private banks, and over 50 per cent of farmers preferred to keep their savings at home rather than deposit them in a bank. Cross [1988: 269] found a particularly active rural credit market in KwaZulu: 'With virtually everyone in the community who was not utterly destitute both borrowing and lending regularly in this informal loan exchange, most men and a great many women had experience of informal loans in the R100–R500 bracket.' Very little is known about the operation of informal credit in other areas of the homelands.

Of the state-run agricultural services within the homelands, those serving independent small-holders (the vast majority of all farmers) were undoubtedly the poor relation, and offered a service that was often inappropriate or inaccessible to the majority of small farmers. Agricultural extension officers, the only link between many farmers and the government service, are widely considered to be poorly trained and biased towards those who conform to their notion of 'real' farmers – that is, full-time male farmers, on substantial holdings, using modern methods to produce for the market. Steyn [1988: 307], for example, relates how extension officers in the Ciskei provided advice based entirely on mono-cropping methods in an aica where inter-cropping was the norm. Fraser [1994: 124] found that the agricultural extension service in Ciskei was understaffed and poorly trained, especially in the area of marketing, and had a disproportionate number of senior (that is, non-field) staff. Only 15 per cent of farmers in the survey sample had any contact with an extension officer. Bembridge [1988: viii] summarises the problems of the extension service in Venda in the following terms:

> Lack of an operational policy, poor management of staff, staff shortages, problems connected with salaries, transport, short periods of service in work areas, poor housing, lack of office accommodation, inadequate record-keeping and reporting systems were all found to be constraints to the efficiency and effectiveness of the extension service. All these factors contributed to the generally low prestige and status of field officers in rural communities, as well as to low staff morale. Field extension staff were relatively young and inexperienced with low formal education. Many staff lack practical farming experience.

The problems facing farmers in the homelands as a result of the inadequacies of the state services are compounded by the shortage, or absence, of services from the private commercial and co-operative sectors. Formal financial services, as already suggested, are absent from much of the homelands, with branches of commercial banks generally confined to the homeland 'capitals'. Private sector services, such as farm supply stores, hauliers and ploughing services are all in extremely short supply and beyond the means of the majority of homeland small-holders. In KwaZulu, however, Lyster [1990: 153] found the supply of seed and fertiliser in the rural areas to be generally adequate, due to the close geographic integration of Natal and KwaZulu, and 'an extensive network of local shopkeepers in KwaZulu who supply a range of inputs at reasonable prices. Transport arrangements are expensive but adequate.'

Farmers' co-operatives have been established in many parts of the homelands, often at the instigation of the homeland governments, but these have a poor track record and, with a few notable exceptions, do no more than provide a rudimentary retail service. Many black farmers therefore depend on 'white' farmer co-operatives in adjoining areas (of which they are not generally members) and which, in recent years, have been extending their retail outlets into the homelands [*Amin and Bernstein*, 1996: 51].

Farmers in the homelands also suffer major problems marketing their crops, although the situation would appear to vary considerably between regions. In Lebowa, Fenyes and Groenewald [1985: 401] found that small-holders who sold crops mainly sold into official single channel markets (for maize, wheat and groundnuts), via local co-operatives, but also sold to shop-keepers and directly to the public. The main problems encountered by producers in this regard were the distance to markets and a lack of transportation. Lyster [1990: 153] comes to a similar conclusion regarding marketing in KwaZulu, where demand for food products in local retail markets was generally high: 'In considering factors inhibiting agricultural productivity, access to land and off-farm wage employment appear to be more important than the marketing function.' Quite different conditions were found by Fraser [1994: 121] in Ciskei, where marketing services were poorly developed. Neither co-operatives nor private stores were involved in purchasing agricultural produce and the government marketing service was either unknown or inaccessible to most farmers. Very little is known about informal agricultural markets within the homelands, which would appear to be considerably more important (in terms of the number of producers and the value of produce involved) than the formal channels mentioned here.

Livestock Farming

Detailed information on questions such as the number of households with livestock, and average herd sizes, are scarce for all the homelands, but the available studies suggests that herds tend to be small, and that a substantial proportion of the rural population do not own any livestock, especially cattle. As with land-holding and crop farming, most studies of livestock have concentrated on the homelands of the eastern seaboard (KwaZulu, Transkei and Ciskei), with relatively little attention being paid to the seven homelands of the interior.

Numbers of livestock per hectare in the homelands are estimated at between 20 per cent and 100 per cent higher than 'white' areas of similar eco-climatic conditions [*van Zyl and van Rooyen*, 1991: 184; *Lyne and Nieuwoudt*, 1991: 198]. With less than 14 per cent of the national land area, the homelands are believed to contain more than one-third of South Africa's cattle, more than half of all its goats, and over one-tenth of its sheep [*Bembridge*, 1990: 22; *DBSA*, 1994: 104].

Studies from various rural districts in Transkei suggest that close to half of all households keep cattle and the great majority of herds are less than ten head. Slightly fewer households keep small stock (sheep or goats) and, again, herd sizes tend to be small. In a survey of 22 farming households in the Shixini area, Heron [1991: 53] found an average of 9.4 Large Stock Units (LSU) per household, and all but one household in the sample kept some stock. Hendricks [1990: 87] estimated that approximately half (46–52 per cent) of the households in the Nyandeni area owned cattle, of which one-third had more than 10 head, and just one per cent had more than 50. A third of households (32 per cent) had sheep, but over a third (37 per cent) had neither sheep nor cattle. Another study of three districts of the Transkei by Leeuwenberg in the 1970s (cited in Southall [1982: 221]), found that 45 per cent of households owned no cattle and 55 per cent owned no sheep. Half the cattle-owning households owned five head or less, and two per cent owned 20 or more; half the sheep-owners owned less than 10 head. Beinart [1992: 182], reviewing the findings of ten local and regional studies in the Transkei, summarises the situation thus: 'in districts as varied as Matatiele, Tsolo, Port St Johns and Bizana, quite similar figures emerge through the period from the late 1970s for the percentage of households with cattle (about 50 per cent) and the percentage with 10 or more (between 10 and 15)'.

A similar pattern is apparent in Ciskei. In two villages in the Peddie district, Steyn [1988: 314] found that approximately two-thirds and one-third of households owned cattle, respectively, with average herd sizes of 6.4 and 4.0. In addition, between a third and a quarter of households owned sheep (average flock sizes of 19.3 and 21.4), while over half (57 per cent and 56 per cent) owned goats (average herd sizes of 10.8 and 17.3). Somewhat higher figures are reported by Bembridge (1987: 118) for the Keiskamma district, where 71 per cent of households kept cattle and the average herd size amongst the study sample was 6.9 head, but this was recorded prior to the severe drought of the early 1980s. Over two-thirds of cattle herds (69 per cent) were smaller than eight head, which Bembridge considers to be the minimum number necessary for the 'primary needs of survival and subsistence', namely the supply of food products and draught power [1987: 119]. Considerably fewer households kept goats (36 per cent) and sheep (25 per cent); average herd size for goats was 13 head, and for sheep, 21.

Studies from KwaZulu show broadly similar conditions, although in some areas the proportion of households with cattle is considerably higher. In a study of Dumisa area (southern KwaZulu), Mpanza and Nattrass [1987: 22] found that 46 per cent of households owned cattle. The average herd size was 4.5, and just five per cent of herds were greater than 10 head. In addition, 33 per cent of households in the study kept goats and seven per cent kept sheep.

Drawing from a relatively large and widely dispersed sample, May [1989: 5] found that 39 per cent of households in KwaZulu had no livestock (large or small), and the average livestock-holding was 5.0 Large Stock Units. Amongst those with livestock, the distribution was, again, highly uneven, with eight per cent of owners holding 32 per cent of all stock. Cobbett [1982: 137], in a study of two villages in the Noodsberg region, found that 45 per cent and 35 per cent of households, respectively, owned cattle, and that three-quarters of these had less than four head each.

Studies from the Nkandla area of KwaZulu report somewhat higher rates of cattle ownership. Ardington [1984: 90] found that 70 per cent of households had cattle, and the average herd size was 7.9. Over two-thirds (69 per cent) of herds were smaller than 10 head, and the largest herd size was 30. Small stock were less common: only 40 per cent of households had goats, and nine per cent had sheep. Ardington estimated that annual off-take of cattle amounted to 7.7 per cent of the total herd: 6.7 per cent for slaughter and one per cent in the form of informal sales within the locality. *Lobola* (bride wealth) was considerably more important in terms of numbers of cattle transferred in and out of herds. Some years later, Cairns and Lea [1990: 80] found slightly more households in Nkandla with cattle (75 per cent), and a slightly larger average herd size, at 8.1 head. The number of households with small stock also showed a small increase (to 51 per cent), but 21 per cent of households possessed no livestock at all. These authors draw attention to the high mortality and low calving rates in the area, which they attribute to the poor condition of the grazing: 'Veld is severely degraded and the stocking rate[9] in the survey area is about four times the recommended carrying capacity. Adult mortality is caused mainly by inadequate nutrition which probably also accounts for the low calving rates' [*Cairns and Lea*, 1990: 99].

Detailed information on livestock holdings in the remaining homelands is relatively scarce, but what is available again suggests that cattle, sheep and goats are owned by a minority of households (possibly even less than in the coastal areas), average herd sizes are small and, amongst those with livestock, the distribution of animals is highly skewed. Even in semi-arid areas, where arable farming is severely restricted, the numbers of animals per household remain low and a sizeable proportion of rural households have no livestock.

In a review of various local studies from Lebowa, Vink and Kassier [1987: 169] reported estimates of the proportion of households owning cattle ranging from 22.3 per cent to 48.8 per cent, and found that the great majority of herds (88 per cent in one study) were below 10 head. In the villages of Mamone and Rantlekane, Baber [1996: 294] found that ten per cent and 16 per cent of households owned cattle, with the average herd size being 8.8 and 8.6 head respectively. Goats were kept by 20 per cent of households in Mamone, and 11 per cent in Rantlekane, with average herd sizes of 7.9 and 4.6 respectively.

In Venda, Pretorius [1994: 58] found relatively high rates of cattle ownership, ranging from 77 per cent to 90 per cent of households in four villages studied, although it would appear that non-farming households (that is, those with neither livestock nor arable land) may have been excluded. Herd sizes were also relatively high, 45 per cent of herds being larger than ten head. In another study of the semi-arid Manenzhe district (northern Venda), just over a quarter (26.3 per cent) of households were found to own cattle, and the average herd size was 11 [Land Research Group, 1995: 8]. Goats were more widespread, being kept by 56.5 per cent of households, although average herd sizes were no bigger, at 10.4. No sheep were found in this study area. In the semi-arid Taung district of Bophuthatswana, Schmidt [1992: 435] found that 80 per cent of households kept livestock, of which two-thirds kept cattle. The average number of cattle per owner was six, and three-quarters of herds contained less than ten head. In Gazankulu, Fischer [1987: 516] found that only 35 per cent of households in a sample from the Mhala district owned cattle, and the average herd size was 10.2 head. Distribution between owners was, again, highly skewed, with the top 15 per cent of owners holding an average of 36 cattle each, and the bottom 35 per cent holding less than five head each. In the Ritavi 2 district, van der Waal [1991: 353] found a somewhat lower rate of cattle ownership, at 26 per cent of the study sample.

Overall, the literature on livestock in the homelands concentrates on cattle, and while some attention is paid to sheep and goats, nothing like a complete picture of their distribution or their contribution to household livelihoods can be formed. Small stock also tend to receive very little attention in rural development planning. The same can be said for other, widely-held livestock, such as donkeys, poultry and pigs, despite their contribution to agricultural production and household nutrition in the form of draught power, manure and food products. From the little information that is available, it would appear that poultry are kept by perhaps 80–90 per cent of households in the rural areas, and the numbers per household are generally small, typically less than ten birds [Mpanza and Nattrass, 1987: 22]. Poultry are kept mainly for meat, rather than for eggs, and are widely traded within local informal markets. Donkeys are found throughout the homelands, and play an important part in transport and ploughing, especially in dryer areas such as Sekhukhune (Lebowa), much of Bophuthatswana and Gazankulu, and northern Venda, although numbers are typically less than 6 per household [Starkey, 1995: 70; van der Waal, 1991: 352]. Pigs are kept by a minority of households in the homelands (probably less than 20 per cent), although in one study from Ciskei Bembridge [1987: 133] found that 50 per cent of sample households kept pigs. Numbers again tend to be very small, typically one or two pigs per owner.

The general condition of livestock-farming in the homelands described in the literature – small herds, concentrated in the hands of a minority of the rural population, with little market activity – has given rise to considerable debate over the function of livestock in rural society, and especially its contribution to household livelihoods. The conventional view is that the homelands are over-stocked, relative to the available grazing resources, which leads to ecological degradation, and that livestock, particularly cattle, are inadequately exploited as an economic resource. This is commonly attributed either to the communal system of grazing, which is held to be antithetical to efficient resource utilisa-tion [*Lyne and Nieuwoudt*, 1991: 198], or to 'traditional' attitudes which treat livestock farming as a socio-cultural rather than an economic activity [*Houghton*, 1973: 73], and which together are said to encourage quantity of animals over quality [*Bembridge*, 1990: 23].

Both main planks of this orthodoxy have been vigorously contested in recent years. Cousins [1996: 200] argues that the relatively high numbers of livestock on communal rangelands are related to the multi-purpose character of small-scale farming, and cannot be compared to the land/animal ratios found in single-purpose dairy or beef herds. Drawing on work by Tapson (for KwaZulu) and Beinart (for Transkei), Cousins [1996: 186]. argues that live-stock numbers in many areas appear to have remained stable over a long period, which suggests they have reached their ecological limit: 'There are indications that herders in South Africa, as elsewhere, pursue opportunistic strategies in their use of rangeland resources and that they base these on a fine-tuned understanding of their environment.'

Shackleton [1993: 66] takes a similar position, arguing that there is little evidence to support fears of widespread degradation of communal grasslands in the homelands:

> It is noteworthy that despite the excessive stocking rates (usually 200–400 per cent of the recommended), most of the communal areas continue to support large numbers of cattle without there having been any cata-strophic decline in total numbers over the last century, except where drought has been identified as the causal factor.

Arguments that livestock, particularly cattle, are underutilised as an economic resource tend to be based either on conventional measures of herd productivity (for example, off-take for sale or slaughter, calving rates, milk yields, herd mortality), herd management practices (for example, disease control and selective breeding), or herd structure (proportion of productive to non-produc-tive animals), all of which are said to compare unfavourably with white-owned herds under similar eco-climatic conditions [*Steyn*, 1988: 374]. Lyne and Nieuwoudt [1991: 198], for example, argue that annual off-take from herds in KwaZulu is only five per cent, compared to 25 per cent amongst white-owned herds in neighbouring Natal. Bembridge [1990: 23] arrives at a similar figure for off-take in Ciskei, and estimates annual mortality rates amongst cattle herds at 20.2 per cent for calves, and 9.5 per cent overall. Vink [1986: 183] found that annual cattle sales in Lebowa accounted for less than 7.5 per cent of herds, and argues that 'the owners of large herds . . . do not keep cattle primarily for the generation of income'.

Arguments to the contrary have tended to take a more holistic approach to the household economy, stressing the multiple benefits conferred by livestock, many of which are realised independently of market mechanisms. In a comprehensive survey of studies from throughout the homelands, Cousins [1996: 181] reaches the conclusion that 'Livestock production in black rural areas today continues to be multipurpose in character'. While the reasons for keeping cattle vary between regions, and between households, sales are consistently found to be less important than 'consumption activities' such as the supply of milk, meat and *lobola* (bride wealth); production activities, such as ploughing and supply of manure; and the use of cattle as a form of savings or investment. Cousins draws on works by Tapson, and Gandar and Bromberger, which suggest that the primary importance of cattle in KwaZulu lies in their supply of milk, rather than meat. Cairns and Lea [1990: 99], however, also speaking of KwaZulu, reach a different conclusion: 'The major economic value of cattle probably lies in their association with the cropping enterprises (draught power and manure) rather than in their ability to produce milk and meat.' In the very different environment of the Taung district of Bophuthatswana, Schmidt [1992: 435] concluded that cattle were kept primarily for their milk, and secondarily as a form of savings.

The sale of cattle is greatly hampered by poorly developed market infrastructure and commercial networks in the homelands. Fenyes and Groenewald [1985: 401] found that in Lebowa only a third (34.8 per cent) of farmers sold any livestock products, and these were largely through private sales within the immediate locality rather than in formal market places. When cattle were sold, it was often as a result of pressing financial problems, rather than as part of a deliberate strategy. In a study of formal cattle markets (auctions) in KwaZulu, Colvin [1985: 388] found that virtually all sales were the result of 'compelling economic circumstances', which obliged owners to sell in order to obtain funds for immediate consumption requirements. The price obtained for an animal sold as beef (dead-weight), Colvin argues, rarely reflected the true (multiple) value of the animal to the farmer, and as a result, the majority of cattle offered at auction sales consisted of the old, the weak and the immature.

Various studies suggest that, when all forms of production are taken into consideration, many livestock-owners in the homelands obtain rates of productivity that can be compared with 'commercial' (that is, white-owned) herds. Shackleton [1993] cites work by Tapson and Rose on KwaZulu which found a total annual off-take from herds on communal lands of 19.9 per cent, of which only a small part went into commercial markets.

> The high proportion of the total off-take channelled into non-commercial pathways highlights the shortfall of many of the previous studies, which tended to focus solely on the value of cattle to the commercial meat market. If all the utility values of cattle in subsistence communities are accounted for, including milk, ploughing, manure, store of wealth, store of food for adverse periods and bride-wealth, then the commercial use and value of cattle in such communities is comparable to intensive commercial farms even though accepted production indices, such as calving and mortality rates, may be low [*Shackleton*, 1993: 71].

The close relationship between livestock-ownership and arable farming found in many local studies has been noted above. Heron [1991: 54], for example, identifies a close correlation between ownership of livestock and crop yields in Shixini (Transkei), which is attributed to access to manure and preferential positions within ploughing companies. Similarly, in Nkandla (KwaZulu), Cairns and Lea [1990: 96] found that households owning cattle used more organic manure, ploughed larger areas, and obtained better crop yields than those without cattle.

As well as being productive assets, however, livestock in the homelands are recognised to be an important form of savings and investment, especially in areas where more conventional forms, such as banks, may not be accessible or, in the case of non-literate people, appropriate. Schmidt [1992: 438] argues that in the Taung district of Bophuthatswana cattle provide a good rate of return compared to more conventional forms of savings, can easily be converted to cash when required, and confer many intangible benefits (including prestige) on owners. Fischer [1987: 516] provides examples from Mhala (Gazankulu) of savings in the form of cattle, and to a lesser extent, goats, being used to meet a range of expenses, including school fees, motor repairs, and basic survival during periods of unemployment. The value of even small herds can be of enormous importance to poor households in the homelands. A study by Gandar and Bromberger (cited in Cousins [1996: 174]) found that the value of the average cattle herd (8.35 head) in Mahlabatini district (KwaZulu) was equivalent to 2.5 times the average annual household cash income.

Finally, it is important to note the contribution of livestock to wealth-generation and social differentiation within the homelands. Vink [1986: 175] found that large cattle-owners in Lebowa tended to be drawn from the ranks of 'the traditional and non-traditional leadership groups', such as chiefs, civil servants, and businessmen, who used their control over land and public resources to entrench their own privileged position. A similar situation is reported from the Transkei by Southall [1982: 221], who found that the larger stock-owners tended to be chiefs or headmen. As Cousins [1996: 181] observes:

Livestock ownership is highly skewed in most areas, is often correlated with higher levels of crop production and with higher levels of income from non-rural sources, and is thus a reasonably reliable indicator of social differentiation. Class formation processes in the former homelands have probably led to a concentration of a significant proportion of livestock in the hands of an elite composed of 'traditional' leaders, bureaucrats and businessmen, some of whom manipulate the communal tenure system for their own benefit.

Control of livestock gives rise to differentiation between households, but also between individuals within particular households, especially between older men, on one hand, and women and younger men on the other. Drawing on work by Ferguson on Lesotho, Sharp and Spiegel [1990: 541] and Cousins [1996: 181] both argue that cattle constitute a special, exclusively male, type of property, that allows migrant workers and others to accumulate wealth that is not necessarily shared with the rest of the household. Indeed, the dominance of men in the ownership of cattle, control of wages and access to land together constitute a highly unequal relationship between the sexes within the household economy: 'women have little or no control over the production process since they lack the ownership of the necessary resources for production, including the means of production (land and implements) and control of labour power' [Levin, Russon and Weiner, 1994: 244].

In summary, these local studies suggest that livestock farming remains widespread throughout the homelands, albeit with wide variations between households and regions. It would appear that somewhere between a quarter and a half of households own cattle, and the great majority of herds are less than ten head. Only a tiny elite own herds of 50 cattle or more. Small stock – sheep and goats – are probably owned by slightly more households, but average herd sizes are not substantially greater. Official policy, which for many decades was extremely hostile to the keeping of cattle in the homelands, is today largely indifferent to the livestock sector, and does little to encourage the economic development of the small-holder livestock sector. Despite official neglect, and recurring predictions of imminent ecological collapse, there is little evidence that livestock numbers are in long-term decline.

Although less important than cropping, livestock contribute to household livelihoods in a wide variety of ways, including food, draft power, bridewealth and a form of savings, all of which tend to be under-estimated (or ignored) by conventional economic analyses.

2.4 THE CONTRIBUTION OF AGRICULTURE TO LIVELIHOODS

From the few detailed studies of livelihoods in the homelands, it is clear that most households depend on multiple sources of income, of which agriculture generally contributes a relatively minor part compared to wages and pensions. Precise estimates of income, however, are notoriously unreliable, given the informal (that is, unrecorded) nature of much economic activity within the homelands and the difficulty of measuring the contribution (direct and indirect) of migrant workers. Equally contentious is the valuation of crop and animal products consumed directly within the household (using notional producer prices or consumer prices), to the point where a number of studies omit this category entirely from their calculations. As Peter Moll [1988: 315] observes, 'valuations of rural incomes are subject to a wide margin of error'. Despite these difficulties, it is clear from the studies cited here that agriculture does provide an important supplementary income to a significant number of households in the homelands, especially those with little access to wage income, and a vital safety net for many in times of crisis.

The results of a number of studies of income, mainly in KwaZulu and Transkei, in the 1980s have been summarised by Peter Moll [1988: 316] and by Nattrass and Nattrass [1990: 526]. The following table shows the range of estimates found under the main income categories.

TABLE 2.3
SOURCES OF HOUSEHOLD INCOME, IN CASH AND KIND (%)

Income Source	Minimum (%)	Maximum (%)
Migrant remittances	33	59
Other wage income	13	57
Pensions	8	26
Agriculture	9	30

All the available studies show that wages (migrant and non-migrant) are the most important source of income for households in the homelands, and it would appear that the importance of wages has steadily increased over recent decades [*Rogers*, 1976: 59; *Nattrass and Nattrass*, 1990: 526]. Most studies show that between 60 per cent and 80 per cent of income is obtained from wages, with between a third and a half of this coming from migrant remittances. Pensions are the second most important source of cash income, contributing between about ten per cent and 20 per cent of average household income. Estimates of agricultural income, in terms of both cash sales and produce consumed directly by the producing household, show the greatest variability, but most studies put it at between ten per cent and 25 per cent of average household income, of which the most part is accounted for by direct consumption.

More recent studies from KwaZulu support these general observations. In a study of eleven hundred households, May [1989: 9] found that 73.6 per cent of household income came from wages (including remittances), 12.7 per cent from pensions, and 7.7 per cent from agriculture. Ardington and Lund [1995: 565] found that 64 per cent of average household income came from wage earnings (48 per cent from local earnings, 16 per cent from remittances), 12 per cent from pensions, and approximately five per cent from 'subsistence' activities (including agriculture). In what they call 'deep rural' areas, however, household incomes were found to be less than half those in peri-urban areas of KwaZulu, mainly due to a much smaller contribution from wages. As a result, these areas were much more dependent on pensions (26 per cent of household income), remittances (24 per cent) and 'subsistence activities' (13 per cent), with wages accounting for 23.5 per cent of total income. In the Transvaal Lowveld, Weiner, Chimere-Dan and Levin [1994: 43] found that 68.4 per cent of cash income came from wages (including 15.4 per cent from remittances), 14.3 per cent from pensions, and 1.9 per cent from agricultural sales. No estimate is provided for the value of produce directly consumed within the household. This study also emphasises the importance of home-based craft activities, such as the production of floor mats, brooms, beer and clothing, as well as hawking, for a minority of households.

All of these studies point to major inequalities in the distribution of income between households. Ardington and Lund [1995: 565] found that the richest quintile (20%) of households in their KwaZulu study earned 47.4 per cent of total income for the sample, compared to 4.5 per cent earned by the poorest quintile. These figures are similar to those found by Nattrass and May [1986: 592] in KwaZulu a decade earlier: then, the top quintile was found to earn 49 per cent of total income (from all sources) and the bottom quintile just five per cent. Levin, Russon and Weiner [1994: 241], drawing on work by First and Neocosmos, argue that, while wages are central to household incomes within the homelands, it is the manner in which wages interact with other, less visible factors, such as access to land, petty commodity production and labour, that underlies the process of social differentiation.

The central importance of wage income for all strata of homeland society, and its importance in determining relative wealth, is emphasised by May [1989: 11]:

> The most important factor which structures the total income of households in all groups is access to wage employment. Indeed, those without this income form the most poor group, with an income which is half the average of the total sample. Peasant production, including the production of commodities does allow a minority of households to increase their income and to save, both in the traditional form of cattle, as well as banks and building societies. Nonetheless, these households are still heavily reliant upon wage income.

Pensions are widely considered to be the second most important source of income in the homelands, but for many households without a wage earner, or receiving only occasional remittances from a migrant worker, they are by far the most important [*Wilson and Ramphele*, 1989: 64; *Delius*, 1996: 151]. The most common form of pension is the state old-age pensions, paid to men over 65 and women over 60 years, but occupational pensions and disability allowances can also be significant. In their study of KwaZulu, Ardington and Lund [1995: 565] found that 34 per cent of households received some form of pension, which accounted for 18.5 per cent of total income, although the figure was considerably higher for female-headed households, for rural households, and for poorer households, and provided an important source of cash for many of the most vulnerable members of rural society:

> pensions are a significant source of income, with marked redistributive effects; they are a reliable source of income, which leads to household security; they are the basis of credit facilities in local markets, further contributing to food security; they deliver cash into remote areas where no other institutions do; they are gender-sensitive towards women; and they reach rural areas as few other services do [*Ardington and Lund*, 1995: 571].

Income from agriculture represents a relatively minor part of livelihoods in the homelands as a whole, but the exact importance varies enormously between households. For many of the very poorest households, it is the principal, or even the only, source of livelihood, whether in terms of cash or kind. For many others, with access to pensions or wage income, it is a useful supplement and a fall-back in times of illness, unemployment or death of an income earner. For a very small minority of households, agriculture provides a substantial livelihood, albeit generally within the context of other income sources, whether wages, pensions or small businesses.

In KwaZulu, May [1989: 9] found that agriculture accounted for 7.7 per cent of household income, 4.2 per cent coming from sales and 3.5 per cent in the form of direct consumption. While only 22 per cent of households obtained a cash income from agriculture, 85 per cent enjoyed some benefits in the form of direct consumption. May also found that households with relatively higher incomes tended to gain more income from agriculture, in absolute terms, and were more likely to sell some of their produce, but were less dependent on agriculture than poorer households. Agriculture accounted for 5.9 per cent of income (in cash and kind) for households in the top income quintile, as compared to 14.7 per cent for those in the bottom (that is, the poorest) quintile. In Nkandla, Ardington [1984: 40] found that agriculture in cash and kind accounted for 15 per cent of average household income, the major part coming from field crops, and the balance from milk and meat. Self-provisioning provided an estimated 11.8 per cent of income to households containing migrant workers, and 25.4 per cent to households without a migrant. In a village study from Ciskei, Steyn [1988: 213] estimated that agricultural sales accounted for six per cent of cash income. Of this figure, virtually all (97 per cent) was from livestock sales, and a minute proportion (three per cent of farm sales, or 0.18 per cent of total cash income) came from crops. In the Transvaal Lowveld, Weiner, Chimere-Dan and Levin [1994: 27] found that only a small minority of households sold any crops (4.4 per cent) or livestock (four per cent) but that for the households concerned the revenue generated amounted to almost half of their total income.

Not surprisingly, some of the highest estimates of agricultural earnings come from the KwaZulu sugar belt although the precise figures vary widely between studies. Weiner, Chimere-Dan and Levin [1994: 42] found that agricultural sales in KwaMakhanya contributed an average of R255 (1994 prices) per household per annum, or 3.8 per cent of total household income. In Gcumisa, Stewart and Lyne [1988: 191] found that seven per cent of cash income came from agricultural sales, compared to 62 per cent from wages and 28 per cent from pensions. Reviewing a range of sources from KwaZulu, Bromberger and Antonie [1993: 423] conclude that less than ten per cent of cash income came from agriculture, with some further contribution in kind. Even under the most favourable conditions, however, 'the total value of crop and livestock sales and subsistence production makes a gross contribution to household incomes of less than 18 per cent'. In what appears to be quite an exceptional case, Cobbett [1984: 374] found that, in the sugar growing area of Noodsberg (KwaZulu), 47 per cent of gross household earnings (R1,436 in 1981 prices) came from crop sales.

Other examples of relatively high agricultural earnings are reported from amongst farmers participating in the Farmer Support Programmes (FSP) in various homelands [Singini and van Rooyen, 1995]. In KaNgwane, FSP participants had a gross average income of R4,389 (1992 prices) from crop sales alone, and agriculture contributed almost 50 per cent of total household income. In Lebowa, the contribution of agriculture was even higher, at 68 per cent, but in Venda it accounted for only 20 per cent. All of these figures represent gross income, however, and do not take account of the considerable expenditures associated with the Programme. The FSP's focus on 'emergent' (that is, better-off) farmers also makes them atypical of farming households as a whole.

In conclusion, the available evidence suggests that, while agriculture is not the principal source of livelihood for the great majority of households in the homelands, it does provide an important supplementary income for a substantial proportion, albeit with a high degree of differentiation between households. Access to land, even relatively small plots or a share of communal grazing, allows households to maintain a diversified livelihood strategy that may include wage employment, pensions, agricultural production (for consumption or sale), and the keeping of livestock as a form of investment, which together enhances their ability to obtain a livelihood under difficult conditions.

NOTES

1. Tapson [1990: 566], for example, suggests that 14 per cent of land in the homelands can be classified as arable, compared to 11.6 per cent of land outside the homelands.
2. Trust farms are land purchased by the South African Development Trust, much of which is also occupied under communal tenure.
3. Abolition of Racially Based Land Measures Act, 1991.
4. Informal village councils aligned to the broad democratic movement.
5. Definitions of 'arable' are those used by the authors cited but generally imply all land currently allocated for cultivation.
6. From 2.3 million to 7.6 million.
7. One bag = c. 90kg.
8. Conventionally, one Large Stock Unit (LSU) = one head of cattle, or five goats or sheep.
9. Number of livestock per hectare.

3

The Land and People of Venda

The former homeland of Venda is situated in the north-eastern corner of the Transvaal, in the Republic of South Africa (RSA). Under the apartheid regime, Venda was declared to be the home of all speakers of the Venda language (*Luvenda*) and became an 'independent' republic in 1979. As with the other three such territories within South Africa (Transkei, Ciskei and Bophuthatswana), Venda's independence was not recognised by the international community and on 27 April 1994 the territory was reincorporated into the RSA. Today it forms part of the new Northern Province and although the area has no formal administrative significance, it retains a distinct ethnic identity and many of its former institutions, including the local bureaucracy, remain more or less intact.

The 'Republic' of Venda consisted of two separate territories, between latitudes 22.15 and 25.24 south, and longitudes 29.50 and 20.31 east, completely surrounded by the RSA (see Map 1). The main block of Venda territory was separated from the Limpopo River, and the border with Zimbabwe, by a narrow strip of territory, the Madimbo corridor, excised from the homeland and occupied by the South African military in the mid-1970s. To the northeast, the Kruger National Park separated Venda from the border with Mozambique. To the south and south-east Venda was bordered by the former homeland of Gazankulu, and to the west and south-west, by the Soutpansberg and Messina Districts of the RSA. The main town and former homeland capital is Thohoyandou, developed in the late 1970s, which embraces the older administrative centre of Sibasa. The area depends for much of its services, however, on the former 'white' towns of Louis Trichardt and Messina and, to a lesser extent, the provincial capital of Pietersburg.

At the time of its 'independence' in 1979, the total area of Venda territory was approximately 520,500 hectares, but this was later increased to 680,700 hectares, or 6,807 square kilometres, by the incorporation of additional South African Development Trust Lands (former white farms, effectively part of the reserves/homeland since the 1950s) and 'black spots' previously scheduled for forced clearance [*DBSA*, 1991: 1]. According to the 1991 Census, the population of Venda was 558,797 people.[1]

For administrative purposes, this territory was divided into four Magisterial Districts, namely Dzanani (in the north-west), Mutale (in the north-east), Thohoyandou (in the centre and south-east) and Vuwani (in the south-west) (see Map 2). The western part of Vuwani (Vuwani II) became the District of Tshitale in the late 1980s but does not feature in most official reports as a separate District. These Magisterial Districts were further subdivided into 25 Tribal Areas and three civil administration zones which served as the basic units of local government during 'independence'.

Compared to the adjoining 'white' areas of South Africa, Venda can be described as extremely underdeveloped in terms of infrastructure, economic activity, health, welfare and education services, and general standards of living.

3.1. PHYSICAL CONDITIONS

Venda can be divided roughly into three physiographic zones – central, north and south – which between them encompass a considerable range of physical and climatic conditions.[2]

Central Venda is dominated by the Soutpansberg Range formed by a succession of volcanic and sedimentary rocks overlying the Archaic bedrock [*RAU*, 1979: 6]. The mountains run for approximately 140 km in an east–west direction, reaching an altitude of more than 1,500m at the western end and 1,300m in central sections. The Soutpansberg is the source of most of Venda's perennial rivers, including the Nzhelele, Nwanedi, Lupepe, Mutale, Tshinane, Mutshindudi, Dzindi and Luvuhvu, which form part of the Limpopo catchment. Rainfall is relatively high on the south-facing slopes of the Soutpansberg, exceeding 2,000 mm per annum on higher ground, and the climate is generally sub-tropical. Climax vegetation is forest but has been largely replaced by grassveld on the mountain tops and by scrubby thornveld, classified as North-Eastern Mountain Sourveld, on escarpments and slopes [*Acocks*, 1988: 43].

North of the Soutpansberg, towards the Limpopo River, lies a semi-arid area comprising dissected river valleys, rocky ridges and the extensive Malonga Flats [*RAU*, 1979: 5]. The geology is predominantly composed of sediments and basalt lavas of the Karoo Super Group. Soils are mainly shallow and stony with areas of red apedal sandy soils of both colluvial and aeolian origin [*ISCW*, 1996]. Climate is very hot with summer temperatures frequently rising above 30°C. Vegetation is mostly short shrubby mopani trees (*Colophospermum mopane*) with scattered Baobab trees (*Adansonia digitata*) [*Acocks*, 1988: 43].

In the south and south-west of Venda lies a region of medium-to-low rainfall, comprising granite plains and foothills of the Soutpansberg, with summer temperatures comparable to those in the north but with cooler winters. Soils are mainly shallow lithosols and soils of the Glenrosa form with red apedal and alluvial soils in parts. Vegetation is predominantly open tree savannah (sourish mixed bushveld), with *Acacia caffra* the dominant tree, while a denser tree savannah (mixed bushveld) is found on hillsides [*RAU*, 1979: 5]. The extreme south of this region forms part of the Letaba River catchment.

Climatic conditions in Venda are generally sub-tropical but, as suggested, show considerable local variation. Rainfall declines dramatically as one moves northwards and towards lower-lying areas, while air temperatures increase, giving rise to relatively cool, wet highlands, and warmer dryer lowlands.

Figure 3.1 (below) shows annual rainfall figures for two meteorological stations just outside Venda, which provide a good indication of the range of conditions found in the north-eastern Transvaal. Levubu station is located south of the Soutpansberg, on the southern border of Venda, and Pafuri station lies in the extreme north-eastern corner of the Kruger Park. Data are also available for stations within Venda (see below) but do not cover such a lengthy period.

Venda lies within the summer rainfall region of southern Africa, with more than 90 per cent of annual precipitation occurring during the six months between September and March, mainly in the form of thunderstorms. Frost, snow and hail are all rare in the area.

The northern Transvaal is prone to periodic droughts, which recur on a roughly ten-year cycle. Pafuri, for which the longest data series is available, shows severe declines in rainfall in 1963/64[3] and 1972/73, while all the stations in the area (Levubu, Siloam, Thohoyandou, Tshandama, Punda Maria and Pafuri) show severe declines in 1982/83 and again in 1991/92. Indeed, the latter year is the driest on record for all the stations. Water reserves in the area remained dangerously low during field work in mid-1995, but by early 1996 the situation had improved dramatically as high rainfall was experienced throughout southern Africa. The limited evidence available, however, suggests that a combination of drought and growing extraction of water for agricultural and other purposes has led to falling levels in all the rivers in the area over the past 50 years (see Chapter 5).

Temperatures in Venda, like rainfall, show considerable variation across the territory. In general, temperatures increase as one moves from the higher ground of the central Soutpansberg to the low-lying areas of the north-east. This pattern may be seen from Table 3.1 (below) which shows average maximum and minimum daily temperatures for January and July, the hottest and coldest months of the year, for three stations in the region: Siloam, Tshandama and Pafuri. These may be taken as roughly indicative of conditions in the Soutpansberg, the valleys of central Venda and the Limpopo basin, respectively.

FIGURE 3.1

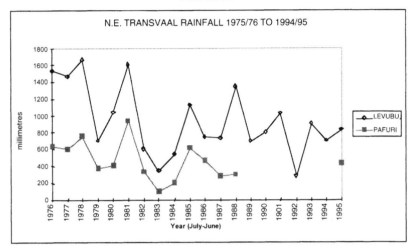

Source: South African Weather Bureau, Station Reports.

TABLE 3.1
AVERAGE DAILY TEMPERATURES, VENDA

Weather Station	Summer (January)		Winter (July)	
	max.	min.	max.	min.
Soutpansberg (Siloam)	29.5	18.4	22.7	7.2
Tshiombo Valley (Tshandama)	31.5	19.3	24.0	6.2
Limpopo Valley (Pafuri)	33.3	22.7	26.3	7.1

Source: South African Weather Bureau, Table WB42.

3.2 HISTORICAL BACKGROUND

The Venda people (*VhaVenda,* or *BaVenda,* in the Venda language), in common with other southern African peoples, are primarily a linguistic grouping, albeit with a distinct cultural heritage and common history. The Venda language (*Luvenda*), part of the Bantu group of African languages, has close affinity with Shona (Karanga) but shows considerable Sotho-Tswana influence [*Lestrade,* 1932: 487; *Kuper,* 1982: 91]. Although concentrated around the

Soutpansberg range, Venda-speakers can be found over much of the north-eastern Transvaal and in the Nuanetsi, Bubye and Gwanda areas of Zimbabwe [*Wilson*, 1969: 167; *Stayt*, 1968: 1].

The Venda are unique amongst the major southern African linguistic groups in not having been the subject of any substantial work of history and sources for both the pre- and early colonial periods are extremely rare. Oral tradition – recorded in the early twentieth century by Wessmann [1908], Lestrade [1932], Stayt [1968] and van Warmelo [1940] – tells of the ancestors of the Venda migrating from an area far to the north of the Limpopo, identified by some sources as the Great Lakes areas of East Africa (i.e. Lake Malawi or Lake Shirwa). After sojourning for a period amongst the Karanga of Zimbabwe, they are believed to have crossed the Limpopo under their leader Dimbanyika (at least as early as the seventeenth century), and subjugated the inhabitants of the Soutpansberg by the beating of a magical drum [*van Warmelo*, 1940: 23]. These conquerors, usually identified as the Singo, built their *Dzata*, or chief's place, in the fertile Nzhelele valley, just north of the Soutpansberg, and established themselves as the rulers of the native people, the Ngona.

Wilson [1969: 170] argues that Venda language, customs and beliefs show strong affinity with the Nyakyusa-Ngonde who inhabit the area north of Lake Malawi, which would tend to support tales of a migration from that region. Ralushai [1977: 29], however, in a critical study of the oral tradition and the early anthropological literature, finds no consensus regarding the origins of the Venda other than that they came from *Vhukalanga* (Zimbabwe), and describes pre-colonial Venda as a 'melting pot' of Zambezian and southern African cultures.

In a study of the documentary sources (mainly Portuguese), Marks [1975: 406] accepts the oral accounts of Singo conquest and relates these events to upheavals within Rozwi society and the rise of the Changamire dynasty north of the Limpopo in the late seventeenth century. Marks views the arrival of the Singo as part of an ongoing process of cultural exchange across the Limpopo, with the invaders adding a new layer of centralised rule over a people with whom they had strong cultural affinity: 'Culturally the Singo conquerors seem to have been assimilated into a distinctive Venda amalgam which had long been in the process of formation, and the Singo impact was principally felt in the political sphere.'

Archaeological evidence points to close links between pre-conquest Venda culture and the iron-age civilisations of Great Zimbabwe and Mapungubwe [*Fouché*, 1937: 44; *Hall*, 1990: 83]. Huffman and Hanisch [1987: 113], drawing on evidence from settlement remains in the area, also link the arrival of the Singo invaders and the building of Dzata to the Rozwi expansion of the late seventeenth century but challenge the assumption that centralised government did not exist before that date. The pre-existing Ngona cultures, they argue, had many features of statehood, such as an institutionalised bureaucracy and a sacred leadership at least as early as the fifteenth century:

> the archaeological evidence demonstrates that the Singo had essentially the same cosmology as the people they conquered. Thus, the Singo contribution to Venda history has been exaggerated in some ways, but not in others. The Singo did not introduce Venda culture, but they did unify the mountainous country for the first and apparently the only time in pre-colonial history.

At some time in their history the Venda incorporated groups of Lemba people (*VhaLemba*), a caste of traders and craft-workers whose origins are unknown but who are referred to in the early literature as displaying Shona or coastal Islamic ('Semitic') influences such as male circumcision and the avoidance of pork [*Lestrade*, 1932; *Stayt*, 1968: 18]. As late as the 1920s, small groups of Lemba, retaining traces of their own language, were to be found throughout the northern Transvaal, not just among the Venda but also among the Northern Sotho and the Tsonga-Shangaans [*Jaques*, 1931: 245]. Ralushai [1977: 226] describes the contemporary Lemba as an endogamous clan composed of a number of exogamous lineages, without chiefs or a language of their own, who constitute perhaps one per cent of the Venda population.

The chiefly line of Ramabulana, which claims descent from the legendary leaders Dimbanyika and Thohoyandou, has been the most powerful of the Venda chieftaincies during the period of recorded history. While leaders such as Makhado in the late nineteenth century were able to dominate neighbouring chieftaincies, there appears to be no tradition of a strong, unitary authority (that is, a paramountcy) encompassing all the Venda-speaking tribes, despite the efforts of twentieth-century propagandists to suggest otherwise. Indeed, Venda history is marked by dynastic struggles both within the house of Ramabulana and between it and other chiefdoms such as Tshivhase, Mphaphuli, Rambuda and Mashau [*Nemudzivhadi*, 1985; *Stayt*, 1968: 17].

The pre-colonial economy of Venda, according to Wilson [1969: 172], was based on 'cultivation, hunting and metal-working', and depended on Lemba craftsmen for woven cloth and pottery. The Venda forged iron hoes, and traded with the Tsonga who dominated the copper trade from Messina and had access to Portuguese traders on the east African coast. They grew grain, originally eleusine (finger millet, or *Eleusine coracana*) and sorghum, and later maize (which came to them via early Portuguese traders) which they stored in underground pits or on raised platforms. They are believed to have kept few cattle, due largely to the prevalence of the tsetse fly [*Stayt*, 1968: 37].

Beer made from eleusine or sorghum played an important part in Venda diet and ceremonial life [*Wessmann*, 1908: 49].

Wilson [1969: 175] argues that the Venda, like the Sotho, are a patrilineal and virilocal people with a preference for endogamous marriage. The institutions of Venda chieftaincy are also considered to be similar to those of the Sotho but show traces of their Karanga inheritance. Ralushai [1977: 16] suggests that early Venda settlements, such as the stone-built Dzata, were located in low-lying areas, and that the custom of living in inaccessible mountainous areas only arose as a result of the *Dlfaqane*, the wars and migrations associated with the rise of the Zulu kingdom from the late eighteenth century. From their mountain fastness, the Venda were able to defend their farmlands on the veld and their elephant hunting grounds in the fly-zone of the Limpopo from occasional attack, and would appear to have survived the upheavals of that period relatively unscathed.

Venda culture has been heavily influenced from an early date by interaction with various Northern Sotho-speaking lowveld peoples, such as the Tlokwa, the Kwebo and the Tswale. The Venda show particularly close affinity to the Lobedu, or Modjadji's people, of the Letaba valley, who are believed to have emerged from a similar imposition of Karanga off-shoots on Northern Sotho communities, although in this case the process of assimilation into Sotho culture has been virtually complete [*Krige and Krige*, 1943: 305; *Kuper*, 1982: 91]. In the east, the Venda have had considerable interchange with Tsonga-speakers who migrated from the coastal belt from the 1830s onwards [*Harries*, 1989: 83].

The arrival of European settlers and traders at Lourenço Marques (Maputo) and Inhambane on the Mozambican coast in the sixteenth century, and at the Cape of Good Hope in the seventeenth, appears to have had little direct impact on the Venda, other than possibly increasing indirect trading opportunities, and it was not until the nineteenth century that the area began to feel the direct impact of European expansionism. The first *trekkers* from the European settlement at the Cape to reach Venda territory were the mixed-race followers of Coenraad de Buys, who settled at the western end of a mountain range they called the Zoutpansberg (literally, Saltpan Mountain, later Soutpansberg) around 1820 [*Wagner*, 1980: 318]. Advance parties of the Afrikaner 'Great Trek', led by Louis Trichardt, Andries Hendrik Potgieter and Johannes van Rensburg, reached the area in 1836, searching for a land route to Lourenço Marques, but most of their parties met an early death either from malaria or at the hands of the local inhabitants.[4] The first substantial white settlement in the area was the town of Zoutpansberg (later Schoemansdal), 15 kilometres west of the present town of Louis Trichardt, founded in 1848 by Potgieter and his followers moving from Ohrigstad [*Thompson*, 1969: 413].

This isolated settlement represented the northern limit of European expansion from the Cape, as further progress was blocked by the tsetse fly country of the Limpopo basin, deadly to both cattle and horses, and the threat of malaria. While the Zoutpansberg settlement was too small and too far from ports or markets to develop as a major producer of crops or livestock, Wagner [1980: 336] argues that it did emerge in the 1850s and 1860s as an important hunting and trading centre – a *jagtersgemeenskap*, or hunters' community – based mainly on ivory. While a few Africans found employment as hunters, or participated in the ivory trade, the Zoutpansberg settlement was experienced by the native people of the area chiefly as 'a raiding state, exercising hegemony over them through annual tribute levies and meeting obduracy with destructive forays, funded out of the attendant plunder' [*Wagner*, 1980: 322]. African communities were, however, brought into contact with merchants from the Cape, Natal, Pretoria and Lourenço Marques, who traded cloth, sugar, coffee, tea, guns and ammunition for salt, skins and ivory [*Das Neves*, 1987: 146]. By the 1860s, the Boers had cleared most elephants from areas accessible on horse-back, and had begun to move into the fly-zone on foot, where they were heavily dependent on hired African marksmen.

To the east of the Zoutpansberg, the ivory trade was dominated by a handful of Portuguese traders, with close ties to the various Tsonga-Shangaan communities in the area and to the powerful Gaza kingdom of southern Mozambique. Foremost among these traders was one João Albasini, a Portuguese–Italian who arrived in the area from Ohrigstad in 1853, building a fort and trading post at Goedewensch on the upper reaches of the Luvuvhu River [*Wagner*, 1980: 326; *Harries*, 1989: 84]. With a foot in many worlds, Albasini, or *Juwawa*, established himself as chief of a large Shangaan community as well as being appointed Portuguese Vice-Consul for the Transvaal and Superintendent of Native Affairs for Zoutpansberg district under the South African Republic (ZAR).

Rivalry over control of a diminishing ivory trade, and attempts to subjugate the Venda chieftaincies, are believed to have contributed to the outbreak of war in 1867, when Venda forces, led by their chief Makhado, defeated a Boer commando under Paul Kruger and destroyed the town of Schoemansdal [*Thompson*, 1969: 442]. The white settlers withdrew in haste to the new towns of Potgietersrus and Marabastad (and later Pietersburg), leaving only a few white hunters, traders and missionaries operating amongst the African tribes between the Limpopo and the Oliphants River. One of the few travellers to pass through Venda territory during this period of relative isolation was the explorer Carl Mauch, who visited the kraals of chiefs Lwamondo and Tshivhase ('Sewaas'), as well as the ruins of Schoemansdal, in 1871 on his way to the Zimbabwe ruins [*Burke*, 1969: 121].

Christian missionaries arrived in the area in the early 1870s, notably the Lutherans of the Berlin Mission Society who had already established themselves amongst the Pedi and the Lovedu. Lutheran missions, operating through the medium of Luvenda, were established in Tshivhase in 1872, at Tshakhuma in 1874, and in Mphaphuli in 1877 and, according to Harries [1989: 92], the Berlin Mission soon became the *de facto* Venda church. At the same time, Presbyterian missionaries of the Swiss Mission were gaining converts amongst the Shangaan-speaking population of the area, establishing missions at Valdezia (1875) and Elim (1879). While the work and lasting influence of the various missionaries merits a major study, it must suffice here to note their role in the creation of the first printed texts in both the Venda and Shangaan (or Tsonga) languages, and what Harries [1989: 92] argues was their contribution to the division of the African people of the northern Transvaal along mutually reinforcing religious, linguistic and geographic lines.

Pressure from white settler-colonists on the remaining independent African peoples south of the Limpopo was renewed following the defeat of the powerful Pedi kingdom under Sekhukhune by the British in 1879, and the restoration in 1881 of the South African Republic (ZAR), which attempted to enforce its claim over the whole of the Transvaal territory. Under Statute No.8 of 1886, land in parts of Soutpansberg and Waterberg districts was surveyed and granted to settlers on condition that they build and inhabit a house on it. White settlement soon spread north from Pietersburg and eastwards along the Letaba River towards the emerging centres of Tzaneen and Duiwelskloof [*Cartwright*, 1974: 44]. Between 1882 and 1895, settler commandos under Joubert fought an almost uninterrupted campaign against those African communities which refused to submit to taxation and move to designated 'locations', defeating the followers of Modjadji and Makgoba (or Magoeba) on the Lowveld between 1890 and 1895 and Chief Malaboch's Hananwa people in the Blouberg in 1894 [*Thompson*, 1971: 281; *Bulpin*, 1965: 377; *Sonntag*, n.d.: 37]. This left the Venda under Makhado as the only independent African people within the territory claimed by the ZAR.

Makhado died in 1895, and was succeeded by his son Mphephu, but there followed a series of violent disputes between Mphephu and other leading chiefs [*Wessmann*, 1908: 120]. Against this background the Transvaal authorities, who had maintained a fort on the Muhododi (Doring) River (the traditional boundary of Makhado's territory) since 1888, were able to secure the submission of most of the Venda chiefs, including Mphaphuli, Tshivhase, Rambuda and Nelwamondo, leaving Mphephu as the only significant leader resisting white authority [*van Warmelo*, 1940]. In October 1898 a Boer Commando under Joubert and Trichardt crossed the Muhododi and erected a laager (complete with portable iron fort) at Tshitandani (Rietvlei, later Louis

Trichardt) [*Bulpin*, 1965: 445]. The following month (November 1898) Joubert's commando of 4,000 Afrikaners plus Swazi and Tsonga allies, and supported by artillery, stormed Mphephu's stronghold of Swunguzwi (Hangklip), and drove the chief and his followers northwards through the Nzhelele Valley [*Wessmann*, 1908: 124]. In December, Mphephu and thousands of followers retreated across the Limpopo and sought refuge in British Rhodesia, only returning in 1901 when the Boer forces were on the verge of defeat by the British. The town of Louis Trichardt was established in 1899 and become the centre of a fast-increasing white presence in the far northern Transvaal [*Bulpin*, 1965: 446].

Very little has been written about the process whereby the native inhabitants of the north-eastern Transvaal were dispossessed of their lands and drawn into working in the white-controlled economy, but it is possible to piece together a broad outline of events. Following the Anglo-Boer war (1899–1902), the Venda were disarmed by the new British administration and their territory divided into three Native Commissioners' areas – Louis Trichardt, Spelonken and Sibasa. The first Sub-Native Commissioner's camp in the area was established at Sibasa in 1902 [*Harries*, 1987: 98]. Much of the Venda territory, particularly to the south and west, was thrown open to white settlers and a greatly reduced area was delimited as 'native locations' for the leading chiefs – Mphephu, Tshivhase, Mphaphuli, Khakhu, Rambuda and Thengwe [*Stayt*, 1968: 19]. These locations were subsequently 'scheduled' under the terms of the 1913 Natives Land Act (that is, reserved for Black occupation only). By 1931, Venda and Shangaan communities had also been excluded from the area of the Kruger Park south of the Luvuvhu River [*Harries*, 1987: 107]. Following the 1936 Native Trust and Land Act, portions of Crown (that is, unsurveyed) Land, particularly the area between the Mutale and Limpopo Rivers, and a number of white-owned farms in southern and western districts were added to the territory reserved for Venda occupation (that is, 'released' in terms of the Act). As much of this land was already heavily populated, however, this did little to alleviate the general land shortage in the 'reserve' [*Harries*, 1989: 98].

Interviews with resettled people and their descendants (in areas such as Manenzhe, Ratombo, Mulima and Ntabalala) in 1995 and 1996 revealed that forced removals began almost as soon as white farmers established themselves in Venda territory and continued in various forms up to the 1980s. The relatively small numbers of white settlers, however, and the acquisition of large tracts of land by absentee owners – both individuals and companies, such as the Consolidated Land and Investment Company – meant that much of the native population was not immediately removed. White settlers were eager for cheap labour and sizeable numbers of the original inhabitants were allowed to remain on the farms as unpaid labour tenants. None the less, restrictions on the amount of land available to tenants for their own cultivation and on the numbers of livestock they could keep, as well as demands for unpaid labour from men, women and children led to a steady flow of labour tenant households off white farms and into the increasingly crowded African reserves and Crown lands.

The Native Economic Commission of 1932 found that soil and grazing in the reserves of the Transvaal was not as severely eroded as in much of the Cape, and in parts of the far north it was considered to be of very high quality: 'In fertility it [the Transvaal] may be said to be rather above the average of South African soil, and in some of the Reserves, notably that of Sibasa in the Zoutpansberg District, where the rainfall is also high, the fertility is exceptionally good' [*Union of South Africa*, 1932: 46]. As part of a lengthy *Addendum* to the main report, Advocate Frank Lucas provided this description of African farm tenants in Zoutpansberg district:

> On some farms the labour tenant is at the beck and call of the land owners and is required to work two days in each week year in and year out. Such a form of contract ties the Native to the farm to such an extent as to make it impossible for him to go out in search of work and thus earn sufficient money to maintain his family on. Natives living on farms under this form of contract are usually in poor circumstances, heavily in debt and unable to pay their Government Taxes. The Native is tied to the farm by the labour contract and is unable to go out to earn money without the consent of his landlord, which is often refused. The big majority of Natives are not in favour of becoming labour tenants owing to their being tied by the labour conditions of contracts.

> This form of contract is not at all popular with the Natives and accounts in a very great measure for the falling off of the numbers who take up residence on farms where such contracts are in vogue. The forms of labour tenancy contracts in this district are as follows:

> (1) 90 consecutive days of service;

> (2) 90 working days spread out over the year.

> The obligation of a labour tenant includes the services of his wives, children and other kraal inmates. No wage in cash or kind is paid unless they are in service on a wage basis after having completed their farm labour obligations and only then in respect of the labour performed over and above their labour contracts. In the majority of instances the labour tenant and his family have to feed themselves whilst in work. The farmer

usually makes it a condition of the contract that he has the use of all the manure from the tenant's cattle kraals. Assistance in ploughing is very seldom given' [*Union of South Africa*, 1932: 200].

Some tenants and other African farmers were, however, able to produce enough crops for their own needs and a surplus for sale. Harries [1989: 86] argues that between 1900 and 1930 the volume of maize marketed by African farmers on white farms, black-owned farms and the reserves in the Northern Transvaal (but not necessarily including Venda) increased dramatically, as did the value of direct taxes paid to the state: 'It is clear that a relatively prosperous, if small, class of African farmers was emerging at the expense of their peers.' This brief flowering of an African peasant class was brought to an end in the 1930s, Harries argues, by a state-led assault on black farmers, which included providing financial aid to white farmers and settling 'poor whites' on 36,000 *morgen* (31,000 hectares) of irrigable land along the upper Luvuvhu. Thousands of African tenant farmers were removed in the process. Government land purchases and support to white agriculture drove up the price of land in the area, and made arable farming attractive to white farmers for the first time. This in turn led white farmers to reduce the amount of arable land and grazing available to tenants, and to increase the amount of labour demanded from tenant households, resulting in what Harries [1989: 97] describes as 'the transformation in the 1930s of a large part of the African peasantry into a landless proletariat'.

Much of what we know about conditions in Venda at this time comes from the writings and speeches of Alpheus (A.M.) Maliba, a stalwart of the Communist Party and the ANC, and one of the founders of the Zoutpansberg Cultural Association, later the Zoutpansberg Balemi (ploughmen's) Association [*Delius*, 1993: 144]. The ZBA had its origins amongst Venda, Shangaan and Northern Sotho workers in Johannesburg, and was active in mobilising opposition to the initial wave of betterment on Native Trust lands after 1937 (see Chapter 2) [*Maliba*, 1981: 138; *Hirson*, 1989: 128]. At the height of its popularity, around 1944, the ZBA claimed over 3,000 members, and had an office and a night school in Louis Trichardt [*Delius*, 1993: 144].

Maliba [1981: 139], writing in 1939, describes life in the Venda reserves in the following terms:

> The people live by means of agriculture, the methods of working the land being traditional. Ploughs are not used, because the greatest part of their land is on hillsides where they cannot use ploughs, and their poverty prevents them from buying such implements. They dig the ground with spades and plant mielies [*maize*], beans, pumpkins, kaffir corn [*sorghum*], and sweet potatoes. They do not sell their produce on

the markets, but use almost everything they grow for their own consumption. When they have a surplus, they barter their produce with the
Indian storekeepers for articles of clothing. They seldom slaughter
cattle, only making use of the milk.

The policy of betterment to which Maliba and the ZBA were opposed was first
implemented in Venda in 1937 with the culling of cattle and demarcation
of arable plots on land acquired for African occupation under the 1936
Native Trust and Land Act. Taxpayers (male heads of households) were at
first allotted two morgen plots, and non-taxpayers (old men, widows and
unmarried men) one and a half morgen, but in 1941 the allocation was reduced
to one and a half morgen for taxpayers and nothing for non-taxpayers [Hirson,
1989: 128]. Maliba and the ZBA held a mass meeting at Piesanghoek to
protest at the restrictions on ploughing and culling of cattle, as well as the
restrictions on cutting firewood, the burden of taxes, and the arbitrary and
extortionate behaviour of local Trust officials, many of them 'poor whites'.
The assembled crowd resolved to ignore the newly demarcated plots and
plough as they did in previous years. The authorities reacted by arresting
Maliba and up to 80 others, but abandoned thoughts of prosecution when faced
with a demonstration of thousands of their supporters outside the Louis
Trichardt courthouse [Hirson, 1989: 129]. Similar protests against betterment
broke out across the northern Transvaal in 1943 and 1944, notably in
Sekhukhuneland, which were forcibly suppressed by the South African police
and military [Delius, 1996: 60].

    Limitations on the amount of land available to Venda households, deterio-
rating conditions of tenancy on the white farms and demands from the state for
taxes meant that Venda men, in particular, were drawn steadily into the market
for wage labour. Apart from a few passing references, however, we know little
or nothing about this process or its impact on Venda life, at least up to the
1960s. Delius [1983: 63] argues that migration to work on white farms in the
Cape was well established among the Pedi as early as the 1860s, but not
among the Venda. The rise of large-scale mining in the 1870s and 1880s
would not appear to have dramatically changed this situation although it is
believed that Chief Makhado's son, Mphephu, was working at Kimberley
when his father died in 1895 [Nemudzivhadi, 1985: 10]. Many of the major
works on mine labour, including Yudelman [1983], Jeeves [1985] and Turrell
[1987] make no mention of Venda workers. The exception is Worger [1987:
72], who specifically excludes the Venda from the first great wave of migration to Kimberley, stating that by 1872 'every black society south of the
Zambezi River, with the exception only of the Venda and Cetshwayo's Zulu,
was represented at the diamond fields'. Murray [1995] provides a vivid

account of 'blackbirding', the illicit recruitment of migrant workers coming from Southern Rhodesia, Nyasaland and Mozambique, at the appropriately named Crooks' Corner on the border of Venda territory during the early decades of this century, but makes no mention of the recruitment of local (that is, South African) labour. Similarly, the ethnographer Hugh Stayt [1968] makes no mention of labour migrancy in his lengthy study of Venda in the late 1920s.

Thus, the available evidence would suggest that Venda workers did not feature prominently among the great waves of recruitment to the mines in the late nineteenth and early twentieth centuries. There is little doubt, however, that over time a growing number of Venda workers found their way to the mines, factories, homes and municipal services of the Witwatersrand and other urban centres, although Wilson [1972: 84] suggests that migration from Venda only reached significant proportions after the Second World War. From the work of Maliba, however, we know that there was a sizeable presence of migrants from Northern Transvaal, including Venda, in the hostels and townships of the Rand, and Maliba himself was variously described as a night-watchman, a factory worker and a baker [*Callinicos*, 1993: 49; *Delius*, 1993: 147]. The army was another source of work, with many BaVenda serving with the Native Army Service Corps in North and East Africa during the Second World War, and the problems faced by servicemen's families was a particular source of grievance to the Zoutpansberg Balemi Association in 1941 [*Callinicos*, 1993: 49]. Direct mine recruitment from Venda was prohibited for many decades in the mid-twentieth century, and it was only in the 1970s that the 'internal labour frontier' for mine recruitment was extended into the African homelands of the Transvaal [*Crush, Jeeves and Yudelman*, 1991: 136]. Interviews with older men in Venda in 1995 and 1996 revealed that many had worked in the cities as household servants, drivers, building workers and municipal employees, but relatively few had worked on the mines.

The administration of the African reserves in the first half of the twentieth century was largely in the hands of Native Commissioners, Magistrates, and officials of the Native Affairs Department. From 1948, however, the National Party government set about establishing a system of 'tribal' administration in the African reserves while continuing to deny political and economic rights to black people in 'white' South Africa (see Chapter 1). For Harries [1989: 105], the system of Tribal Authorities was the cornerstone of the new government's native policy: 'It attempted to consolidate and bolster the power of the chiefs, and to give them an element of self-government, by increasing and modernising their access to a means of patronage. This necessitated extending their land area and expanding their tax base.'

The first Tribal Authorities in Venda were established in 1954, in Mphephu,

Tshivhase, Mphaphuli and Rambuda Areas, followed by Tshikonelo, Mulenzhe, Thengwe and Tshimbupfe in 1959 [*Nemudzivhadi*, 1985: 28]. Three Regional Authorities – Ramabulana, Spelonken, and Vhembe – were established to cover the Venda-speaking territories, but Vhembe, in particular, included a sizeable number of Tsonga-speakers such as the Makuleke people of the Pafuri triangle and others living south of the Luvuvhu River. By 1962, the foundations had been laid for the division of the African population of the northern Transvaal along ethnic lines with the creation of three Territorial Authorities: Thohoyandou, under the chairmanship of Chief Mphephu for the Venda-speaking population, Matshangana (later Gazankulu) under Chief Mhinga, for Tsonga-Shangaan speakers, and Lebowa for Northern Sotho-speakers [*Hill*, 1964: 15]. Given the widespread inter-mingling of peoples in the region, many Venda- and Tsonga-speakers, in particular, found themselves on the 'wrong' side, and conflicts arose over the allocation of land, the assignment of positions of responsibility on tribal authorities and school boards and the language medium to be used in schools [*Horrell*, 1973: 8]. Tensions were exacerbated by the policy of the Ntsanwisi regime in the new Gazankulu of encouraging thousands of 'Tsonga-Shangaans' living in Venda and Lebowa to come 'home' [*Harries*, 1989: 107].

According to Desmond [1971: 184], once Tsonga people started abandoning Venda areas the Venda chiefs demanded that Venda-speakers be moved from Tsonga areas to replace them. Thousands of Vendas are reported to have been forcibly removed from the area of Mavambe, south of the Luvuvhu River in 1968, while large numbers of Tsonga were removed from Tshakhuma Lutheran Mission farm and other villages in Sibasa District [*Desmond*, 1971: 185]. The process of homeland consolidation and boundary-fixing continued throughout the 1970s and into the 1980s. In 1977 the Madimbo corridor was occupied by the South African military, to counter the perceived threat of infiltration from Rhodesia-Zimbabwe, leading to the removal of a number of settlements [*Surplus People Project*, 1983: 164]. In 1978, the area around Elim Hospital, with a long tradition of mixing between Venda-, Shangaan- and Northern Sotho-speakers, was split between Venda and Gazankulu, leading to the relocation of much of the Venda-speaking population [*Horrell*, 1973: 8; *Land Research Group*, 1995: 11). With Venda's 'independence' in 1979, many Northern Sotho-speakers were obliged to leave the territory out of fear of losing access to welfare services and own-language education [*Surplus People Project*, 1983: 164].

The Surplus People Project [1983: 164] suggests that 'tribal' consciousness only became a problem in the northern Transvaal with the imposition of the system of Tribal Authorities, which gave government-approved tribal leaders the power to grant or withhold employment, pensions and other benefits within their areas and to discriminate against members of other ethnic groups. Similarly, Harries [1989: 82] argues that the creation and fuelling of ethnic consciousness was an integral part of 'separate development' and class formation, and tribal chiefs and others viewed self-government as a means of competing more successfully with rival 'ethnic' groups and of accumulating personal wealth. The process of 'retribalization', accompanied by an upsurge of 'national' culture through the press, radio and schools, boosted the material and symbolic position of the chiefs, and created opportunities for an emerging petty bourgeois class who wished to take advantage of the emerging business and administrative opportunities offered in the homelands.

Forced removals from 'white' districts of the northern Transvaal also increased following the establishment of the 'homelands'. The sustained attack on 'squatters', which began in other parts of the country with the 1913 Natives Land Act, and intensified following the passage of the 1936 Native Trust and Land Act, was not implemented in the northern Transvaal until the late 1960s due to the opposition of farmers and tenants [Surplus People Project, 1983: 120; Delius, 1996: 143]. From about 1966, tens of thousands of black families were evicted from white farms throughout the region, often with considerable violence, and dumped in the reserves, a process vividly described by Cosmas Desmond [1971] and Muriel Horrell [1973]. The relocation of Venda-speakers was concentrated in the western parts of Venda, particularly in those areas acquired by the Native Trust after 1936 and within commuting distance of white farming districts [Surplus People Project, 1983: 165]. Farm workers, now officially resident in the reserves, were obliged to spend lengthy periods on white farms without their families and without access to the ploughing and grazing land they had formerly used as tenants. Within the crowded Venda reserves, removed families were rarely given access to arable plots, or entitled to keep livestock, and found themselves in competition with longer-standing residents for very limited resources and services [Schutte, 1984: 12].

Forced removals were not confined to white farms, however. Mission stations,[5] where black communities enjoyed a degree of autonomy and in some cases freehold title to their lands, as well as urban townships, were targeted by apartheid's social engineers using the powers of the Group Areas Acts of 1950 and 1966 [Desmond, 1971: 160]. One of the largest removals occurred in 1969 when the Pafuri triangle was incorporated into the Kruger Park, and over 3,000 Makuleke were moved south to Ntlaveni, part of Mhinga Tribal Authority [Harries, 1987: 107]. As late as 1979, over twelve thousand people were cleared from 'black spots' in the northern Transvaal in a single year [Surplus People Project, 1983: 161]. In the black township of Tshikota, adjacent to the town of Louis Trichardt, the authorities set about removing

each of the so-called 'national' groups to their respective 'homelands'.
Between 1982 and 1984, over twelve hundred Venda-speaking families were
moved to the new 'township' of Vleifontein, 20 kilometres away, and a similar
number of Shangaan-speakers were moved to Waterval, adjacent to Elim
Hospital.[6] The relatively small Indian population of Louis Trichardt was also
removed to a separate township, Eltivillas, on the outskirts of the town.

Within the reserves, the policy of betterment which had been implemented
intermittently since the late 1930s was applied with new energy following the
introduction of self government. Across Venda, on Trust land and within the
older 'tribal locations', dispersed rural settlements were regrouped into tighter,
grid-like villages, standard-sized arable plots were allocated to approved
households, grazing lands ('camps') were demarcated and fenced, and attempts
were made to impose a rotational grazing system. Households of long-standing within older locations such as Mphephu, Tshivhase and Mphaphuli were
generally able to secure grazing and ploughing rights, although not necessarily
in proportion to their original holdings. For those without land rights at the
time of betterment, however, and especially the tens of thousands of households moving into Venda from surrounding areas, there was little chance of
obtaining an arable plot or access to communal grazing. Investigating the
process of forced villagisation in the north-west of Venda, Schutte [1984: 12]
found that the pre-existing social structure, based on extended patrilineal kin-
networks, was not accommodated in the new settlements and prospects for
obtaining agriculture-based livelihoods were much reduced following betterment. Wilson [1972: 84] (writing in the early 1970s), provides a first-hand
account of the burgeoning closer settlements in Venda:

> . . . within the space of three or four years the whole of Vendaland
> from Mara 30 km west of Louis Trichardt to Sibasa in the east has
> seen the mushrooming of closer settlements housing anything from a
> few hundred up to 10,000 or more people . . . First of all the people
> are responsible for building their own houses and so the settlements
> look like enormous villages whose inhabitants have varying amounts
> of arable land at distances up to several miles from the homelands
> [*probably 'homesteads'*]. Secondly the amount, and in some places the
> quality, of the arable land is nowhere near sufficient for the families
> living in the settlements to eke out even subsistence level of existence.
> Thus according to those who know the settlements the general rule is
> for the homelands to be inhabited by women, children and old people.
> Most of the able-bodied men are away in the work centres such as
> Phalaborwa, Pietersburg or the Witwatersrand.

By 1972, 78 per cent of the land area of Venda was reported to have been replanned [*Horrell*, 1973: 9] and the process of forced villagisation was still proceeding ten years later [*Schutte*, 1984: 12].

Following the lead set by the Transkei, the Thohoyandou Territorial Authority was replaced by a Venda 'legislative assembly' in 1971 and two years later was granted the status of a 'self-governing territory' within the Republic of South Africa, with Chief Mphephu as Chief Councillor [*Horrell*, 1973: 42]. Elections to the legislative assembly were held in 1973 and 1978. On both occasions, the majority of contested seats were won by the Venda Independence People's Party (VIPP), led by Baldwin Mudau, but Mphephu's Venda National Party (VNP) managed to hold on to power through the support of nominated chiefs [*Surplus People Project*, 1983: 19]. This manipulation of the electoral process set the tone for the next decade, as the Mphephu regime engaged in systematic intimidation of the opposition and the accumulation of considerable personal wealth. In September 1979, Venda declared its 'independence', a status recognised by no democratic country in the world, and Chief Mphephu had himself declared *khosikhulu* (paramount chief) and subsequently 'Life President'. In the elections of 1984, Mphephu's VNP won an unlikely 41 out of 45 elected seats amidst strong protests of vote-tampering from the opposition VIPP. As violent opposition to apartheid spread to the homelands in the mid-1980s, the Mphephu regime acquired a growing reputation for corruption and violence, which included the death in detention of several anti-government activists [*Cadman*, 1986: 83].

Mphephu ruled until his death in 1988 and was succeeded as State President by Frank (F.N.) Ravele amidst growing popular opposition to the regime.[7] Anti-government demonstrations broke out in August 1988 when students protested against alleged corruption and ritual murder by members of the cabinet [*Koch and Ritchken*, 1988: 48]. In 1990, following the release of Nelson Mandela and the unbanning of the ANC, marches, demonstrations, strikes and stay-aways by government workers, students and supporters of the United Democratic Front brought the homeland to a virtual standstill, with demands for the dismissal of Ravele and his ministers, an end to martial law and the re-incorporation of the territory into South Africa. This period of political turmoil was also marked by a wave of violence (including many murders) against people accused of witchcraft, not only in Venda but across the northern Transvaal [*Delius*, 1996: 203; *Northern Province*, 1996]. Faced with mass popular opposition to his rule, Ravele was ousted by the chief of staff of the Venda Defence Forces, Colonel Gabriel Ramushwana (with support from the South African Defence Forces), who backed the popular calls for reform and for re-incorporation [*National Land Committee*, 1990: 12]. There followed four years of military dictatorship, and widespread strikes and anti-government demonstrations, during which the state structures and public services in Venda virtually collapsed.

Along with the nine other homelands, Venda was reincorporated into a unified South African on 27 April 1994. In the elections of that month, the ANC won an overwhelming majority (92 per cent) of the vote in the new Northern Province and all but one of the seats in the provincial parliament [*Indicator SA* 1994: 37]. In November 1995, the ANC again triumphed in elections to the newly-formed local councils, winning all the seats in the former Venda

3.3 DEMOGRAPHY AND SETTLEMENT

Population estimates for Venda, as for the other former homelands, must be treated with considerable caution. Poor survey methods, the prevalence of migrant labour, and a history of forced removals have tended to result in under-estimates of the black population, especially in rural areas [*DBSA*, 1993a: 29]. Frequent changes in homeland borders add to the uncertainty, especially when attempting comparisons between censuses. Bearing these points in mind, the following table shows the available population statistics for Venda since 1970, broken down by Magisterial Districts.

TABLE 3.2
POPULATION OF VENDA, BY MAGISTERIAL DISTRICT

	1970[1]	1978[2]	1985[3]	1991[4]	1996[5]	Increase 1970–96 (%)
Dzanani	63,611	74,536	108,400	123,035	129,261	103.2%
Mutale	27,726	32,099	47,400	55,141	57,931	108.9%
Thohoyandou	123,114	175,371	203,000	244,532	256,905	108.7%
Vuwani	70,799	78,247	118,600	136,089	142,975	101.9%
TOTAL	285,251	360,253	477,400	558,797	587,072	105.8%

Notes: [1] Total 'Black' population from 1970 census [*RAU*, 1979: 30], including an upward adjustment of 4.7% for under-enumeration. [2] From RAU (1979: 30). [3] 1985 Census [*DBSA*, 1989]. These figures have been rounded to the nearest hundred. [4] 1991 Census [*Republic of Venda*, 1993a]. [5] Preliminary results of the 1996 Census (as supplied by the Central Statistics Office, April 1998).

The population of Venda in 1991, according to the census of that year, was 558,797, which represents an increase of 95.9 per cent over the figure for 1970, with the highest rate of growth in the period 1978–85. It is not possible to say how much of this increase is due to natural factors, and how much to forced movement of people into the area, although clearly both played a part.

These figures represent an average growth rate over the period of approximately 3.4 per cent per annum, compared to three per cent for the black population of South Africa as a whole and 2.7 per cent for the entire South African population [*DBSA*, 1993a: 102]. The population density of Venda in 1991 was 82.5 persons per square km, less than that of the neighbouring homelands of Lebowa and Gazankulu, but thirteen times the density of the non-homeland (that is, 'white') portion of the northern Transvaal [*DBSA*, 1993a: 102].

As with other former 'homeland' areas, population structure in Venda is skewed in favour of women and the young, which is usually explained in terms of the out-migration of adult male workers. The following table shows the composition of the population by age and sex for 1970 and 1985.

TABLE 3.3
POPULATION COMPOSITION BY AGE AND SEX, VENDA 1970–85 (%)

Census	0–14 Years		15–64 Years		65+ Years		TOTAL
	male	female	male	female	male	female	
1970	25.3	25.1	12.2	33.2	1.5	2.7	100
1985	23.9	23.9	15.9	30.9	1.7	3.7	100

Source: RAU [1979] and DBSA [1993a].

The main changes evident between 1970 and 1985 are: a drop in the proportion of the population under 15 years of age (from 50.4 to 47.8 per cent); a rise in the proportion of males in the population as a whole (from 39 to 41.5 per cent) but especially in the 'economically active' age group (15 to 64 years); and an increase in the proportion of the population aged 65 years or older. All of these trends continued in the 1991 Census, indicating a move towards a more 'balanced' population structure. Although the available data are insufficient to allow any firm conclusion, they are at least consistent with a drop in the birth rate, an increase in life expectancy and a drop in out-migration over the period in question.

The manner in which the Venda territories have been demarcated during the twentieth century, and the successive waves of population movement within the region, have resulted in a high degree of cultural and linguistic homogeneity amongst the population. The 1991 Census found that 95.2 per cent of the population spoke *Luvenda* as their first language, with the only significant linguistic minorities being Shangaan/Tsonga (two per cent) and Northern Sotho (1.9 per cent) speakers. Afrikaans is understood by many people, particularly older people with experience of working on white farms, and was the principal language of administration up to the 1970s. English is now the preferred medium of communication with non Venda-speakers, especially amongst the younger generation and within the administration, although it is not spoken by much of the rural adult population. Understanding of English or Afrikaans is generally higher amongst men than amongst women.

While Venda is generally considered to be 'deep rural', a growing proportion of the population is becoming functionally urbanised within the five 'proclaimed' towns and the many rapidly growing 'closer settlements' created under betterment [*DBSA*, 1993a: 46]. Of the 'urban' areas, the most important is the new town of Thohoyandou, which was developed during the 1970s and 1980s as the capital of the 'independent' Venda, and embraces the older administrative centre of Sibasa and the townships of Shayandima and Makwarela. The population of Thohoyandou urban area (including informal settlements) was 21,998 in 1991 [*Republic of Venda*, 1993a]. The much larger Thohoyandou Magisterial District accounted for 43.8 per cent of the population of Venda, and further large concentrations of population are found between Thohoyandou and Louis Trichardt, in the Magisterial Districts of Vuwani and Dzanani. The largest Magisterial District, Mutale, in the northeast, accounts for less than ten per cent of the total population.

Apart from Thohoyandou, the only areas with any substantial commercial or industrial development are the town of Makhado (Dzanani District), Tshikondeni mine (Makuya Area), and Muraleni, in Kutama Area, adjacent to the former 'white' town of Louis Trichardt. The township of Vleifontein, in western Vuwani, with an official population of 2,891 in 1991, is effectively a displaced suburb of Louis Trichardt with few social or economic facilities of its own, while other emerging towns such as Vuwani, Mutale, Masisi and Tshitale are little more than rural trading posts with some government offices and scattered settlements.

Venda has an estimated 420 so-called rural settlements, ranging from remote villages to informal towns [*Mutshekwane*, 1993: 69]. The majority of these were subjected to 'betterment' planning in the 1960s and 1970s, either as 'agricultural villages', whose inhabitants had access to some arable and grazing lands, or 'closer settlements', for households without land. Most houses in the rural areas are of traditional build, with round, mud-brick walls and thatched roofs, but there is a strong trend towards concrete-block walls and tin roofs. Very few data are available on household or family structure in Venda. In a study of two areas, Naledzani [1992: 45] found an average household size of 5.4 persons in Khakhu and 7.0 in Mashamba. In a study from Tshikundamalema, van Nieuwenhuizen [1984: 8] found that the average number of inhabitants per 'hut group' was 6.18. A recent study by SALDRU [1994: 21] found that the average household size for Africans in the Northern Province as a whole was 5.4 persons.

3.4 ECONOMIC AND SOCIAL CONDITIONS

The general lack of investment and economic development in Venda, and the ways in which its people have been incorporated into the South African economy, have left it heavily dependent on the major industrial and commercial centres for employment and the provision of goods and services. While attempts were made during the independence period to produce 'national' economic indicators (for example, Gross Domestic Product, Gross National Product and per capita income), these must be treated with caution due to the open nature of the economy, the prevalence of 'informal' (that is, unrecorded) activities and the sometimes questionable survey methods. The Development Bank [*DBSA*, 1993b: 4] estimated the Gross Geographic Product (GGP) for Venda in 1988 at R535.2 million and per capita GGP at R1,060. This latter figure was substantially higher than the comparable figures for the neighbouring homelands of Gazankulu and Lebowa, but only 15 per cent of the figure for the 'white' (that is, non-homeland) portion of the northern Transvaal. Throughout the independence era (1979–94), the greater part of budgeted government expenditure (70–80 per cent) was provided by the South African government [*Moody and Golino*, 1984: 5].

The formal economy is heavily biased towards the tertiary (that is, service) sector, which largely addresses welfare concerns – health, education, pensions – and is dominated by the public sector. Government services accounted for an estimated 54 per cent of GGP in 1990, followed by construction (10.1 per cent), trade and tourism (9.9 per cent), agriculture (8.3 per cent), manufacturing (6.4 per cent) and financial and business services (5.3 per cent) [*DBSA*, 1993b: 4]. Venda is heavily dependent on wages remitted from outside the territory, which Schutte [1984: 5] estimated probably outweighed the entire value of goods and services produced within Venda in the early 1980s. The Development Bank[*DBSA*, 1993a: 41] estimates the male absentee rate in the age group 15-64 at 48.1 per cent and puts the total number of migrants from Venda, male and female, at around 80,000. Labour migration from Venda is mainly to the Witwatersrand (Gauteng Province), with smaller numbers going to the industrial centres of the northern Transvaal, such as Pietersburg, Messina and Phalaborwa. Formal employment opportunities are estimated to exist within Venda for less than a quarter of the available workforce (excluding migrants). The Development Bank [*DBSA*, 1993a: 96] estimated that in 1991 over half of the labour force (53.5 per cent) was engaged in the 'subsistence' sector, 23 per cent in 'formal' employment and 7.3 per cent in 'informal activities', with 16.2 per cent classified as 'unemployed'.[8]

At 'independence', Venda was poorly supplied with education, welfare and communications services. The territory had only two tarred roads, totalling

131 km – one running from Louis Trichardt to Punda Maria, with a 5 km spur to Thohoyandou; the other, dating from the late 1970s, running from the Messina-Louis Trichardt road to Pafuri on the Mozambique border, via Tshipise [*RAU*, 1979: 127]. The western tip of Venda is traversed by the Pietersburg-to-Messina railway line, but there are no stations within Venda territory. Recent years, especially the period since 1990, have seen rapid improvements to the road network and considerable progress in the supply of electricity to private dwellings, although many areas have yet to be served. The telephone system still extends little beyond the main urban areas, with a small number of 'farm lines' to outlying government offices and local notables. Piped water is supplied to most homes in urban areas and is slowly being extended to the rural areas. This tends to be in the form of communal standpipes, and in many rural areas even these are frequently dry, leaving people dependent on streams and springs for their household water supplies.

Formal education in Venda has expanded dramatically since independence, especially at the secondary level, aided by an extensive school-building programme. By 1991, the number of primary pupils was up 57 per cent on the figure for 1978 (roughly in line with population growth), while the number of secondary students had increased dramatically (albeit from a very low base) by 336 per cent [*DBSA*, 1993a: 165]. As with other public services, quality of delivery is marked by enormous differences, with many rural children still receiving their education under makeshift shelters and suffering severe shortages of basic educational materials.

The numbers of hospital beds, nurses, clinics and doctors per capita are also far behind the levels for 'white' South Africa. At 'independence', Venda had three hospitals – Donald Fraser, Siloam and Tshilidzini – all founded by missionary societies, with a total of 1,263 beds. In addition, 39 clinics functioned as satellites of the hospitals, and the entire territory was served by ten doctors [*RAU*, 1979: 56]. Since then, health care provision has been considerably improved through the extension of the village clinic system under the supervision of the three main hospitals. Women's self-help groups ('Care Groups') have also been mobilised in many areas to raise awareness of health and nutritional issues [*Mfono*, 1989: 495].

Detailed statistics are not available for welfare indicators such as life expectancy or literacy for Venda alone, but a general impression may be obtained from figures for the African population of the Northern Province as a whole. By virtually every indicator, the African population of the province represents the least favourable case for all races and all regions in South Africa. For example, life expectancy at birth and adult literacy are the lowest in the country, while rates for infant mortality, births to teenage mothers and total (lifetime) fertility for women are the highest [*DBSA*, 1993a: 121;

SALDRU, 1994]. The Development Bank [*DBSA,* 1994: 18] found that personal income per capita, at R725 in 1993, was only slightly over half that of the next poorest province, the Eastern Cape, placing Northern Province firmly at the bottom of its Human Development Index.

Venda today, unlike many of the other homelands, is characterised by its remoteness from large urban centres, its relative cultural homogeneity, and the high proportion of households that continue to have some access to agricultural resources. Although the past 20 years have seen the emergence of a new elite based around the public service and private business sector, Venda remains a poor area within the poorest region of South Africa. The sense of geographic and linguistic isolation of the area was, if anything, intensified by the experience of 'independence' which, however unpopular politically, has left the population with a strong sense of their own identity within the 'new' South Africa.

NOTES

1. Preliminary results from the 1996 Census put the population of the four Venda Magisterial Districts at 587,072.
2. See RAU [1979] for a detailed description of all regions and sub-regions.
3. Desmond [1971: 182] provides a vivid description of the impact of drought in the region during this time.
4. The *voortrekkers* under Louis Trichardt, along with the de Buys, are believed to have assisted Ramabulana to overcome his rival Ramavhoya for the leading Venda chieftaincy, and the Boers at Schoemansdal intervened again to assist the succession of Makhado after Ramabulana's death in 1864 [*Thompson,* 1969: 441; *Wagner,* 1980: 329)]
5. Ramphele [1995: 6] provides a rare account of life on a mission station in the Soutpansberg at this time.
6. Tshikota is today being rebuilt and reoccupied, mainly by the original inhabitants.
7. See van Kessel [1993: 598] and Delius [1996: Ch. 6] for more detailed accounts of related events, particularly the rise of the UDF, in the neighbouring homeland of Lebowa.
8. These categories are not defined in the source.

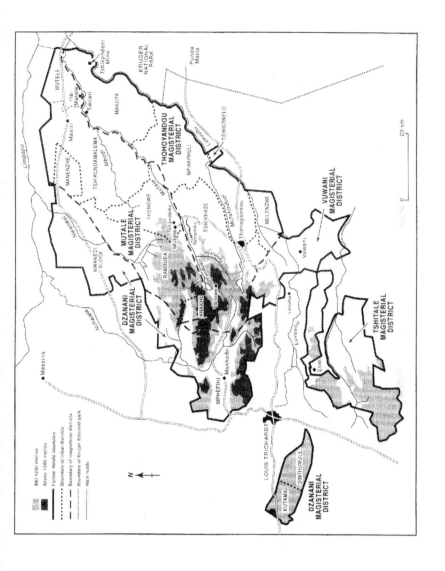

4

Agriculture in Venda

Agriculture was at the heart of the pre-colonial economy of Venda and, until the 1950s, Venda would have been considered a largely agrarian society, albeit one that was being progressively incorporated into the broader industrial economy of South Africa. Virtually nothing has been written, however, about the transformation of society and economy in Venda that began with the arrival of white hunters, traders and missionaries in the nineteenth century. This process accelerated rapidly after the Anglo-Boer war with the loss of territory, the absorption of labour into white-controlled agriculture and industry and the imposition by the colonial authorities of new financial obligations on the native population.

Despite the challenges to the old order posed by colonialism (and later apartheid), it did not immediately eliminate the central place of agriculture in the life of most BaVenda. The great majority of households within the demarcated 'locations', and later on Trust lands, continued to have access to some land for agricultural purposes, while in the areas of white settlement, at least until the 1960s, many BaVenda managed to retain a precarious link to the land as labour tenants. The conditions under which the Venda were incorporated into the colonial economy, however, meant that a prosperous semi-independent peasantry, of the kind described by Bundy [1979] for the eastern Cape and Natal and Keegan [1986] for the Highveld in the late nineteenth century, did not emerge.[1] Possible explanations for this include the relatively developed state of white agriculture (in terms of integration into markets for land, inputs and agricultural produce) by the time Venda was annexed, the very limited market for agricultural produce within the northern Transvaal and the determination of the white authorities to discourage competition from black farmers and restrict economic activity within the tribal 'reserves' in the decades following the Anglo-Boer war. Furthermore, the area had relatively few mission stations, and little sharecropping, both of which provided important channels for accumulation by black peasants in other parts of the country. As the economy of the northern Transvaal came to be dominated by a relatively few large-scale white farmers, generously supported by the state, smallholders within the reserves were left with little option but to produce mainly for domestic consumption, with very limited quantities of fresh produce and livestock being traded on local informal markets.

Apartheid policies of influx control, betterment, forced removals and evictions of farm tenants, coupled with a high natural rate of population growth, mean that today probably close to half of all households in Venda do not have access to agricultural land or livestock. For those who do, farming generally provides a relatively minor part of their livelihoods.[2] Large-scale commercially-oriented farming emerged in Venda only in the 1970s and until the late 1980s was confined almost entirely to the state-controlled sector, either in the form of direct production by state-owned companies or through the leasing of state-owned lands to selected individuals and corporations. Only in the latter stages of Venda's 'independence' did there emerge a small elite of larger 'private' farmers, most of whom had substantial non-farm resources and close ties to the homeland regime.

4.2 A NOTE ON SOURCES AND TERMINOLOGY

Information on land holding and agricultural activities in Venda, as for the other former homelands, is very limited and not always reliable (see Chapter 2). The main sources of statistical information for the period 1979–94 are the publications of the Venda Agricultural Corporation Ltd. (Agriven), the South African Bureau for Economic Research: Co-operation and Development (BENSO) and the Development Bank of Southern Africa, particularly the *Venda Information File [DBSA*, 1986] and *Development Information: Region G [DBSA*, 1991]. All of these organisations (with the possible exception of Agriven) rely heavily on agricultural censuses and routine reports by government field officers (rather than original research). They also tend to be heavily biased towards farmers on government-supported schemes supplying formal agricultural markets and neglect the mass of independent small-scale farmers producing mainly for home consumption and informal markets. Little independent verification of this data is carried out and it must be treated with considerable caution. For example, Dederen [1992: 12] found that participants in the Farmer Support Programme in Venda routinely tended to understate crop yields, and local officials to overstate them, giving rise to major discrepancies between what farmers actually produced and what ended up in official reports. Other weaknesses in reporting systems were found on the Tshiombo irrigation scheme (see Chapter 6) where Agricultural Officers used 'standard' (as opposed to actual) estimates of inputs, yields and income, all deduced from areas planted. Information on more complex aspects of rural livelihoods – such as off-farm incomes, unemployment rates, household expenditure patterns and the like – is extremely scarce and, where it exists, tends to be based on very small samples and questionable reporting methods.

A variety of non-official studies shed additional light on aspects of agriculture in Venda, including academic works by Thormeyer [1989], Naledzani [1992], Dederen [1992] and Pretorius [1994]; short studies for the Second Carnegie Inquiry by van Nieuwenhuizen [1984], Moody and Golino [1984] and Schutte [1984]; and a recent report by the Land Research Group [1995] for the Land and Agricultural Policy Centre. Such local studies provide valuable qualitative (and some quantitative) information on rural conditions, especially processes of social and economic change, that are largely absent from the official record.

Despite the availability of such material, there remain large gaps in the literature on agriculture and related issues in Venda. No reliable figures are available for the total number of households with arable or grazing land, for example, or how such land is distributed between households. Key indicators of farming activity, such as total numbers and distribution of livestock and annual crop output, are reported periodically (at least for the 1980s), but the information is far from complete and little or no data are available at the village or household level.

An additional problem confronted in the study of homeland agriculture is the terminology used in most official and quasi-official sources, which tends to be misleading, inconsistent and ideologically loaded. Agriculture in the homelands is commonly divided into a 'commercial' sector, comprising large-scale state projects and individuals heavily supported by the state, producing for sale in formal markets; and a 'subsistence' sector, comprising smaller-scale farmers integrated poorly (if at all) in to state support systems or formal agricultural markets – in short, a modified form of the discourse more commonly used to distinguish agriculture in the homelands as a whole from agriculture in the rest of the country [*DBSA*, 1986, 1987, 1991; *Bembridge*, 1988].[3] The main difference evident when these sources discuss distinctions *within* the homelands is the addition of a new intermediate category, the 'emergent' (commercial) farmer, but the crude dichotomy of subsistence versus commercial farmers, and a unilinear path of 'development' between the two, is effectively reproduced. Interestingly, in the 1990s, with the conversion of much of the development establishment to a 'small farmer path', the terms 'commercial' and 'subsistence' have largely disappeared from the discourse, to be replaced with the general (and seemingly all-embracing) category of 'smallholder' [*Singini and van Rooyen*, 1995: 12].

There is little to suggest that the existing 'white' farming sector is the most suitable model for understanding (or for 'developing') agriculture in the former homelands. Indeed, the conventional dichotomy between 'commercial' and 'subsistence' farming is largely based on the racist assumption of the essential superiority of farming as currently (and historically) practised by white farmers and a failure to appreciate the political factors which have shaped the agricultural economy within (and outside) the homelands. Scarcity of alternative data sources dictates that much of what follows is based on the official, or conventional, view of agriculture in Venda but it is important to move beyond these narrow categories towards a more objective analytical framework.

4.3 LAND

The total land area of Venda in 1986 was 680,700 hectares (6,807 square kilometres) [DBSA, 1991: 38]. The greater part, 82 per cent, was considered suitable only for stock-grazing and 11 per cent (74,655 hectares) suitable for arable purposes, of which only a small portion (probably less than a tenth) was under irrigation. The remainder was made up of forests (approximately 10,000 hectares), protected natural areas (19,400 hectares) and land used for non-agricultural purposes (for example, industrial and residential). Bembridge [1988: 20] describes the agricultural potential of Venda as follows:

> the high rainfall central areas of Venda including the southern parts of the Thohoyandou District which comprise about 13 per cent of the total area of Venda have a high agricultural potential as yet relatively underdeveloped, which is suited to a wide range of crops, including sub-tropical fruit and vegetables under dryland conditions. Medium rainfall parts of the northern, southern and western areas (46 per cent) are more suited to livestock production supported by drought resistant crops, while the drier extreme northern and western areas (41 per cent) are suited to semi-extensive livestock production.

Most land in Venda is classified as 'communal' land, including much of the land used for agricultural projects. Legal title to all non-privately owned land was transferred by the South African government to the government of Venda on the eve of 'independence', under Proclamation R200 of 1979. This included all the 'Scheduled Areas' set aside for tribal occupation under the 1913 Natives Land Act and 'Trust' land acquired under the provisions of the 1936 Native Trust and Land Act. The only lands of which the Venda government did not acquire ownership at this time were the relatively small areas of privately-owned land (approximately 24,000 hectares, or 3.5 per cent of the total) which had been bought and registered in the names of various chieftaincies in the early decades of the twentieth century, or acquired by mission churches, either for their own use or on behalf of their followers [RAU, 1979:

123; *Mutshekwane*, 1993: 8]. Land formally incorporated into the territory of
Venda after 1979 as part of the policy of homeland consolidation, mainly
former white farms acquired by the South African Development Trust,
remained state (that is, Venda Government) land (as opposed to communal
land). This included the Northern Farms (in Dzanani and Mutale Districts) and
the area surrounding the township of Vleifontein (Tshitale District). Since
reincorporation into the Republic of South Africa in 1994, all state and communal lands in Venda are nominally owned by the government of South
Africa.

The system of communal tenure found in Venda is similar to that in other
former homelands, as described in Chapter 2. Land can be acquired only from
a Tribal Authority, usually on the recommendation of a village headman
(*Nduna* or *Gota*). Newly allocated agricultural land is usually surveyed by the
Department of Agriculture and registered with the Tribal Authority and the
Magistrate's Office, where Permission to Occupy (PTO) may be issued,
although in recent years the system of registration appears to have broken
down. Such land cannot be sold or otherwise alienated, but can usually be
passed on between generations with the agreement of the village headman.
Land is officially granted only to household 'heads', which usually means
married men, but women can sometimes acquire land in their own right. Since
1990, a small number of private individuals have acquired exceptionally large
areas of communal land from the Tribal Authorities. As of May 1996, at least
one such individual, with 150 hectares under irrigation, was reported to have
approached Tshivhase Tribal Authority with a view to acquiring (whether by
grant or purchase) some form of permanent private tenure (freehold or lease-
hold), but this was being resisted by the tribal leaders (Interview with the
District Director, Department of Land, Housing and Local Government,
Thohoyandou, March 1996).

On smallholder projects run by the Department of Agriculture, Tribal
Authorities appear to have some influence over landholding, although the
actual allocation of plots is made by Departmental officials (see Chapter 5).
Officially, Tribal Authorities have no influence over state land and large-scale
Agriven projects but the allocation of land by government agencies was (at
least until 1994) highly politicised, which often meant preferment for tribal
leaders, politicians or business figures close to the homeland regime.

As noted in Chapter 3, most of Venda was subjected to betterment planning
during the 1960s and 1970s, whereby rural communities were reorganised into
'agricultural villages' and 'closer settlements', resulting in a relatively uniform pattern of landholding. In those areas classified as 'agricultural villages',
typical dryland allocations were in the range of one to three hectares, with one
hectare being the most common. In areas defined as 'closer settlements', only

residential sites, ranging from 0.1 to 0.5 hectares, were allocated but cultivation of a part of these plots is widespread. On state-run irrigation projects, households were generally allocated plots of between 0.25 and 1.5 hectares each, with 1.2 hectares (1.5 *morgen*) being the most common size.[4] In agricultural villages, communal grazing was restricted to certain demarcated areas but this system has now largely broken down and in most villages all non-residential and non-cultivated land can be used by the inhabitants for grazing purposes as well as for the collection of firewood and other natural materials.

Despite these attempts at regulation of landholding, it is impossible to say with any certainty how many households (or individuals) in Venda have access to agricultural land or are involved in production of crops or livestock.[5] In part this is due to a lack of accurate centralised record-keeping but also because of problems of conceptualisation and definition, especially with regard to very small-scale producers. Not everyone with formal rights to land actually uses their land, while many people without formal land rights are active farmers. Bembridge [1988: 28] suggests that as of 1988 there was no detailed statistical information on landholding in Venda and the system of land registration was 'not yet operational'. The collapse of the homeland regime and the abolition of apartheid-era land laws in the early 1990s has certainly made matters worse [*Cross and Rutsch*, 1995: 23]. Furthermore, many producers of crops or livestock in Venda do not consider themselves 'farmers', both in the sense that farming is not their principal source of livelihood and because the English word is used by Venda-speakers very specifically to signify large-scale white farmers [*Dederen*, 1992: 6]. This study does not try to define terms such as 'farmer' but takes an inclusive view of agricultural activities and the ways in which they contribute to livelihoods.

Various studies have provided estimates of the number of households engaged in arable and livestock farming in Venda. RAU [1979: 144] estimated the number of 'families with farming rights' in 1978 at 24,739, or 35.6 per cent of the total number of 'families' in Venda. Similar figures were reported by Moody and Golino [1984: 10], who calculated that 23,443 out of 69,000 'families' in Venda (34 per cent) had 'rights to agricultural land' in 1979 (precisely what these rights may have been is not explained). The main Development Bank sources on agriculture in Venda [*DBSA*, 1986; *DBSA*, 1991] have virtually nothing to say on agricultural activity outside the 'commercial' sector, but do provide one estimate of the total number employed in the 'informal and subsistence sector': 38,186 persons, which may mean (or include) small farmers [*DBSA*, 1991: 7]. One subsequent publication [*DBSA*, 1993a: 103] puts the number of 'subsistence farmers' in Venda at 42,316 in 1992, but this category is explained only as 'the number of people involved in the peripheral sector'. If this figure is taken as an indication of the total number of households engaged in agriculture, then it is quite high (but not implausibly so), representing approximately 45 per cent of the total number of households in Venda. With no indication of how this figure was arrived at, it is of little use, other than to add to the impression that a sizeable minority of rural households are involved in agriculture to some degree.

Local studies add considerable detail regarding the pattern of landholding in Venda. Dederen [1992: 6] estimates that in Tshitale District 54.2 per cent of households have access to arable land, with the proportion dropping to 38.2 per cent in the Muila Area. Naledzani [1992: 76] found average dryland holdings of 1.1 hectare per household in Mashamba and 0.9 hectares in Khakhu, while Pretorius [1994: 49] found average holdings ranging from 0.5 to 1.6 hectares, or 1.1 hectares overall, in village studies from four different parts of Venda. Schutte [1984: 11] found that in an unnamed part of Nzhelele, in 1983, only 31.4 per cent of households had access to arable land following betterment, of whom only a fifth had more than one hectare. Non-systematic interviews by the author in villages throughout southern and western Venda in 1995 and 1996 (including Ntabalala, Tshimbupfe, Tshituni and Tshakhuma Areas) revealed that the standard allocation of arable land was in most places around one hectare but a sizeable proportion of households in all areas visited appeared to be without land.

4.4 THE DEVELOPMENT OF AGRICULTURE AND THE ROLE OF THE STATE IN VENDA

It has been argued above that the South African state (including its homeland proxies) has played a decisive role in shaping the pattern of landholding and the development of agriculture in the African reserves/homelands, especially in the period after 1948. In Venda, this has produced a considerable variety of farm types, including large corporate estates, private 'commercial' farmers, smallholder irrigation schemes, extensive livestock farms, private orchards, dryland cropping (predominantly small-scale) and a stratum of very small-scale farmers producing crops and livestock in residential areas and on unallocated land.

Interventions by the state in the agrarian economy of Venda date from the earliest years of annexation but very little has been written about events prior to the 1960s. The earliest government activities appear to have been restricted to the livestock sector, with the construction of cattle-dipping tanks and the introduction of compulsory dipping from about 1915 [*Nemudzivhadi*, 1985: 26]. From the writings of Alpheus Maliba, leader of the Zoutpansberg Balemi Association, we know that by the early 1940s state officials were attempting to restrict ploughing on Trust land, which led to widespread resistance in western areas of Venda (see Chapter 3). Forestry plantations were established at Thathe Vondo and on nearby Crown lands by the South African Department of Forestry in the 1930s and 1940s, but this was driven more by the needs of the South African economy for timber than by a desire to develop the local economy [*RAU*, 1979: 114]. Maliba [1981: 143] states that seven headmen and their people were removed from Crown land in the Zoutpansberg district between 1928 and 1938 to make way for forestry schemes.

Under the apartheid regime from 1948, and especially in the wake of the Tomlinson Commission's Report [*Union of South Africa*, 1955], the South African state became directly involved in the promotion of particular forms of agriculture in the reserves (see Chapter 2). The key government agency concerned for half a century was the South African Native Trust (later Bantu Trust, later still Development Trust), created in 1936, which operated under the direction of the Native Affairs Department and its successors. In addition to acquiring land for expansion of the Reserves, the Trust was involved in the implementation of 'betterment', the creation of agricultural projects such as irrigation schemes and sisal plantations, the funding of public services (particularly health services) and the promotion of black-owned businesses, either directly or through subsidiary organisations such as the Bantu Investment Corporation [*Horrell*, 1973: 65].

In Venda, the earliest examples of state agricultural projects were smallholder irrigation schemes on the Dzondo, Luvuvhu, Mutale and Nzhelele Rivers, begun in the mid-1950s, and seven large-scale sisal projects dating from the 1960s [*Horrell*, 1973: 88; *RAU*, 1979: 112; *Thormeyer*, 1989: 8]. A rudimentary agricultural extension and training service was initiated by the Bantu Affairs Department in the 1960s and was expanded by the new Venda Department of Agriculture following the granting of 'self-government' in 1973.

The move towards self-government brought a shift in official policy in favour of large-scale, prestigious agricultural projects, funded at first by government agencies and later jointly with private (non-Venda) capital, a policy which emphasised raising production, employment, and state revenues rather than promoting independent farmers (see Chapter 2). In 1975 the Venda Development Corporation (VDC) was founded to promote economic development in the homeland and took over many of the functions previously carried out in the area by the Corporation for Economic Development (formerly the Bantu Investment Corporation) [*BENSO*, 1979: 68]. The VDC became involved in the development of agro-industries, many of them as joint enterprises with the private sector or South African government agencies. These included the Phaswane coffee plantation and the Tshivhase tea estate, operated by the Sapekoe company, as well as a number of pig and poultry-breeding projects. Agro-processing plants were also established, included an *achar* (pickle) factory at Shayandima (wholly owned by VDC) and the NTK Roller Mills at Shayandima, the first major 'tripartite' venture involving the VDC, 'external' corporate capital and individual share-holders [*BENSO*, 1979: 129]. In 1977, the VDC became the first organisation to offer production loans to farmers in Venda.

During the period of self-government (1973–79), the Venda Department of Agriculture and Forestry provided a range of support services to farmers, such as tractor ploughing, marketing assistance, provision of agricultural inputs and agricultural extension and training. By 1979, however, there were still only 60 extension officers to cover the entire territory and their efforts were largely directed towards farmers on state-managed schemes [*BENSO*, 1979: 125]. As well as managing older projects, such as small-holder irrigation schemes and sisal projects, the Department initiated a number of new projects at this time, including two sub-tropical fruit farms, two small irrigation schemes on the Mutale River, cattle-breeding projects at Musekwa, Nwanedi and Masia, a nursery at Thathe Vondo and a fishery project at Dzindi [*BENSO*, 1979: 128]. It also established the Madzivhandila Agricultural College at Dimani (in 1978) and opened agricultural research stations at Sigonde, Tshiombo and Lwamondo. In the area of livestock, the Department was responsible for cattle-dipping services and arranging cattle auctions, and provided certified bulls for breeding purposes [*BENSO*, 1979: 124]. All state forestry in Venda was taken over by the Department of Agriculture and Forestry in 1973. By 1978, the area under forestry had been expanded to 4,175 hectares in four projects – Thathe Vondo, Tshamanyatsha, Joubertstroom, and Phiphidi – producing mainly pine and some bluegum (eucalyptus). The Department also operated the Pumalanga saw-mill at Thathe Vondo [*RAU*, 1979: 114].

Following 'independence' in 1979, the Venda government service, and particularly the parastatal sector, was greatly expanded and became more directly involved in agricultural production. Agriven (the Venda Agricultural Corporation Ltd.), an off-shoot of the VDC, was founded in November 1981 specifically to initiate, finance and manage agricultural projects until they were ready for take-over by private entrepreneurs [*Dederen*, 1992: 13].

To this end, Agriven took over some of the previous functions of the Department of Agriculture and the VDC but also initiated many new projects, especially in the form of joint ventures with the private sector, and quickly came to dominate the 'formal' agricultural sector in Venda. Sizeable irrigated farms were created (or, in one case, taken over from white owners) at Nwanedi, Makonde, Tshandama and Lambani, producing cotton, tobacco, vegetables, grass seed and sub-tropical fruit. Bananas, avocados, guavas, macadamia nuts, mangoes and litchis were grown on the Tsianda and Barotta farms, and grapes and peaches were produced at Kutama. Dairy projects were initiated at Tswinga, Rembander and Elim, poultry and pig farms at Tswimi and Nwambedi, and cattle feedlots at Muledane and Mannamead. Two major new estate farms were also established, the Mukumbani Tea Estate and the Damani Coffee Estate, both joint ventures between Agriven and the Sapekoe company [*Agriven*, 1988: 18].

In addition to its agricultural projects, Agriven became involved in developing agro-industries, either on its own account or in partnership with private investors. These included a tomato-canning factory at Makhadu, an animal feeds factory, the Zetpro macadamia nut-crushing plant (a joint venture between Agriven and the 'white' Levubu Co-operative) and Venteco, a joint venture between Agriven and Sapekoe to market tea and coffee from their estates. A packing house for sub-tropical fruit was also established at Tshakhuma [*Agriven*, 1988: 16].

Agriven provided a range of technical and commercial services to farmers on various projects, such as tractor ploughing services, agricultural extension and training, and assistance with irrigation facilities, as well as supplying agricultural inputs through its depots at Nwanedi and Makonde [*Agriven*, 1988: 4]. Commercial services offered by Agriven included the marketing of sub-tropical fruit in South Africa and overseas and arranging contracts between farmers, transporters and processing plants. The parastatal also controlled the Venda Livestock Board, which acted as support buyers at cattle auctions and operated facilities for fattening cattle, although numbers handled would appear to have been very small [*Bembridge*, 1988: 27]. In the absence of any lending facilities from the commercial or government banks, Agriven was for many years the sole source of credit for farmers in Venda. Long-term loans were provided for the establishment of 'viable farming units' such as orchards, livestock herds or irrigation works, while revolving credit was made available mainly to farmers on recognised irrigation or dryland projects [*Agriven*, 1988: 4]. Bembridge [1988: 27] reported that, by 1988, Agriven's Department of Co-operative Development had made long-term loans to 167 farmers and had supplied short-term credit to approximately 6,000 small-scale farmers.[6] Naledzani [1992: 55] states that, by 1992, 180 long-term loans (worth R3.4 million) and 15,997 'revolving credit loans' (worth R14.4 million) had been agreed, but it is likely that this latter figure refers to the total number of transactions rather than the actual number of farmers involved. Agriven's lending programme was severely curtailed in 1992–93 following substantial losses.

In the late 1980s, agricultural policy in all the homelands began to shift away from large-scale state-run projects (see Chapter 2). In Venda, this led to two major developments: the gradual sub-division of Agriven's projects and their leasing to individual farmers, a process referred to as 'privatisation'; and the introduction of an integrated Farmer Support Programme.

Moves towards privatisation were initiated in 1987, and saw the withdrawal of Agriven from direct agricultural production on most of its projects [*Agriven*, 1988: 17]. The sprinkler irrigation schemes at Nwanedi and Makonde were divided into plots of 10 to 75 hectares and leased to individual farmers. Much larger areas were leased to private farmers for grazing on the Nwanedi Block, some with herds of 100 cattle or more. The largest of the dairy projects, at Tswinga, was leased to a white farmer, a senior figure in NTK in Venda.

Interviews with senior Agriven management in April 1996 revealed that only two major productive enterprises – the Barotta and Tsianda fruit farms – were still under the direct control of the parastatal, along with a number of 'strategic' facilities such as the Tshakhuma packhouse and a small experimental farm at Sinthumule. While Agriven's objective was that these too would be privatised, suitable buyers had yet to be found. Agriven was continuing to provide support services such as ploughing, extension advice, credit and marketing advice to farmers, particularly those on its own (former) projects, on what was intended to be a full cost-recovery (that is, 'commercial') basis.

The second component of the neo-liberal retreat from the big state (and big state projects) within the homelands was the adoption of a 'small farmer path' to agricultural development. Independent 'subsistence' farmers, long excluded from the benefits of state assistance, were now discovered to be efficient users of limited resources who could, with a little help, be moved along the road towards 'commercial' agriculture.

The principal manifestation of this new policy was the Farmer Support Programme (FSP), introduced to Venda in 1988 as a joint project between Agriven, the Venda Department of Agriculture and Forestry and the Development Bank of Southern Africa (DBSA). It was implemented in three areas – Mulima, Mashamba and Khakhu – which had previously formed part of the Venda Dryland Crop Production Scheme. All of these areas had been subjected to betterment in the 1960s and typical arable holdings were between one and three hectares [*Dederen*, 1992: 5]. The version of FSP applied to Venda was intended to be a 'comprehensive support programme' for small-scale maize farmers, involving the improvement of local infrastructure, the upgrading of government extension services and the provision of a 'package' of credit, ploughing services, agricultural inputs and technical advice. These were to be delivered through specially created 'primary co-operatives' in each FSP area [*Kirsten, Sartorius von Bach and van Zyl*, 1995: 73]. A 'secondary co-operative' (actually a state-run supply centre), established at

Shayandima in 1985, was to act as a wholesale supplier to the primary co-operatives,

A passage in the Agriven house journal from 1988 shows a bureaucracy still struggling with the idea that small farmers can be trusted to know their own interests when it describes the new FSP as

> an aid programme for farmers to promote structural changes in the agricultural industry of Venda. Farmers will be made aware of the advantages of commercial production . . . The structuring of the project will largely consist of decision-making by governmental and semi-governmental departments which are transferred to the co-operative or individual level [*Shuma*, Dec. 1988: 8].

From the limited information available (including interviews with officials and farmers in two of the programme areas), it was clear that the FSP did not lead to 'structural changes' in the small-holder sector, and had ceased to operate as an effective programme at least as early as 1994. The Development Bank's own evaluation of the FSP in Venda [*Kirsten, Sartorius von Bach and van Zyl*, 1995: 95] attempts to draw some favourable conclusions but the figures it presents demonstrate that the programme provided very few benefits to the participants, either in terms of cash income or supply of maize for domestic consumption. For the year studied (1990/91), FSP participants in Venda produced an average of 12.03 bags of maize, compared to 7.92 bags for non-participants in the same areas, and sold an average of 3.89 bags, thereby generating an average cash income of R144.59 (gross). The authors of the evaluation include this figure for income in calculations of total household income, alongside items such as wages and pensions, as if it were disposable (that is, net) income. This is clearly inappropriate, as the average cost of purchased inputs amongst FSP members amounted to R181.06 and the average loan incurred was R213.70. Thus, the average *net* cash income (that is, profit) from crop production amongst this group (disregarding all non-cash inputs and benefits) was actually negative (that is, a loss of R36.47, or more if total loan repayment is taken into consideration). While the FSP may well have boosted maize production, maize sales and the use of purchased inputs, as the authors claim, it certainly did not make the participants more commercially 'successful'. In the words of the report itself, 'The reason that FSP farmers sell maize is mainly to be able to repay their production loans and to cover other costs incurred in production' [*Kirsten, Sartorius von Bach and van Zyl*, 1995: 86].

In an alternative analysis of the same programme, Dederen [1992: 28] agues that the FSP had little positive impact on farmers because it failed to address the fundamental conditions under which agricultural production is carried out, particularly the size of plots allocated under betterment: 'The bottom line is that commercial farming with staple crops on limited one hectare plots needs to be reconsidered seriously'. Central elements of the programme, including credit, tractor ploughing and extension services were in place before the introduction of the FSP and were not improved by including them as part of a new 'package'. At the same time, the expressed demands of farmers for assistance with marketing services, particularly bulk transport, were ignored [*Dederen*, 1993: 10].

By 1995, the three 'primary co-operatives' associated with the FSP were still in operation, but interviews with local farmers revealed that they were being run as retail stores and ploughing service centres by government-appointed managers with little or no participation from the membership. They were 'co-operatives' only in so far as they were registered with the Venda Registrar of Co-operatives, but the Registrar's office reported that it was excluded from any involvement or oversight of their affairs.[7] The 'secondary co-operative' had collapsed by 1992 due to 'financial problems' according to the DBSA evaluation [*Kirsten, Sartorius von Bach and van Zyl*, 1995: 93], or 'bad management and uncontrolled debts' according to the Venda Registrar of Co-operatives (Interview, April 1995). The premises were subsequently taken over by NTK (*Noord-Transvaalse Kooperasie*, or Northern Transvaal Co-operative) as a (retail) farmer supply store, which was generating an annual turn-over of R9 million by 1994/95 (Interview with NTK management, Shayandima, April 1995).

Elsewhere in the territory, the Venda Department of Agriculture has had difficulty providing even rudimentary services in recent years. Agricultural projects have stagnated as tractors went unrepaired or unfuelled, irrigation pumps remained unserviced, fences on grazing camps lay unrepaired and a top-heavy bureaucracy failed to reach the mass of farmers in the field [*Land Research Group*, 1995: 34; *Lahiff*, 1997: 64]. In a study of the extension service in Venda in the 1980s, Bembridge (1988: 61) found a great many inadequacies, particularly in the areas of policy, training and resources:

> the lack of an operational agricultural policy, poor management of staff, staff shortages, problems connected with salaries, short length of service in work areas, poor housing, office accommodation, as well as inadequate record-keeping and reporting services, are all major constraints to efficiency of the extension service.

Extension staff were found to have an 'inadequate' knowledge of applied technology, farm management and extension methods to perform their tasks effectively, while the Department lacked sufficient professional specialists in keys areas such as agronomy and animal husbandry. Field officers were found to suffer from poor pre-service and in-service training and a lack of simple leaflets or bulletins on crop, horticulture or animal production. This led to poor levels of communication with farmers, excessive concentration on 'progressive' farmers (with little demonstration effect for others), few 'Farmers' Days' or field visits and excessive time spent on administrative tasks. The agricultural research stations run by the Department did not, in Bembridge's opinion, have adequate staff or other resources and did not provide usable knowledge to farmers or the agricultural service.

Interviews with farmers and extension officers throughout Venda in 1995 and 1996 indicated that the problems outlined by Bembridge still prevailed. Farmers in many parts of Venda (including areas as diverse as Tshimbupfe, Mphephu, Makuya and Ntabalala) reported that they had never had contact with an extension officer, while others reported that the officers were incapable of providing even basic advice on issues such as the selection of seed varieties or pest control.[8]

Outside the state sector, Venda has seen little in the way of development in terms of either agricultural production or support services. Twenty-four farmers' co-operatives have been started since the 1970s, but most remain extremely weak, and by 1995 only those at Tshiombo and Tshino (and possibly Khakhu, post-FSP) were functioning effectively as member-run organisations with their own premises (see Chapter 5). None of the co-operatives was engaged in marketing its members' produce and none was in a position to offer its own credit facilities.

The private commercial sector is also poorly developed in Venda and offers a very limited range of services to farmers. The principal private investment in the local agricultural economy, outside the NTK mill and the large plantations, is the Giants food-processing plant at Makhado, which buys tomatoes and other produce from farmers in Venda but depends on white farmers in adjoining districts for most of its raw materials. The most common private commercial service utilised by farmers is transport, provided by numerous truck-, van- and taxi-owners throughout Venda. Private tractors are also offered for hire in a growing number of villages but, as with transport, the individual enterprises are small and poorly capitalised. While the main South African banks have offices in Thohoyandou, they do not generally provide credit services to farmers on communal lands. The main supplier of inputs to the agricultural sector is the NTK store at Shayandima which is legally defined as part of a co-operative but, as far as its customers in Venda are concerned, is effectively a private retail operation.

Farmers outside the state projects and support programmes tend to operate on a very small scale, but a number of exceptions have emerged in recent years. Along the lower Mutale River, in the remote north-east of Venda, more than 50 farmers have created their own irrigation systems on plots of up to 25 hectares. They are engaged in intensive production of tomatoes, vegetables and fruit, with little or no support from the state [*Lahiff*, 1997: 88]. In the same area, a small number of individuals have accumulated large cattle herds (of between one and five hundred head), but remain poorly integrated into formal markets and have little access to veterinary or other support services. Since 1990, upwards of a hundred township dwellers at Vleifontein (south-west Venda) have unofficially occupied plots of between one and ten hectares on land granted to members of the former Venda administration. Interviews with a number of these farmers in 1995 and 1996 revealed that they were already engaged in cultivation of dryland crops, without any support from the state, and were willing to invest in irrigation infrastructure if they could obtain some security of tenure and technical advice. Along the Mbwedi River, in central Venda, one private investor has developed a tomato farm encompassing 150 hectares under drip irrigation with his own nursery, packing sheds, trucks and close to 200 employees. With the notable exception of this single enterprise, financed with capital acquired through urban-based retail businesses, virtually all farmers outside government projects (and many within them) suffer from severe shortages of capital, technical training and commercial advice and are largely ignored by the state agricultural services.

4.5 QUANTIFYING THE AGRICULTURAL SECTOR: THE OFFICIAL VIEW

As noted above, information on agriculture in Venda has been produced by a variety of sources over the years including the Venda Government, BENSO, and its successor, the Development Bank of Southern Africa. The most important single source is probably the Development Bank's *Venda Information File* [*DBSA*, 1986] which provides a range of data on state and private sector farming, both arable and livestock.[9] This information was compiled largely from reports supplied by various agencies of the Venda Government and is marked by the general inadequacies of collection and presentation discussed above. It is also now considerably out of date, being based on data for the agricultural year 1984/85. No revision of these data has been published, however, and the collapse of much of the Venda administration around 1990 means that very little information of any kind is available after this date. Therefore, the material contained in the *Venda Information File* is, despite its limitations, worth considering in some detail. In the discussion that follows, information from this source is used in conjunction with the limited amount of more up-to-date information available from Development Bank, Agriven and Venda Government sources.

For the year 1985, agriculture and related activities contributed an estimated R30.2 million to the Gross Domestic Product of Venda, or 12.3 per cent of the total [DBSA, 1987: 111]. Of this, roughly two-thirds (65.2 per cent) originated from the 'non-market sector' and one third (34,8 per cent) from the 'market sector' (these terms are not explained in the source). In terms of employment, 9,200 people, or 13.8 per cent of the 'economically active population', were engaged in the agricultural sector (presumably the 'formal' sector) while the number engaged in the 'informal and subsistence sector' (which probably refers mainly to small scale agriculture) was, at 38,186, over four times as great [DBSA, 1991: 7].

The total value of output from the market sector for the year 1984/85, according to the Development Bank's *Statistical Abstracts* [DBSA, 1987: 116], was R9.3 million, of which the great majority (89.4 per cent) came from field crops and horticulture and the balance (10.6 per cent) from animal products. Of the R8.3 million in the market sector derived from crops, well over half (62 per cent) came from tea, followed by cotton (11.3 per cent), beans (7.1 per cent), vegetables (6.3 per cent) and maize (5.8 per cent). The Development Bank's *Venda Information File* [DBSA, 1986: Table 7.1.8] gives a slightly higher figure for crop output in the market sector, at R8.9 million, of which most (82 per cent) was produced by 'Agricultural Projects' (mainly corporate or parastatal enterprises), with just 18 per cent coming from 'Private Individual Farmers' (see below for discussion of these terms). Four years later (1988/89), the reported value of agricultural output was considerably higher, at R49.9 million (at contemporary prices) [DBSA, 1991: 7]. Livestock made up almost one-third of this figure (32.1 per cent) but, as it appears to include a considerable 'non-market' share, it is not comparable with the figures for live-stock given for 1984/85.

Table 4.1 (below) combines information from a number of tables in the *Venda Information File* [DBSA, 1986] to provide a summary of agriculture in Venda as portrayed by the official sources circa 1985. Like the documents it draws on, this table relates exclusively to what might be termed the 'formal' (or 'official') agricultural sector – that is, the minority of farming enterprises (individual and corporate) in Venda that operate within a formal government structure such as a state-run project or support programme.

The principal categories used in the table below are defined by the Development Bank [DBSA, 1986: 7–10], as follows:

An *agricultural project* can be defined as an agricultural activity managed by a public institution (for example, the Department of Agriculture and Forestry or Agriven), or a private company which is either involved in the farming activities or supplies only technical and professional support. The main objective could be to operate the project on a profitable basis or to establish individual farmers who can farm for commercial purposes.

Private commercial farmers can be defined as those farmers who receive only technical, professional and/or financial [by means of loans] assistance from other institutions. The farming activities are managed privately by the individuals themselves or by co-operative committees.

Community gardens can be defined as gardens cultivated by the community on a co-operative basis while *home gardens* are cultivated by a family.

TABLE 4.1
FORMAL AGRICULTURE IN VENDA, 1985

Type of Activity	Number of Units	Total Area (Ha)	Average Area per Unit (Ha)	Value 1984/85[10] (R millions)
Agricultural projects				
Dryland	7	1,238	176.9	–
Irrigation	10	1,421	142.1	–
Dryland/Irrigation	5	1,826	365.2	–
Nursery	3	6	2.0	–
Dairy	3	657	219.0	–
Cattle breeding	3	3,335	1,111.7	–
Other livestock	5	53	10.6	–
Total (crops and livestock)	36	8,536	237.1	8.607
Private commercial farmers				
Dryland	1,762	1,819	1.0	0.193
Irrigation	1,968	2,733	1.4	1.356
Orchard	563	3,759	6.7	0.018
Plantation	3	125	41.7	–
Total (crops only)	4,296	8,436	2.0	1.567
Plantations	10	7,706	770.6	–
Community/Home Gardens	1,155	–	–	–

Source: DBSA [1986: Tables 7.1.2 and 7.1.7].

Agricultural Projects

The category of *Agricultural Projects* contains 72 projects run directly by the Venda Department of Agriculture, Agriven or private corporations. This appears to be a reasonably distinct and comprehensive category, in that the official sources do not exclude any projects that meet the above definition. This category clearly out-weighs the private (or individual) 'commercial' sector in terms of land area used and total value of output. The above table does not, however, compare like with like. Of the total area under agricultural projects, nearly half (47 per cent) is used for livestock farming, mostly in the form of extensive grazing, leaving just 4,491 hectares available for cultivation. The figures for private commercial farmers relate only to cultivation and make no allowance for grazing available to this group – probably communal grazing in the main, and therefore hard to estimate, but likely to be considerable none the less.

The following information on the various sub-categories of Agricultural Projects has been extracted from the *Venda Information File* [*DBSA*, 1986: Tables 7.1.3, 7.1.4 and 7.1.5]:

The *Dry-land* category is made up of seven sisal projects run by Agriven, ranging in size from 106 to 206 hectares, located in southern and western Venda (Vuwani and Dzanani Districts).

Irrigation is dominated by the large Agriven farm at Nwanedi (660 ha) growing cotton, fruit and vegetables, with smaller units at Lambani and Tshakhuma, growing a mixture of fruits and tobacco, and small-scale food-plots at Nesengani.

Dry-land/Irrigation is dominated by the Makonde-Tshandama project on the Mutale River (850 ha in total), producing cotton, wheat, tobacco and vegetables, and the Tsianda and Barotta sub-tropical fruit farms, all of which are run by Agriven.

The *Nursery* category contains three small nurseries – two run by Agriven, at Joubertstroom and Tshakhuma, and one run by the Department of Agriculture and Forestry at Thathe Vondo – which between them produce sub-tropical fruit trees, vegetables, ferns and cycads.

Dairy comprises three dairy farms, all run by Agriven, the main ones being Elim and Tswinga.

Cattle breeding comprises three projects, two in the extreme north of Venda (Musekwa and Nwanedi), and one at Masia, in Vuwani District, all run by the Venda Department of Agriculture and aimed at upgrading the indigenous cattle herd.

The category *Other Livestock* is made up of feedlots for cattle and sheep, run by Agriven, and various pig and poultry farms run as joint ventures between Agriven and private investors.

Private Commercial Farmers

Unlike the agricultural projècts discussed above, the category *Private Commercial Farmers* is ambiguous for a number of reasons. This category comprises 1,762 dryland farmers, most with just one hectare of land, in 21 villages; 1,968 irrigation farmers, most with just 1.2 hectares, on 21 state-run schemes; and 563 farmers with orchards, mostly of five hectares. While the latter two sub-groups could be said to be reasonably distinct and inclusive, there is nothing obvious to distinguish the first sub-group from the tens of thousands of dryland farmers in Venda. Moreover, as argued below, the use of the term 'commercial' for many of these farmers appears arbitrary and inappropriate.

The *Dryland* category (1,762 farmers) is composed almost entirely of farmers with just one hectare each. Among the larger concentrations are 209 farmers at Dzwerani (Lwamondo), 120 farmers at Mulima and 123 farmers at Tshisahulu (Tshivhase), all with one hectare apiece. While a few isolated individuals have holdings of up to ten hectares, the only example of a concentration of farmers with more than one hectare is at Phiphidi where 18 farmers have plots of three hectares each. The main crops shown in nearly all cases are maize and sorghum or, in just two villages in Mphephu Area, sorghum alone.

Irrigation (1,968 farmers) is largely composed of farmers with plots of 1.2 hectares each, including 813 farmers at Tshiombo and 354 farmers on seven schemes in the Nzhelele Valley (Mphephu Area). The exceptions are 137 units of 0.5 hectares on the Folovhodwe and Klein Tshipise schemes (both in Mutale District), 43 plots of 2.5 hectares on the Garside and Mamuhohi schemes (Mphephu Area) and 16 five-hectare units on the Sanari and Mutele schemes on the lower Mutale River. Produce is invariably shown as maize and vegetables.

The category *Orchards* (563 farmers) is composed of holdings considerably larger, on average, than the dryland or irrigated plots held by individual farmers. The majority of holdings are of five hectares, 48 orchards (8.5 per cent of the total) are ten hectares or greater and the largest is 23 hectares. Most of these orchards produce mangoes or avocado pears, with smaller numbers growing oranges, peaches, bananas, pineapples, litchis, apples and macadamia nuts [*DBSA*, 1986: Table 7.1.6]. Orchards are heavily concentrated in Thohoyandou and Dzanani Districts, with just 12 per cent in Vuwani and less than one per cent (four orchards) in Mutale District.

It should be noted that by 1991 the Development Bank had changed its definition of *Private Commercial Farmers* in Venda to exclude the *Dryland* sub-category, leaving only *Irrigation, Orchards and Plantations*. The total number of farmers in these sub-categories increased from 2,534 in 1985 [*DBSA*, 1986 Table 7.1.2] to 2,738 in 1986/87 [*DBSA*, 1991: Table 6.5b], due to a small rise in the number of farmers in the *Irrigation* category and a more substantial increase (almost a third) in the *Orchard* sub-category. The additional orchards would appear to have been substantially larger than those already in the sub-category as the average size overall increased from 6.7 hectares [*DBSA*, 1986: Table 7.1.2] to 8.8 hectares [*DBSA*, 1991: Table 6.5b].

The category *Plantation* (private) contains just three privately-run forestry plantations, amounting to 125 hectares in all, on communal land at Phiphidi, Vhufule and Khubvi, but no further details are given.

Plantations (Corporate)

This category comprises ten forestry plantations run by the Venda Department of Agriculture and Forestry, covering a total of 7,706 hectares [*DBSA*, 1986: Table 7.1.10. Over half of this area (4,309 hectares) is accounted for by the largest, and oldest, plantation at Thathe Vondo. Subsequent publications show that by 1988/89 the number of forestry plantations had risen to 16, covering a total area of 13,646 hectares [*DBSA*, 1991: 15]. The total value of forestry and logging products in Venda in 1985/85 amounted to R1.2 million [*DBSA*, 1986: Table 7.1.10, rising to R3.2 million in 1988/89 (in contemporary prices) [*DBSA*, 1991: Table 6.48].

Community/Home Gardens

This category is made up of 14 'community schemes', with a total of 479 members and 14 hectares between them, and 1,141 'home gardens', but no explanation is provided for how these figures were derived [*DBSA*, 1986: Table 7.1.11]. There can be little question that tens of thousands of people in Venda cultivate 'gardens' next to their homestead, many using improvised forms of irrigation, but no indication is given as to how or why this particular group was selected. No information is available on the types of crops grown or the volume (or value) of output on either community schemes or home gardens.

Land Use

The total cultivated area for all categories in the 'formal' sector amounts to just 29 per cent of the overall amount of arable land in Venda (officially estimated at 74,655 hectares) [*DBSA*, 1991: 7]. No information is available on the relative quality of land held by the 'formal' sector but it is likely that much of the best land is occupied by farmers in this category.

The situation regarding irrigated land is quite different. No figure is given in the *File* for the total amount of irrigated land in Venda, although an amount is shown for each corporate project and each group of private farmers. These two categories together contain 4,154 hectares of land under irrigation: 1,421 hectares on projects and 2,733 hectares among individual farmers. This total corresponds closely to the figure of 4,181 hectares given in subsequent reports for the total area under irrigation in Venda [*DBSA*, 1991: 7]. Closer examination of individual projects (detailed in DBSA [1986: Table 7.1.3]), however, reveals that the amount of irrigated land on *Irrigation Projects* alone actually amounts to 1,700 hectares, with an additional 687 hectares *under irrigation* in the *Dryland/Irrigation category*, mainly at Makonde-Tshandama. The total area of irrigated land on official projects thus amounts to 2,586 hectares [*DBSA*, 1986: Table 7.1.3].

The sum total area under irrigation on individual projects (2,586 ha) and among private farmers (2,733 ha) is, therefore, 5,319 hectares, which can be taken as an estimate of the total amount of land under irrigation within the 'formal' agricultural sector in Venda. It is not possible to say what proportion of the total area of irrigated land in Venda this represents, but it is likely to be close to 100 per cent.[11]

Livestock

Far less information is available on livestock than on crop farming in the official sources on Venda. What data exist, however, appear to be relatively inclusive, in that total numbers of livestock in various categories – derived from cattle dipping records and agricultural censuses – are reported regardless of scale or type of ownership (that is, 'project' or 'individual', 'formal' or 'informal'). While the available statistics are likely to suffer many of the same problems as other agricultural data with regard to collection and reporting, they do not appear to exclude a large portion of the sub-sector.

Table 4.2 (below) shows the total numbers in the main categories of live-stock in Venda during the 1980s, as reported by the Development Bank. All figures relate to the month of March in the relevant year.

The number of grazing stock fluctuates greatly from year to year, largely as a result of changes in rainfall. Figure 4.1 (below) shows the number of cattle and goats in Venda for the period 1981 to 1989. It may be noted that the drop in cattle numbers in the period from 1984 to 1986, attributable to the severe drought of 1982/83, was accompanied by a major increase in the

FIGURE 4.1
LIVESTOCK NUMBERS IN VENDA, 1981 TO 1989

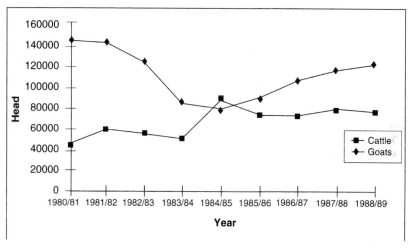

Source: DBSA [1991: Table 6.30].

TABLE 4.2
LIVESTOCK IN VENDA 1981–89

	1981	1985	1989
Cattle	146,338	83,485	136,339
Goats	45,710s	89,550	77,960
Sheeps	2,516s	1,915	3,202
Equines	–	7,097	5,845
Pigs	8,533	12,635	3,512
Poultry	81,831	198,784	336,366
LSU[12]	154,376	98,729	149,866

Source: DBSA [1986: Table 7.1.9; and 1991: Table 6.34].

TABLE 4.3
LIVESTOCK PRODUCTION IN VENDA, 1982–87

Year[14]	1982	1983	1984	1985	1986	1987
Value (R millions)	9.508	12.905	10.517	8.147	9.337	14.302

Source: DBSA [1991: Table 6.29].

number of goats. Whether this was due to natural causes (for example, reduced competition for grazing or reduced incidence of diseases in dry years), or to owner behaviour (for example, slaughtering less goats), could not be determined.

The official sources suggest that stocking rates in Venda (that is, the numbers of livestock per hectare), as in the other homelands, are well above recommended levels (see Chapter 2 for a critical discussion of these concepts). The carrying capacity of unimproved grazing (the average amount of land required per animal) is estimated at 8.4 hectares per Large Stock Unit across Venda as a whole, but this varies from 6.0 hectares in Thohoyandou District to 12.0 hectares in Mutale. In 1989 (not an exceptional year) grazing in Venda was carrying more than twice the recommended number of stock, ranging from 390 per cent of the recommended number in Vuwani District to 159 per cent in Mutale District [*DBSA*, 1993a: 109].

Information on the distribution of livestock between households, and on livestock productivity, is very limited and is likely to be less reliable than the overall census numbers shown in Table 4.2 (on the assumption that it is easier to count livestock at a point in time than to calculate movement in and out of a herd or flock over the course of a year). The Development Bank [*DBSA*, 1991: 168] estimated the total number of *cattle-owners* (in March 1989) at 10,653. If this figure is taken as one owner per household, it suggests that somewhere in the order of 11–14 per cent of households in Venda own cattle and that the average herd size is 12.8 head.[13] This latter figure appears very high, and the number of households with cattle very low, relative to the estimates for Venda and other homelands given in Chapter 2. The following table shows the gross value of livestock production in Venda for the period 1982 to 1987.

The gross value of livestock production in 1988/89 was reported to be R16 million, which included a gross value of cattle slaughtered of R8 million [*DBSA*, 1991: 7]. This figure (and those in Table 4.3) would appear to include both 'market' and 'non-market' components. It is not clear to what extent these production figures take into consideration informal sales and private slaughter of cattle and other livestock but they are unlikely to fully represent the situation outside formal markets and official schemes. The figure for 1988/89 is equivalent to approximately half the gross value of crop production in Venda for that year (R33.9 million including both market and non-market components) [*DBSA*, 1991: 7].

Unlike dryland and irrigated cropping, there were no examples (at least prior to 1990) of private farmers raising livestock as part of government programmes. Officially-run stock sales are also few and far between and are not popular with many producers [*Lahiff*, 1997: 83]. Loans are generally not available for development of herds (apart from intensive feed-lots) and few farmers have access to veterinary services. Overall, with the exception of the dipping programme, very little has been done by the state to develop the small-scale cattle sector and nothing at all to promote the production or marketing of goats, which are more important than cattle to many poorer households.

Thus, virtually all livestock farming in Venda can be described as 'informal' (see below). Exceptions to this are the handful of intensive pig and poultry projects established as joint ventures between Agriven and private investors and the three government cattle-breeding stations which provided stud bulls to private (individual) farmers. These breeding services would appear to have reached relatively small numbers of cattle-owners in Venda.

4.6 THE INFORMAL AGRICULTURAL SECTOR

There can be little doubt that the stratum of farmers represented in the official reports on agriculture (above) represents a small minority of all those engaged in agriculture in Venda. As noted, the highest estimate that could be found for the number of farmers in Venda was 42,316 households, or 45 per cent of the total number of households [DBSA, 1993a: 103], and there is no reason to believe this is an overestimate. Only 4,296 farmers are recognised by the official record (or 6,000 in Bembridge's 1988 estimate), leaving the vast majority (possibly in the order of 90 per cent) of households engaged in agriculture virtually unaccounted for. While some acknowledgement of this is made in the official sources, very little information is available on the activities or the extent of what might be referred to as the informal agricultural sector.

From the little that has been written on the subject [van Nieuwenhuizen, 1984; Pretorius, 1994; Land Research Group, 1995; Lahiff, 1997], and on the basis of direct observations, it is possible to say with a reasonable level of confidence that most households involved in the informal agricultural sector grow small quantities of dryland crops for their own consumption and a minority have very small garden plots under irrigation. Many farming households possess the standard plots assigned under betterment, typically one hectare, but others have as little as one-tenth of that amount. An unknown number of households have obtained plots of various sizes from village headmen since the late 1980s, when betterment rules would appear to have lapsed in many areas, or cultivate patches of unallocated land without official permission, but again few of these holdings exceed one hectare. In common with many of the farmers in the 'formal' sector, it is likely that very few in the informal sector depend on agriculture as their principal source of livelihood, and those that do so are probably among the very poorest.

Dryland cropping patterns are remarkably uniform throughout Venda, with most farming households producing a cereal crop inter-cropped with ground nuts, dry beans, pumpkins or melons [*Land Research Group*, 1995: 28; *Lahiff*, 1997: 92]. The main cereal is maize but sorghum and millet are also grown, especially in the dryer areas north of the Soutpansberg. Ploughing, whether by hired tractor, donkeys or hand hoe, is carried out after the first rains, generally between September and November, and usually just one crop is produced in a year.

For most small-scale farmers, dryland crops are produced entirely for domestic consumption. Pumpkins and melons are not widely marketed in Venda, and while a ready (informal) market exists for groundnuts, few small-holders produce sufficient to make selling worthwhile. For sorghum and millet, relatively minor crops in all but the far north, no formal or informal market could be found operating anywhere in Venda.

Formal markets do exist for maize, via the former Maize Board channels, but remarkably few farmers appear to use them. Throughout the period of fieldwork (see Chapter 5), and my meetings with hundreds of farmers (including many on official irrigation schemes and participants in the maize-oriented Farmer Support Programme), not a single farmer with *less* than five hectares of arable land reported selling any maize through formal channels in the previous five years. A small number of larger farmers reported that they occasionally sold maize, and a number of smaller farmers said they had done so in the past, but the available evidence would suggest that the staple crop in Venda remains largely untraded. This has major (and largely unacknowledged) implications for agricultural development policies, especially those such as the Farmer Support Programme which aim to increase the commercial orientation of farmers through increasing maize output (see above).

Indeed, virtually nothing has been written about how farmers in Venda dis-pose of their maize crop. Up to about twenty years ago, it appears certain that a high proportion was stored within households as grain, and pounded by hand (by women) as required from day to day. In a typical rural household, with perhaps one hectare of arable land, this might be expected to supply half of the household requirement of staple food (that is, about six 80 kg bags) as well as a supply of fresh cobs during the growing season. Smaller amounts of grain and by-products of the pounding process would probably have been fed to chickens or used for brewing beer.

Since 1979, NTK has operated a large-scale roller mill at Shayandima which attracts farmers from a wide radius. The mill is a public company, run by NTK on a management contract. Turnover for 1994/95 was reported to be in excess of R20 million, most of which was accounted for by sales of maize meal with a much smaller proportion coming from the sale of animal feeds (Interview with NTK management, April 1995). A growing proportion of the mill's sales goes to state and NGO feeding schemes which have been operating throughout the northern Transvaal since the late 1980s. The main advantage of this mill to farmers, apart from its central location, is its storage capacity (that is, silos), which allows farmers to deliver their maize harvest in one load and to obtain in return good quality maize flour as and when required. This system, known as *stoormielies*, operates on the basis of vouchers which can be redeemed for an appropriate volume of maize on payment of a milling fee [*Dederen*, 1993: 11]. Farmers are thus relieved of the responsibility of storage and the attendant risk of spoilage. The disadvantages are the scale of the milling fees (R23.72 for 80 kg of 'special' meal in 1995) and the loss of milling by-products.

Up to 1995, NTK was the only 'formal' buyer of maize in Venda. NTK management reported that the mill purchased no more than 1,000 tonnes of maize annually within Venda, or about five per cent of its requirements. Many times this amount (exactly how much was not clear) was delivered by Venda farmers for milling on the voucher system. According to the mill management (and confirmed in interviews with producers), it was not unusual for farmers to have upwards of 50 bags of maize (that is, close to five tonnes) in storage with the mill at any one time and there were suggestions that some farmers sold maize meal to consumers outside official channels. Farmers interviewed were highly critical of the prices paid by the mill for maize, which many of them believed to be below the price obtained by white farmers, and were generally unwilling to sell to the mill.[15] Those wishing to sell maize generally preferred to take advantage of the substantial difference between producer prices (for maize) and consumer prices (for maize meal) by converting their maize to flour, either for household consumption or for (informal) sale to consumers. In Mulima, farmers reported selling maize to a local shopkeeper in order to save on the costs of transporting it to the nearest mill (Soutpansberg Millers, in Louis Trichardt), although this did not appear to be a widespread practice.

Since 1990, a number of modern electric mills have been established by private entrepreneurs in and around Venda (for example, at Tshiombo and at Chabani). These offer a high quality service, but no storage facilities, and appear to have captured a large part of the market in their areas, especially amongst smaller producers. Neither NTK nor these new mills have totally displaced older and smaller forms of milling (tractor-powered mills and hand stamping), however, which continue to be used by poorer households and those without motor transport. Overall, the economics of maize in former homeland areas such as Venda are little understood and require urgent investigation.

Irrigated cropping outside official projects is mainly limited to small gardens on residential sites, watered by hand or by hose-pipe, from standpipes, boreholes or streams. The most common garden crops are green-leaf vegetables, such as cabbage or spinach, followed by sweet potatoes, tomatoes, onions and beans. Once again, cultivation tends to be restricted to the hotter, and wetter, summer season.

In most cases, garden vegetables are consumed fresh within the household or dried in the sun and stored for the winter. As noted above, however, a number of relatively large-scale 'independent' irrigators have emerged in recent years who make use of both informal markets (hawking) and formal channels such as the Giants canning factory at Makhado [*Lahiff*, 1997: 88].

Most livestock is raised (and traded) in the informal sector, but the few studies of agriculture in Venda provide only glimpses of this activity. In a study from the Tshikundamalema Area, van Nieuwenhuizen [1984: 15] found that 34.1 per cent of households kept cattle, 45.1 per cent kept goats, 22.0 per cent kept pigs and 71.4 per cent kept poultry. Average herd sizes were 12.6 for cattle and 8.1 for goats. In two areas where the FSP was implemented, 54 per cent of households were found to keep cattle, although cattle did not form part of the Programme [*Kirsten, Sartorius von Bach and van Zyl*, 1995: 76]. The average number of livestock per household (including households without any livestock) in Mashamba was 4.0 cattle, 0.6 goats, and 9 chickens, while in Khakhu the average numbers per household were 2.6 cattle, 0.4 goats and 1.0 chicken. In the four villages studied by Pretorius [1994: 59], the proportions of households owning cattle were remarkably high, falling between 77 per cent and 88 per cent, and the average number of cattle per household (including those without cattle) ranged from five to 13. In a study of the Manenzhe area (northern Venda), the Land Research Group [1995: 8] found that just over a quarter (26.3 per cent) of households owned cattle: the average herd size was 11.9 and the largest cattle herd was 70 head. Goats were more widespread, being kept by 56.5 per cent of households, although average herd sizes were no bigger, at 10.4 head. Lahiff [1997: 88] reported a number of individuals with exceptionally large herds of cattle (100–600 head) in the neighbouring Mutele and Tshikundamalema Areas.

None of the local studies cited provide much detail about livestock productivity or the importance of livestock sales but interviews with farmers throughout Venda suggest that sales, especially of cattle, are extremely low. The only 'formal' markets for livestock within Venda are government-organised cattle auctions but even larger farmers tend to sell mainly 'informally' to consumers or to local butcheries [*Lahiff*, 1997: 82]. No formal marketing channels exist in Venda for smallholders' goats, sheep, pigs or poultry.

Income from farming, whether in cash or kind, is extremely difficult to estimate for small-holders in the homelands, and Venda is no exception (see Chapter 2). Accurate records of production, sales and consumption are not kept by most farmers and rural households generally obtain income from more than once source, making it difficult to quantify either total household income or the relative importance of agriculture. The few detailed local studies from Venda, and from neighbouring homelands, suggest that agricultural income among smallholders is extremely low, both in absolute terms and as a proportion of total household income.

Writing in the early 1980s, van Nieuwenhuizen [1984: 17] estimated the average cash income from agricultural produce and livestock in one community in Tshikundamalema at R4.78 per month, or 5.7 per cent of total household cash income. Some years later, Thormeyer [1989: 27] found, that amongst households on the Tshifhefhe irrigated food plot scheme (in Vuwani District), agricultural sales contributed an average of R11.4 per month (in 1986 prices) or seven per cent of total household cash income. At Khumbe, the same author found that agricultural income was somewhat higher, averaging R16.9 per household per month or 13.6 per cent of total cash income. All of these figures are exclusive of non-marketed farm produce (that is, direct consumption), which the authors accept is probably quite substantial.

4.7 RECENT DEVELOPMENTS

Most recent developments in the agricultural sector have occurred as part of broader reform processes dating from the late 1980s or early 1990s, rather than as a direct result of the transition to democracy in South Africa. The biggest change in recent years at the national level – the liberalisation (deregulation) of agricultural markets – has brought little if any direct benefit to farmers in Venda. Producer prices for maize for most crops have not risen significantly as a result of price liberalisation, while consumer prices (of much greater importance to the vast majority of rural households) have continued to rise [*SAIRR*, 1996: 548]. The reduction in state support to agriculture generally [*Bernstein*, 1996: 19] has had little direct impact on farmers in Venda, who were excluded from most of its benefits anyway. Other current reforms, such as the subdivision and leasing of Agriven's projects, predate the transition to democracy and have to be seen as top-down processes, benefiting a small elite, rather than as products of a new democratic politics.

Of greater potential importance are new and proposed forms of assistance targeted specifically at small or black farmers, such as credit schemes, settlement grants, tractor purchase schemes and projects funded under the national government's Reconstruction and Development Programme (RDP). Increased pension allowances, government drought relief programmes and some improvement in public sector wages (including more reliable payment) since the early 1990s have also been of considerable (if as yet unquantifiable) benefit to specific groups of rural people. Otherwise, political (re)integration has had little effect on the local economy which was, in monetary and trade terms, already fully integrated into the South African national economy.

In the area of land reform, claims for restitution of expropriated lands are being prepared by many communities but they have yet to receive significant material support from the state. Given the likely opposition from existing owners, such claimants face a long and complicated legal process. Despite the availability of sizeable areas of state land in and around Venda, none of this has yet been made available to black farmers and there have been no moves by the Provincial Government to acquire additional land (by purchase or otherwise) for redistribution to black farmers (or would-be farmers). The very slow progress reported from the Pilot Land Reform Programme on state land at Gillemberg, outside Potgietersrus, suggests that major changes in land-holding in the Province are still a long way off.

The integration and reform of state agricultural services in four former jurisdictions has posed a major challenge to the new government of the Northern Province. The provincial Department of Agriculture is, in the words of one senior official, committed 'to addressing the needs of small and emergent farmers', but while some internal restructuring had been put into effect by June 1996 (and brave new 'organograms' and 'mission statements' were taking shape), there were few signs of any shift in strategic objectives or in the quality or range of services being delivered to farmers in the former homelands. The budgetary crisis which had crippled the Venda agricultural service since the early 1990s appeared to be resolved by mid-1996, however, with the release of funds for vehicles, fuel and salary increases.

The future role of the three Agricultural Development Corporations (ADCs) in the Northern Province was the subject of considerable debate within the provincial administration during 1996 and there were proposals to merge them into a single organisation, to be called the Northern Province Agricultural and Rural Development Corporation. The precise functions of such an organisation, however, had not yet been announced.[16] According to the Chief Executive of Agriven, the Corporation still has a role to play in 'empowering the small-scale farmer', particularly in providing services not yet offered by the private commercial sector.[17] Agriven is coming under increasing pressure from government to be self-financing, however, and is targeting its services at more 'progressive' farmers, particular those on its former projects, who are more likely to be able to pay for them. It was suggested that such farmers would eventually join the ranks of South Africa's 'commercial' farmers, and gain access to main-stream financial services, but how this was to be achieved under a communal land system was not clear.

Another change since the early 1990s has been the increased involvement of non-governmental and welfare organisations in agricultural development projects. A number of 'income-generating' schemes, such as small-scale irrigation projects, bakeries, piggeries and brickyards, have been funded by national (South African) organisations such as the Independent Development Trust (IDT), Operation Hunger and the National Nutrition and Social Development Programme (NNSDP). These projects, at least in Venda, have tended to suffer from organisational and financial problems, and many have yet to deliver any material benefits to their participants [*Land Research Group*, 1995: 8; *Lahiff*, 1997: 87]. More successful have been women's Care Groups, of which 249 were established in Venda between 1980 and 1990 by the Department of Health with support from international donors [*Mfono*, 1989 : 495; *Gaigher, van Rensburg and Bester*, 1995: 225]. As well as promoting primary health care, these groups have had some success in setting up communal gardens, with the aim of improving the supply of fresh vegetables in rural communities, but have been less successful with income-generating products such as knitting and wire-fence making.

The period since 1990 has also seen the emergence of independent organisations within the agricultural sector. After a number of false starts, a Venda Farmers' Union (VFU), allied to the National African Farmers' Union, was established in 1995, and is led by a former senior official of the Venda Department of Agriculture. Interviews with the VFU leadership in May 1995 revealed that their main demand was for a new state credit scheme, targeted specifically at black farmers. To this end, the VFU was working with the provincial government to set up official Credit Boards in each Magisterial District. The leadership stated that they were generally unhappy with the rate of change in official policy over the previous two years, saying that there was little evidence of a 'black voice' within the provincial administration and that even newly appointed black officials showed little understanding of their needs. As an example, they reported that they had been repeatedly advised by officials to bring their demands to the Land Bank and the Agricultural Credit Board, despite the fact that, according to the VFU, neither institution would deal with farmers on communal lands or those aged over 55 years, effectively excluding the vast majority of black farmers.

On land reform, the VFU is in favour of the government making loans available to selected individuals, or small groups of experienced farmers, to purchase white-owned farms but they are strongly opposed to the whole-scale resettlement of communities. The leadership stated that they were in favour of reducing the power of the chiefs over land in the communal areas as much land was, in their opinion, under-utilised at present. They did not believe, however, that it was necessary to move to a fully individual form of tenure, stressing that communal land should continue to be available without charge to those who needed it.

While the Union appears to be an initiative of mostly larger farmers in the 'formal' sector, the emergence of any farmers' organisation is an important step in the reform process. Few if any locally-based farmer organisations exist in Venda, although attempts were being made in June 1996 to create a plot-holders' committee on the Tshiombo irrigation scheme (see Chapter 5). The spread of democratic politics to the countryside, in the form of elected Local Councils (since 1995) and village-level 'civics'[18] (since the early 1990s), may mean that rural communities become more vocal in their demands for local development. As yet, however, these organisations have concentrated on the provision of basic services, such as water, electricity and housing, rather than on agricultural issues [*Lahiff*, 1997: 106].

The future of the few farmers' co-operatives still in operation in Venda is in doubt in the face of competition from Agriven and NTK stores. Since acquiring the former secondary co-op at Shayandima in 1992, NTK has rapidly expanded its presence in Venda, taking over the premises of failed co-operatives, at Dzondo, Tshikinini and Rambuda as retail outlets. Up to 1994, NTK has operated purely as a commercial organisation in Venda, as it had no black members and did not fall under the authority of the Venda Registrar of Co-operatives. It is not known how many black members it has attracted since 1994, but it is unlikely to be many. The NTK store in Louis Trichardt adopted a policy of employing black cashiers and advertising in Venda and Shangaan languages in 1994, and reported a major rise in the number of black customers as a result. A similar increase in black business was reported from NTK stores at Vivo and Alldays, but some white members were reported to have resigned from the co-operative when black members were admitted (Interview with NTK management, Louis Trichardt, April 1995). Levubu Co-operative, which is also used by many Venda farmers, had three black members by 1995 (Interview with Levubu Co-operative management, April 1995).

Members of the independent co-operatives in Venda believe that they face unfair competition from Agriven's farmer supply stores, which are heavily supported by the state and obtain more favourable terms from suppliers. Senior management at Agriven, interviewed in 1994 and 1996, were scornful of the independent co-operatives and their members whom they described as 'illiterate', 'disorganised', 'badly managed' and 'prone to corruption'. An exception was made for the Agriven-supported 'primary comparatives' of the Farmer Support Programme (FSP), which were said to be well-run and 'fully independent'. The Venda Registrar of Comparatives was of the opposite opinion, stating that the FSP co-operatives, particularly those at Mulima and Mashamba, were 'completely controlled' by Agriven with minimal involvement by the membership (Interview, April 1995). Agriven executives stated that the corporation would be willing to work with the black co-operatives once they had reached a satisfactory level of efficiency but were reluctant to do anything to help them achieve this. They were also contemptuous of attempts to form independent black farmers' organisations, with one senior figure describing those involved as 'diary farmers' who should be spending 'more time in the fields and less in meetings'.

4.8 CONCLUSION

There can be little doubt that more than 30 years of involvement by the state has done little to change the fundamental position of agriculture within Venda, especially in terms of household livelihoods. While the majority of households outside the main 'urban' areas and denser settlements are still engaged in agriculture to some extent, it is likely that it contributes a smaller proportion of household livelihoods than ever before. The direct involvement of the state in agricultural production has effectively ceased with the demise of the homelands, leaving a select group of farmers facing an uncertain future on projects which have yet to prove themselves economically viable. With the failure of the Farmer Support Programme, there are now no state agricultural programmes aimed specifically at small black farmers and the vast majority of farmers, including many on formal government-run schemes, continue to have access to only the most rudimentary agricultural services.

This is not to suggest, however, a uniform, downward trajectory for the agricultural economy. Agriculture has undoubtedly allowed a minority of households, particularly on government projects, to earn some additional income and has allowed a small 'elite' to obtain a reasonable livelihood. Furthermore, as will be argued below, agriculture takes on varying importance at different points in people's lives. Many of the most active and successful farmers in Venda are men over 50 years of age who became full-time farmers only after many years in non-farm (migrant) employment. Many of them have, with the passage of time, absolved themselves of some of the more onerous responsibilities of house-building, child support and care of parents. This would appear to allow them to settle for an income, and lifestyle, that might be unattractive to a younger person, but which offers other less tangible rewards. For another group, the very poor, agriculture represents a safety net, a means of survival between periods of employment or following the loss of a pensioner or other breadwinner. All of these issues are explored in more detail in the case of Tshiombo in the following chapters.

NOTES

1. Harries [1989: 96] describes a short-lived response to the expanding market for agricultural produce by a class of African farmers in the northern Transvaal in the 1930s, but it is not known whether this included Venda areas.

2. Cobbett [1987: 69] suggests that, in 1985, Venda was second only to Transkei amongst the homelands in terms of the contribution of agriculture to 'national' income (estimated at 22.8 per cent). As will be shown below, however, the majority of 'formal' (recorded) agricultural income accrued to the corporate sector (state and private), not to 'households'.

3. Watkinson [1996] provides a valuable critique of this discourse, and traces its grip on official thinking from the time of the Tomlinson Report in the 1950s through to the Farmer Support Programmes of the 1980s (see Chapter 2).

4. This allocation (1.5 *morgen*) is remarkably consistent, not just in Venda but throughout the former homelands [*de Wet*, 1995: 83; *Bembridge*, 1986: 361], and seems to have been adopted as standard at least as early as the 1950s. It was almost certainly related to the concept of an 'economic unit', whereas one hectare of dryland – a typical 'betterment' allocation – was probably intended to do no more than supplement household food supply (see Chapter 2).

5. Much attention was paid in the days of apartheid (and before) to the largely futile exercise of estimating the 'optimal' number of households that could be supported by the land in the communal areas and various essays in social engineering ensued. RAU's *Planning Proposals for Venda* [1979: 144] suggested that Venda could support a maximum of 14,000 families at 'optimal farming level', and Moody and Golino [1984: 10] came up with a similar figure for the number who could gain what they call 'an adequate livelihood' from agriculture. The topic will not be pursued further in this study, other than to note the pervasive influence of such ideas amongst contemporary rural development planners.

6. This is the highest estimate in the literature for the number of farmers receiving any form of government service.

7. Interview, Venda Registrar of Co-operatives, April 1995.

8. Even those areas falling under the FSP were poorly served. In Mashamba in 1995, farmers reported that the extension officer in the area was only concerned with cattle, and no advice was available on the use of the recommended package of crop inputs. In Mulima, farmers resorted to asking the author for advice on the control of *Vhuri*, a common maize parasite (witch-weed, or *Striga lutea*).

9. See Watkinson [1996: 49] for a critical appraisal of the DBSA *Files*.

10. The *Value* column is derived from Table 7.1.7 of the *File* which shows value of output by categories of private farmers for the year 1984/85. Output from Project Farming is broken down somewhat differently, into Agronomy (R6.6M), Horticulture (R0.62M) and Fruit (R0.15M).

11. Areas of 'independent' (or 'informal') irrigation have been established along the lower reaches of the Mutale River (in Makuya and Mutele Areas) and along the Mutshindudi and Mbwedi Rivers (Mphaphuli Area) (see Map 2), but most of this would appear to have occurred since 1990 [*Lahiff*, 1997: 88].

12. Large Stock Units. In this instance, the Development Bank appears to be defining an LSU as one head of cattle, or six sheep or goats, and ignoring all other types of livestock.

13. Based on the 1985 and 1991 censuses and assuming an average household size of six persons.

14. It is not clear from the source whether this refers to calendar year or agricultural year.

15. NTK management reported that the producer price for maize paid by the mill in 1993/94 was

R350 per tonne. The Maize Board price for the same year was R417 [*Maize Board*, 1994: 1]. Mill management and many farmers were under the impression that the maize market in Venda was subject to the provisions of the 1968 Marketing Act but this could not be confirmed.

16. Interviews with senior officials of the Northern Province Department of Agriculture, Pietersburg, May 1996
17. Interview, May 1996.
18. Informal village councils, aligned to the broad democratic movement.

Introduction to the Tshiombo Case Study

The aims of this study, as outlined in Chapter 1, are to investigate the position of agriculture in household livelihoods in one of South Africa's former homelands and to recommend ways in which public action can contribute to the development of the rural economy and the improvement of household incomes. The first section of the study has provided an overview of agriculture and rural livelihoods in the homelands, based largely on published sources, with particular emphasis on Venda. In this and subsequent chapters, the results of a case study of the Tshiombo irrigation scheme in central Venda are presented and analysed. Together, the two sections provide the basis for a discussion, in Chapters 8 and 9, of the prospects for agricultural reform and development at Tshiombo and in the former homelands more generally.

This chapter outlines the reasons for selecting the case study site, provides an overview of the Tshiombo area and discusses the methodology used in the household survey.

5.1 SELECTION OF THE CASE STUDY SITE

Preliminary visits were made to Venda in April 1994, shortly before the formal re-incorporation of the territory into the Republic of South Africa, and again in the following month. This time was spent touring Venda, gaining familiarity with the physical and social geography of the area and meeting a range of people with knowledge of agriculture and rural life, including government officials, farmers and representatives of non-governmental organisations (NGOs) (see Appendix). On the basis of these preliminary visits, the main phase of fieldwork was planned for the period January to July 1995, the aims of which were to investigate agricultural conditions in Venda in some depth and to plan and carry out a detailed case study, focusing on individual households.

The initial stages of field research (roughly mid-January to mid-March 1995) employed a highly opportunistic, multi-method approach that drew on the techniques associated with the Rapid Rural Appraisal (RRA) methodology, including interviews with key informants, group discussions and transect

walks [*McCracken, Pretty and Conway*, 1988: 18; *Chambers*, 1992: 6].
Particular efforts were made to balance official (that is, government) with non-official informants, in the hope of obtain a diversity of opinions and in order to avoid identifying the study too closely with (or being too influenced by) 'the government' (itself a somewhat fluid concept during this period of political transition, but one that carried a lot of meaning for most informants none the less).

'Official' contacts began with meetings with senior officials of the Provincial Department of Agriculture in Pietersburg and Thohoyandou and with senior managers of Agriven, the public institutions most closely involved with agriculture in Venda. Both provided information on agricultural conditions in Venda and on the activities of their organisations, as well as facilitating visits to a selection of field projects and introductions to field officers, representatives of agricultural co-operatives and individual farmers.

'Non-official' contacts began with meetings with NGOs active in the northern Transvaal, including the Independent Development Trust, the Mvula Trust, the Akanani Rural Development Association and the Northern Transvaal Land Research Group, as well as academics at the University of Venda (Univen). These contacts provided valuable insights into the social and economic conditions of rural Venda, the main development initiatives in the area and the ongoing process of political and administrative transition. They also facilitated introductions to a range of community-based organisations, such as 'civics', women's groups and youth organisations, many directly involved with local development projects. Discussions with these groups supplied an important counter-balance to 'official' accounts of local affairs and some insight into the issues of concern to people working 'at the grass-roots'. Formal interviews were supplemented by village walks and visits to farmers' lands, as well as attendance at community meetings (at headmen's kraals and tribal offices) and 'Farmers' Days' organised by the Department of Agriculture.

During the initial, extensive, phase of the study, a short-list of villages (and some wider areas) that might be suitable for the planned case study was complied. In this, two key issues had to be considered – the wide variety of ecological (and thus agricultural) conditions found in Venda and the fact that, as far as could be ascertained, agriculture was extremely marginal to livelihoods over much of the territory. This raised important questions about how representative any one village could be of Venda as a whole and how effective a study of a relatively minor aspect of the broader local economy could be in understanding rural livelihoods. Selecting a case study site from the semi-arid periphery of Venda, where households struggled to raise even a few livestock or to produce a single crop of maize in a year, might reveal a lot about rural poverty, but relatively little (over the lifetime of the study) about the function-ing of the agricultural sector. Alternatively, selecting a site from an area of relatively high agricultural potential in central Venda, where government support services were concentrated and at least some households were believed to obtain a sizeable portion of their livelihood from agriculture, might be more productive in terms of data collection, but unlikely to reveal much that could easily be generalised to the rest of the territory.

After much consultation, it was decided that, of the two scenarios, the latter – a relatively developed agricultural area – was more likely to generate the type of information required on agriculture and livelihoods and thus meet the objectives of the study. As a result, the search for a study site now concen-trated on areas of relatively high agricultural potential where initial contacts suggested the researchers would obtain the co-operation of local leaders and officials and gain access to sufficient numbers of farming households. The focus on small-scale farming with which the study had began, however, remained paramount.

One of the areas visited during the early stages of fieldwork (in February 1995), and that stood out as an area of strong small-holder activity, was the Tshiombo irrigation scheme. Although larger than what originally was envisaged as a case study site, covering as it did six villages and over one thousand hectares of irrigated land, Tshiombo was difficult to ignore (see Map 3). It was the largest and one of the oldest schemes of its kind in Venda, if not in South Africa, and its farmers were described by officials as 'commercially-orientated'. It differed from the large-scale, parastatal projects of the 1970s and 1980s, however, in that typical holdings were in the order of one to two hectares and production was in the hands of private individuals. As a research proposition it offered many attractions, not least amongst them the fact that it had been established for over thirty years and that land appeared to be clearly demarcated and allocated to identifiable households. The area exhibited a mix of farming types, with many households keeping livestock or combining irri-gated agriculture with dryland (that is, rainfed) cropping off the scheme. A number of small private orchards were also in evidence. Thus, the potential for learning about a wide range of agricultural activities from a substantial number of farming households seemed good.

The key questions that had to be answered before the final decision could be made, however, were: are the conditions found at Tshiombo qualitatively different from those in the rest of Venda, and does Tshiombo, as a relatively sophisticated and long-established agricultural project, hold potential lessons for rural development in other parts of Venda and beyond?

Initial interviews and investigations at Tshiombo suggested that, while the area had many unique features, particularly in terms of the overall scale of the irrigation scheme and the high degree of support it received from the state, it also appeared to suffer from many of the problems found elsewhere in Venda. Despite the presence of irrigation plot-holders were said to be short of water, certain government services, particularly ploughing, were reported to be barely functioning and formal marketing structures appeared to be virtually non-existent. Of particular importance, however, and something on which all informants were agreed, was that agriculture was not the main source of livelihood for the majority of plot-holders at Tshiombo. This was generally attributed to the small size of holdings and the limited marketing opportunities for farmers' produce. This suggested that, in one crucial aspect at least, plot-holders at Tshiombo did not differ greatly from the mass of rural households in the rest of Venda.

Thus, after considerable reflection, it was decided that while Tshiombo did contain much that was unique it also had much in common with other parts of Venda and that an in-depth study could yield useful information about agriculture and rural livelihoods which was likely to have implications for smallholders over a wide area. On this basis, Tshiombo was selected as the location for the proposed case study. A period of three weeks was then spent conducting a preliminary survey of the entire Tshiombo scheme, developing a research strategy suited to the area and to the aims of the study and negotiating access to plot-holders, officials and local leaders.

Gaining access to any rural community in Venda, especially for a white researcher affiliated to an unfamiliar foreign institution, is a delicate business at the best of times. Local leaders and officials maintain a close watch on comings and goings within their communities and many rural people have a well-developed distrust of outsiders, especially whites, who it is assumed are in some way connected with 'the government'. Preliminary visits to Tshiombo were in the company of people who were well known in the area and were not connected with the government service. This allowed the researchers to by-pass senior officials and 'traditional' leaders and make direct contact with farmers, extension officers and other members of the community. Once the decision was taken to make Tshiombo the main focus of the study, however, it was thought prudent (and more productive) to seek the approval and assistance of the official structures, particularly the Department of Agriculture, while at the same time building relations with non-governmental organisations and individuals in the area. This approach had considerable success, as it facilitated direct access to all officials connected with the scheme, both at the District Office in Thohoyandou and at Tshiombo itself, all of whom were highly co-operative and provided valuable assistance throughout the course of the study.

The first weeks of the case study proper were spent learning about the organisation of the irrigation scheme as a whole and gathering information about social and economic conditions in the surrounding area, prior to proceeding with the household survey. On the 'official' side, formal interviews were held with the Acting Regional Director, the Regional Director of Field Services and the District Controller of the Department of Agriculture in Thohoyandou. At Tshiombo itself, meetings were held with the scheme Superintendent, the Agricultural (extension) Officers and the Chief Water Bailiff. Between them, these contacts provided a comprehensive overview of the irrigation scheme, the range of government support services available and the main forms of agriculture practised in the area. Visits were also paid to all six village heads (*mahosi*)[1] to explain the purpose of the study. All gave their permission for the study to continue, and while this may not have been strictly necessary, it pleased the local officials and helped assure respondents that the survey had the approval of all the relevant authorities. All the *mahosi* had plots on the irrigation scheme and were themselves a useful source of information about past and present conditions in the area.

On the 'non-official' side, a wealth of information and opinion on social, economic and political conditions in the area was obtained through meetings with the committee of Tshiombo Co-operative, members of village civics, clergymen, health workers, teachers and shop-keepers. First-hand accounts of agriculture on the irrigation scheme were supplied in informal interviews with prominent farmers introduced by the Chief Water Bailiff and other (less prominent) individuals encountered during walks in the fields with the extension officers.

These discussions and observations provided a good working knowledge of the Tshiombo scheme and suggested a number of ways in which the study could proceed. It had been decided in advance that the principal research instrument of the case study would be a detailed household interview, covering all sources of income and agricultural activities, and a draft questionnaire had been prepared and piloted in various parts of Venda during the first exploratory phase of fieldwork. Attention was now given to modifying the draft questionnaire to suit conditions at Tshiombo (particularly regarding the irrigation scheme and the range of government support services), as well as working out how best to select a sample from amongst the households at Tshiombo for interview.

Details of the design and implementation of the household survey are discussed below, but first it is appropriate to provide a more detailed overview of social, economic and environmental conditions at Tshiombo.

5.2 OVERVIEW OF THE TSHIOMBO IRRIGATION SCHEME

Tshiombo irrigation scheme is situated at the western end of the Tshiombo valley, on the upper reaches of the Mutale River in central Venda (see Map 2). The irrigated lands cover an area of 1,196 hectares, divided into 930 plots of approximately 1.28 hectares (1.5 *morgen*) each. The plot-holders, with a few exceptions, reside in the six 'betterment' villages situated alongside the scheme. The Tshiombo scheme was, until 1994, under the control of the Venda Department of Agriculture and Forestry and the Department of Works, but it now falls under the authority of the new Northern Province administration.

The Tshiombo valley is a broad, almost flat, area approximately 33 kilometres long and four to seven kilometres wide, at an altitude of 600 metres above sea level. The valley is bounded to the north by the Soutpansberg range and to the south by a smaller line of hills, part of the central Venda highlands. It is bisected by the Mutale River, which rises in the sacred lake Fundudzi ten kilometres to the west and marks the historical (that is, nineteenth century) boundary between the chieftaincies of Tshivhase, to the south, and Rambuda and Thengwe to the north. The valley covers some 18,800 hectares, 80 per cent of which is classified as footslopes (*Terrain Type 4*) and 20 per cent as valley bottom (*Terrain Type 5*) [*ISCW*, 1996: Land Type Ba60]. Some 29 per cent of land in the valley is considered to be unploughable due to stoniness and/or shallowness of the soil, but slope, at less than 12 per cent throughout, does not present a barrier to cultivation. The geology of the valley is quaternary sand and alluvium overlying sandstone and quartzite of the Soutpansberg Group [*RAU*, 1979: 22].

Soils are predominantly red, well-drained sandy loam soils, with some grey, poorly drained soils of a higher clay content, as shown in the following table.[2]

TABLE 5.1
MAIN SOIL TYPES, TSHIOMBO VALLEY

Description	Depth (mm)	Soil Types	Percent
Shallow red sands	200–400	Clansthal Hu24 Bontberg Hu25	20
Deep red sands	> 1000	Bontberg Hu 25 Msinga Hu26	21
Grey plinthic sandy clay loams	400–900	Longlands Lo21 Albany Lo22 Devon We22 Sibasa We13	35

Source: ISCW 1996: Land Type Ba60.

Rainfall for the Tshiombo valley is well above average for the Transvaal. Annual (calendar year) rainfall was estimated by RAU [1979: 22] at between 800 and 900 mm, but more recent statistics from the Tshandama weather station show a lower figure of 688 mm. Rainfall for the agricultural year (the so-called seasonal total, measured July to June), however, shows considerable deviation from this mean. In the two severe droughts of the past 15 years, 1982/83 and 1991/92, seasonal totals fell to 394 mm and 240 mm respectively, while in the wetter years of 1984/85 and 1987/88 they reached as high as 1094 mm and 1120 mm. Exceptionally high rainfall was again experienced in 1995/96 and 1996/97, but precise details were not available at the time of writing.

The following figure shows the seasonal rainfall (July to June) recorded at Tshandama for the period 1982/83 to 1992/93.

FIGURE 5.1

ANNUAL RAINFALL, TSHIOMBO VALLEY

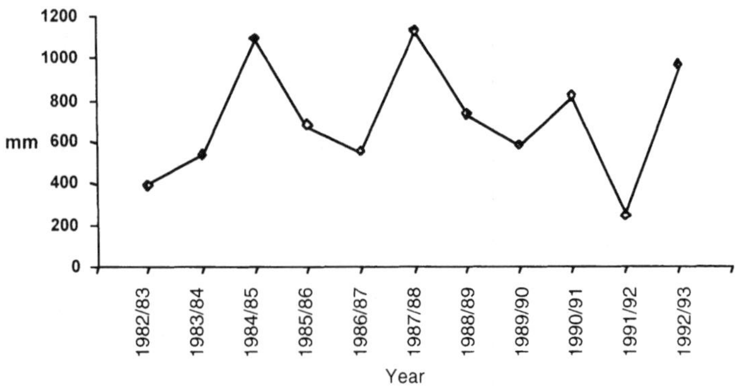

Source: South African Weather Bureau Station Report, Tshandama.

Rainfall is heavily concentrated in the summer months, with 82 per cent of the annual total on average falling in the period October to March. Monthly averages range from a high of 131 mm in February to a low of 9 mm in June, as shown in Figure 5.2.

Temperatures in the Tshiombo valley are generally sub-tropical and frost is virtually unknown. Average daily temperatures range between 14.9° Celsius in June and 31.5° in January. The lowest temperature on record is –3.4° (June 27 1983) and the highest is 43.2° (24 December 1988). Figure 5.3 (below) shows average daily minimum and maximum temperatures throughout the year, recorded at Tshandama weather station over the period 1982 to 1990.

FIGURE 5.2

AVERAGE MONTHLY RAINFALL, TSHIOMBO VALLEY

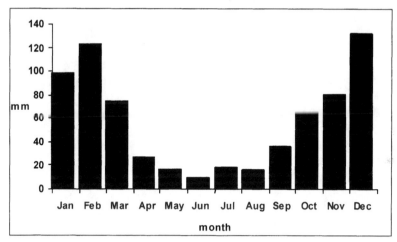

Source: South African Weather Bureau WB42, Tshandama: 1982–90.

FIGURE 5.3

AVERAGE MAXIMUM AND MINIMUM DAILY TEMPERATURES, TSHIOMBO
VALLEY (DEG. C)

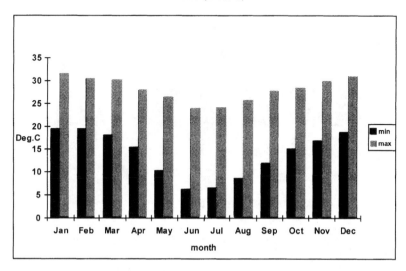

Source: South African Weather Bureau WB42, Tshandama: 1982–90.

At the time of writing, the Mutale remains one of the few perennial rivers in South Africa that has not been the subject of a comprehensive hydrological study.[3] Figures for the monthly volume of water flowing in the Mutale River, measured at Thengwe (Streamflow Gauge A9M04), are available, however, with some gaps, for the years 1932 to 1993. For the 38 years for which complete data are available, the average flow was 82.68 million cubic meters per annum and in 29 of these years flow exceeded 50 million cubic meters.

The following chart shows the volume of water flowing in the Mutale for all years for which data are available for ten months or more.[4] Examination of the monthly trend suggests that the missing data are unlikely to make a significant difference to the overall pattern shown. Annual totals are for the period October to September.

FIGURE 5.4

MUTALE RIVER FLOW 1932/33–1992/93

(MILLIONS OF CUBIC METRES)

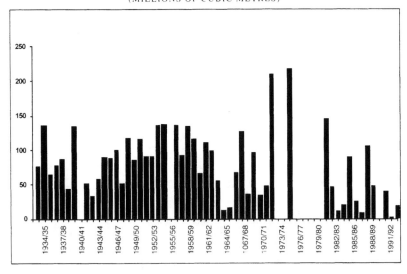

Source: Department of Water Affairs and Forestry, Tzaneen.

These streamflow data show a cyclical pattern, with exceptionally high points in the mid-1950s and mid-1970s and low points in the early 1960s, the early 1980s and the early 1990s. In five years out of the last ten shown (that is, 1982/83–1993/94) annual flow in the Mutale fell below 30 million cubic metres, less than half the average for the previous 50 years. The only other time this happened was in the years 1963/64 and 1965/65, but in both cases data are available for only 10 months out of 12.

The lowest confirmed figure for annual flow in the Mutale is 1.28 million cubic metres (for 1991/92). Less than 50,000 cubic metres (that is, virtually no flow) was recorded for each month from February to October 1992. Informants living on the Mutale's lower reaches (around Masisi) reported that the river dried up completely in 1992, the only time that they could recall this happening.

There is no single explanation available for the dramatic decline in water volumes in the Mutale River in recent years, but a number of possibilities suggest themselves. Most obvious is the changing rainfall pattern in the region, which seems to be in long-term decline (see Chapter 3). To this must be added, however, the increasing extraction of water for irrigation schemes and private irrigators, both from the Mutale itself and from its tributaries [*Lahiff*, 1997: 99]. In addition to the 8.14 million cubic metres required every year by the Tshiombo scheme, Murray, Biesenbach and Badenhorst [1989: 32] estimate that four million cubic metres are extracted for the Makonde irrigation scheme and a further 1.8 million cubic metres between Tshiombo and Thengwe for animal and human consumption. Another likely cause of decline is the damming of the Tshirovha River, a tributary of the upper Mutale, in the mid-1980s, in order to provide irrigation water for the tea plantations at Mukumbani, on the southern side of the mountains.

Whatever the reason, or combination of reasons, the general pattern of decline fits that described by O'Keeffe, Uys and Bruton [1992: 288] for rivers (like the Mutale) draining through the Kruger National Park:

> Reductions in the flow of South African rivers, due to river abstractions as well as impoundment, have compounded the effects of catchment degradation and have converted a number of southern Africa's perennial rivers to seasonal rivers. Some of the most striking examples are the rivers that flow through the Kruger National Park. These rivers all rise to the west of the park boundary, and many have been heavily exploited before they flow into the park. Although there are no formal hydrological records, very reliable observations since the first half of the century are available from park rangers' notebooks. These indicate that all the main rivers (Luvuvhu, Great Letaba, Olifants, Sabie and Crocodile) were formerly perennial. In recent years the flow in the Letaba River has been so reduced that it flows for only a few months each year. The Luvuvhu River first stopped flowing in 1948, and again in 1964–65, but it now stops flowing in most years.

As yet, the Mutale itself has not been dammed, but the threat facing all of the rivers in the region, and the people and ecologies that depend on them, would appear to be same. It is worth noting that no reference to a threat to water levels in the Mutale could be found in any official publications, or in conversations with government officials in Pietersburg or Pretoria, and it would appear that conservation of water resources was not a prominent policy under the former homeland regime.

Development of the Irrigation Scheme

The Tshiombo irrigation scheme was developed by the South African Department of Native Affairs between 1959 and 1964, on 'communal' land under the control of Tshivhase Tribal Authority. Arable plots were allocated as early as 1961 and the scheme was fully operational by about 1964, although interviews with plot-holders suggested that not all plots were occupied until the late 1960s or early 1970s.

The creation of the scheme involved relocating the population of the area, which then lived in dispersed settlements, into six new, compact villages, namely Matangari, Tshiombo,[5] Mianzwi, Maraxwe, Muhotoni and Mutshenzheni, each under its own headman (or headwoman). The villages are all located south-west of the main road that runs the length of the scheme, and to the south of the arable lands (see Map 3).

Older people in the villages remembered the early days of the scheme as a time of plentiful employment, with the construction of the irrigation infrastructure and the clearing of land for ploughing, but also as a time of considerable disruption as households were forced to relocate to the designated residential areas. One informant recalled that white overseers and Pedi (that is, Northern Sotho) workers came to construct the scheme, but when it was finished, 'they all went away and we were left with the plots'. A number of households, not wishing to join the scheme or not understanding what was happening, are said to have left the area ('they ran away', said one old man), and an unknown number of Shangaan-speaking households appear to have been forcibly removed around the same time. One elderly Shangaan-speaker reported that he had left Tshiombo in 1949 to work in Johannesburg, and when he returned in 1975 nearly all of the Shangaans were gone. Another Shangaan couple said they had resisted removal from the area, and an elderly Shangaan woman – who was born in Thengwe – stayed because her husband was a Venda-speaker. Overall, however, it appears that most households in the vicinity of the scheme were able to obtain an irrigated plot if they so desired, as were a considerable number of people from other parts of the emerging Venda 'homeland' and adjoining 'white' farms.

Although little documentation could be obtained regarding the origins of the

Tshiombo scheme, it would appear to be an early, and relatively elaborate, example of the policy of 'betterment' implemented throughout the black reserves/homelands in the late 1950s and early 1960s (see Chapter 2). De Wet [1995: 48] argues that after 1954 the South African government abandoned its earlier policy (and the recommendations of the Tomlinson Commission) of developing agriculture in the reserves through the creation of 'economic' holdings, which had included the culling of cattle and the forced removal of 'surplus' (that is, landless) population. Instead, the apartheid regime concentrated on establishing more effective control over the rural population, which meant bolstering the position of the 'tribal' institutions (including the chieftaincy and the system of communal land) and 'stabilising' the rural economy through the development of irrigation schemes, small-holder sugar-cane production, forestry and fibre (cotton, flax and sisal) projects. Culling of cattle and any changes to the 'tribal' land system, such as the introduction of private tenure or mass dispossession, were rejected on the basis that they would undermine the position of the chiefs who were essential to the emerging policy of retribalisation. De Wet [1995: 51], for example, observes that:

> Locations were still divided into residential, arable and grazing areas, but plans were modified to cater for all the inhabitants of a location as the surplus population was to remain. This meant that only a few, and in some cases, no families, received economic units, as it was policy in the application of the revised planning strategy that no one should lose rights to occupy land as a result of the implementation of Betterment.

While the Tshiombo scheme would appear to fit de Wet's description closely, it went far beyond the typical 'betterment' project, particularly in terms of the scale of infrastructural works (and the amount of public investment it implies) and the number of households directly involved. This suggest a relatively serious attempt (by homeland standards) to 'uplift' at least part of the rural population, albeit against a background of widespread repression and dispossession of the African population. Unlike similar schemes in other parts of the country, Tshiombo does not appear to have been aimed directly at the tribal elite (Chief Tshivhase and his circle, based at Mukumbani, 20 km away), nor did it involve the original inhabitants being replaced by new settlers [*Watkinson*, 1996: 41]. Indeed, as will be show below (Chapter 6), the largest group of beneficiaries appears to have been those people already living and working on the land that was incorporated into the scheme.

At 1.5 *morgen* (1.28 hectares) each, the irrigated plots were certainly capable of providing a substantial contribution to household food requirements and, under ideal conditions, employment for one or two persons. Given the number of people dependent on each plot, however (both today and, presumably, in the past), and the limited marketing possibilities in the area, it appears highly unlikely that a household could ever have hoped to obtain its livelihood from agriculture alone. Moreover, the prevailing policy of one plot per household effectively precluded the possibility of accumulation within agriculture, at least in the early years of the scheme, while the fixed number of plots on the scheme ensured that the number of households involved could not increase over time. Overall, considering the limited opportunities available to black rural households in the 1960s, a scheme such as Tshiombo probably represented a relatively attractive foothold in the homeland, but with the small plot sizes and the limits to accumulation, there can be little doubt that households were, from the beginning, obliged to send members into paid employment for longer or shorter periods.

Social and Economic Conditions at Tshiombo

Tshiombo lies within the relatively well-developed zone of central Venda, 20 km from the 'capital', Thohoyandou, and has reasonably good commercial services and communications. A tarred road passes close by the irrigation scheme, running from Thohoyandou to Mutale township, via a bridge over the Mutale at Makonde. A well-maintained gravel road runs from Makonde through the villages of Matangari, Tshiombo, Mianzwi, Maraxwe and Muhotoni, continuing via another bridge to Rambuda. A smaller and poorly maintained track runs to the most westerly village on the scheme, Mutshenzheni.

Public transport – in the form of buses and mini-bus taxis – is generally good in the area, at least as far north as Mutale township. Taxis serve all the villages between Makonde and Rambuda, with the exception of Mutshenzheni. Telephone services are restricted to a few farm-lines (manual exchange), mainly to government offices. An assortment of shops, petrol stations and other services are located along the main tarred road, at places such as Khubvi and Makonde, but the main concentration of services in the area is at Mutale township. This has a magistrate's and other government offices, a police station, a post-office, a variety of shops, a fresh produce market and a collection of small craft workshops built by the Venda Development Corporation.

Agriculture is the dominant economic activity throughout the Tshiombo valley, and there are two other irrigation schemes in addition to the one at Tshiombo. The Rambuda scheme, located on the opposite bank of the Mutale, was developed at the same time as Tshiombo and comprises 120 hectares under irrigation, divided into 102 plots. Irrigation is provided by means of a canal from the Tshala River. Adjacent to the Tshiombo scheme, at Makonde and Tshandama, an irrigation scheme of approximately 570 hectares was developed by Agriven in the 1980s. Since 1988, this project has been subdivided into plots of between eight and 25 hectares and leased to individual farmers. Irrigation is by large central-pivot sprinklers, supplied by diesel-powered pumps directly from the Mutale River. Production on this scheme is heavily market-orientated and farmers receive substantial support from Agriven, ranging from advice on production and marketing to credit, plough-ing and transport services. Apart from these state-supported projects, small areas of 'informal' (that is, private) irrigation may be found on both banks of the Mutale River and along tributaries such as the Sambandou and the Tshiombedi.

Dryland (rainfed) agriculture predominates in other parts of the valley, particularly the eastern end. The main dryland crop in the area is maize, usually grown in mixed stands with pumpkins and various kinds of squash. Smaller areas of groundnuts and sorghum are also grown. Livestock farming, both cattle and goats, is widespread, but not on the scale found in more northerly parts of Mutale District. Grazing south of the Soutpansberg is largely classified as *sourveld*, meaning that the grass loses its nutritional value in winter. To the north of the mountains, grazing is largely *sweetveld* and so pro-vides year-round nutrition. Officials of the Department of Agriculture esti-mated that no more than a quarter of households in the Tshiombo valley kept livestock, with cattle slightly out-numbering goats. There are no established sales points for livestock in the area and informal sales – to butcheries and direct to consumers – were reported to be on a very small scale.

All land within the Tshiombo valley is officially classified as communal land and is under the control of the various Tribal Authorities. On the govern-ment-run irrigation schemes a degree of control has been acquired by Agriven and the Department of Agriculture, but this has not fundamentally altered the form of land ownership or tenure (see Chapter 6).

Agriculture and related services in the Tshiombo area generate considerable economic activity for non-farmers as well as for farming households. At least eight private tractors were available for hire on the Tshiombo scheme, and many more people provide transport services using one-tonne *'bakkies'* (pick-up trucks). Large numbers of merchants, mostly with their own transport, and smaller-scale hawkers, many using public transport, operate in the Tshiombo area, supplying Thohoyandou and other towns with fresh produce. Additional enterprises serving the agricultural sector at Tshiombo include a new, electrically-powered maize mill, which offers an accessible alternative to the roller-mill at Shayandima, and the Tshiombo Co-operative which sells a wide range of agricultural and household requisites (see Chapter 7).

The only industrial activity of any note in the Tshiombo area is brick-making, and brickyards have started in many of the villages in recent years. Some are privately owned, but others are community-based projects, started with assistance from non-governmental organisations such as the Independent Development Trust (IDT). This development is in response to the rising demand for brick-built houses, which have begun to replace the traditional mud and thatch huts in many areas. There is also considerable self-employment in services and hand-crafts such as motor mechanics, panel-beating, dressmaking, shoe-repairs and hairdressing. Apart from the government service, however, there are no major employers in or around Tshiombo and the great majority of people in wage employment must travel to work outside the area, either commuting to Thohoyandou or migrating to the industrial and commercial centres of Gauteng Province, principally Johannesburg and Pretoria.

All six villages at Tshiombo are laid out on the grid pattern typical of 'betterment' planning and are provided with rudimentary services. Each has a small general store and between them they share eight primary schools, two secondary schools and one clinic. A doctor from Donald Fraser Hospital attends the clinic once every fortnight and a mobile clinic tours the area every two months. The only other shops within the area of the scheme are the Tshiombo Co-operative and a number of small 'spaza' shops, located in people's homes and in roadside shacks. All the villages have been fitted with communal water taps (stand pipes), but supply is unreliable and households mainly rely on the irrigation canal and natural springs for their domestic water requirements. The nurse at the Tshiombo clinic reported that the general health of people in the area was good compared to other parts of Venda, but that cases of bilharzia were common, especially amongst children, due to drinking (and swimming in) untreated water. Domestic toilets are of the pit-latrine type. Mains electricity first reached the area in 1993, but by mid-1996 only a minority of houses had paid to be connected.

Most homesteads consist of a number of traditional-style *rondavels* (round huts), made of mud bricks and thatched with grass. A sizeable number of modern houses, with concrete bricks and tiled roofs, have been built in the area in recent years, however, and many homesteads display a mix of traditional and modern styles.

The population of the Tshiombo villages, according to the 1991 census, was 7,992, as shown in the following table [*Republic of Venda*, 1993b]. Assuming an annual growth rate of 3.5 per cent, as used by the Venda Statistical Department, the population for 1995 would have been in the order of 9,170. These figures are for the *de facto* (actually present) population only and exclude migrants and others absent at the time of the census.

It was not possible to determine the precise number of households at Tshiombo. The 1991 Census, however, found that the average household size for Venda was 5.58 persons, or 5.54 for the rural portion of Thohoyandou

District (which includes Tshiombo) [*Republic of Venda*, 1993a].[6] These figures suggest that the number of households at Tshiombo is likely to be at least 1,400. As the total number of plots on the irrigation scheme was only 930, it was expected that a sizeable number of households would be without land (or at least without irrigated plots) and this was indeed found to be the case. Estimation of the extent of landlessness was complicated, however, by some households holding multiple plots on the irrigation scheme and the use of so-called waste land around the margins of the scheme. Further details of land-holding and household composition are presented in Chapter 6.

TABLE 5.2
POPULATION OF TSHIOMBO

Village	Population
Matangari	2,992
Tshiombo	1,127
Mianzwi	1,338
Maraxwe	1,069
Muhotoni	988
Mutshenzheni	478
Total	7,992

Local Administration

Administratively, Tshiombo falls within the Tshivhase Tribal Area and the Thohoyandou Magisterial District and until 1994 the principal organs of local government were the Tshivhase Tribal Authority and the Thohoyandou District Council (Regional Authority). Each village falls under the jurisdiction of an unelected headman (or in one case, a head woman) and a village council, which in turn come under the authority of the Chief Tshivhase and the Tshivhase Tribal Authority. As in the other former homelands, both Tribal Authorities and District Councils in Venda were dominated by (unelected) 'traditional leaders' (chiefs and headmen), which despite support from some sections of the population were widely seen as ineffective and lacking in legitimacy [*Surplus People Project*, 1983: 17]. Tribal Authorities had (and continue to have) considerable, if ill-defined, powers in the area of land alloca-tion and the administration of tribal courts. District Councils in Venda had no revenue-raising powers and their main function seems to have been to make representations to government on the provision of services in their area [*Eales*, 1993: 150]. What public services existed at the local level were provided by the line departments of the homeland government.

As part of the transition to democracy, local government in Venda has been substantially reorganised and Tshiombo, somewhat incongruously, now forms part of the Greater Thohoyandou Urban Council, while the rest of the Tshiombo Valley and large areas to the north and east fall under the Rural Council of Mutale, Masisi and Vutshwema. At the time of fieldwork it was not clear what powers, if any, these primary-level local councils would have, as most revenue-raising and regulatory powers, and control of services, had passed to the line departments of the Provincial Government and the new, indirectly elected, Northern District Council [*Lahiff*, 1997: 19]. The former Thohoyandou District Council was technically abolished along with the rest of the homeland government structure in 1994, but continued in a care-taker capacity until the local government elections of November 1995.

The emergence of democratic local government in Venda, as in the other former homelands, has been greatly complicated by the continued existence of Tribal Authorities and the plethora of 'traditional leaders'. Since the local government elections of 1995, there effectively exist two parallel systems of local governance in Venda, resulting in enormous confusion and growing conflict around issues such as the allocation of housing plots, control of communal land and the right to negotiate on behalf of communities with higher level authorities. By the end of fieldwork (June 1996), no provision appeared to have been made for the transfer of functions from the old 'tribal' structures to the new 'democratic' ones, and little was being done by government to clarify the respective powers and responsibilities of these two sets of institutions.

Landholdings

Land at Tshiombo can be divided into four categories, namely, residential 'stands' (sites), arable plots on the irrigation scheme, arable land off the irrigation scheme and communal grazing land. When the area was reorganised under 'betterment' in 1959/60, only the first two categories were catered for and, unlike other villages in the area, no lands were officially demarcated for dryland agriculture or for grazing. Limited amounts of both these activities, however, are today carried out on the margins of the irrigation scheme (see below).

With the exception of about 50 houses in Matangari village which are located on a small 'island' amongst the irrigated lands, all houses in the six villages at Tshiombo are situated in a narrow (100–500 m) strip of land between the main road and the hills on the southern fringe of the scheme. Residential stands are roughly 40 metres square and are arranged in a regular grid pattern. Stands contain between one and ten huts and many have sizeable areas used for fruit trees, vegetable plots and animal kraals (enclosures). Stands are allocated, in principle, by the village headman, within the area officially demarcated for residential purposes. Up to about 1990, residential stands could be registered at the local Magistrate's office (in Thohoyandou), where the boundaries of the stand and details of the householder were recorded, and with the Tribal Authority (at Mukumbani) where householders were granted 'Permission to Occupy' (PTO), sometimes in writing but usually verbally. Registration and PTO did not confer any legal title to the land, but were widely seen as securing the position of householders in the event of a dispute with the headman or neighbours. By 1995, however, the system of allocation was showing signs of breaking down, as 'the youth' were reported to be building houses without permission from the village headmen. This can be seen as part of a growing tension between 'traditional' authorities and supporters of the democratic movement organised around the local civics and the new (ANC-controlled) local council.

Land on the irrigation scheme is divided, for administrative purposes, into four main Blocks (1 to 4), and in recent years these have been further sub-divided into twelve sub-Blocks, each under the supervision of an Agricultural (Extension) Officer.[7] Blocks ranged in size from 48 plots (Block 1) to 143 plots (Block 3A). Some mention was made of an additional Block (3B) by officials at Thohoyandou Regional Office, and judging from the size of Block 3A it may have been their intention to split this Block into two (Blocks 3A and 3B) at some stage, but this had not yet occurred.

Plots on the irrigation scheme are allocated jointly by the village headman and the Agricultural Officer for the Block. Plot-holders pay an annual charge of 12 Rands (R12) per plot to the government, described by plot-holders as 'rent' and by officials as 'irrigation fees', an amount that has remained fixed since the beginning of the scheme.[8] Examination of the records for one Block (Block 3) in June 1995 showed widespread arrears in payments of annual fees. Out of 59 plots, 32 had not yet paid for 1994 and some had arrears stretching back to 1991. Despite the role of officials in the allocation of plots and the charging of annual fees, the system of land-holding on the scheme does not differ greatly from other land allocated under the 'communal' (or 'tribal') system. Occupants are given permission to use the land and are usually allowed to pass their plots to other family members on their death or retire-ment, but are given no title deed and cannot sell or (officially, at least) sub-let their plots. All of the Agricultural Officers on the scheme reported a demand for plots, both from within Tshiombo and from surrounding areas, and eight of them kept waiting lists of applicants for land. Turn-over of plot holdings is extremely low, however, although there were reports of households surrender-ing land in recent years due to the lack of irrigation water. Most plots have remained in the possession of the same family or household since the scheme began. An official policy of 'one man one plot' operated (with some exceptions) for about the first ten years of the scheme, but in recent years this appears to have broken down and a minority of plot-holders have been able to acquire multiple irrigated plots as well as areas of 'waste land' adjacent to the scheme (see below). As far as could be ascertained, there were no effective means of repossessing a plot, even if it was unused, unless an occupant surrendered it.

No land at Tshiombo, other than the irrigation scheme itself, was formally designated as arable land. None the less, sizeable areas on the margins of the scheme, particularly marshy areas between the scheme and the Mutale River, referred to by local officials as 'waste land', were being cultivated.[9] Interviews with users suggested that cultivation of such land has intensified greatly since the late 1980s. Plots are allocated by the village headmen, one of whom said that he consults informally with the agricultural officers as to the suitability of the land and of the household in question.

From the information available, it appeared that no land was ever formally demarcated for grazing purposes at Tshiombo. To a large extent, this can be explained by the geographical setting, as virtually the entire valley bottom (on one side of the river) is given over to the irrigation project, with the residential areas squeezed into a narrow strip between the plots and the steep hillsides to the south. Older inhabitants reported that ownership of cattle and donkeys was widespread before the scheme began and that they were used for ploughing and transport purposes. Ploughing with animal traction remained common in the early years of the scheme, but was said to have been strongly discouraged by the (white) officials of the time and was gradually replaced by tractor ploughing. Informants were agreed that livestock numbers in the area declined greatly as a result. Goats were said to have been relatively rare in the area in the past and were actually banned from Tshiombo for many years after 'betterment' because they were considered a nuisance to arable farmers, but this rule appears to have lapsed in recent years. Today, goats are grazed mainly on the hillsides behind the residential areas, whereas cattle and the few remaining donkeys are grazed on the margins of the irrigation scheme and the residential areas, along the river bank and on irrigated plots after harvest. Livestock may not be grazed on cultivated lands, or on other people's house-stands, and anyone infringing this rule is liable to be reported to the agricultural officer or village headman and fined by the Tribal Court. Otherwise, there appeared to be no restrictions on the number of livestock that may be kept by villagers, or on the use of unallocated (that is, common) land for grazing.

The Irrigation System

The method of irrigation used at Tshiombo is a gravity-fed canal and furrow system, supplied with water from the Mutale River by means of a purpose-built barrage and piece pipeline up-stream from the irrigated lands. The main concrete-lined canal follows the contour along the southern edge of the scheme for 15.2 km, roughly parallel to the road. The canal decreases in size from a top width of 2.0m and a depth of 0.85m at the beginning, to a width of 0.66m and a depth of 0.31m at the end [*Murray, Biesenbach and Badenhorst,* 1987: 30]. There is no main reservoir, but a limited water storage capacity is provided by nine small buffer reservoirs ('ground dams') situated at points along the scheme. Typical flow rates in the canal were estimated in 1987 as 510 litres per second in the upper reaches, dropping to 120 litres per second after the first 4.7 km [*Murray, Biesenbach and Badenhorst,* 1987: 30].

From the main canal and buffer dams water is supplied to the arable plots by a series of concrete-lined secondary canals. The flow of water into the secondary canals is controlled by means of division boxes ('DBs'), fed by small-diameter pipes, which are opened and closed using improvised stoppers – usually a mix of grass, twigs, plastic bags or other available debris. Plot-holders direct water into their plots by temporarily damming the secondary canal using an object such as a large stone or fertiliser sack. This causes the water to overflow via one of the indentations placed at regular intervals (approximately every ten metres) in the canal side. Each indentation corre-sponds to a single cultivation strip, or crop 'bed', within the plot. Depending on their shape, plots have between 10 and 16 such crop beds, 12 being the most common number. Once water is diverted into the plot, it is channelled in earthen furrows between crop ridges as required, an extremely laborious process that involves constant opening and blocking of furrows using hand tools. The system drains back into the Mutale River.

Officially, every Block on the scheme receives water once a week, usually for about six hours, on a rota basis. When water is particularly scarce, as was the case during much of 1993 and 1994, supply is reduced to one period every two weeks and limits are imposed on the number of beds that may be irrigated on each plot. Agricultural Officers said the limit was half a plot (six beds) but plot holders claimed that the supply was in fact sufficient for only two or three beds. Unauthorised use of water appeared to be widespread, especially at night and during the weekends when the water bailiffs were off duty. Excessive water extraction in the upper portions of the canal inhibits the rate at which the lower ground dams are replenished and reduces the supply to users on lower Blocks. A similar problem occurs along the course of the secondary canals during the authorised irrigation period, as users closer to the junction with the main canal have first claim on the water and supply diminishes considerably further down-stream.

The shortage of water in the irrigation system was a source of constant complaint amongst plot-holders and the situation was particularly bad on the lower reaches of the scheme (especially Block 4C), which were said to be frequently dry for the entire period from May to September. Various proposals have been put forward over the years by the Venda Government, Eskom (the South African electricity company) and the Development Bank of Southern Africa for the construction of a dam on the Mutale River and the upgrading of the irrigation infrastructure, but as of mid-1996 none of these had come to fruition.

Government Services

The state provides a wide range of services at Tshiombo, relating to the maintenance and operation of the irrigation system and support to individual farmers. The main agencies involved up to 1994 were the Venda Department of Works, which maintained the irrigation infrastructure and provided tractor services, and the Department of Agriculture and Forestry, which provided the agricultural extension service and ran the small Research Station. Both Departments have now been incorporated into the new Provincial government service.

The key officials in the day-to-day management of the scheme, and in the co-ordination of government services on the ground, are the Agricultural Officers, each of whom is responsible for one of the 12 Blocks. The Agricultural Officers advise farmers on various aspects of crop production, particularly the selection and use of seed and fertiliser, optimal times for planting and harvesting and control of pests. They also organise farmer training and demonstrations, co-ordinate the provision of tractors and other services on their Blocks and deal with applications for new plots or transfers of plots between members of a household. Some of the Officers assisted plot-holders with marketing their crops, but this appeared to be a matter of personal initiative. The Officers report to the Scheme Superintendent, who divided his time between Tshiombo and the District Office at Thohoyandou.

Working closely with the Agricultural Officers were fifteen water bailiffs, who supervise the daily allocation of water to the various Blocks and are expected to prevent unauthorised water use, albeit with little success. Other staff involved in the operation and maintenance of the scheme included fence repairers, office cleaners, a team of (approximately 20) labourers to maintain the irrigation canals and a clerk who receives revenue for tractor hire and annual irrigation fees. During the early 1990s, these staff were supplemented by teams of labourers employed under the national drought relief programme, who were engaged in the cleaning of the main and secondary canals and repair of roads around the scheme.

An important component of the Tshiombo project since its inception has been the fleet of government tractors which provide ploughing services to plot-holders for a fee. In the early days of the scheme, survey respondents reported, many households preferred to plough using animal traction, but this was discouraged by scheme officials. According to the scheme Superintendent there were six tractors stationed at Tshiombo in 1995, but no more than two appeared to be working at the time of fieldwork. Plot-holders were unanimous in the opinion that the government ploughing service had deteriorated severely in recent years, particularly since 1990, and during much of 1995 there were long delays in obtaining government tractors at Tshiombo. Officials on the scheme confirmed that the tractor service suffered from lengthy delays in routine maintenance and repairs, despite the presence of full-time mechanics on site. Mechanical problems were compounded by recurring shortages of diesel fuel, caused by budgetary problems in the former homeland administration in 1994 and 1995, but these appeared to have been resolved by the end of my fieldwork in 1996. Occasionally, tractors based on projects elsewhere in Venda are available for hire by plot-holders at Tshiombo, but not during the period of peak demand in early summer when priority is given to dryland farmers.

A small agricultural research station is located at Tshiombo, but no actual research was being carried out at the time of fieldwork. In June 1996, trial plantings of various maize varieties were being planned, in collaboration with a commercial seed supplier. Otherwise, the station is used for occasional demonstrations by the Agricultural Officers and some individual beds are allocated to households awaiting plots on the scheme in order to give them practical experience of irrigation.

In addition to the agriculture-related services, the Department of Agriculture, through its Home Economics division, also employs a Development Officer and four local assistants, charged with promoting small-scale income-generating schemes amongst women at Tshiombo. In her first year at Tshiombo (1994/95), the Development Officer's activities focused on egg-laying and sewing projects, which operated in all six villages on the scheme.

Non-Governmental Organisations and Services

The most important non-governmental service at Tshiombo is undoubtedly the Tshiombo Co-operative. This was founded in 1973 as a collective purchasing organisation for farmers and provides a rare example of a (relatively) successful independent co-operative in a former homeland. The founding members of the Co-operative reported that they received advice and help from the Agricultural Officers on the scheme, but insisted that it was their own initiative from the beginning. The Co-operative had 630 members in 1995 and the annual membership fee was R10, up from R5 in 1990. It is run by a management committee, elected annually by the membership, and employs a full-time staff of six. Members are entitled to a five per cent discount on purchases and in good years receive a dividend related to value of purchases. The Co-operative building, originally a storage shed for harvested produce, is leased from the Venda government, and some instruction is given by the Registrar of Co-operatives' office in tasks such as book-keeping and the preparation of annual reports, but otherwise the Co-operative is independent of the state apparatus.

The Tshiombo Co-operative is essentially a retail operation, its main activities being the sale of agricultural inputs, such as fertiliser, seed and pesticides; petrol (it has the only filling station in Tshiombo); and household supplies such as cooking pots, candles, paraffin, soap, mealie meal (maize flour) and waterproof clothing. The management of the Co-operative reported that it was having problems competing with the Agriven-run stores at Makonde and Malavule and the 'white' co-operatives in the region (NTK and Levubu Co-operative) due to the poor terms they obtained from suppliers and because Tshiombo was not in a position to offer credit facilities to its members. The Co-operative did act for a number of years as a facilitator for Agriven's rotating credit scheme, whereby it supplied farmers with inputs and was subsequently refunded by Agriven. This facility was withdrawn by Agriven in 1992, reportedly due to large-scale non-payment by farmers, leading to a considerable drop in business, according to the Co-operative manager. The Co-operative shares a site with one of the agricultural offices on the scheme, the tractor service station and the agricultural research station, making it the focal point of the Tshiombo scheme.

As noted above, a number of private operators offer tractor and transport services in and around Tshiombo, but it was not possible to establish how many individuals were involved in this business. One further privately-funded intervention in the local economy was the establishment, in 1994, of a substantial electrically-powered mill, located across the road from the Co-operative. At the time of fieldwork, the mill appeared to be doing a roaring trade, with customers coming from Tshiombo and from surrounding villages to mill their maize. Some farmers on the scheme, however, complained that the mill was not capable of producing the very finest grade of maize meal which they preferred.

Apart from the Co-operative, no effective forms of organisation could be identified amongst plot-holders at Tshiombo. A Central Committee for the scheme was said to meet from time to time, but it was unclear how its members had been elected (or selected) or what their functions were, and most plot-holders appeared to be unaware of its activities. Decisions regarding the development of the scheme and the day-to-day running of the irrigation system were made by government officials and there appeared to be little or no tradition of consultation with plot-holders. The difficulties of forming representative structures at Tshiombo became apparent towards the end of the final period of field work, when officials on the scheme attempted to organise the election of representatives from each Block to form the committee of a new farmers' organisation. At its first public meeting, in May 1996, the newly-elected representatives and their chosen chairman met with considerable hostility from plot-holders, leading to the abandonment of the meeting. The newly-formed Venda Farmers' Union was also attempting to form a branch at Tshiombo in 1996.

5.3 METHODOLOGY OF THE HOUSEHOLD SURVEY

The preliminary study of resources and institutions at Tshiombo, discussed above, provided the basis for the final design and implementation of a formal household survey. The principal research instrument used was a detailed interview with a sample of plot-holders, using a semi-structured questionnaire. This was designed to ensure that a minimum set of questions was asked in every interview, while allowing flexibility of response and scope for whatever supplementary questions might be appropriate. A draft questionnaire had been prepared in advance and was tested in pilot interviews with an *ad hoc* selection of 12 households at Tshiombo during the preliminary stages of the case study. On the basis of this experience, the questionnaire was modified to produce the 'Household Questionnaire, Version 2 (Tshiombo)' (see Appendix), which was then used for all interviews in the survey proper.

When selecting Tshiombo as the case study site, it was decided (perhaps erroneously in retrospect) to restrict the survey to households with plots on the irrigation scheme. As there was a total of 930 plots it was necessary to find a way in which a representative sample of plot-holders could be selected for interview. On the basis of the pilot interviews, and in the light of the limited resources available for the study, it was felt that a sample size of ten per cent of plot-holders would be both manageable and sufficiently comprehensive.

Following consultations with Agricultural Officers on the scheme, it was decided that the official plot numbers would provide a suitable sampling frame from which to select households for interview. These plot numbers, which ran from 01 to 930, were known to the plot-holders and have remained fixed since the beginning of the scheme, and therefore appeared to offer a reliable and accessible basis for selection. An official Register, showing the name of every plot-holder, was kept by each Agricultural Officer, but these were not used as they were said to be out of date and a number of the persons named on the register were deceased. Selected plot numbers were, therefore, provisionally matched to households with the help of the Agricultural Officers and sub-sequently matched to individual plot-holders following consultation with household members (see below). In other words, plot numbers, which were unambiguous, were used as a proxy for plot-holders (the individuals to be interviewed), as no precise list of such persons was known to exist [*Casley and Lury*, 1987: 187]. While this method contained an element of imprecision and subjectivity, subsequent experience did not suggest that it was in any way inaccurate, and named plot-holders were identified in all cases without great difficulty.

A sample of ten per cent of plots on the irrigation scheme was generated by means of interval (or systematic) selection of every tenth plot number, starting with a randomly selected number between '1' and '10' (drawn from a hat).[10] This produced a total of 93 elements, but on examination it was found that two of the plots selected were held by the same household, so the initial sample size (that is, the total number of possible interviews) was reduced to 92. Occupation of multiple plots was subsequently found to be common amongst the sample, but this was the only case where two plot numbers drawn by the interval selection were held by the same household.

Interval selection was chosen for two reasons. First, it was generally agreed by informants during preliminary research that agricultural conditions gradually deteriorated from the beginning to the end of the irrigation scheme. That is, lower plot-numbers (nearer the head of the canal) tended to receive more water and thus to be more productive, than higher numbers (those further from the water source). Therefore, an even distribution of plot-holders across the entire scheme was considered most likely to represent accurately the full range of physical conditions. Such a sampling method cannot be described as truly random, as once the starting number has been chosen, the remaining elements in the frame no longer have an equal chance of being selected, but the resulting sample is likely to share the characteristics of a random sample. Where the elements in the sampling frame are pre-arranged according to some non-random order – in this case geographic – a systematic selection results in what Casley and Lury [1987: 61] describe as 'a rudimentary stratification' of the sample.

Second, it was important that the method of selection used was comprehen-sible, and acceptable, to all those concerned with the survey – selected plot-holders, excluded plot-holders and the various intermediaries who would be depended upon to arrange the interviews. From experience gained during the pilot study it was clear that many parties had their own ideas regarding the 'best' people for interview, and that whatever sampling method was used was likely to be contested and would have to be defended vigorously.

As expected, the sample selection procedure was readily understood and accepted by most people involved with the study and seemed to offer some reassurance to those plot-holders selected (and those who were excluded) that the method of selection was 'blind' and did not reflect on them personally (either positively or negatively). Local officials also expressed satisfaction with the sampling method, although they disparaged some of the plot-holders selected as 'poor' (as opposed to 'progressive') farmers. None the less, the vast majority of officials and others encountered during the course of the study were extremely co-operative at all times.

Once the sample of households had been selected, a rough interview schedule was drawn up in co-operation with the Agricultural Officers. Every Monday morning a meeting was held with one (occasionally two) of the Block officers, who informed the relevant households that we (researcher and translator) would be working on their Block during that week and invited them to participate in the survey. The aims and format of the study, and the names and affiliations of the researcher, were explained more fully at the time of interview. In cases where individuals were reluctant to participate, or required more information, the translator would attempt to meet them and encourage them to become involved in the study. Where plot-holders were not available during the week in question, attempts were made to arrange a more suitable time. Indeed, the last three weeks of fieldwork were devoted to tracking down plot-holders who had been unavailable or uncontactable during the first round of interviews.

Up to this point, plot numbers had only been matched to households, as prior to actually meeting with the household concerned it was not possible to determine who might be the most relevant person, or persons, within the household to be interviewed (although the Agricultural Officers usually had a good idea of who this might be). The key person as far as this study was concerned was what I loosely designated as the 'plot-holder', the person within the household with operational control of the agricultural holding and its products (see Chapter 6). Households selected for interview were invited to nominate the person who knew most about agriculture and the overall financial position of the household, and were told that this did not have to be the 'head' of the household. In the majority of cases, the nominated person was subsequently identified as the plot-holder, and where the person nominated was clearly not the plot-holder, the interview was generally postponed until he or she were available. In a small number of cases, wives or mothers of migrant workers, who had day-to-day control of agriculture but were not themselves the plot-holders, were interviewed in lieu of the absent plot-holder. In many cases, additional members of the household also participated in the interviews and this was generally encouraged.

Household interviews were conducted over a period of three months, from May to July 1995. This is the early dry season in the northern Transvaal and marks the beginning of the annual cropping cycle. Few if any crops remain to be harvested and most plot-holders spend this time preparing the ground for the first planting of the year – typically early maize or green leaf vegetables. By squeezing the interviews into this relatively short period it was hoped to be able to focus discussion on the same time frame (approximately April 1994 to March 1995) in all cases and minimise the risk of confusion between different agricultural seasons.

Interviews took place in respondents' homes, in their fields, or at the Block office, as they preferred. Interviews generally lasted between one and two hours and two to three interviews were conducted on a typical day. The preferred method was to complete the interview in a single visit, but a few cases required a second or third visit, either because the interview was interrupted for some reason, or because the respondents wished us to speak to additional members of the household.

All of the interviews were conducted by the author and the translator (Mr Lawrence Phala) who was fluent in all five languages of the Northern Province (Afrikaans, English, Northern Sotho, Shangaan and Venda). During one week we were joined by an anthropologist from the University of Venda (Mr Godfred Dederen), who assisted us by raising a number of interesting supplementary questions and correcting some mistaken impressions we had formed, particularly with regard to the naming of crops and the meaning of certain familial relationships. We were escorted and introduced to most respondents by a government officer, but officers generally left us alone to conduct the interviews and did not participate in any way.

Most interviews were in the Venda language, with immediate point-by-point translation into English. Two respondents preferred to be interviewed in Shangaan and a number of men chose to conduct some or all of the interview in English. All notes were taken in English. Tape recording of interviews was attempted in the early stages, but was found to distract respondents and to be ineffective in the open air, where most interviews took place, and so was abandoned. Interview notes were written out in full each evening, along with comments about the conduct of the interview and any additional observations about the respondents' or their plots.

Survey respondents were asked a total of thirty-two pre-set questions, under six main headings, with various supplementary questions as appropriate. Part

One of the questionnaire dealt with family history, place of origin, amount of land held and date when it was acquired. Part Two covered household composition, the age, sex and occupation of each household member and sources of household income. Part Three dealt with all aspects of agricultural production over the previous twelve months, including output, sale and consumption of produce, methods of transport used and the use of household and non-household labour. Part Four dealt more specifically with purchased agricultural inputs, including seed, fertiliser and pesticides, methods of ploughing and access to credit. Part Five covered all aspects of livestock farming, including the numbers of cattle, goats, donkeys, poultry and other stock owned by the household, access to grazing, purchased inputs used and the sale and consumption of animals and animal products. Part Six contained a series of open-ended questions which sought respondents' opinions on issues such as the quality of government services and their perceived needs in terms of the development of agriculture and the local economy. The individual questions, and the problems associated with them, are discussed in subsequent chapters.

Successful (that is, more or less complete) interviews were carried out with 83 of the 92 selected households. There were various reasons why the remaining nine households were not interviewed and it is difficult to estimate what bias, if any, their omission may have introduced to the survey results. Only two of these 'failures' were due to outright refusals – in each case, we met the plot-holder and explained the purpose and form of the study, but they declined to be interviewed. It should be pointed out that varying degrees of persuasion were required in many other instances, so these represent only the most extreme cases. One plot in the sample was reported to have been abandoned, the last occupier having died some time ago. It was unused at the time of our visit and other members of the household could not be found. Interviews could not be arranged with six other plot-holders during the period of the field study, despite numerous attempts. Two of these lived outside Tshiombo, were said to visit their plots infrequently and could not be contacted. Four others were working in Gauteng and were not expected back for many months, and no other members of their households were available or willing to meet with us. Attempts to obtain these last remaining interviews eventually had to be abandoned when the time allotted to the survey expired. Thus, the effective sample size, as far as data collection and analysis are concerned, was 83 (n=83) and this is the sample that is referred to throughout the rest of this study.[11]

Once all the interviews were finished, the completed questionnaires were numbered from 01 to 83, in the same order in which they occurred on the scheme (that is, in order of plot number) and these, rather than the actual plot numbers, are the 'Respondent Numbers' referred to throughout the rest of this study. The approximate position of individual respondents on the scheme can be seen from the following table.

TABLE 5.3
LOCATION OF SURVEY RESPONDENTS ON THE IRRIGATION SCHEME

Respondent Numbers	Main Block	Sub-Blocks	Plots Numbers
1–20	1	1, 1A, 1B	1–233
21–39	2	2, 2A, 2B	234–444
40–57	3	3, 3A	445–646
58–83	4	4, 4A, 4B, 4C	647–930

A separate semi-structured questionnaire was devised for interviewing the Agricultural Officers on the scheme (see Appendix). The questionnaire design was based on informal interviews with four of the officers at Tshiombo and others in various parts of Venda, conducted during the preliminary stages of fieldwork (February–March 1995). The purpose of this questionnaire was to capture specific information about each Block, in a standard fashion, which could subsequently be used for purposes of comparative analysis. As all 12 Agricultural Officers were to be interviewed, no sampling was necessary. Formal interviews with the officers were conducted immediately prior to interviews with plot-holders on their respective Blocks, but informal meetings and discussions continued throughout the period of fieldwork.

Roughly a year after the household survey, a second period of eight weeks was spent at Tshiombo (April–June 1996), during which further interviews were conducted with some of the original survey respondents, the Agricultural Officers, a number of plot-holders not included in the original survey and various others. The aims of this phase of fieldwork were to present a provisional analysis of the household survey data for discussion with interested parties, to conduct further research into a number of social groups which had been inadequately covered during the first visit, particularly agricultural labourers and crop merchants, and to observe what changes might have occurred on the scheme over the course of the year. All the Agricultural Officers were re-interviewed, along with a number of village headmen, the newly elected councillor for the area, members of civics and a variety of other informants. Group interviews were held with farmers on four of the twelve Blocks on the scheme, to which the Agricultural Officers were given discretion to invite participants. Out of 32 plot-holders who attended these meetings, 13 had participated in the original survey and 19 were new to the study. Provisional survey findings were presented for discussion at these meetings, allowing for considerable debate and clarification of issues on the part of researchers and plot-holders.

5.4 THE QUESTION OF THE HOUSEHOLD

This study (both theoretically and methodologically) treats the household as the central social and economic unit around which livelihoods are constructed, one which combines within it important elements of production, reproduction, consumption and access to resources. It is necessary, however, to recognise that households are far from homogeneous entities and tend to be highly differentiated both internally (between individuals) and externally (between households), as well as being subject to considerable change over time. It is equally important to recognise that the household is not the sole site of economic and social activity, and cannot be treated as synonymous with all the interests or actions of its various members. Individuals clearly pursue many activities which do not contribute directly to the collective welfare of their primary household and may occupy positions simultaneously or sequentially in more than one household. Employment, trade, kinship and a plethora of other social and economic relations integrate households with other households and with the wider world.

The wide variety of household forms, and the problems of defining households in practice, have featured prominently in recent studies of the southern African periphery [*Brown*, 1983: 122; *James*, 1985: 163; *Martin and Beittel*, 1987: 218; *van der Waal*, 1996: 31]. Murray [1981: 48], for example, writes of the multiple meanings of the term 'household' in Lesotho and argues that neither co-residence nor kinship are reliable guides to household composition under conditions of extreme dependence on migrant earnings. Nonetheless, he argues, 'the household remains the unit of economic viability whether or not its members are physically dispersed at any one time'. In his study of Transkei, Spiegel [1986: 17] highlights the 'fluidity' of households in areas supplying migrant labour which, it is argued, arises from 'the distribution and re-allocation of people between households as those units' access to sources of income fluctuates over time'. This dynamic aspect of rural households leads Spiegel to caution against static notions of the household drawn from one-off survey material.

On a practical level, the most pressing issue for this study was to come up with a working definition of the household that would minimise debate or confusion at the point of interview and facilitate subsequent analysis of households as social and economic units. Clearly, such a definition needed to include a residence dimension (members would have to be actually resident, or show a long-term commitment to residence) and some degree of reciprocal or dependent relationships between members. It was, however, an aim of the study to *develop* a functional definition of the household, based on the concrete forms that were encountered in the survey, and it was therefore important that any pre-set definition would remain flexible and could be adjusted and refined over the course of the study. Thus, the guiding questions in defining specific households for the purposes of fieldwork were: Who lives in this household?; Who contributes to it?; and Who is supported by it? Respondents were encouraged to take a liberal interpretation of these categories, in order to arrive at the broadest possible definition of a household. Once this had been done, the other central issues of the study could be investigated – the assets and sources of income available to the household and the various activities pursued by household members in order to obtain a livelihood.

Along with the definition of the household itself, the concept of 'head of household' also requires some clarification. This concept is widely used in household surveys, not only because it helps to define a household in terms of relationships between the 'head' and other members but also because it facilitates comparative analysis of households on the basis of characteristics such as age, sex, education or employment of that key individual [*Casley and Lury*, 1987: 161]. Of particular mportance in the context of widespread male migrancy is the somewhat ambiguous position of women, many of whom are effectively in charge of households for lengthy periods but rarely attain the formal title of 'head'.

Preliminary fieldwork in Venda suggested that the concept of 'head of household' in general, and of the 'female-headed household' in particular, were of quite limited practical or analytical value. While many households were run by women on a day-to-day basis, virtually all households had a man – a husband, a son, or a father – who played some role in the household and who would invariably be described as the head, regardless of age or economic status. Widows of male heads did not, generally speaking, inherit that position from their husbands, although in practice they often took over many of their late husbands' responsibilities.

Such situations have led some authors to distinguish between *de jure* and *de facto* heads, but these distinctions are inevitably arbitrary [*Spiegel*, 1986: 20]. Some improvements on this approach are offered by James [1985: 168] who employs the concept of the 'matrifocal' household to describe cases where a male head occupies a relatively marginal position, and by Ardington [1984: 16] who refers to widows and deserted wives as 'permanent' heads of households in order to distinguish them from the wives of migrants who occupy the position of head only in their husbands' absence. Useful as these categories are, none of them seemed to capture the range of conditions found within households in Venda.

Rather than trying to impose such categories on the survey sample, this study attempts to analyse households along various lines, such as overall size, the presence of adult men and adult women, the number of wage earners and so on. Probably the most useful approach, however, both in terms of exploring gender issues and social relations more generally was to focus attention on what I call the 'plot-holder', the person within the household (not necessarily the head) with most responsibility for agricultural matters. By focusing on the plot-holder, I have effectively avoided the question of head of household altogether and have concentrated instead on the functional roles of men and women within households and the specific problems faced by women-only households.

NOTES

1. While the Venda term for a headman is generally given in the literature as *gota* (or *nduna*), and the term for a chief as *khosi* (singular) [*Jeannerat*, 1997: 88], the village headmen (and one head woman) at Tshiombo were invariably referred to, collectively, as *mahosi*.
2. I am indebted to Mr Gary Patterson of the ISCW for interpretation of the *Land Type Inventory*.
3. Officials of the Department of Water Affairs and Forestry in Pretoria suggested that such a study was planned for 1997/98.
4. Of the 51 annual estimates shown, eight are based on data for only 11 months, and five on data for 10 months.
5. Elsewhere in this study, the name 'Tshiombo' is used to mean the irrigation scheme as a whole, including all six villages, in keeping with local practice, unless otherwise indicated.
6. The average household size reported by the household survey (below) was substantially higher as, unlike the census, it included migrant workers and others temporarily absent from the household.
7. One of the Agricultural Officers was said to be in dispute with the Department of Agriculture and he did not participate in the study. His Block was being served by an Officer from another Block.
8. The South African unit of currency is the Rand (R). In 1995, the exchange rate was approximately R5.5 to UK£1. The charge of R12 was easily borne by most plot-holders in 1995, but it represented a substantial sum in the early 1960s. Workers on drought relief programmes in the northern Transvaal, for example, were receiving only R14 per month at that time [*Desmond*, 1971: 148].
9. Most quotations in this part of the study have been translated from the original Venda into English, but many technical terms, such as 'waste land', are part of a standard English vocabulary used by officials and others on the scheme.
10. The actual plot numbers have been kept confidential in order to offer some anonymity to the survey respondents.
11. The survey found that the average number of plots held by households in the sample was 1.52, which suggests that there were a total of approximately 608 households with land on the irrigation scheme. Therefore, the initial sample size of 92 probably represented around 15 per cent of total households, and the number of completed interviews (83) approximately 13.6 per cent of households, in excess of the original target of ten per cent.

MAP 3: TSHIOMBO

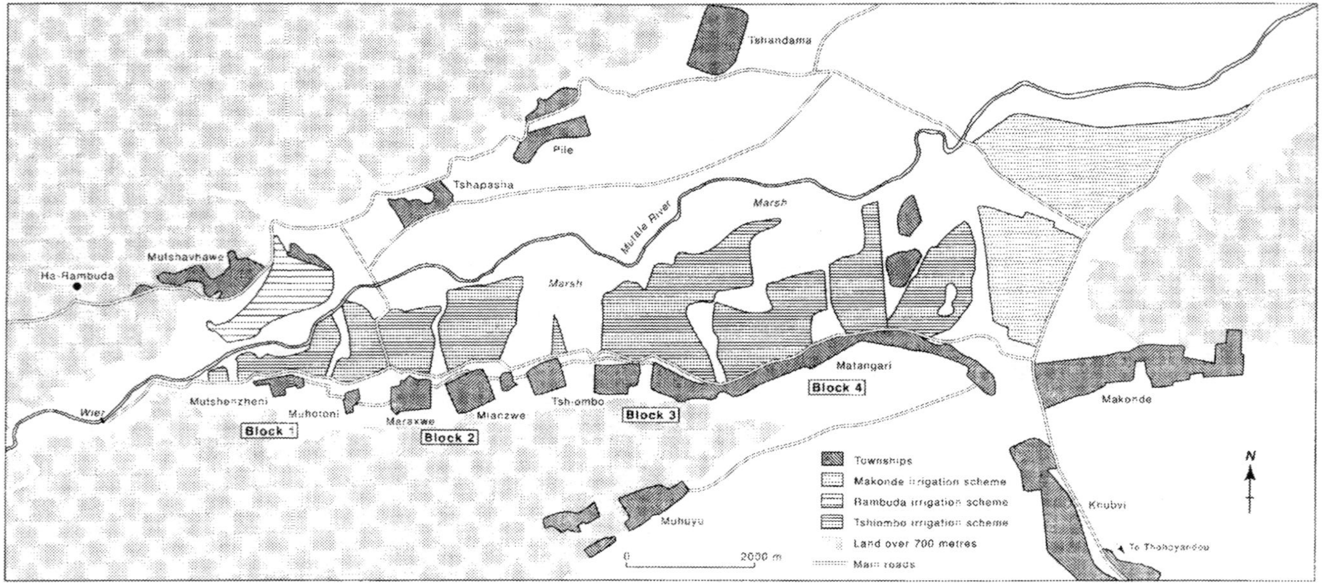

Legend:
- Townships
- Makonde irrigation scheme
- Rambuda irrigation scheme
- Tshiombo irrigation scheme
- Land over 700 metres
- Main roads

Block 1
Block 2
Block 3
Block 4

Ha-Rambuda
Mutshamhawe
Mutshekezheni
Mulhotoni
Meraxwe
Miaczwe
Tshiombo
Mulhuyu
Matangari
Makonde
Knubyi
To Thohoyandou
Tshiandama
Pile
Tshaonsha
Mutale River
Marsh
Wei

0   2000 m

6

Household Composition, Income and Assets at Tshiombo

The previous chapter outlined the methodology and context of the survey conducted amongst plot-holding households on the Tshiombo irrigation scheme. In this chapter, survey findings regarding household composition, sources of income and agricultural assets – land and livestock – are presented and analysed.

6.1 HOUSEHOLD SIZE AND COMPOSITION

Survey respondents were asked to provide details about everyone who lived within the household for some or all of the year or who supported it financially (see Chapter 5). While this left much scope for discussion with respondents over who was to be included or excluded, most cases were easily resolved through applying a broadly 'inclusive' approach – that is, all persons currently residing within the household (for at least a month) and others described as members of the household were included unless they had definitively left and established a permanent home elsewhere. Married migrants (effectively men) whose spouse resided in the household, and who returned at least once a year, were included, but those who had migrated with their spouse were not. Unmarried migrants were included if they returned at least once a year and supported other household members financially (again, effectively men only). Children who were sent away for schooling (mainly to Soweto) but continued to be supported by the household were included in the household. Children who lived with their grandparents or other relatives while both parents stayed in the city were included even if their parents were not, as in most cases the children had been born in Tshiombo and simply stayed behind when their father or mother left. The breadth of this definition of the household is taken into account in the analysis that follows.

The total population of the 83 households surveyed, according to the above definition, was 636, an average of 7.7 persons per household. The actual number of persons per household ranged from one to twenty-one persons, but two-thirds of households contained between five and ten members and the median household size was seven persons. The following figure shows the distribution of household sizes at Tshiombo.

FIGURE 6.1

PERSONS PER HOUSEHOLD AT TSHIOMBO

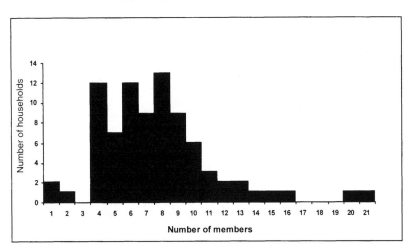

Differentiating between children and adults within households presented a number of problems. Standard categories used by the Census of Venda and other sources define all persons under 15 years of age as children and those of 15 years and older as adults. While this has the advantages of clarity and exactitude, it does not provide socio-economic categories that are particularly useful in trying to understand households in an area such as rural Venda. If childhood is understood as a state of economic dependence on parents or guardians, then it clearly does not end neatly at 15, but earlier in some cases, and substantially later in many more. Widespread poverty, a poorly-resourced school system, a lack of employment opportunities and the political disturbances of the late 1980s and early 1990s have meant that many pupils do not finish school until they are well into their twenties.[1]

For the fortunate few, full-time education (and economic dependence on family members) may be extended into the tertiary level, in the form of teacher training college, Technicon or University. Eight households in the sample (9.6 per cent) had somebody in third-level education. On the other hand, many people under 15, especially girls, drop out of school to assist in the family home or fields, while an apparently high incidence of teenage pregnancy means the early onset of adult responsibilities for many others. Van der Waal

[1996: 37], writing of fieldwork in the neighbouring homeland of Gazankulu, expresses a similar dilemma, when he says that he 'quite arbitrarily categorised as children everyone up to age 19 years, even though at one extreme, some 16-year-old girls were already married mothers staying with husbands and functioning as adults, while, at the other extreme, there were 28-year-olds who were still at school and dependent on others for support'. For the purposes of this study, all persons under eighteen years and neither married, caring for their own children nor in full-time paid employment were classified as children, along with those over 18 and under 21 in full-time education. According to this classification, 42.6 per cent of the sample population were adults, and 57.4 per cent were children.

Of the adults in this survey, 41.3 per cent were male and 58.7 per cent were female. Such a preponderance of adult females over males is a recurring feature of studies of the southern African periphery, and is usually explained in terms of the system of oscillating labour migration, which keeps a proportion of men away from their homes for most of the year. In this study, however, men who migrated to the industrial centres for work but left their families behind in the village were included in the definition of the household, suggesting that there may be other factors influencing this disparity between the sexes.

The survey uncovered a significant number of women (ten in all) who described themselves as 'abandoned' or 'divorced' by their migrant husbands, which suggests that migration leads to the permanent (or semi-permanent) absence of a minority of men from their home villages. Spiegel [1986: 25], writing of Transkei, describes such men as 'absconders', migrants who have 'been lost in Johannesburg' (see Brown [1983: 373] and Moodie [1994: 149] for similar findings). Secondly, there was a large proportion of widows within the sample, but few widowers, suggesting that wives tend to outlive their husbands. Whether this is because of women's greater longevity, or because wives tend to be younger than their husbands, could not be conclusively demonstrated on the basis of this study, but anecdotal evidence suggests that both factors play a part. Thirdly, a number of younger, unmarried male migrants may have slipped through the survey 'net' if they were omitted by their parents and did not leave wives or children behind to suggest their presence in the household. Finally, the definition of 'adult' and 'child' used in this study probably (unintentionally) boosted the number of females defined as adults, and reduced the number of males, especially if, as appears to be the case, women marry younger than men. For example, a 17-year-old girl caring for her child would have been counted as an adult, but her 20-year-old brother or boyfriend attending school would not. All of these factors are likely to have exaggerated the number of female adults relative to the number of male adults.

Overall, however, the pattern suggests that Tshiombo tends to lose males to the cities and that women tend to outlive their husbands, thereby creating a permanent predominance of women over men in the area.

Households in the survey took a wide variety of forms. Most contained three generations of the same family and a minority was organised around polygynous marriages. The average number of adults per household was 3.2 and four-fifths of households (80.8 per cent) contained between two and four adults. All households had at least one adult and the highest number reported in a household (one case) was ten. The number of children per household ranged from nil (four cases) to 16 (one case), and the average for the sample was 4.4 children per household. The majority of households (63.8 per cent) contained between three and six children. Thus, it is possible to speak of a 'typical' Tshiombo household that contains three or four adults and four or five children: a quarter of households (21 out of 83) fitted this description.

At Tshiombo (and elsewhere in Venda), it is considered the norm for women to continue living in their natal household at least until they have had their first child and to return there for subsequent confinements. Women generally go to live with their husband after the birth of their first child, or eventually establish a home of their own if they remain unmarried.[2] As noted above, it is common for relatively young women (14–17 years) to bear children while unmarried and resident within the parental homestead, although this may be a temporary arrangement. In a number of cases, women with young children said they were not married and no mention was made of a male partner, so the issue was not pursued further.

It is less common for a woman to marry and to live with her husband within her natal household, but examples of this were found within the survey and would appear to be associated mainly with wives of migrant male workers. Natal households also have a tendency to partially reconstitute themselves, sometimes after many years, as widowed, abandoned or divorced women return to live with their parents.

Men tend to remain part of their natal household at least until they marry, and long after in many cases. It is common practice for the youngest son of a household to reside there and to take responsibility for ageing parents.[3] Other sons, however, may also continue to live within the homestead with their wives and children after marriage: the leading example of this was a household comprising a couple in their seventies with four married sons, their wives and a total of 11 grandchildren, all inhabiting the one, much-enlarged homestead. It is not uncommon for this pattern to be continued into a fourth, contemporary generation, as one or more grand-child marries and/or has children of their own while remaining within the household.

Children in the sample generally lived with their mother or with their grandmother (maternal or paternal) and although this survey lacked a longitudinal dimension, it was apparent from the accounts of respondents that there was considerable mobility of children between households. Van der Waal (1996: 45) describes the high incidence of fostering and the mobility of children between households in the neighbouring homeland of Gazankulu as 'a levelling mechanism whereby the burden of childcare is distributed in terms of the availability of resources (shelter, the presence of an adult, food and clothing) that are extremely limited' (see also Spiegel [1986: 23] for details of fostering in Transkei). Overall, however, the evidence from this one-off study would suggest that households at Tshiombo were not as vulnerable to fracture and dissolution as in many other parts of the former homelands and that the irrigation scheme offered a reasonably stable livelihood base around which relatively large extended households could grow up.

Polygynous marriage is a long-standing feature of Venda life, commonly associated with the chiefs. The practice has been strongly opposed by the missionary churches, but it still survives, particularly amongst non-Christians and the followers of independent 'Africanist' churches. In the course of the survey, 19 examples of polygynous marriage were encountered, all involving men with two wives,[4] although examples of men with up to six wives were encountered outside the survey sample. Polygynous households fell into two broad types: the more common situation (14 cases) was where wives lived within the one household (albeit in separate huts), and the less common (five cases) was where wives lived in different households (usually in different villages), with the husband alternating between the two. In some of these latter cases, it appeared that the first wives had effectively been abandoned or divorced by their husbands but, as Murray [1981: 127] observed for Lesotho, 'it is not always easy to distinguish genuine polygyny, serial monogamy and monogamy combined with an informal relationship of cohabitation'. While most of the men concerned were relatively elderly (that is, in their sixties or seventies), cases of polygynous husbands in their forties and fifties were also found. Women, as noted above, tended to be younger than their husbands and, in the case of second wives, differences of 20 years or more were common.

Men in the survey reported marrying for the first time between 20 and 40 years of age, typically after securing their first paid (local or migrant) employment. Second marriages tended to occur much later, commonly on a man's retirement from migrant labour in his forties or fifties. As a result, some men continued fathering children until quite an advanced age – one example was found of a man aged 77 with two wives, one in her sixties and one in her forties, with children in primary school. Overall, roughly one-sixth of men in the survey sample had more than one wife, far higher than the figures reported from most other parts of southern Africa [*Murray*, 1981: 127; *Brown*, 1983:

372]. An exception is Ardington's [1984: 15] case study from KwaZulu, which found that 22 per cent of marriages were, or had been, polygamous.[5]

The preponderance of adult women over men suggests that a sizeable number of women live without male partners, which, despite the prevalence of polygyny, was indeed the case. One consequence of the extended family structure, however, was that relatively few households at Tshiombo were entirely without an adult male member (that is, over 21 years): only five (six per cent) of households in the sample did not contain an adult male. Of these cases, one was an elderly widow who lived alone, two were widows with young children and two were women abandoned by their husbands, one who lived with her children and her (widowed) mother and one who lived with her children and her husband's mother (also widowed). This latter situation was said to have arisen as a result of conflict between the man, who was unemployed, and his wife. When the man wanted to throw his wife out of the household, his mother reportedly intervened and persuaded (or possibly ordered) him to leave instead. The strong inference from both women's accounts of these events was that, because they shared responsibility for domestic work and for cultivation of a single irrigated plot, with little or no contribution from the man, they had a vested interest in staying together and preferred to live without the man rather than break up the household.

One middle-aged man also lived alone, having being abandoned by his wife and children, the sole example of a household without an adult female member.

6.2 OCCUPATIONS AND INCOME SOURCES

Survey respondents were asked to describe the occupations of all household members. On the basis of the information supplied, the adult population of the sample has been divided, for analytical purposes, into three mutually exclusive occupational categories: pensioners, persons in wage employment and persons engaged primarily in the household economy (domestic or agricultural), as shown in the following table.

The largest occupational category was made up of persons primarily engaged within the household economy, which accounted for 127 persons, or 46.9 per cent of all adults in the sample. This included people involved in both domestic and agriculture work, various forms of petty commodity production and those described as 'unemployed' (see below). Pensioners accounted for 29.9 per cent of adults (81 persons),[6] and wage workers made up the remaining 23.2 per cent (63 persons). These broad categories clearly mask a large degree of internal differentiation, the most important of which is the radically different occupational structures for men and women.

TABLE 6.1
ADULT POPULATION, BY SEX AND OCCUPATION

	Male	Female	Total	Percent
Pensioners	27	54	81	29.9
In Wage Employment	53	10	63	23.2
Domestic/Agricultural	32	95	127	46.9
Total	112	159	271	–
Percent	41.3	58.7	–	100

Note: All percentages are as a proportion of 271, the total number of adults in the sample.

Looking first at adult women, over half (59.8 per cent) were primarily engaged within the household economy (domestic and/or agricultural work), one-third (34 per cent) were pensioners and the remainder (6.3 per cent) were in paid employment outside the household economy. In reality, of course, there was considerable overlap between these (analytical) categories. Most female pensioners and women in paid employment had some role in the household economy, while many household workers said they obtained occasional informal employment outside the home, or worked on their own account as hawkers. Collecting firewood and fetching water were among the more laborious tasks carried out almost exclusively by women (and girls) at Tshiombo, along with a host of domestic duties such as child care, cooking, cleaning and washing clothes.

Of the ten women in paid employment, one was a nurse, one worked in a clothing factory, one worked in a brickyard, one was a cleaner and another a labourer, both employed by the government on the irrigation scheme, one was a tribal official and four were primary school teachers. All ten lived at Tshiombo and worked within 20 km of their homes. Unlike the situation in many other homelands, casual employment on white farms, in towns, or on parastatal-run agricultural projects was not generally available for women in this 'deep rural' part of Venda [*van der Waal*, 1991: 351; *Sender and Johnston*, 1995: 11].

Thus, it can be said that women were heavily concentrated within the household economy, with a relatively high proportion of pensioners and a very low incidence of extra-household employment. It is striking that no women migrants featured in the survey, but this does not mean that women do not migrate from Tshiombo to the main urban centres. Indeed many respondents spoke of female family members who worked in the cities, particularly Johannesburg. What was apparent from the household interviews, however, was that migration meant different things for (and presumably to) men and women. Whereas many male migrants could sustain, and remain part of, a rural household, women tended to go to the city either with their husbands, or alone if unmarried. In either case, female migrants, unlike men, tended to be described by those remaining in the rural area as members of new, urban-based households, even if some or all of their children were left behind in the care of others.

The occupational structure for men at Tshiombo was very different, being heavily weighted towards non-farm (extra-household) employment, with a relatively small number of pensioners. The proportion of adult men in paid employment (47.3 per cent) was nearly seven times that of women, or nearly five times the absolute number. Of the 53 men in employment, 21 (39.6 per cent) were migrant workers (meaning that they were in permanent employment at some distance from their home, returning home no more than once per month, but as little as once a year in some cases), and 32 (60.4 per cent) were employed locally, within daily or weekly commuting distance. Of the second category, all worked within 150 km of Tshiombo, and all but one of them within Venda. The majority of men in local employment (24 out of 32) worked in some branch of the government service – tractor drivers, hospital orderlies, soldiers,[7] teachers, labourers and watchmen, four of them on the irrigation scheme itself. Of the others, one worked in a shop at Thohoyandou, one at a filling station in Messina, one as a minister of religion at Tshiombo, one at Tshikondeni mine (north-east Venda), one on the Mukumbani Tea Estate, one as a builder's labourer and two as taxi drivers.[8] Migrant workers were employed in a wider range of jobs in the public and private sectors, mostly in skilled and semi-skilled manual trades – drivers, plumbers, construction workers, machine operators and the like – and three former migrants had worked for long periods (10, 18 and 23 years) on the South African railways. As much of the information regarding the work (and earnings) of migrant workers, and some local workers, was obtained second-hand (that is, from other members of their households, in their absence), however, it was not as comprehensive as had been hoped.

The proportion of men receiving pensions was well below the figure for women (24.1 per cent compared to 34 per cent) and in absolute terms male pensioners were outnumbered two to one by female pensioners. This difference can, in part, be explained by the fact that women qualify for the state pension at 60 years of age, whereas men must wait until 65. It is also con-sistent with the hypotheses that women at Tshiombo outlive men and that a number of male migrants permanently abandon their rural homes. The remain-ing 32 men (28.6 per cent) – those without pensions or wage-employment – have been crudely categorised as occupied within the household economy. As was the case with women, however, this category covered a wide range of individual situations. In particular, it included two occupational descriptions that were applied by survey respondents exclusively to men: 'full-time farmer' and 'unemployed'.

A total of 19 men under 65 years of age described themselves as full-time farmers, meaning that farming was their principal occupation and their main source of income. Many women could, by the same criteria, be included in this category, but they did not describe themselves in the same terms and appeared to view agriculture more as an extension of domestic duties rather than as a 'profession'. A number of male pensioners could also be described as full-time farmers, but, for purposes of this analysis, they too have been excluded from this category. All but one of the full-time farmers had been in full-time paid employment at some time in the past, for periods of between three and 35 years. Two had been full-time farmers since the very beginning of the scheme (1961 and 1963 respectively), as had a number of others who were now pensioners. Some of these individuals approximated to Murray's [1981: 41] description of the successful migrant in Lesotho: 'The paradigm of the successful migrant career for a man is to establish his own household and to build up a capital base, through the acquisition of land, livestock and equipment, to enable him to retire from migrant labour and to maintain an independent livelihood at home' (although Murray found that this idyll was rarely attained).

The concept of 'unemployment' is clearly problematic in the context of a predominantly informal economy with widespread under-employment and periodic breaks between labour contracts [*Standing, Sender and Weeks*, 1996: 68; *Todaro*, 1989: 242]. In the household survey, 13 men described themselves (or were described by others within the household) as unemployed. Supplementary questioning revealed that this description was generally applied to younger men (mainly in their twenties, some of whom had never been in paid employment), both married and unmarried, who had finished formal education and were looking (or waiting) for work outside the household economy. Some of these were engaged in agriculture on household plots, but viewed it as a temporary strategy, although a few said they would continue farming on a part-time basis if they could find paid employment locally. Others played no part in agriculture, or any other productive activities within the household. In practice, there was often no discernible difference between those describing themselves as 'unemployed' and 'full-time farmer', and in many cases this distinction appeared to represent little more than different perspectives (possibly related to age) on a similar situation. For most of the older men, a farming lifestyle was something they had long aspired to and was only attained once other obligations – marriage, child-rearing, house-building and the like – had been met. For younger men, who had achieved few of these things, farming was generally seen as a poor substitute for full-time paid employment.

Apart from agricultural activities (discussed in detail below), a minority of households in the sample (11 households, or 13.6 per cent) had a member engaged in a craft or other small-scale income-generating activity. The most common activity mentioned was dress-making, carried out by six women in the sample; other examples included the occasional supply of a van or donkey cart and casual building work. In none of these cases did such activities constitute the main source of household income. It is worth noting that, despite the extremely low income reported by many households in the survey, there were no reports of people working on other households' plots, an activity that would appear to be confined to members of landless households (see below). There can be little doubt, however, that a one-off, interview-based survey of this kind is unlikely to capture the range of casual, or opportunistic, livelihood activities engaged in by people at Tshiombo over the course of a year.

Of potentially greater importance, in income terms, are shebeens (informal liquor outlets), which were observed at two of the households in the survey. In each case, both bottled (that is, commercially produced) and home-made beer were on sale. As the respondents in the households concerned made no reference to this trade during interview, however, and supplementary questions were met with silence, little more can be said on the subject, other than to confirm the presence of shebeens and the legendary reluctance of their owners to discuss business with strangers.[9]

In addition to questions about wages, pensions and informal income-generating activities, survey respondents were asked if they had any other (non-farm) means of supplementing their household income. Seven households (8.4 per cent of the sample) reported that they received occasional financial support from sons living in Johannesburg or surrounding areas, two of whom were teachers and five manual workers. In only one case was this the main source of household income, as the other six all obtained income from pensions and one had a member in full-time (local) employment. In three of these cases, children of the urban-based workers lived with their rural grandparents, which suggests that the extended family retains considerable social and economic importance despite the physical separation imposed by migration.

6.3 NON-FARM INCOME AND DEPENDENCY RATES

The most important sources of income for households in the survey were wages, from both migrant and local workers, and pensions. Agriculture contributed a relatively minor share of income in the majority of households, as will be shown in subsequent chapters.

Over half the households in the sample (61.4 per cent) had at least one person in paid employment (including migrants) and three-quarters (74.7 per cent) had at least one person in receipt of a pension. The majority of households in receipt of wage income (41 out of 51) had just one member in employment, while nine had two wage-earners and one household had four. The average number of persons in wage employment over the entire sample was 0.76 per household. Similarly, the majority of households in receipt of pension income (45 out of 62) contained just one pensioner, but 16 contained two pensioners and one household had three. The average number of pensioners per household across the entire sample was 0.98. Not surprisingly, there was considerable overlap between these two sources of income and close to half of all households (48.2 per cent) received both wage and pension income. This still left 12 per cent of households (ten out of 83) without any income from either wages or pensions.

The average number of regular off-farm incomes (wages and pensions) amongst households in the sample was 1.7, the distribution of which is shown in the following table. Note that only the total *number* (as opposed to the value) of non-farm incomes per household are shown and these figures are not, therefore, a reliable guide to relative wealth.

TABLE 6.2
NUMBER OF OFF-FARM INCOMES PER HOUSEHOLD

Number of Incomes	Number of Households	Percentage of Households
0	10	12.0
1	25	30.1
2	32	38.6
3	13	15.7
4–6	3	3.6

Wages and Remittances

Obtaining precise information on wage income presented a number of difficulties. First, many migrant workers were not available in person at the time of interview and other people within the household stated that they did not know how much the absent workers earned, or were unwilling to discuss the matter. Second, there was a great reluctance, even amongst wage earners who were interviewed in person, to say anything about their earnings, and those that did often did so only in the most vague or general terms. 'I earn almost nothing' was a common response.

Monthly wage rates for local employment reported by survey respondents ranged from R400 (for a labourer or watchman on a government project) to R1,400 (a junior civil servant), with most falling in the range R500–1,000. Wages for migrant workers were considerably higher, ranging from R650 per month to at least R1,800 (for an experienced truck driver with a supermarket chain in Johannesburg), with most falling in the range R1,000–1,400. A handful of workers, including a school headmaster, undoubtedly earned more than this upper figure, but were not willing to provide details on income. For analytical purposes, however, it was necessary to attribute some income to workers for whom detailed information was not available. For professional workers (for example, teachers) this was done by reference to prevailing wage rates in the area (via informants in the public service). For unskilled or non-specified workers, a uniform rate was imputed, based on the information supplied by other respondents, the figures used being R750 per month for local workers and R1,200 for migrants.

While some information was obtained on migrant workers' earnings, the question of what proportion was shared with the rest of the household, in the form of remittances or otherwise, proved much more problematic. Both migrants and their families were particularly reticent on this topic, but given the multiple financial responsibilities of migrants, some with dependants in both town and country, it appeared that even they themselves were hard-pressed to calculate their financial contribution to the rural household over the course of a year. Resolving this was, in large part, a question of definition. The broad definition of 'household income' applied at the outset of this study included all income (cash and kind) accruing to members of the household, but without any suggestion that such income is pooled or shared equally between household members. Indeed, the distribution of income within households was not directly investigated by this study. According to this definition, the entire earnings of a migrant worker could be included as 'household income', but this is unrealistic given the considerable costs associated with migrancy.

The conventional approach to this question is to include only the amount actually remitted to other household members as 'household' income [*Ardington*, 1984: 46; *May*, 1989: 9], but this effectively treats the migrant as an *external* source of income, rather than an integral part of the household. It also tends to exaggerate the difference between the contribution of migrants and that of non-migrant (local) workers, whose entire earnings are routinely included within the definition of 'household' income. While there are considerable costs associated with migrancy – particularly accommodation and travel – which can reasonably be excluded from the household account, it does not follow that all non-remitted income should be disregarded. As Baber [1996: 284] argues, migrants contribute to the welfare of their households in many ways, directly and indirectly, over the course of their working lives, although the value of such contributions may vary considerably between migrants and over time. Examples of indirect contributions (those in addition to remittances) include savings accounts controlled by the migrant, capital goods such as a car or livestock and the often considerable spending by migrants during visits home on food, school uniforms, ploughing fees and maintenance of the homestead. Expenditure on such items by a migrant is neither more nor less beneficial to the 'household' than it would be in the case of a locally-based worker (and in many cases is very beneficial indeed) and there is no case for treating it differently. Furthermore, by providing for his own subsistence while away from home the migrant worker is effectively relieving the 'household' of a substantial burden and this needs to be taken into account.

Among the households surveyed at Tshiombo, very few reported that migrants remitted a fixed sum every month. The most common practice, especially for migrants who returned regularly every one or two months, was to take care of certain expenses on their visits home – such as food, school uniforms, ploughing fees and fertiliser – and, depending on circumstances, to leave a sum of money with their wife or mother on departure. Migrants who returned home less often – and absences of up to a year were not uncommon in the sample – were reported to occasionally send money home between visits, usually via relatives, but this did not appear to be a common occurrence. In the case of illness or other unexpected household crisis, it was more likely that a migrant would make an unscheduled visit home in person. Despite the problems of travel and communications, examples were found of migrant workers arriving in Tshiombo from Johannesburg, a distance of over 500 km, less than 24 hours after the sudden death of a family member. Thus, while migrants may be physically removed from their households for long periods, most retain a close involvement in its affairs.

If, as appears to be the case, direct remittances account for only a portion of migrants' contribution to the income of rural households, there remains the problem of establishing this empirically, and the methodology of this study was not adequate to do this for more than a small minority of the households concerned. Thus, for purposes of calculating total household income it was necessary to impute a figure for the proportion of migrant earnings included within the definition of 'household income', and the paucity of data in this area suggested that a uniform figure be used across all households in the sample. After much consideration, this was set at 50 per cent of migrants' cash earnings, and this figure is used in all further discussion of wage earnings and household income. A substantially lower figure would put migrants' households at the bottom of the income ladder, something that was not supported by other evidence in the survey, and would suggest that migrancy would be a last resort rather than the expressed work preference of many men at Tshiombo.

Pensions

Pensions were a more common source of income than wages and, in gross terms, were worth approximately half the value of wages. There can be little doubt, however, that pensions are worth considerably more than wages to many households in terms of disposable (cash) income and tend to be distributed amongst members in quite a different way [*Ardington and Lund*, 1995: 571]. Pensions received at Tshiombo included state old-age pensions (paid to women at 60 and men at 65), employer pensions and state disability pensions, but for the purposes of this study they were treated as one. The state old-age pension for men and women in 1995 was R430 per month.

Despite the disruptions to public services in Venda in recent years, pensions were being paid out on a regular basis, and pay-out points attracted a lively gathering of hawkers selling meat, cloth, household utensils, agricultural implements and a range of other goods.[10] Many people reported problems obtaining a pension in the first place, however, due to a lack of knowledge about the system on the part of would-be recipients (many of whom were non-literate) and lengthy delays within the former homeland bureaucracy. A number of women over 60 years had not applied for pensions and many others, both men and women, reported waiting a year or more prior to receiving their first payment (see Van der Waal [1991: 351] for similar findings from Gazankulu).

Total Off-Farm Income

Combining income from all the above sources, households in the survey were found to have a total off-farm income ranging from zero to an estimated R48,000 for the year in question, or an average of R10,463 (R872 per month). Of this, approximately half (50.8 per cent) came from wages (including remittances), slightly less from pensions (47 per cent) and the balance (2.2 per cent) from other sources, such as petty commodity production and remittances from non-household members. Almost two-thirds of wage income came from local employment (as opposed to migrant remittances), an extremely high proportion by homeland standards.[11]

The following table shows the breakdown of off-farm income for households in the sample, divided into income quintiles (fifths). The first quintile represents the top (that is, 'richest) 20 per cent of households (in terms of off-farm income only) and the fifth quintile the bottom (that is, 'poorest') 20 per cent. The proportion of income from each source (wages, pensions and other income) is shown as a percentage of the total for each quintile.

TABLE 6.3
HOUSEHOLD OFF-FARM INCOME AT TSHIOMBO, BY QUINTILES

Quintile	1st (n=17)	2nd (n=16)	3rd (n=17)	4th (n=16)	5th (n=17)	Total (n=83)
Migrant Wages (R)	4,569	1,800	1,694	900	0	1,822
%	23.6	14.3	15.4	13.4	0	17.4
Local Wages (R)	6,494	5,775	2,824	2,475	0	3,499
%	32.9	46.0	25.6	36.9	0	33.4
Total Wages (R)	11,153	7,575	4,518	3,375	0	5,320
%	56.5	60.3	40.9	50.3	0	50.8
Pensions (R)	8,499	4,838	6,374	2,580	2,125	4,911
%	43.1	38.5	57.8	38.5	96.8	46.9
Other (R)	70	150	141	750	72	231
%	0.4	1.2	1.3	11.2	3.2	2.2
Total Off-farm Income (R)	19,722	12,562	11,033	6,705	2,195	10,46

Off-farm income was distributed highly unevenly between households, with 38.6 per cent of the total accruing to the top 20 per cent of households, as opposed to only 4.3 per cent to the bottom 20 per cent. This is largely due to the unequal distribution of wage income (local and migrant), which was shared between less than two-thirds (61.2 per cent) of households. Pensions were more evenly distributed, reaching three-quarters (74.7 per cent) of households in the sample.

Households with the highest levels of off-farm income achieved this through a combination of pensions, migrant employment, and local employment, for both men and women. All the households in the top income quintile contained at least one pensioner and ten out of seventeen had two or more. All but one households in this group also contained at least one wage earner and four had both men and women in wage employment. The very top earning household in the sample (with 20 members in all), contained three men in local employment and one migrant, plus a male and female pensioner, bringing in a total income of R39,120 per year (R3,260 per month).

While the top 80 per cent of households (by income) obtained, on average, over half their off-farm income from wages, the bottom quintile was distinguished by the total lack of wage income. Eight households out of 17 in this group contained a pensioner, but nine had no regular source of off-farm income and were entirely dependent on agriculture and assistance from relatives and neighbours. Like households in other income quintiles, however, these households differed considerably in terms of agricultural income (see Chapter 7).

Dependency Rates

Overall welfare of a household obviously depends not only on the number of income sources, or their combined value, but also on the number of people dependent upon such income. A crude dependency rate was calculated for each household in the sample by relating the number of income-earners to the total number of persons in the household. Here, I follow the example of Ardington and Lund [1995: 570], who treat pensioners as income-earners, rather than the more conventional approach which is to treat them as dependants, in light of the relative importance of pensions to household income within the homelands. Table 6.4 (below) shows the breakdown of households according to the percentage of dependants (that is, children and adults with no non-farm income) in the household.

The extremes on this scale are represented by two households with no dependants (one widowed pensioner living alone, and a married couple, both pensioners) and ten households with no regular source of off-farm income. Of this latter group, one obtained occasional remittances from a former member of the household but all the others depended entirely on agriculture. Income from this source varied widely, however, and this group included one of the most productive farmers on the scheme, with an agricultural income of over R10,000 a year, and four households that earned less than R2,000 in the year and were close to destitute (see Chapter 7). The average household dependency rate for the sample was 74.8 per cent: that is, three-quarters of household members, on average, did not earn off-farm income, or each off-farm income supported approximately four persons.

TABLE 6.4
HOUSEHOLD DEPENDENCY RATES

Dependency Rate (%)	Number of Households	Percentage of Households
100	10	12.0
80–99	25	30.1
60–79	34	41.0
40–59	12	14.4
0–39	2	2.4

6.4 CHARACTERISTICS OF PLOT-HOLDERS

An important aim of this study was to be able to differentiate between households in terms of social and economic factors such as land-holding and income, demographic composition and the various livelihood strategies and opportunities available to them. In particular, it was considered important to be able to distinguish between households where land and agriculture were controlled by men and those where they were controlled (or at least managed by) women.

Once the study was under way, however, it became apparent that control (or 'ownership') of land could not always be attributed to a single individual within the household and was not a reliable guide to control of agriculture (that is, land use). Although plots on the irrigation scheme are registered in the names of individuals, the registered tenant does not necessarily have any direct involvement in agriculture, whether due to old age, lack of interest or prolonged absence from the area, and may even remain on the register many years after their death. In the early years of the scheme, it would appear that plots were allocated almost exclusively to male 'household heads', but this has changed somewhat over the years, as a number of women have been allocated plots in their own right and others have acquired them from male relatives (but have not necessarily registered them in their own name). Not all wives inherit land holdings on the death of their husbands, however, and there is a strong tendency for women, unlike men, to transfer 'ownership' to a son once he reaches adulthood. Thus, the effective control of land tends to be obscured within a complex of cultural and official conventions which emphasises the position of men within the household and in the wider community and down-plays the position of women.

As neither the registered 'owner' nor the 'head of household' was considered to be a good guide to the actual control of agriculture (or an adequate basis for inter-household comparisons), it was necessary to identify for each household in the sample what I call the 'plot-holder' – that is, the person who appeared to have most control over the use of land and its produce. Casley and Lury [1987: 188], following the practice of the Food and Agriculture Organisation (FAO), define a plot-holder as 'the person who exercises control over the operations of the holding and is responsible for the utilisation of available resources', while stressing that it is overall decision-making power that distinguishes the holder from the day-to-day user.

In keeping with this definition, a distinction is made throughout this study between *access* to land (that is, 'ownership', or entitlement to land) and the *use* of 'available resources'. In many of the households where women were judged to be the 'plot-holder', both men and women were adamant that the land itself 'belonged' to a male 'head', but that the use of that land was delegated to a woman. In effect, the identification of 'plot-holders' used here was probably biased towards short-term (day-to-day) control of agricultural production (that is, in favour of women) and may understate the involvement of male absentees over the longer term.

In practice, the 'plot-holder' was not difficult to identify in most households in the sample: many respondents were quite clear who the user of the plot was, even if the 'owner', or the 'head of the household' was somebody else. Where a plot-holder could not be identified directly by the respondents, a judgement has been made on the basis of available information, such as the person or persons who worked on the plot, who purchased inputs, who decided what and when to sow, who sold the produce and who received the income. Of the 83 households surveyed, 62 nominated such a person themselves, while in the remaining 21 a judgement was made on the basis of information supplied by the household. As a result, 48 'plot-holders' (57.8 per cent of the sample) were found to be men and 35 were women (42.2 per cent).

Amongst the households with female plot-holders were the five that contained no adult male. Other female plot-holders were the wives or mothers of migrant workers, the wives of pensioners, or, in two case, the mothers of local (that is, non-migrant) workers. In all these cases, the men referred to were described as the head of the household, but none of them was directly involved in agricultural production.

Age of Plot-holders

As with many other issues in this survey, not all respondents, especially older women, were able to be precise about their age and in such cases a variety of means were employed to arrive at an approximate age [*Peil*, 1982: 102]. The date on which old-age pension was first received was usually the most convenient guide, but children's ages and the opinions of family members and local officials were also used to estimate the approximate age of each plot-holder.

Table 6.5 (above) shows the breakdown of plot-holders in the sample by age group. Plot-holders ranged in age from 26 to 77 years. More than half (55.4 per cent) were over 60 years and just five (six per cent of the sample) were under 40 years of age. The average age of plot-holders in the sample was 58.1 years.[12]

TABLE 6.5
AGE OF PLOT-HOLDERS AT TSHIOMBO

Age in years	Number of plot-holders	Percentage of plot-holders	Cumulative percentage
70+	17	20.5	20.5
60–69	29	34.9	55.4
50–59	16	19.3	74.7
40–49	16	19.3	94.0
30–39	4	4.8	98.8
20–29	1	1.2	100.0

6.5 ORIGINS OF HOUSEHOLDS

Plot-holders in the survey were asked where they originated and when their household first acquired a plot on the irrigation scheme. As women in Venda generally move to their husband's home (or home village) on marriage, in most cases the husband's home village was taken as the origin of the household. For households that came to Tshiombo from elsewhere, the place they lived immediately prior to moving to Tshiombo was taken as the place of origin.

While it appears that the irrigation scheme was at first intended primarily for the inhabitants of the immediate Tshiombo area (see above), over the years people from a wide area have migrated to live and work there. Survey respondents and other local informants suggested that it took about ten years from the beginning of the scheme for all the plots to be occupied. A number of respondents reported having cleared their plots 'from the bush' in the late 1960s, implying that they were the first occupants of these plots, while others reported taking over plots from previous occupants who had abandoned them (for reasons unknown) around the same time. The majority of households in the survey (59 per cent) acquired their plots in the early years of the scheme – that is, prior to 1966 – and most others (27.7 per cent) acquired them during the decade 1966–75. The last twenty years have seen few new arrivals on the scheme and, on the basis of the household survey, it would appear that the great majority of plots that changed hands since 1976 went to existing plot-holders rather than to newcomers (see below).

It should be noted that survey respondents did not, in many cases, have a precise recollection of when they arrived at Tshiombo, or when they acquired land. For example, a number of respondents stated that their households came to Tshiombo 'at the beginning of the scheme', or had acquired land 'a few years after the scheme began'. The scheme itself was officially opened in 1963, although it would appear that some local people had been allocated plots as early as 1961.

For analytical purposes, the history of the scheme has been divided into three periods – up to 1965, 1966 to 1975 and 1976 to 1995. Respondents who reported that they had acquired plots at or around the beginning of the scheme generally dated this to between 1960 and 1965, while those who dated their arrival to the late 1960s or after spoke of the scheme as already in operation. Thus, for convenience, the period up to 1965 has been treated as the initial wave of allocations and anybody saying they arrived at or near the beginning of the scheme has been allocated to this category. The two subsequent periods correspond roughly to different phases in the settlement of the scheme, namely a phase of consolidation (1966–75), during which the last remaining plots were allocated, and a phase of accumulation (1976–95), during which a minority of plot-holders were able to acquire additional (that is, multiple) plots.

The following table provides a breakdown of households on the scheme according to their place of origin and the period in which they obtained their first plot on the scheme.

TABLE 6.6
ORIGIN OF HOUSEHOLDS AND DATE OF JOINING THE IRRIGATION SCHEME

	Tshiombo	Tshivhase	Venda	White Farms	Total	Percent
Pre-1966	21	16	8	4	49	59.0
1966–75	4	14	4	1	23	27.7
1976–95	1	6	4	0	11	13.2
Total	26	36	16	5	83	–
Percent	31.3	43.4	19.3	6.0	–	100.0

Note: Both columns and rows are totalled and all percentages are as a proportion of the total sample (n = 83)

Places of origin are classified as follows:

• *Tshiombo*: the village of Tshiombo and the five other villages directly adjacent to the irrigation scheme;

• *Tshivhase*: the entire Tshivhase tribal district, excluding Tshiombo;

• *Venda*: the entire territory of Venda (1994 borders), excluding Tshivhase district;

• *White Farms*: so-called white rural areas lying outside Venda.

Three-quarters of households in the sample originated either in Tshiombo or elsewhere in the Tshivhase Tribal Area. This is not surprising given that this constitutes the immediate hinterland of the scheme and that the tribal leaders have considerable influence over the allocation of land for cultivation and residence at Tshiombo. Tshivhase is also by far the most populous Tribal Area in Venda.

The origin of households joining the scheme has changed considerably over time. In the early years of the scheme (that is, pre-1966), a relatively high proportion of plots was allocated to residents of the Tshiombo area, but over time, and as the availability of plots on the scheme has decreased, an increasing proportion of new plot-holders came from outside the immediate vicinity. Of those households which obtained plots prior to 1966, 21 (or 42.9 per cent) originated in Tshiombo, while 28 (57.1 per cent) came from outside. For those joining the scheme between 1966 and 1975, the proportion coming from Tshiombo falls to 17.4 per cent, and for the period after 1975 just one household out of 11 (9.1 per cent) came from Tshiombo.

Of the five households in the sample that originated in what were then 'white' farming districts, four arrived in Tshiombo before 1965 and the fifth reported arriving 'over twenty years ago'. This is in line with what is known about the ending of labour tenancy and the forced removal of black labour tenants ('squatters') from white farms, a process which entered its decisive phase in the northern Transvaal in the late 1960s (see Chapter 3). Evidence from other parts of Venda points to an influx of experienced and relatively well-resourced former tenants at this time, many of whom were able to acquire land within the homeland to continue, or even expand, their agricultural activities [*Lahiff*, 1997: 82]. One survey respondent reported that her late husband came to Tshiombo from a white farm in Levubu around 1960, bringing with him cattle, ploughs and 'his own wealth', and eventually accumulated ten plots on the irrigation scheme.

The reasons for coming to Tshiombo also appear to have changed over the years. Many people who moved into the area, especially in the early years of the irrigation scheme, said they were attracted by the prospects of irrigated land and government support, and came with the intention of becoming full-time, commercially-oriented farmers. 'I was tired of living in Johannesburg', said one early arrival at Tshiombo. 'I heard the government was giving out land and I decided to go for farming. It's a healthy life and I thought it would give me a good income.' In recent years, however, the attraction of agriculture as a source of livelihood seems to have diminished, and all four plot-holders who joined the scheme from outside the area since 1980 did so for what could be termed 'social' rather than 'economic' reasons. Three of these were widowed women who moved to be closer to family members; the fourth was a married man who came to care for a sick relative, and all subsequently obtained plots on the scheme. While this shift may be due in part to the dwindling supply of new plots, it is also possibly connected to changing perceptions of the relative economic potential offered by the scheme. In this regard, the population at Tshiombo could be said to have become stabilised by South African standards, as people no longer move in and out of the area for 'special' reasons (that is, because of the irrigation scheme), but for broadly the same reasons as people move in or out of any black rural area.[13] In an interesting example of reverse migration, one respondent, a woman in her twenties who was born and raised in Tshiawelo (Soweto) and had married a migrant worker from Tshiombo, described how she had been shocked to discover that she was expected to work her husband's 'farm' with a hand hoe, but said that after five years she was getting used to it.

6.6 LANDHOLDINGS

As noted above, households at Tshiombo have access to two types of agricultural land: plots on the formal irrigation scheme and land adjacent to the scheme, referred to locally as 'waste land'. Most households also cultivate portions of their residential stands, but these are not considered here. Households make use of uncultivated land for grazing livestock, and a small minority of households had access to grazing in other villages where their livestock were cared for by relatives (including wives). One household was also found to hold arable land on another government-run scheme elsewhere in Venda, and a second had done so in the recent past. As these types of land are not easily comparable, findings on each will first be presented separately, before looking at combined holdings.

Plots on the Irrigation Scheme

All households within the survey had, by definition, at least one plot on the irrigation scheme. These averaged 1.28 hectares each, although there were some variations between plots. A policy of 'one man one plot' seems to have been part of the original plan for the scheme, but this does not appear to have been enforced uniformly. While many respondents stated that it was forbidden to hold more than one plot, others reported that they had acquired additional plots at various times since the beginning of the scheme. From the late 1970s or early 1980s there appears to have been a further relaxation of the 'one plot' rule and many more households were able to obtain additional plots on the scheme as well as areas of 'waste land' surrounding the scheme.

The largest number of plots held by any household in the survey sample was six, although one respondent reported that her late husband had held ten plots at one time. A sizeable majority of plot-holders (63.9 per cent), however, conformed to the original project design in that they had only one plot on the scheme. The total number of plots held by the sample was 127, an average of 1.53 plots (approximately 1.96 hectares) per household. The distribution of irrigated plots amongst the households in the sample is shown in Table 6.7.

TABLE 6.7
IRRIGATED PLOTS PER HOUSEHOLD

Number of Plots	Number of Households	Percentage of Households
1	53	63.9
2	21	25.3
3	7	8.4
4	0	0.0
5	1	1.2
6	1	1.2
Total	83	100

Plot-holders with multiple plots on the scheme were mainly men and tended to be somewhat older than average. Amongst men in the sample, 42 per cent held two plots or more, compared to 27 per cent of women, and the nine largest land-holders on the scheme (six men and three women) were all over 50 years of age. Households in this latter group were also distinguished by their relative lack of wage income, especially from migrant workers. Of the six households in this group with a male plot-holder, none had any wage income (including remittances), although five did contain a pensioner. The three women plot-holders in this group were themselves all pensioners and each had a son in wage employment (two locally and one migrant).

Waste Land

In addition to plots on the irrigation scheme, 21 households held additional arable land off the scheme. According to the Agricultural Officers at Tshiombo, this so-called waste land was deemed unsuitable for cultivation when the irrigation scheme was created, either because it was swampy or because it could not be reached by the irrigation canals, and the prohibition on its cultivation appears to have remained in force until the late 1980s.

Holdings of waste land ranged from a quarter of a hectare to ten hectares and averaged 2.4 hectares (n=21). These figures are based on land-holders' own estimates, given either in hectares or in terms of an equivalent number of 'beds' on the irrigation scheme (roughly 0.1 hectare each). Table 6.8 shows the distribution of waste land amongst the households in the sample.

TABLE 6.8
WASTE LAND PER HOUSEHOLD

Land Area (hectares)	Number of Households	Percentage of Households
Nil	62	74.7
0.1 – 0.9	9	10.8
1.0 – 4.9	7	8.4
5.0 – 9.9	3	3.6
10.0+	2	2.4

Waste land at Tshiombo is used for a wide range of crops and many respondents described their waste land as being more productive than their plots on the formal irrigation scheme. One plot-holder had given up trying to irrigate his two plots on the scheme, using them solely for rain-fed cropping, and was concentrating on irrigating his five hectares of waste land.

Drier areas of waste land were generally used either for rain-fed crops such as maize or for orchards. In fact, six of the larger holdings of waste land (all greater than one hectare) were being used for mango or avocado orchards. In wetter, low-lying areas, between the irrigation scheme and the river, land-holders were taking advantage of water running off the irrigation scheme to grow vegetables, and two farmers (with one and three hectares respectively) had constructed their own 'informal' irrigation furrows. Three others, each with at least six hectares of waste land, were irrigating their land using diesel-powered pumps which drew water directly from the Mutale. The location of many of the waste-land plots, between the scheme and the river, and the effectiveness of some of the private irrigation supplies, meant that these plots were often irrigated as well as those on the scheme proper, and many of the same crops – such as tomatoes, cabbage, maize – were grown on both. In the hills above the scheme, one of the village headmen had a particularly fertile piece of land on the banks of a stream, where he grew rice, sugar cane and bananas, as well as the usual range of cereal and vegetable crops.

As was the case with plots on the formal irrigation scheme, men were more likely than women to acquire waste land and their holdings tended to be larger, but the age profiles of the land-holders were quite different. Of the five households in the sample with five hectares or more of waste land, four were men and one was a woman, and all were aged between 44 and 55 years, well below the average age for the sample. As before, the occupational structure of households in this group was heavily oriented towards agriculture and away from wage employment. Three of these five land-holders were full-time male farmers, one woman was also effectively a full-time farmer and one was a man who combined agriculture with local employment. This household was the only of this group in receipt of any wage income (containing two teachers). Of the other four, one contained two pensioners, another a single pensioner and two were without any source of off-farm income.

Combined Landholdings

The inequality in land-holding at Tshiombo suggested above becomes even more pronounced when we look at combined holdings per household. The following table shows the distribution of land between households according to the number of plots held on the formal irrigation scheme, and suggests that households with multiple plots on the scheme have been considerably more successful in obtaining land off the scheme than those with just one plot.

TABLE 6.9
COMBINED LANDHOLDING PER HOUSEHOLD

Plots	Number of Households	Average Waste Land (ha)	Average Total Holding(ha)
1	53	0.13	1.41
2	21	1.08	3.64
3-6	9	2.33	6.88

Note: 1 plot = approximately 1.28 ha.

Amongst households with one irrigated plot, only 11 (out of 53) had acquired additional areas of waste land, the average holding being 0.64 hectares (or 0.13 ha. across the whole group). Amongst those with two irrigated plots, seven (out of 21) held additional land, averaging 3.25 hectares each (or 1.08 ha. for the whole group). Of the nine households with three or more irrigated plots, three had additional land off the scheme, averaging 7.0 hectares each (or 2.33 ha. for the whole group). This correlation between the size of land holding on and off the scheme suggests a continuing process of accumulation by a small minority of households.

Overall, approximately half the households in the sample (41 out of 83) had acquired something more than a single plot of land, and the average combined holding of arable land (that is, on and off the scheme) for the sample as a whole was 2.57 hectares. This is relatively high by homeland standards, especially considering the high proportion under irrigation (see Chapter 2).

Survey data and interviews with other local informants suggested that the accumulation of land by households at Tshiombo accelerated during the 1980s and has continued in the 1990s. Of 44 additional plots (that is, in excess of one plot per household) on the irrigation scheme held by households in the sample, two were obtained during the 1960s, 12 during the 1970s, 22 during the 1980s and eight during the 1990s (1990–94). At the beginning of the 1980s, only 14 households in the sample (reportedly) had multiple plots on the scheme and the highest number of plots held by any one household was three. By 1995 there were 30 households with multiple plots and the highest number of plots had risen to six. Indeed, since 1990, only households which already had multiple plots obtained (further) additional plots, suggesting that the principle of one plot per household has been thoroughly undermined and that the effective criteria for obtaining land had moved decisively in favour of households with above average holdings over those with single plots or, indeed, new entrants to the scheme.

Looking at the reverse process, only two households in the sample reported losing any land over the whole period of the scheme. In one case, an elderly widow revealed that her late husband had occupied ten plots on the scheme, but following his death seven of these were repossessed 'by the Agricultural Officers' and allocated to other households. In the other case, a male pensioner reported that he had rented a plot from a neighbour for a number of years, but had returned it when it became too much for him to work on his own. The accelerating pace at which plots are being acquired on the scheme, however, suggests that many more households are in fact losing land. In the period since 1980, seven plots have been allocated to households joining the scheme, and 30 more to households already on it. Extrapolated to the scheme as a whole, this would suggest that somewhere in the order of 274 plots, or close to a third of all plots on the scheme, have changed hands over a 15-year period. Given the virtual absence from the sample of households that have lost land, it would appear likely that such households have quit the scheme altogether, possibly because they could not work the land, or because the plot-holders concerned died or moved away from the area.

As with plots on the irrigation scheme, the accumulation of non-scheme land also appears to have accelerated in recent years. Thirteen households in the sample stated that they held additional (off-scheme) land prior to 1990, the largest holding being 1.5 hectares and most being between a quarter and half a hectare. Since 1990, however, eight further households have acquired additional land and these holdings have all been between one and ten hectares. Indeed, a total of 42 hectares of waste land, or 82.8 per cent of the total area held by households in the sample, has been acquired since 1990 alone, again suggestive of a considerable change in the pattern of land-holding at Tshiombo and rapid accumulation by a small minority of households.

How this process works in practice may be illustrated by reference to four individual examples from the household survey. The first three are amongst the largest landholders in the sample, while the final example could be described as an average land-holder.

Respondent Number 52 was the largest land-holder in the sample, with a total of 17.7 hectares of arable land at Tshiombo.[14] He was born in a village adjacent to Tshiombo in 1940, and worked as a clerk in Johannesburg from the age of 18 to 25. In 1965 he returned to Venda and obtained a single plot on the Tshiombo scheme. He obtained a second plot in 1975, two more during the 1980s and a fifth and sixth in 1991, all through application to the Tribal Authority. In 1991 he also obtained ten hectares of waste land at Tshiombo, which he irrigates himself using a diesel pump, drawing water from the Mutale River. The household consisted of the plot-holder, his parents (both pensioners), two wives who worked in the home and on the land, and 11 children, ranging from three to 24 years of age, all but the youngest of whom were in full-time education. Five agricultural labourers were employed full-time. This household also owned a herd of 25 cattle, which were grazed in the plot-holder's natal village by a relative.

Respondent Number 55 was a male plot-holder, aged fifty-one, who lived with his mother (a pensioner), his two wives and ten children. The plot-holder worked as a shop assistant in Tshiombo for twenty years before inheriting his father's plot in 1980. He obtained a second plot in 1985, three more in 1990 and 10 hectares of waste land in 1994, all 'from chief Tshivhase'. In 1995 he obtained credit worth R6,000 from NTK, as part of the Agricultural Credit Board programme for small farmers (see Chapter 7). He owned his own bakkie and, along with his wives, used it to sell vegetables (from his own plots and purchased from others) in neighbouring villages. This household kept 10 cattle and 15 goats up to two years ago, when they were sold to pay debts. Labour was supplied by the plot-holder, his two wives and three full-time hired labourers. The plot-holder had been a tenant on the Agriven farm at Makonde in the early 1990s, but quit due to heavy debts.

Respondent Number 60 was a female plot-holder in the process of bringing 8.5 hectares of land under irrigation. She was born at Mudunungu (Tshivhase Area) in 1946 and married there in 1964. After ten years she was abandoned by her husband, so, with her children, she moved to join her parents who had acquired two irrigated plots at Tshiombo. Both plots passed to the current holder on her father's death in 1985. In 1994, with the help of her eldest son (who had recently graduated from university), she acquired six hectares through the Tribal Authority, which she began irrigating using a diesel pump obtained through her brother in Louis Trichardt. In 1995 she obtained R14,000 worth of credit under the Agricultural Credit Board Scheme, which was spent on diesel for the irrigation pump, hire of tractors for ploughing and other agricultural inputs. At the time of interview, agriculture was the only regular source of income for this household, supporting the plot-holder and her five school-going children. It was clear, however, that substantial financial support was provided from time to time by relatives for university fees and other expenses. Most agricultural labour was provided by the plot-holder and her children, but in 1995, for the first time, she hired two day labourers to work her much-extended holding. The household owned no livestock, but did have a bakkie which was used to carry produce to market at Thohoyandou and to the tomato-processing factory at Makonde.

Respondent Number 40 was born in Tshiombo in 1927 and worked on the railways in Johannesburg for 32 years. He lived with his two wives and eight school-going children. In 1969, while still a migrant, he inherited a plot on the irrigation scheme from his father, who had obtained it at the beginning of the scheme, and this was worked by his wives while he was in Johannesburg. In 1987 he retired on an employer's pension, aged 60, whereupon he obtained a second plot and devoted himself to agriculture. All agricultural work was done by the farmer, his wives and his children, without the use of hired labour.

These examples illustrate a number of important points about the acquisition of land at Tshiombo, particularly the importance of inheritance, by both sons and daughters, and the ability of (a few) women with dependants to acquire substantial areas of land and make a living from agriculture. In addition, they show the growing importance of 'waste land' in the last five years, coupled with the rise of independent (or informal) methods of irrigation. All of these plot-holders could be described as full-time, active farmers, which would appear to be a key factor in the accumulation of above-average land holdings.

Very little information could be obtained regarding the precise process by which land is allocated, either on or off the irrigation scheme. Survey respondents reported that they had obtained land by applying either to the village headman, the Tribal Authority or the Agricultural Officer, and it would appear that all three parties are involved at some stage of the process. Very few critical voices were raised against either the system of land tenure or the method of land allocation, but this should not be altogether surprising amongst a sample of households which had managed to increase its combined land-holding by over 60 per cent since 1980, at a time of growing landlessness in Venda as a whole. Further research amongst non-land-holding households in the area might be expected to come up with quite different results. As a long-standing state project, it might be expected that plots on the Tshiombo scheme would be allocated in a manner different from other, non-project, forms of communal land. The evidence of this study, however, particularly the success of a small minority of households in accumulating land both on and off the scheme, would suggest that the allocation processes are in fact quite similar. While the state played an important role in the development of the scheme and the original allocation of plots, this has not led to the establishment of a radically different form of land tenure. In the early years of the scheme, plots differed from other, 'communal' land in the availability of irrigation, the role of (white) state officials in their allocation and, perhaps most importantly, the charging of an annual fee. Over the years, all three features have declined in importance, as the supply of irrigation water has become more problematic (see Chapter 5) and other forms of (independent) irrigation have become available. White 'outsiders' have also been replaced by local Venda speakers (especially since 1979), and the annual fee of R12 has become devalued to a tiny fraction of its former worth. Thus, it would seem that land on the Tshiombo project has, over time, become less distinguishable from other ('tribal') land, and subject to similar 'customary' forms of allocation. This process has accelerated greatly in recent years (that is, post-1990), a time of profound political change and uncertainty in Venda. The virtual collapse of the central (that is, Venda) state at this time appears to have given the Tribal Authorities greater power over land allocation and created opportunities for certain individuals at Tshiombo to accumulate sizeable land-holdings in a relatively short period, particularly so-called waste land that had previously been kept out of production by local officials.

Demand for Land

Plot-holders in the survey were asked if they had enough land for their own use, and nearly three-quarters (73.5 per cent) stated that they were satisfied with the amount of land they had at present. Some of these stated that they would like to have more land, but that with the mix of other resources currently available to them – particularly labour, cash and water – they would not be in a position to use it. In other words, they were unable to generate a satisfactory income from the amount of land currently available to them, but neither did they see more land in itself as the solution to their problems. Others, particularly older people, stated that they had enough land for their own use, but that there were younger family members or neighbours who were unable to obtain land. Subdivision of plots did not appear to be a common response to this situation, which perhaps can be explained by the nature of the extended household, which allows household members to share the benefits of a plot of land without the need for subdivision. One respondent had allocated half of his plot to his brother, and another had a similar arrangement with his married son, but in both cases those sharing lived in separate households.

Over a quarter of plot-holders in the survey (26.5 per cent) reported that they were not satisfied with the amount of arable land currently available to them and believed they could use more land. Most of these (16 out of 22) stated that they would be satisfied with a total holding of two to three hectares under irrigation, which was commonly said to be as much as a single house-hold could manage. These respondents generally felt that more land should be made available for cultivation within the Tshiombo area, but had few concrete suggestions as to how this could be achieved. The remaining six plot-holders in this group, all full-time male farmers in their forties and fifties, took quite a different position, saying that they required between 10 and 25 hectares. This small minority of respondents, all interviewed separately, stood out from the rest of the sample for their grasp of current political developments, their wish to become what some called 'real farmers' and their insistence that the level of public resources previously given exclusively to white farmers should now be extended to black farmers. In particular, they demanded that the new govern-ment should make government land in formerly white areas available to 'pro-gressive' black farmers on favourable (that is, subsidised) financial terms. This was clearly not a plea for the upliftment of black agriculture as a whole, of which some of this group were quite scathing, but for the rights of 'pro-gressive' individuals to become 'real farmers, like the Boers'.

Amongst larger land-holders there was some mild criticism of what was seen as the under-utilisation of land by many plot-holders, especially older women, whom they disparaged as 'part-time farmers'. One of the larger land-holders (with three plots on the scheme) suggested that the annual rental should be increased to R50 to encourage the redistribution of plots to those who were in a position to use them more productively. On the other hand, just one respondent (who was sharing his single plot with his brother) felt that land should be taken away from those with multiple plots and redistributed to those who did not have any.

Little evidence could be found of any informal, or temporary, redistribution of land amongst plot-holders, but as sub-letting is not permitted on the irriga-tion scheme (nor under 'communal' tenure), it is possible that there was some under-reporting in this area. Two plot-holders did admit, however, that they had sub-let land in the past. One elderly couple had allowed a neighbour to use their plot when they were ill, simply in return for paying the annual fee

(R12). Another larger plot-holder (with three plots of his own) said that he occasionally used a neighbour's plot during the winter, and in return would plough it for her for the summer season.

In summary, we can say a number of things about the pattern of land-holding and the process of land acquisition at Tshiombo. First, following a relatively egalitarian period in the first decade of the scheme, the accumulation of additional irrigated plots by a minority of households has gathered pace in recent years. Secondly, the accumulation of so-called waste land, which was held by only a small minority of households prior to 1980, and in relatively small quantities, has also accelerated, but most dramatically in the period since 1990. Thirdly, there is a high correlation between these two groups, which serves to accentuate the differentiation between households in terms of land-holding. Combining both forms of land, it was found that the top six land-holding households (7.2 per cent) controlled a total of 65.6 hectares on and off the irrigation scheme, almost a third (30.8 per cent) of all land held by house-holds in the sample. Those accumulating land were largely (but not exclu-sively) full-time male farmers in their fifties and sixties, with relatively low levels of (household) off-farm income. Most plot-holders were satisfied with the system of land-holding, although many stated that it was not possible to obtain a livelihood from agriculture under present conditions. Only a small minority, all of them men with many years experience of farming, expressed a strong interest in acquiring substantial additional land. It is certainly significant that the two largest land-holders at Tshiombo both acquired sub-stantial holdings on another state project in recent years (albeit temporarily in one case), persuasive evidence of a desire for expansion amongst a small farm-ing 'elite'.

6.7 LIVESTOCK

As noted above, livestock farming was never an integral part of the Tshiombo project, either in its own right or as an adjunct to crop farming, and has been strongly discouraged by state officials. The keeping of large stock (cattle and donkeys) appears to have declined dramatically since the irrigation scheme began, due to restrictions on grazing, the introduction of tractor ploughing, recurring drought and the growth of formal education, which has meant that children are no longer available for herding duties. The keeping of small stock (sheep and goats) was prohibited by state officials in the early years of the scheme, but some goats (though no sheep) are now kept at Tshiombo. Poultry are kept by many households, but recurring bouts of disease (particu-larly Newcastle disease) have caused large fluctuations in numbers in recent years.

Cattle

Virtually all households in the survey sample reported keeping cattle at some time in the past, but at the time of the survey only 20 households (24.1 per cent of the total) kept cattle, mostly indigenous Nguni and Afrikander breeds, with some admixture of Brahman. Among households keeping cattle, the number of head ranged between two and 45, with an average of 14.6 per cattle-owning household (or 3.5 head per household across the entire sample). Over four-fifths of all cattle (241 out of 291) were concentrated in the hands of the 11 largest owners, as shown in the following table.

TABLE 6.10
DISTRIBUTION OF CATTLE AMONGST HOUSEHOLDS AT TSHIOMBO

Number of Cattle	Number of Households	Percentage of Households	Percentage of Cattle
Nil	63	75.9	0
1–10	9	10.8	19.2
11–20	7	8.4	45.1
21+	4	4.8	35.7

Various reasons were given for the reported decline in cattle-owning at Tshiombo. A number of households stated that they had sold off their cattle when they first came to join the scheme, or over the years to pay debts, while others said they had sold off their cattle due to a shortage of household labour, especially as children grew up. One woman plot-holder said that she had sold off all her late husband's cattle to send her sons to university. A number of respondents reported that the cultivation of waste land around the irrigation scheme in recent years had led to a reduction in grazing, but this was not a widespread complaint. The recurring drought of the 1980s and early 1990s also took a heavy toll of cattle in the area, and one household reported losing twenty cattle over the previous five years. Farmers at Tshiombo depend on natural replacement to rebuild their herds, and once herds are lost completely they tend not to be replaced. Official disapproval of livestock farming at Tshiombo would appear to have abated in recent years but there was still opposition from some non cattle-owners who expressed strong feelings about cattle damaging their crops and suggested that the area was simply unsuitable for cattle-farming.

Underlying these contingent factors, however, there was evidence of changing attitudes towards cattle-owning at Tshiombo. As a form of bride-wealth (*lobola*), as an indicator of wealth or social status, as a source of income, or even as a form of savings, cattle have been effectively replaced by other more accessible, more flexible and more productive forms of property obtained through participation in the market economy. Farming households at Tshiombo are today more likely to invest in capital and cultural goods, such as vehicles, agricultural inputs, clothing or education, which are more highly regarded or capable of generating a higher return than cattle, while bride-wealth, if it is paid at all, is most likely to be paid in cash. With the growing importance of the cash economy over many decades, and the multiple daily demands on households for cash, tying up household wealth in cattle is no longer seen by many people at Tshiombo as an appropriate use of available resources.

Most herds at Tshiombo were built up slowly over many years, but no cases were found of households taking up cattle farming for the first time in the previous ten years. This may be related to an ageing population, but it also suggests that cattle are of declining importance to households at Tshiombo. One former migrant related how he had bought a single cow after going to work in Johannesburg in 1965 and now owned a herd of 21 cows. He sells all his bull calves to local butchers, or swaps them with other farmers for heifers, and relies on scrub bulls for breeding. Only one owner reported buying in stock in the past year, in this case two heifers and a cross-bred Brahman bull purchased to replace animals lost due to the drought. While cross-bred bulls of various types were common, none of the owners reported taking systematic measures to improve the quality of their stock through selective breeding, and most owners depended on scrub bulls.

Cattle are generally kraaled at night and are taken out only after the dew has lifted, often as late as midday. They are grazed on the margins of the irrigation scheme and the residential areas, along the river bank and on crop residues on the irrigation plots after harvest. No fodder crops are grown. Cattle are dipped regularly throughout the year in a tank operated by the Department of Agriculture, once a week in the rainy seasons and once a fortnight in the dry season, to prevent tick-borne diseases such as redwater and heartwater. They are also vaccinated by veterinary officials against foot-and-mouth disease and anthrax. Most owners do not have access to regular veterinary services, how-ever, and some cattle were reported to have died from redwater disease follow-ing the heavy rains of 1995/96 which rendered dipping ineffective. A number of cattle-owners reported feeding purchased 'stimulants' to their cattle to increase appetite and promote weight-gain.

Cattle farming at Tshiombo remains very uncommercialised and, on the basis of the limited survey data, overall off-take from herds would appear to be quite low. Only half the cattle owners in the survey (that is, ten) reported sell-ing stock in the past year, each selling between one and six head. This repre-sents an average of 1.6 head per owner, or 10.9 per cent of the total cattle population. Sales were all confined to the Tshiombo area, most to private individuals and a few to local butcheries. Cattle prices reported were in the range R1,200 to R1,500 per head in 1994/95. Nine households reported slaughtering cattle in the past year, three of them slaughtering two animals each and the remaining six households a single animal each, bringing the total off-take up to 15.1 per cent. In two cases cattle were slaughtered on the occasion of a funeral within the household and another for a wedding, with the rest being killed for family gatherings at Christmas or Easter. A number of other cattle-owners insisted that they never slaughtered their cattle, although they said they would consume them if they died, and would consider selling them only in an emergency. Off-take of milk for human consumption would appear to be very low (although this topic was not investigated in any detail) and none of the cattle-owners in the survey reported selling milk.

Households owning cattle differed from those without cattle in a number of important ways, most notably with regard to size of their land-holdings and the sex of the plot-holders. Amongst households with cattle, the average land-holding was 3.5 hectares and, for the eleven largest cattle-owners (that is, those with more than ten head of cattle) the average holding was 4.3 hectares, compared to an average of 2.3 hectares for those without cattle. Male plot-holders were somewhat more likely to keep cattle than women and tended to have considerably larger herds. Thirteen male plot-holders (27 per cent of the total) kept 239 cattle between them, an average of 18.4 each, while seven women plot-holders (20 per cent of the total) kept 52 cattle between them, an average of just 7.4 each. Of the plot-holders with eleven cattle or above, ten were men who were permanently resident at Tshiombo. Four described themselves as full-time farmers, three were pensioners and two were in local employment. By contrast, none of the five households in the sample without an adult male member kept cattle (although one did keep goats).

As a form of property, cattle tended to be associated with men in a way that other forms of property (such as homesteads and arable plots) were not, and although a few widows owned cattle, both men and women in the sample tended to speak of cattle as male property. Three women respondents stated that their late husbands had owned cattle and that after their deaths these had passed to male relatives outside the household. In two other cases, women reported that their husbands had abandoned them and taken their cattle with them. Thus, whether for cultural or economic reasons, men appeared to be more successful than women at accumulating cattle and keeping them as personal, rather than household, property.[15]

Goats

Ownership of goats at Tshiombo is even less widespread than cattle: just six respondents (7.2 per cent of the sample) reported keeping goats at the time of the household survey, all of them of the short-eared 'Boer' variety. Grazing land for goats is even more limited that for cattle, being almost entirely restricted to the rocky outcrops to the south-west of the irrigation scheme. Goats were extremely unpopular with scheme officials and most plot-holders and many informants told of goats damaging crops in their home gardens and irrigated plots.

Five of the six households with goats owned between two and 17 each, while the other kept a herd of 100. The owner of this large herd was the only one who reported selling any goats, disposing of approximately 50 every year to consumers in the local villages, at between R100 and R120 each. He also reported spending upwards of R2,000 per year on supplementary fodder, purchased from NTK. Other owners said that they sold goats from time to time when they were in need of cash, and all had consumed at least one goat within the household during the previous year.

Households that kept goats were not significantly different from the remainder of the sample in terms of land-holding, household size, off-farm income or sex of plot-holder. Goats did, however, tend to be associated with other forms of livestock – half the households with goats also kept cattle and all of them kept poultry.

Donkeys

Donkeys were reported to have been widely used at Tshiombo up to the 1970s for tillage and transport purposes but numbers would now appear to be in severe decline.[16] Only three households (3.6 per cent of the sample) kept donkeys at the time of the survey, owning four, six and six animals respectively. Just one of these households relied on donkeys for ploughing, but the other two used them for harrowing following tractor ploughing. Two households also earned occasional income by hiring out their donkey teams and equipment to other plot-holders. None of these owners had bought or sold donkeys in the past year, or indeed in recent memory. All three donkey-owners also kept cattle, grazing and kraaling both types of animals together.

The reported decline in donkey numbers at Tshiombo can largely be put down to the wide availability of tractors and motor transport and, as with changes in cattle-owning, appears to have been accompanied by a considerable shift in attitudes amongst plot-holders. All three donkey-owners believed that their neighbours looked down on them for using animal traction and said that the younger members of their households refused to be seen with either a donkey cart or plough.

No horses or mules were kept by any households in the survey and none was apparent at Tshiombo.

Pigs

Pigs are not widely kept in Venda and there is a strong (cultural) antipathy to them in many areas. A small number of pigs were in evidence around Tshiombo, but, of the survey respondents, just one reported keeping a pig, which was being kept for consumption by the household.

Poultry

Chickens were kept by less than half the households in the survey (45.8 per cent). Numbers ranged between two and 25 per household, with the exception of a single owner who kept 50 birds. These surprisingly low figures are in part attributable to the effects of Newcastle disease, which was widespread in the area for the three years prior to the survey, but observations at respondents' homesteads suggested that there may have been considerable under-reporting of chicken numbers. Chickens are generally kept for domestic consumption of meat, rather than for eggs or for sale. Households with poultry tended to have slightly less land, higher off-farm income and more cattle than those without poultry.

Only two plot-holders, both men, reported selling any chickens during the previous year. One sold an average of one bird per week and the other sold 50 birds every two weeks. Not surprisingly, this latter owner was also the only respondent who regularly purchased young stock, buying 50 chicks at a time from a hatchery at Levubu at R12 apiece. These factory chickens were allowed to roam freely within his yard for two weeks and were fed on purchased feed, producing a bird that was said to taste much better than those from larger, intensive poultry farms, and could fetch R18 on the local market.

Chicken eggs are not widely exploited by the farmers of Tshiombo, either as food or for sale, and the local varieties of birds were not considered reliable layers. Efforts have been made by the Department of Agriculture, however, to promote egg production in the locality. A female Home Economics officer based at Tshiombo assists women by providing them with a dozen laying hens (three to four weeks old) and initial feed supplies for an investment of about R300. Three households within the survey were participating in this scheme – two with 12 hens each, producing on average ten eggs a day, and one with 24 hens, producing an average of 20 eggs per day. As with most other small-scale income-generating schemes encountered in the area, however, little thought had been given to the marketing aspects and all the producers reported difficulty disposing of even these small quantities.

Income from Livestock

In order to arrive at an estimate of the amount of income derived from live-stock, cash values have been imputed to all livestock consumed within households, and these have been added to actual sales revenue where appropriate. Livestock consumed within households were valued at R1,500 per head of cattle, R100 per goat and R18 per fowl, the most common prices mentioned by households who sold such animals. It should be noted that no account is taken of overall value of livestock in hand, a considerable asset in many cases.

A total of 49 households in the survey (59 per cent) obtained an income (in cash or kind) from livestock during the previous year, ranging from R36 (two chickens consumed) to R11,550 (50 goats and three head of cattle sold, four goats and one head of cattle consumed). Average income from livestock amongst these 49 households was R1,257 (or R742 per household across the entire sample). The following table provides summary information on households with *above* and *below* R1,000 income from livestock for the year, showing the average land-holding, average off-farm income, average age of plot-holders and the number of male and female plot-holders for each stratum.

TABLE 6.11
ESTIMATED LIVESTOCK INCOME PER HOUSEHOLD (PER ANNUM)

Livestock Income	Number of H'holds	Average Land-holding (ha)	Average Off-farm Income (R)	Average Age of Plot-holders	Sex of Plot-holder	
					M	F
R1,000+	15	3.8	9,672	60.9	12	3
R0–999	68	2.3	10,638	57.5	36	32
TOTAL	83	2.6	10,463	58.1	48	35

Households earning above R1,000 per year from livestock tended to have substantially more land than the rest of the sample and a high proportion of male plot-holders. Indeed, the top seven earners of livestock income in the sample were all men, which is in line with earlier comments on the control of livestock, particularly cattle, by men.

Little difference was found between the two groups shown above in terms of off-farm income, which suggests that off-farm income in the current period (as opposed to historical earnings) is not a major factor in livestock production. Households in the survey generally accumulated livestock slowly, by natural increase rather than by purchase, and careful stock management would appear to be just as important to this process as cash income. Livestock-owners (particularly men) thus tended to maximise their herd size, and their income from this source, only after they ceased off-farm employment and devoted themselves full-time to agriculture. Off-farm income for these top households therefore came largely from pensions and from the wages of plot-holders' sons and daughters.

With few exceptions, little information could be obtained on the costs associated with livestock production. Many owners said they spent nothing on their livestock other than the R2 per annum fee for cattle-dipping, but others quoted figures equivalent to between ten per cent and 30 per cent of the income derived from their livestock. In order to arrive at a rough estimate of net income from livestock, however, it was necessary to impute some figure for costs, and a figure equivalent to 20 per cent of livestock income has been used for this purpose. The resulting estimate of 'Net Livestock Income' is used in subsequent Chapters for the computation of overall household income.

Net livestock income was thus found to range from zero to R8,660, with only 12 households obtaining more than R1,000 in the year. Average net live-stock income for those with livestock (49 households) was estimated at R1,257, or R557 for the sample as a whole (n=83).

In conclusion, livestock farming at Tshiombo can be said to be relatively unimportant either as a source of income or as an input to arable farming and, with the exception of dipping, livestock farming has received virtually no support over the years from the government service. Ploughing with animal traction is now a rarity and animal manure is not used by a majority of plot-holders (see Chapter 7). Only two households in the survey said they obtained a regular (that is, monthly) cash income from livestock, and even the contribu-tion to household diet was minimal in many cases. In terms of income, cattle were by far the most important form of livestock, although cases were found of households making substantial income from goats and chickens as well. Plot-holders with above-average earnings from livestock tended to be non-migrant men in their fifties and sixties, the same group which was most successful in accumulating arable land. The following chapters will explore the relationships between livestock farming and other livelihood activities in more detail and the contribution of livestock to overall household income.

NOTES

1. For similar conditions in Lebowa see Delius [1996: 160] and Baber [1996: 280].
2. See Murray [1981: 110] for similar findings on Lesotho, and Brown [1983: 375] on Botswana.
3. See James [1985: 164] for a description of a similar custom in Lebowa.

4. This included a case of two widows of the same husband, and their children, who shared the same household and arable plot.
5. This topic is widely neglected in studies of the South African homelands, and many studies specifically concerned with women and the household make no reference to polygyny: for example, James [1985] on Lebowa, and Sharp and Spiegel [1990] on Transkei and QwaQwa.
6. Persons of pensionable age accounted for 12.7 per cent of the entire sample population, which is extremely high even by homeland standards (see Ardington and Lund [1995: 563]).
7. Military service was a recurring theme in many of the interviews, something that has not featured in any other homeland study to the best of my knowledge. Two men in the sample had served in the former Venda Defence Forces, and one in the ANC's *Umkhonto we Sizwe* (MK), all of whom were incorporated into the reformed South African defence forces after April 1994. Two former migrants had worked as civilian cooks in barracks in Johannesburg and Pretoria, and two pensioners had served with the South African forces in Kenya and North Africa during the Second World War. One of these was particularly bitter that, unlike his white comrades, he had never received a war pension, and had to wait twenty years to obtain the land he had been promised. By contrast, only one former policeman was found in the survey, who had served for 28 years in Johannesburg.
8. In fact, these two men – a father and son – owned their own taxis, and are most accurately described as self-employed, but for the purposes of this analysis they have been included in the category of wage workers.
9. It should be noted that not all respondents were visited in their homes, so for the sake of consistency this analysis is restricted to information that was supplied voluntarily by respondents, while bearing in mind its often incomplete nature.
10. See Davidson and Stacey [1988: 245] for details of pension-day markets in Bophuthatswana.
11. This figure includes only 50 per cent of migrants' earnings as 'household income', as discussed above. If 100 per cent of migrant earnings were included, they would constitute 51 per cent of total wage income, and 29.7 per cent of total off-farm income. This is still remarkably low.
12. The category of plot-holder, unlike that of 'full-time farmer' discussed above, includes both women and pensioners. It should also be noted that while land (and hence agriculture) in the former homelands is widely said to be dominated by the elderly, no comparative data could be found regarding the age of farmers or plot-holders (as opposed to 'heads of households').
13. See Ardington [1984: 9] for KwaZulu; van der Waal [1996: 51] for Gazankulu; de Wet [1995: 171] for Ciskei; Spiegel [1986: 20] for Transkei.
14. During follow-up interviews, it was learned that this plot-holder also held eight hectares of irrigated land on the nearby Agriven scheme at Makonde, but as little information could be obtained regarding this land or how it was used, it has been excluded from the analysis.
15. Writing of Lesotho, Ferguson [1994: 151] describes cattle and donkeys as 'men's animals', over which women have little or no control, while pigs and fowl are considered to be women's property.
16. See Starkey [1995: 22] for the widespread decline in the use of donkeys throughout the former homelands.

Agricultural Production at Tshiombo

This chapter presents survey findings on aspects of agricultural activity at Tshiombo for the agricultural year 1994/95, including land usage, the types and volumes of crops grown, methods of ploughing, agricultural labour, purchased inputs, marketing of agricultural produce and the role of the government extension service. It also examines the wide disparities between plot-holders in terms of agricultural output and attempts to explain these in terms of the different assets, income, cropping strategies and demographic composition of households in the sample.

7.1 LAND USAGE

As shown in the previous chapter, over a third of households in the survey (31 out of 83) had multiple plots on the irrigation scheme, while a quarter (21 households) had waste land away from the scheme. Allowing for overlap between these categories, this left approximately half the households (42) with just a single irrigated plot at their disposal. Apart from a relatively small area of waste land used for orchards, most arable land at Tshiombo, both on and off the scheme, is used for the production of annual (or seasonal) field crops.

Crop production at Tshiombo is based on a two-phase cycle – that is, summer and winter, or rainy and dry seasons – although not all households grow crops in both seasons. The summer season is generally defined as the months of October through March, and winter as the months of April through September. Considerable variation was found between households regarding the types of crops grown in each season, and the precise times of planting and harvesting.

The extent of land use on the scheme varies widely over the course of the year, but some crop production occurs in every month. The following chart shows the pattern of land use on one Block at Tshiombo (Block 1B) over the course of the agricultural year covered by this study – April 1994 to March 1995. The total area of arable land on this Block was 110.6 hectares, divided into 87 plots.

FIGURE 7.1

AREA OF LAND CULTIVATED, TSHIOMBO BLOCK 1B 1994/95 (HA)

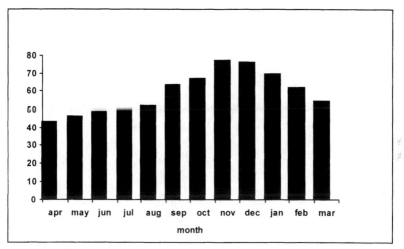

The area of land used on this Block varied between 43.1 hectares (40 per cent of the total) in April and 68.8 hectares (62.2 per cent) in January. The rate of land use followed roughly the same pattern in all 15 years for which records were available, peaking in the period November to January and reaching a low point between April and June. The lowest land usage on record was in 1992/93 (at the end of a severe drought), when no more than 44.9 hectares (40.6 per cent) were cultivated in any month.

In the household survey, plot-holders were asked how much of their land they had cultivated in the two seasons immediately preceding the survey – winter 1994 (approximately April to September 1994) and summer 1994/95 (October 1994 to March 1995). The precise definition of the seasons, and allocation of particular plantings to one season or another, was left to the individual respondents. Responses to this question showed considerable variation between households, between different parts of the scheme and between summer and winter seasons.

The vast majority of households (94 per cent) planted at least one summer crop in the 1994/95 season, nearly three-quarters (73.5 per cent) planted at least one winter crop and just three households (3.6 per cent) planted nothing at all over the course of the year.[1] One of these had not ploughed since 1991 due to the lack of irrigation water, one had not ploughed since 1992 and appeared to have little interest in agriculture and the third, a couple in their late sixties, had not ploughed since 1990 due to ill-health. All had alternative sources of (off-farm) income and two appeared to be running shebeens, although this was not explicitly stated (see Chapter 6).

The following table shows the average proportion of arable land cultivated by survey respondents on each of the four main Blocks on the irrigation scheme, in summer and winter seasons 1994/95.

TABLE 7.1
AVERAGE PROPORTION OF IRRIGATED LAND CULTIVATED PER
BLOCK, PER SEASON

	Summer (%)	Winter (%)	Annual (%)
Block 1 (n=20)	67.5	45.0	56.2
Block 2 (n=19)	75.0	57.9	66.4
Block 3 (n=18)	69.4	45.8	57.6
Block 4 (n=26)	64.4	30.8	47.6
Total (n=83)	68.7	43.7	56.2

Note: 'Total' is the arithmetic mean of all 83 households in the sample, rather than the mean of the four Block averages shown. 'Annual' is the average of summer and winter usage.

Overall, respondents used an average of 68.7 per cent of available land in summer and 43.7 per cent in winter, or 56.2 per cent over the two-crop cycle. There were two reasons for this: one, because fewer households planted a winter crop; and two, because those who did plant in winter tended to use less land than in summer – winter growers in the sample used on average 52.4 per cent of their land, while summer growers used 68.3 per cent. Only 13 households (15.7 per cent of the sample) reported using all available land in both summer and winter.

The pattern of land use also varied considerably between the main Blocks on the irrigation scheme. Block Two had the highest land usage, in both seasons, with Blocks One and Three showing somewhat lower rates. Block Four clearly had the lowest land usage in both seasons. These results partially confirm the popular opinion at Tshiombo that agricultural conditions deteriorate as one moves down the Blocks (that is, from the 'top-end' to the 'tail-end' of the main canal), but do not explain why plots on Block One appear to be used less intensively than those on Block Two. The explanation offered by some of the Agricultural Officers at Tshiombo was that Block One was the farthest from the main road and thus tended to be neglected by crop-buyers, thus partially offsetting its advantageous position with regard to water supply. Reasons given by plot-holders for not using all available land included the need for periods of fallow, shortages of a particular input, such as irrigation water, tractors or cash (for seeds, fertiliser or chemicals), or temporary abandonment of agriculture due to ill-health of the plot-holder or the expectation of drought.

Information regarding waste land was not as comprehensive as for the irrigation scheme, but the pattern of land use appeared to be broadly similar. Only those farmers with their own irrigation pumps grew crops in both seasons, and the proportion of land used tended to be less in winter than in summer. Only those households with the very smallest holdings of waste land (that is, 0.5 hectares or less) reported using all available land in either season.

7.2 CROPS GROWN AT TSHIOMBO

The irrigation system and the range of agricultural services available at Tshiombo have allowed plot-holders on the scheme to expand the range of crops, extend the growing season and generally intensify production compared to dryland farmers in other parts of Venda. For most plot-holders, however, it has not totally transformed the choice of crops or methods of production. In the early years of the irrigation scheme, the main crops were reported to be those with which local farmers were already familiar, such as maize, cabbage, spinach and beans, all grown from farmers' own (retained) seed. Crops such as tomatoes and groundnuts were introduced gradually over the years, along with inorganic fertilisers, chemical pesticides and hybrid seeds. Veterans of the scheme reported that there were no established market-places in Venda when the scheme began and, although a few plot-holders managed to get contracts to supply local hospitals and other institutions, most produce was destined for domestic consumption. Over the years, plot-holders at Tshiombo have adopted new crops and a wide range of modern technologies, and now dispose of a high proportion of their produce on local (that is, Venda) markets.

Obtaining detailed (and accurate) information on current crop production and disposal, including areas planted, yields and sales revenues, presented many practical difficulties. Complete up-to-date records were kept by none of the officials on the scheme and the quality of records that were available varied widely from Block to Block. Most showed considerably less production than was reported by plot-holders themselves, and prices for crops sold tended to be 'official' (that is, notional) prices decided by the Department of Agriculture rather than the prices actually obtained by producers. Prices and volumes of purchased inputs – seed and fertiliser in particular – were also 'standardised' in this way in official records, being estimated on the basis of the land area cultivated rather than the amounts actually used by individual plot-holders. Summaries of the area of crops planted and harvested on each Block are filed with the Department by the Agricultural Officers every month, but the methods of estimation used meant these reports could only be used as a general guide to activity on the scheme.

Without doubt, the single most important crop, in terms of area planted, is maize, the local staple food, which accounts for 40–50 per cent of the total cultivated area on the irrigation scheme. Following this, a group of seven crops between them account for around 40 per cent of the area under production, namely groundnuts, China spinach, *muxe* (a local variety of spinach), tomatoes, sweet potatoes, dry beans and cabbage. [2] Other crops, such as chilli peppers, pumpkins and onions, account for relatively small areas (in the range 1–2 per cent each), while jugo beans, tobacco, sugar cane, sweet melons, millet (for ceremonial beer), carrots, lettuce and okra are grown in even smaller quantities.

The following section draws together information on the main crops grown at Tshiombo, based on interviews with Agricultural Officers and crop merchants and on the results of the household survey. Details of crop production at the household level are discussed in subsequent sections.

Maize

Maize was grown by every household in the sample that planted a crop but, in the case of those with multiple plots, not necessarily on every plot. The planting season for maize extends over a lengthy period, running from May to November, and a minority of households (15.7 per cent) planted two crops in the year, on different land – typically in May/June and again in August/September. Most plot-holders had strong preferences for when they would plant maize, with dates such as 15 May, 15 June and 25 July being mentioned frequently, apparently based on long-standing family traditions. Just two plot-holders in the survey said that they deliberately spread out their maize production over the season in order to ensure a steady supply of fresh produce, each planting one or two 'beds' every month from May to September. Growing time in the cool, dry winter season is longer than in the relatively warm, wet summer months, with the result that the maize harvest is largely concentrated in the period December to March, with small volumes harvested as early as October and as late as April. During follow-up interviews in 1996, a number of plot-holders said that they had taken advantage of very late rains to plant maize in January (1996) and were hoping to harvest in May.

Farmers on irrigated lands such as Tshiombo have a comparative advantage over those in dryland areas in the production of early (or winter) maize, for which there is a strong demand throughout Venda. Early maize is generally either sold, or consumed within the household, as fresh cobs (green mealies, or *zwikoli*), rather than being milled for meal. Later in the season (from about February onwards), the demand for fresh maize in the region is much diminished as the dryland crop is harvested, and summer maize (*mavhele*) is therefore largely retained for home consumption (as maize meal). Much symbolic importance is attached to summer maize compared to winter maize and other crops. Summer is the traditional maize season in the region, when yields are higher and more reliable than in winter, and summer maize is widely seen as the staple crop around which the agricultural year is organised, and on which the well-being of the household in the year ahead may depend. Winter maize, by contrast, is seen as a relatively 'new' crop, entails greater risk (due to unfavourable climatic conditions), tends to be grown largely for sale and generally carries less of the cultural associations of *mavhele*.

Larger and better-off producers at Tshiombo generally take their summer maize to the NTK roller mill at Shayandima where it is deposited, milled and withdrawn as required, under a voucher system known as *stoormielies* (see Chapter 4). Smaller producers and those without their own transport mainly rely on small tractor-powered mills, or the new electric mill at Tshiombo, neither of which has storage facilities. It is now extremely rare at Tshiombo for households with more than about a bag (80 kg) of maize to stamp it in the traditional fashion, by hand.

In good harvest years maize may be sold outright to the NTK mill (part of South Africa's official maize marketing system until 1995), but no plot-holders reported selling maize to the mill in the three years prior to the survey. As noted above (Chapter 4), farmers at Tshiombo, and throughout Venda, were highly critical of the prices offered by the mill, and many were convinced that they were being paid less than white farmers at mills elsewhere. Small volumes of dry mealies are sold informally or exchanged for sweet potatoes within the locality, fetching between R60 and R80 per 80 kg bag. Plot-holders using the Tshiombo mill usually dry their maize and store it as cobs within the homestead, later shelling and soaking the grain as and when they wish to mill it. Households in the survey generally stored maize loosely piled, or in bags in domestic huts, and only one household reported storing it in traditional-style underground storage pits.

Green mealies are generally sold directly to consumers within Tshiombo and surrounding villages, or to hawkers at markets in Thohoyandou or Sibasa. Prices quoted for this trade were between R1,500 and R3,000 per bakkie-load of cobs (probably in the order of 0.5–0.75 tonnes).

Precise per hectare yields of maize at Tshiombo, as with all other crops, were difficult to ascertain. Agricultural Officers' records on one Block (1B) for the period 1990–95 showed average annual yields for summer maize ranging between 14 bags (1,120 kg) and 35 bags (2,800 kg) per hectare, as shown in Table 7.2 (below).

TABLE 7.2
SUMMER MAIZE YIELDS, BLOCK 1B

Year	Bags per Hectare	Kg per Hectare
1990/91	35	2800
1991/92	31	2480
1992/93	16	1280
1993/94	14	1120
1994/95	16	1280

The average yield for this Block over the period, according to the official record, was 1,790 kg per hectare. As noted above, Block One is probably the Block with the highest agricultural potential on the scheme, but these figures are still considerably higher than the yields reported by many of the plot-holders themselves.

In the household survey, plot-holders across the entire scheme reported harvesting between 20 and 30 bags per plot (roughly 1,600 to 2,400 kg per hectare) in 1990/91 and 1991/92 summer seasons, but many lost their entire crop to drought in 1992/93 and 1993/94 and few reported harvesting more than the equivalent of 12 bags.[3] The 1994/95 summer season showed some improvement, with plot-holders in the sample reporting yields of between six and 20 bags. In 1995/96, maize was reported to have been severely stunted due to excessive heat.

All but one of the households in the survey stated that they aimed to be self-sufficient in maize, but the majority failed to achieve this in the year under investigation or at any time in the previous five years. The extent of self-sufficiency is obscured by the fact that many households both buy and sell maize (or maize products), and it would certainly appear to be economically rational for farmers at Tshiombo to sell fresh cobs during the winter and buy maize meal. Three-quarters of respondents (62 households) reported buying some maize meal in the previous year. The typical maize meal requirement appeared to be in the order of two 80 kg bags per person per year, or one bag a month for a household of six persons.

Tomatoes

Extensive cultivation of tomatoes is a relatively recent development in Venda, but over the last twenty years it has become a significant source of income for farmers with irrigated land and a widespread addition to the popular diet. This trend has been boosted by the establishment of a tomato-canning factory at Makhado (north-west Venda), but a large informal market for tomatoes also exists in the area.

Tomatoes can be grown at Tshiombo throughout the year, but most planting occurs between March and June, with harvesting concentrated in the period July to August. Agricultural Officers' records suggest that tomato yields fluctuate enormously, both between seasons and between growers. In 1991, official records show that growers on the scheme produced the equivalent of between one and five tonnes per hectare; in 1992 virtually the entire crop was wiped out by drought; while exceptionally high harvests were recorded by a number of farmers in 1993 and 1994, with many exceeding 10 tonnes per hectare and one grower producing 20 tonnes from a single plot.[4] One survey respondent claimed that he had regularly obtained yields of 100 tonnes or more from two plots (2.56 ha) during the 1980s, which is in line with yields achieved by white farmers supplying the Giants canning factory (see below).

Tomatoes are generally sold either to the canning factory, to hawkers and merchants who come to the fields, or directly to consumers at Tshiombo and surrounding areas. In past years, Agricultural Officers at Tshiombo arranged for the hire of trucks to transport tomatoes to the factory (a distance of some 80 km) and handled payments from the factory on behalf of producers. This arrangement broke down in 1994, seemingly due to farmers' dissatisfaction with the low prices obtained from the factory relative to the cost of transportation and having to wait until the end of the season for payment (see below). The factory was reported to be paying producers R230 per tonne in 1994/95, and R300 in 1995/96, although many producers reported receiving less than these amounts, possibly on grounds of quality or because the amount delivered weighed less than the producers had expected. Substantially better prices could be obtained on the informal market, where tomatoes sold for between R10 and R15 per case during this period, equivalent to R400-600 per tonne.

Groundnuts

Groundnuts are strictly a summer crop at Tshiombo and are commonly grown with little application of fertiliser or pesticide. Considerable labour is required, however, for both weeding and harvesting. Planting occurs during the months September to January, and groundnuts are harvested during the period January to April.

Agricultural Officers' records showed yields ranging from 700 to 1,800 kg per hectare for the period 1990/91 to 1993/94. Yields for 1994/95 were generally higher, with producers reporting yields of between 2,000 and 4,000 kg per hectare. In 1995/96 the harvest was reported to be extremely poor due to flooding in early 1996.

Prices for groundnuts have been rising steadily in recent years: an 80 kg bag sold for R80 in 1993 and R100 in 1994, while some growers reported obtaining as much as R120 per bag in 1995, equivalent to R1,500 per tonne. Groundnuts not consumed within the household are nearly all sold to small-scale hawkers who call at the plot-holders' homes.

Sweet Potatoes

Sweet potatoes are grown over a prolonged season, with the most planting between January and May and harvesting from June to August. Planting may continue up to September, however, and harvesting until February. Producer prices have improved considerably in recent years, from R10 per crate (approximately 25 kg) in 1992, to R15 in 1995, with occasional reports of R20 per create. Few respondents were able to provide detailed estimates of yields, as harvesting and sales were usually done piecemeal, but Agricultural Officers suggested that typical yields for sweet potatoes were in the range of two to five tonnes per hectare. One survey respondent said he produced 15 van loads (probably in excess of 10 tonnes) from a single plot in 1994, which he sold in Thohoyandou for R230 per load. Sweet potatoes were reported to have suffered badly from drought in early 1994 and from excessive rain in early 1996.

Cabbage

Cabbage is widely grown as a winter crop at Tshiombo, being planted mainly between the months of February and June and harvested between July and September. A small number of plot-holders also grow cabbage over the summer season, planting in November and December and harvesting in February and March, although the crop is vulnerable to excessive heat. Survey respondents reported yields ranging from 10,000 to 30,000 head of cabbage per plot (1.28 ha), with a market value of R6,000 to R20,000.

China Spinach and Muxe

China spinach and *muxe* are widely grown on the Tshiombo scheme and constitute an important element of the local diet. They are grown under similar conditions and fetch similar prices, although *muxe* is more likely to be reserved for home consumption. These crops are grown all the year round: various respondents reported planting in every month from February to October and harvesting from May to January, although the main season is the period April to July. Prices for spinach and *muxe* were reported to be R10 per crate in 1993 and R15 in 1994. Agricultural Officers estimated a typical income of R1,500 to R2,000 per hectare over the course of a season, with continuous harvesting.

Fruit

Fruit trees are an integral part of the landscape at Tshiombo, both on residential stands and around the edges of arable plots, but are more likely to be grown for shade and domestic consumption of fruit rather than for commercial purposes. While 41 households reported having fruit trees on their arable land, only 18 of these (21.7 per cent of the sample) had ten trees or more and only one had more than 50 trees. Many of the smaller orchards were located on the irrigated plots – either down the middle in a single line, or around the edges – but the larger ones were all on non-irrigated waste land. The largest of these comprised 900 mango trees on five hectares and belonged to a local school teacher. The most common type of fruit grown was mangoes, followed by bananas, guavas, lemons, avocados and paw-paws. Some mango growers sold fruit to *achar* (pickle) factories at Levubu and Shayandima, but most reported that their fruit was either consumed within the household or sold within the local villages. Mango trees were reported to have been badly affected by blight in recent years, resulting in extremely poor yields.

Other Crops

Little specific information was obtained regarding the less popular crops grown at Tshiombo, but what is known is summarised here.

Onions are mainly planted in the period April to June and harvested between August and November. Prices were R10 per 10kg bag in 1993 and R15 in 1994.

Beans (also known as dry beans) are planted mainly in the months of April and May and harvested July to September. Reported yields were in the range of one to two tonnes per hectare and prices at Tshiombo (in 1994/95) were between R80 and R100 for a 25 kg bag.

Chilli peppers (*peri-peri*) are planted between December and August and harvested from May to January. Reported yields were in the range of 1.5–2.5 tonnes per hectare and prices varied from R35 to R45 for a 10 kg bag.

Sugar cane is grown all around the project, often on waste ground and along the river bank, mainly for domestic consumption, but small amounts are sold to consumers along the road-side at Tshiombo.

FIGURE 7.2

CROPPING SEASONS AT TSHIOMBO

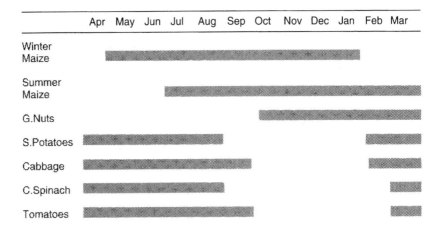

Virtually all households at Tshiombo organise their agricultural year around the production of maize. Planting of maize begins in late May and peaks in the period June to August, prior to the summer rains, as shown in Figure 7.2 (above). Groundnuts are the other main summer crop. They are usually planted in October, after the rains begin (and after maize planting has been completed), and mature during the wettest, hottest months of the year. Production of all the other main crops – sweet potatoes, cabbage, China spinach and tomatoes – is concentrated in the cooler, dryer months. These crops are usually planted in March or April, at the end of the rainy season and before maize planting commences. All of these crops come to maturity during the cool, dry months of mid-winter (July–August) and are generally harvested after maize has been planted.

7.3 CROP OUTPUT

The above section has provided an overview of crop production on the Tshiombo scheme as a whole. This section looks at production at the household level, using information gathered through the household survey.

As noted above, the most common crops (by area and by number of producers) were maize, groundnuts, China spinach, *muxe*, tomatoes, sweet potatoes and cabbage. Virtually all plot-holders in the sample (80 out of 83) grew at least three different crops in the year and over three-quarters (78 per cent) grew five or six crops. It proved difficult to ascertain what were the most productive crops (in terms of gross return per hectare) given the widely different yield estimates by growers for the same crops. All of the crops listed here were reported to have produced gross income in excess of R3,000 per hectare, but the highest reported returns came from green maize, tomatoes and cabbage, each of which produced gross income in excess of R5,000 per hectare in at least one case. Exceptionally high incomes were also reported for chilli peppers, but only two plot-holders in the sample grew this crop, on just one bed and four beds respectively. Mangoes were the only fruit to make a significant contribution to agricultural incomes but the small numbers of trees grown (in most cases), the long cycle of maturation and widely different yield estimates made it difficult to assess its performance relative to field crops.

Most households in the sample planted no more than three beds of any one crop, with the exception of summer maize, which was commonly planted on four or five beds. Those with larger holdings obviously had more opportunity for extending the area under particular crops, but there appeared to be limits on how much of any one crop plot-holders were willing (or able) to grow. Only four farmers grew more than one full irrigated plot (or equivalent on waste land) of any crop: two growing maize (three hectares and two hectares respectively), two growing cabbage (one full plot in each case) and one growing tomatoes (again, one full plot).

The main reason for this diversification of crop production, according to survey respondents, was the desire to minimise the risk of crop failure and to ensure a supply of staple foods (and cash income) over many months. By growing a range of crops, spread out over one or two seasons, households were able to spread the demand for cash (for seed, fertiliser and ploughing) and household labour over the year and use the income from one crop to finance the next. Irrigation alone demanded a high labour input and, without the use of hired labour, most households were hard pressed to tend to more than two or three beds at any one time. Different crops tended to overlap, as may be seen from the Crop Schedules shown below, but the most labour-intensive tasks, such as planting, irrigating, weeding and harvesting, could usually be staggered so that no more than one crop required attention at any one time.

The estimation of crop yields (and values) at Tshiombo was highly problematic, as noted above, for reasons connected with local farming practices and the limitations of this study. None of the plot-holders in the survey kept written records and many were unable (or unwilling) to provide precise estimates of past harvest volumes. No independent measurement of yields was attempted. Most farmers could, however, recall the area planted to various crops, usually in terms of the number of beds, which themselves varied considerably in size. The main units of crop measurement used by plot-holders were bags (usually meaning an 80 kg maize meal sack, or occasionally a 25 kg sack) or bakkie-loads (approximately 0.5–1.0 tonne), which again were far from precise. Crop quality rarely featured in discussion of yields, although it undoubtedly influenced the prices that could be obtained by producers.

The exceptions were those crops which were stored after harvest, and those which were sold (or processed) through formal channels, and therefore could be quantified. Groundnuts, for example, were uniformly packed (in the shell) in 80 kg maize bags, and were generally sold (informally) to hawkers directly from the home or in the market place at Thohoyandou. Similarly, summer maize was generally dried and packed (as grain) in 80 kg bags, whether it was to be milled at Tshiombo or deposited at the NTK mills. Tomatoes, as noted above, could be sold to the Giants canning factory at Makhado, while mangoes could be sold to achar factories in Levubu or Shayandima. In either case, the weight of produce sold (or processed) was generally known to the plot-holder, but such sales often accounted for only a portion of the total amount harvested and were not therefore a reliable guide to total yield.

Attempts to estimate yields were further complicated by the fact that perishable crops tend to be harvested piecemeal over a prolonged period, whether for sale or for consumption within the household. Daily consumption of crops typically begins well before the formal harvest and continues throughout the period of harvesting and selling, as in the well-documented case of green mealies [*Lipton*, 1977: 73; *Marais*, 1989: 361]. Thus, although most crops are divided between household consumption ('subsistence') and marketed share ('surplus'), the exact breakdown between these could not always be ascertained.

On the basis of the information provided by survey respondents, an attempt has been made to calculate the total value of crop production per household, bearing in mind the limitations to the estimation of crop output outlined above. This involved imputing a monetary value to each crop produced over the course of the year (on and off the scheme), based on prevailing farm-gate prices at Tshiombo, regardless of whether the crop was actually sold or consumed within the household. As most produce was sold informally and in relatively small quantities, there was little effective difference between producer prices and consumer prices for households at Tshiombo. Therefore, it was decided to use a standard method of valuation – producer prices – across all households and all crops, based on prevailing prices reported by plot-holders in the survey.[5]

Table 7.3 (below) provides a breakdown of households in the survey according to estimated total crop output, showing the average land-holding (on and off the scheme) for each stratum.

The total (imputed) value of crops produced by households in the survey for the year 1994/95 varied enormously, from zero to R42,000, and the mean value per household was R4,674. A substantial majority of households (62.7 per cent) produced crops with a gross value of less than R5,000, and only the top six producers (7.2 per cent of the sample) came close to obtaining an income from crops that could conceivably meet their household subsistence requirements. Overall, 70.6 per cent of crop output (by value) was sold and 29.4 per cent consumed within households. Over three-quarters of households (65 out of 83) reported selling at least half of their produce.

TABLE 7.3
ESTIMATED CROP OUTPUT PER HOUSEHOLD, 1994/95

Crop Value (R)	Number of Households	Percentage of Households	Average Land Holding
10,000 +	6	7.2	8.29
5,000 – 9,999	25	30.1	2.60
2,000 – 4,999	36	43.4	1.96
0 – 1,999	16	19.3	1.55

The annual agricultural cycle, the range of cropping patterns and the wide variation in output between producers may be illustrated by summarising data on four individual households, selected to be approximately representative of each of the income strata shown above. The following examples show the main cropping activities for the year 1994/95, starting with the lowest stratum, those producing crops worth less than R2,000. Note that the category 'Consumed' includes produce consumed directly by the household or stored for future consumption and seed retained for future planting.

Example 1: Respondent Number 78, Block, 4C (R0-1,999)

This household comprised a female plot-holder in her fifties, her three school-going children and an adult daughter with two young children. It was one of the five households in the sample with no adult male member. The household was dependent upon the earnings of the daughter, who worked as a cleaner in Thohoyandou, and on the produce of their single plot. The plot-holder inherited the plot from her father in 1981. This household produced crops worth an estimated R1,550 in 1994/95, of which 54.2 per cent was sold and 45.8 per cent was consumed directly within the household. Due to lack of water on this part of the scheme (Block Four), crops were grown only during the summer and no green vegetables were produced. Eight out of 11 crop beds were utilised during the year, or 36 per cent of the total number possible over two seasons. All labour was supplied by members of the household.

CROP SCHEDULE 1
RESPONDENT NO.78

Month	Main Activity	Value (R)	
		Consumed	Sold
April			
May			
June	Harvest sweet potatoes: 40 crates	200	400
July	Plant maize: 3 beds		
August			
September			
October	Plant groundnuts: 2 beds		
November			
December			
January	Plant sweet potatoes: 3 beds		
February	Harvest maize: 5 bags	400	–
March	Harvest groundnuts: 5 bags.	110	440
	Four sold at R110 per bag		
TOTAL		710	840

Example 2: Respondent Number 12, Block 1A (R2,000-R4,999)

At 26, this male farmer was the youngest plot-holder in the sample. He lived with his wife, two young children, his brother who attended school and his widowed mother. This man had worked full-time on the plot since leaving school in 1986 and in 1994 his mother registered it in his name. He had never been in paid employment, but said he was looking for work locally. The household depended for its livelihood on the mother's pension and the produce of its single plot. This plot-holder was unusual in that he grew more crops in winter than in summer, which could be attributed to the advantageous position of the plot close to the top end of the irrigation canal. In 1994/95, maize was grown only in winter and all of the harvest was sold as fresh cobs. Additional supplies of maize for domestic consumption were acquired later in the year by bartering sweet potatoes and tomatoes. All eleven crop beds were utilised in winter, and six in summer, an annual land usage of 77.3 per cent. The total value of crops produced on this holding in 1994/95 was estimated at R4,550, of which 87.5 per cent was sold and 12.5 per cent was consumed within the household (including R180 worth of bartered goods).

CROP SCHEDULE 2
RESPONDENT NO.12

Month	Main Activity	Value (R)	
		Consumed	Sold
April	Plant China Spinach: 2 beds		
May	Plant maize: 6 beds		
June	Plant tomatoes: 2 beds		
	Plant onions: 1 bed.		
July	Harvest sweet potatoes; 42 crates		
	20 sold at R15; 12 bartered for 4 bags of maize	150	480
August	Harvest china spinach: 30 bags.		
	20 sold at R15 per bag, 10 bags consumed.	150	300
September	Harvest onions: 18 bags from 1 bed.	–	180
	All sold all R10 per bag		
October	Harvest tomatoes: 30 crates from 2 beds.	50	250
	25 sold at R10 per crate		
November	Plant groundnuts: 3 beds		
December	Harvest Maize. Two bakkie-loads	–	2,000
	sold as green mealies		
January	Plant sweet potatoes: 3 beds		
February			
March	Harvest groundnuts: 9 bags from 3 beds		
	7 bags sold at R110 per bag.		
	1 consumed, 1 retained for seed	220	770
TOTAL		570	3,980

Example 3: Respondent Number 36, Block 2B (R5,000–R9,999)

This household comprised a female plot-holder in her sixties, her elderly husband, who was in poor health, and her unmarried son who was in the army. It was a relatively affluent household, as it contained two pensioners and one wage-earner. The total land-holding of this household comprised one plot on the irrigation scheme and 1.5 hectares of waste land. Approximately one third of available land was used during the winter, and two thirds during the summer, or 50 per cent over the course of the year. Labour was supplied by the plot-holder herself, with occasional assistance from her husband and son, and two labourers were employed for two or three days a month to assist with planting and harvesting. Total crop income was estimated at R7,530, of which approximately 83.9 per cent was accounted for by cash sales and 16.1 per cent by direct consumption.

CROP SCHEDULE 3
RESPONDENT NO. 36

| Month | Main Activity | Value (R) | |
		Consumed	Sold
April	Plant China spinach: 2 beds		
May	Plant sweet potatoes: 1 bed		
	Plant winter maize: 2 beds		
June	Plant tomatoes: 8 beds		
	Harvest beans: 4 bags. Sold at R2 per cup	–	300
July	Plant *muxe*: 1 bed		
	Plant summer maize: 4 beds on waste land		
August	Harvest China spinach	100	500
September	Plant groundnuts: 4 beds, on waste land		
October	Harvest *muxe*		
	Harvest sweet potatoes: 20 crates	50	350
		45	255
November	Harvest tomatoes: 120 crates	–	1,200
December	Harvest winter maize	–	600
January	Harvest mangoes: 20 trees	–	800
February	Harvest summer maize: 10 bags		
	Harvest Ground Nuts	–	800
		220	2,310
March	Plant beans: 2 beds		
TOTAL		1,215	6,315

Example 4: Respondent Number 54, Block 3A (R10,000+)

This plot-holder was a 60-year-old man, who lived with his two wives and three school-going children. They were entirely dependent on agriculture for their livelihood. Land-holding comprised three plots on the irrigation scheme and no waste land. The plot-holder worked as a cook in a Johannesburg army barracks for ten years, until he obtained a plot on the Tshiombo scheme in 1967 and decided to become a full-time farmer. He received two more plots when he married his second wife in 1977.

CROP SCHEDULE 4
RESPONDENT NO.54

| Month | Main Activity | Value (R) | |
		Consumed	Sold
April	Plant sweet potatoes: 1 plot		
May	Plant winter maize: 1 plot		
June			
July	Harvest tomatoes: 360 crates		
	All sold at R10 per crate	–	3,600
August	Plant summer maize: 2 plots		
September	Harvest sweet potatoes: 1 plot	200	4,500
October			
November			
December	Harvest winter maize: approximately 1.5 tonnes		
	All sold as green cobs	–	2,800
January	Harvest mangoes: 5 bakkie-loads	–	1,500
February	Plant tomatoes: 1 plot		
March	Harvest Summer Maize: 30 bags	2,400	–
TOTAL		2,600	12,400

This plot-holder restricted his production to maize, tomatoes and sweet potatoes, using all of his land in winter and two thirds of it in summer – an annual usage of 83 per cent. He was one of only two plot-holders in the sample who ploughed by animal draught, keeping a pair of oxen specifically for this purpose. Most of the work on these plots was carried out by the plot-holder and his wives, but two labourers were hired at harvest times. In addition to growing crops, this household kept a herd of 100 goats and 36 cattle. The total value of crops produced in 1994/95 was R15,000, of which 82.7 per cent was sold and 17.3 per cent was consumed directly within the household (including 30 bags of maize deposited at the NTK mill for future use).

The above examples show the considerably diversity of cropping and pro-longed land use typical of the majority of households in the sample. All of these plot-holders grew at least three crops in the year (the highest number grown was nine) and all but one had at least one crop under cultivation in every month of the year. All sold a slightly higher proportion of their crop than the overall sample average, but serve to illustrate how even relatively small producers tend to sell the greater part of their produce. The next sections examine each of the main aspects of agricultural production at Tshiombo, before looking in more detail at the wide differences observed between plot-holders in terms of total output, with particular focus on the larger producers in the sample.

7.4 HIRED LABOUR

Agriculture in the former homelands is generally seen as a 'household' activity and the results of this study would support that impression. A majority of plot-holders in the survey (59 per cent) did not hire any labour in the previous year, depending entirely on household members to work their plots. A total of 31 households (37.3 per cent) hired some labour over the course of the year and, of these, two depended entirely on such labour, with no contribution from household members (although these were among the smaller producers in the sample). As noted above, the three remaining households did not use their land at all over the course of the year.

The majority of households that hired labour reported employing just one worker at a time, but a sizeable minority employed two or more and the highest number employed by a single household at any one time was five. Table 7.4 (below) shows a breakdown of households in the survey according to the maximum number of workers employed at any time during the previous year.

TABLE 7.4
NUMBER OF HIRED WORKERS PER HOUSEHOLD

Number Of Workers	Number Of Households	Percentage Of Households
Nil	52	62.7
1	19	22.9
2	9	10.8
3+	3	3.6

Respondents used a variety of terms to describe the form of hired labour used, including 'full-time', 'seasonal', 'part-time', 'occasional' and 'piece-work', and the differences between these categories were not always clear. The main distinction appeared to be between workers who were hired only for specific tasks, such as harvesting or planting, and paid a piece-rate or daily wage, and those who were employed for more routine work, such as weeding, spraying and irrigating, and were paid by the month. Just nine plot-holders in the survey (11 per cent) employed workers all the year round and six of these said they hired additional seasonal labour as required.

Most employers paid their workers between R120 and R250 per month, which is comparable to wage rates on white farms in the Province [*Standing, Sender and Weeks*, 1996: 255] but well below rates in the 'formal' economy, which start at about R400 per month. Some plot-holders also provided their workers with meals, as well as with a bag or two of produce at the end of the harvest, so the effective wage rates were probably somewhat higher than the above figures would suggest. Rates for piece-work, such as weeding or harvesting a single crop bed, were generally in the range of R25–40, for what could be two to four days' work. Daily rates ranged from R7 to R10. Reports were received of Mozambican refugees and Zimbabwean migrants at Tshiombo being paid even less than this, or just provided with food, but none were encountered during the survey. One plot-holder reported that she occasionally had to pay her workers in kind (that is, a share of the harvest) when she was unable to find a buyer for her crops but added that this form of payment was generally not acceptable to workers.

Opinion was divided amongst labour-employing plot-holders regarding the relative merits of male and female labour. Women tended to be paid somewhat less than men (typically R120–180 per month) and outnumbered male workers by two to one, but many plot-holders considered men to be more effective workers. The highest paid agricultural worker encountered was a man, employed all the year around, who earned R300 per month.

Six agricultural workers – four women and two men – were interviewed in the course of the study. None had any land on the irrigation scheme, although four lived at Tshiombo. One elderly woman said her late husband had his own plot many years ago, but had given it up because it was too dry. Another young man reported that his parents had moved to Tshiombo after the scheme had started and had not received a plot because the village headman considered them 'outsiders', but he was hopeful of obtaining a plot of his own in the near future.

Households hiring labour tended to differ from the rest of the sample in a number of ways, particularly in terms of the size of arable land and crop income, as shown in the following table.

TABLE 7.5
CHARACTERISTICS OF HOUSEHOLDS WITH/WITHOUT HIRED LABOUR

	Household With Hired Labour (n=31)	Households Without Hired Labour (n=52)
Average Size of Holding (Ha)	3.66	1.92
Average Off-farm Income (monthly) (R)	919	844
Average Crop Income (R)	7,715	2,940

Households hiring labour had, on average, almost twice as much land (on and off the irrigation scheme) and over twice the crop income as those which did not hire labour. There were, however, a number of notable exceptions to this general pattern, as amongst those employing labour were households with only a single plot and households with no source of off-farm income (but not both). Not surprisingly, eight out of the ten largest land-holders in the sample employed labour, as did eight out of the top ten crop-producers. Households hiring labour had only marginally more off-farm income than those not hiring and, of these, the majority (21 out of 31) had themselves a member in (off-farm) wage employment. Seven more had only pension income to supplement what they earned from agriculture, and three households employing labour were entirely dependent on agriculture for their livelihood. Two women pensioners depended entirely on a hired labourer to work their plots on their behalf, and three women employed by the government on the irrigation scheme (two as office cleaners and one as a general worker on the Research Station) employed full-time labourers (two of them men) but also worked on their plots themselves in their spare time.

No clear relationship could be identified between household size and the use of hired labour. Households hiring labour ranged in size from one to 14 persons, and those not hiring were similarly diverse. Attempts were made to estimate available household labour per household, but these did not prove satisfactory due to the multiple responsibilities of many household members, and the difficulties of determining why certain members of the household who appeared to be 'available' did not, in fact, make any contribution to agricultural production.

Within households, the most common agricultural tasks – cultivation, planting, weeding, irrigating, harvesting – were generally shared between the sexes, although not necessarily equally. A number of specific tasks, notably the highly laborious process of picking groundnuts from their stalks, appeared to be almost entirely performed by women and children. Ploughing, the task most commonly associated with men in southern Africa, has effectively been removed from the control of the household with the advent of hired tractors (themselves owned and operated exclusively by men). In the two households in the survey where ploughing was done using animal traction, this work was carried out by men. Men also tended to dominate ancillary agricultural activities, such as buying inputs, transporting produce to market or to the mill and arranging for the hire of tractors, but in households where the plot-holder was a woman, she generally took responsibility for such matters. Two male farmers insisted that their wives had no role in the fields and were engaged only in domestic work.

Children make a considerable contribution to agriculture at Tshiombo, but again it was difficult to quantify this and many plot-holders (male and female) insisted that their children did not (and should not) work in the fields while they were still at school. It was clear from observations, however, that children did make a contribution to household labour on most plots during key points in the agricultural cycle, particularly at planting and harvest time, and women plot-holders, especially those without a husband, appeared to make greater use of children's labour than men.

7.5 METHODS OF PLOUGHING AT TSHIOMBO

The intensive use of farm machinery is one of the principal factors that distinguishes state-sponsored projects such as Tshiombo from agriculture in other parts of Venda. Since the beginning of the scheme, ploughing services have been provided by the state, latterly by the Venda (now Provincial) Department of Public Works, using tractors and drivers based permanently on the scheme. It was widely reported that the state service had deteriorated severely in recent years and that plot-holders were obliged to turn increasingly to the hire of privately-owned tractors. The parastatal agricultural corporation, Agriven, which maintains its own fleet of tractors, has also been offering these for hire at Tshiombo in recent years, particularly from the Farmer Support Programmes at Khakhu and Mashamba. None of the households in the survey had a working tractor of their own, but two plot-holders possessed old tractors which they said they could not afford to repair.

Soil preparation by tractor is usually done in two stages: ploughing and discing (harrowing). Each process is charged for separately by the various providers and a minority of plot-holders, especially those on sandier soils, use only the ploughing service, preferring to harrow using animal draught and their own implements. No evidence could be found of plot-holders using any form of machinery for planting, weeding, harvesting, or application of fertiliser.

TABLE 7.6
PRINCIPAL METHODS OF PLOUGHING AT TSHIOMBO

Method	Number of Households	Percentage of Households
Private hire tractor	59	71.1
Government tractor	18	21.7
Animal draught	2	2.4
Hand-hoe	1	1.2
Nil	3	3.6

Note: 'Government tractor' includes Departmental and Agriven services.

The household survey found that over 90 per cent of plot-holders had used hired tractors for ploughing in the previous season (that is, summer 1994/95) and, of these, less than a quarter had used the government service, as shown in Table 7.6 (above).

Various explanations were offered for the decline in the government service, but most pointed to a general collapse in the homeland administration in the period after 1990. For the tractor service at Tshiombo, this meant acute shortages of spare parts, lengthy delays in effecting repairs and, most definitively of all, periodic shortages of diesel, all of which kept the tractors out of operation for months at a time. Difficulties in obtaining tractors for ploughing were amongst the leading problems reported by plot-holders in the survey, second only to the shortage of irrigation water (see Chapter 8).

The decline in the state ploughing service in recent years has meant that plot-holders have been subjected to considerable additional expense and frequent disruptions of production, but it has created opportunities for some local entrepreneurs. Over the last four years, at least eight individuals at Tshiombo (but none in the survey sample) have acquired tractors and begun offering them for hire on the irrigation scheme. Private tractor-owners charged considerably more than the government rates and were widely criticised by plot-holders for using inappropriate implements and unskilled drivers. The charge for government tractors (including Agriven) was R137 per plot for ploughing and R79 for discing, while that for private tractors was between R150 and R240 for ploughing and R120 for discing. Both charged proportionately less for single beds. At least one man with a team of donkeys, from outside Tshiombo, was offering ploughing and harrowing services for R10 each per bed (R120 per plot), but this was not being used by any of the plot-holders in the sample.

The unreliability of the state tractor service was compounded for plot-holders by its charging policy – customers were required to pay in advance (at the time of booking) and were not refunded or compensated if services did not materialise. When this happened, plot-holders were often not in a position to pay a second time (and at a higher rate) for a private tractor, and even those who could afford to pay again often chose not do so, effectively gambling on the government tractor showing up before the planting season was over. Every plot-holder interviewed at Tshiombo reported some delays in planting over the last three years due to problems in obtaining tractors and a number had missed out completely on certain crops for a whole season. One plot-holder, who had paid for a government tractor and could wait no longer for it to arrive, reported that he had tilled two beds by hand, while another had hired a team of donkeys to plough a portion of her land for the first time in many years.

Despite the problems of recent years, plot-holders at Tshiombo greatly preferred the Departmental tractors over the private operators, due to the higher skills of their drivers and the lower (that is, subsidised) prices they charged. Agriven tractor services were also rated highly by the plot-holders, but, as their principal commitment is to Agriven projects, they are only available to other farmers for limited periods and cannot meet the demand from plot-holders at Tshiombo.

By June 1995, fuel supplies had been restored for the government tractors and by May 1996, three tractors belonging to the Department of Works were in operation on the scheme. The general opinion amongst plot-holders, however, was that at least ten tractors, each with a full set of implements, would be required to service the entire scheme adequately.

The use of draught animals, until recent decades the back-bone of African agriculture, appears to be reaching the final stages of extinction at Tshiombo. Ploughing with cattle or donkeys is not a skill shared by the younger generation of plot-holders and even households with livestock do not generally possess the specially-trained teams, or the implements and harnesses, required for effective ploughing. Starkey [1995: 70], however, found considerable use of animal traction in Venda and other parts of the Northern Province and suggests that donkeys have gradually replaced cattle, especially for ploughing, due to recurring drought and the limited amount of grazing available.

Only two households in the survey used animal traction on a regular basis – one a man in his sixties with three plots (Respondent No.54) who used a team of two oxen, the other a man in his seventies with two plots (Respondent No.1) who used a team of six donkeys. Both sets of animals were kept especially for ploughing purposes. The owner of the oxen stated that his animals required six months of training before they could be used in the field and had to be replaced every seven years. The owners reported themselves well-satisfied with the quality of ploughing, which they suggested was as good as what could be achieved with a tractor, especially in sandy soil. One of these men earned additional income by hiring out his donkey team to other plot-holders, but insisted that this was on a very small scale, 'just a few beds' in a year. Five other plot-holders reported that they occasionally used cattle or donkey traction for the final stages of soil preparation (harrowing), as it was cheaper and more effective than using a tractor. As far as could be established, animal traction was not used for weeding or other post-planting operations anywhere on the scheme.

7.6 AGRICULTURAL INPUTS AND PRODUCTION COSTS

Information on the volumes and types of purchased inputs used by plot-holders provides insight to two areas of interest: the commercialisation (or market integration) of agriculture (in terms of backward linkages) and its technical sophistication. The Tshiombo household survey dealt with three categories of inputs – fertiliser, seeds (including seedlings) and agro-chemicals (pesticides) – and respondents were asked how much of each they used, of what types and where they purchased them. It was found that every plot-holder who had planted a crop in the last year (80 out of 83) had purchased and used at least one of these inputs.

Fertiliser

Chemical (that is, inorganic) fertilisers have gradually been adopted by plot-holders at Tshiombo and today the vast majority use them on at least some of their crops. In the household survey, 91.6 per cent of plot-holders reported that they had used chemical fertiliser in the past year and over two-thirds (69.9 per cent) indicated that they had used close to the quantities (and types) recommended by their Agricultural Officer.[6] Various formulas of mixed (or aggregate) fertiliser (N-P-K) were applied at planting time, most commonly *2-3-2*, *2-3-1* and *3-2-1*. For most parts of the scheme, extension officers were advising the use of approximately 500 kg of mixed fertiliser per hectare at planting, but plot-holders applied anywhere between 250 kg and 1000 kg.[7]

Approximately three-quarters of plot-holders applied a second application of fertiliser as top dressing on some or all of their crops, usually *KAN* (calcium ammonium nitrate) or, in a handful of cases, urea, typically using approximately half the quantities applied at planting.

Sample prices of fertiliser at Tshiombo Co-operative in April 1996 were as follows (50 kg bags in all cases):

KAN 28	*R53.39*
Superphosphate 10.5	*R43.25*
Urea 46%	*R78.61*
3.2.1 (25) with 0.5% Zn	*R59.00*

Organic fertiliser (animal manure) was used by only a minority of plot-holders in the survey (26, or 31.3 per cent) and was not used by all those keeping livestock. Kraal manure, either from donkeys or cattle, was used by 23 households and three used chicken manure. Just over half of the plot-holders using manure (14 out of 26) obtained it from their own kraals, four bought it from neighbours and eight obtained if from neighbours or relatives free of charge. Typical rates charged were in the range R50–100 for a bakkie-load of manure, or R200–300 for the whole contents of a kraal.

While animal manure was rated highly as a fertiliser by those using it, only one plot-holder in the survey relied exclusively on it, all the others combining it with chemical fertiliser. Of those plot-holders not using animal manure, a few said they would use it if they could obtain it cheaply, but most did not consider it a priority. One younger farmer was strongly opposed to the use of kraal manure, saying that it introduced excessive amounts of river grasses and other weeds to the arable plots.

Seed

As with fertiliser, the use of purchased seed has gradually become established at Tshiombo. Many plot-holders, however, remain unconvinced of the superiority of the purchased varieties and even those plot-holders using purchased seed for one crop did not necessarily use it for all the crops they grew.

A majority of plot-holders in the survey (69.9 per cent) had purchased maize seed in the previous year, but less than half of these (27 out of 58) used it for their entire crop. All the others said they had mixed it with retained seed (from past harvests), in various proportions. Many of the plot-holders not using purchased maize seed said they had done so at some time in the past, but did not buy it every year. Maize seed (*Pioneer 64*) was on sale at Tshiombo Co-operative for R10.50 per kg.

Tomatoes and cabbage were grown mainly from purchased seed, but a number of the larger tomato-growers reported buying seedlings from nurseries in the Tzaneen area (100 km to the south). Sweet potatoes were generally grown from 'runners', either produced on the plot or, in the case of plot-holders planting half a hectare or more, purchased from (white) farmers in the Levubu area. Groundnuts, china spinach and *muxe* were all grown entirely from retained seed. The exchanging of seed (and seedlings) was one of the few inter-household agricultural activities reported in the survey, with many women, in particular, saying they exchanged seedlings – such as cabbage, tomatoes and sweet potatoes – with other plot-holders.

Agro-Chemicals

The use of agro-chemicals (insecticides and fungicides) was less widespread than other types of purchased inputs. Many plot-holders did not appear to have a good understanding of these products, or said they could not afford them. While the price of inputs generally was the subject of frequent complaint throughout the survey, plot-holders tended to treat fertiliser as a higher priority than pesticides. Overall, 71.1 per cent of plot-holders surveyed reported using pesticides on at least one crop over the previous twelve months, although in many cases the amount used was well below the levels recommended by the suppliers and the extension officers.

The most commonly used sprays were the insecticide *Nuvacron 400 SL,* which was used against bagrada bugs in cabbage, stalk-borer in maize and red spider mites in tomatoes, and the fungicide *Bravo 500* which was used against blight on tomatoes. Various granular preparations were used against cutworm and stalkborer in maize, but little specific information on pest control was collected. No weed-killer (herbicide) was used by plot-holders in the survey.

Other pests mentioned by plot-holders, against which they had very little remedy, were river rats, bush pigs and termites.

Source of Inputs

Tshiombo is highly unusual, in Venda and in the former homeland generally, in that it possesses a functioning farmers' co-operative that is actually owned and run by the members, as opposed to by the state (see Chapter 5). The co-operative carries a supply of the basic goods required by farmers, such as fertiliser, seed, pesticides, hand-tools, sacks and boots, as well as a limited range of household requisites, including tinned food, toiletries, candles and cooking utensils. Although it carries only a fraction of the range of the white farmer co-operatives in surrounding districts, and is not particularly cheap, the ready availability of basic goods at a convenient location makes Tshiombo Co-operative very popular with households in the area.

Plot-holders in the survey were asked what was their principal source of purchased agricultural inputs and what other sources they had used during the previous year. Three-quarters of respondents (75.9 per cent) reported that they used the Tshiombo Co-operative as their main source of purchased agricultural inputs, 18.1 per cent used the NTK store at Shayandima and just two plot-holders (2.4 per cent of the sample) reported that they used the Agriven store at Makonde. Price was the most common reason given for purchasing from outside Tshiombo, but a comparison of prices in all three outlets revealed little overall difference. The wider range of goods, agricultural and household, available at NTK, however, and its proximity to Thohoyandou and the Shayandima roller mills, may make it a more attractive proposition for some plot-holders, especially those with their own transport. The availability of credit facilities at NTK during the 1994/95 season is also likely to have been a factor in attracting customers from Tshiombo (see below).

A minority of plot-holders (10.8 per cent) stated that they supplemented purchases from the above sources with occasional purchases from specialist suppliers, particularly of seeds and seedlings. Three respondents reported that they had purchased tomato seed directly from the canning factory at Makhado during the previous year, while six had bought seedlings (tomatoes and sweet potatoes) from nurseries in the 'white' farming districts of Tzaneen, Moketsi, Levubu and Louis Trichardt. All were amongst the ten top producers in the sample (by value of agricultural output).

Production Costs

Having considered the main categories of inputs, it is possible to construct some sample budgets for crop production at Tshiombo. The following examples, drawn from specific holdings in the sample, illustrate typical costs associated with four of the main crops grown at Tshiombo. Only the direct costs of production are included, with no allowance made for other costs such as labour, transport and annual plot rental (R12).

TABLE 7.7
PRODUCTION COSTS FOR ONE PLOT OF MAIZE (1.28 HA)

Item	Description	Price (R)
Ploughing	Private hire tractor	200
Discing	Private hire tractor	120
Seed	5 kg Pioneer 64	55
Fertiliser (first application)	400 kg 3.2.1	472
Fertiliser (top dressing)	200 kg KAN	214
Agro-chemicals	2.5 litres Nuvacron	89
	1kg cutworm powder	45
Total		1,190

A typical harvest of 1,500kg of maize could be sold as green mealies for between R3,000 and R5,000, a gross profit of between R1,810 and R3,810. Milling this quantity of maize meal (at R25 per 80kg and allowing for 20 per cent loss in weight), would cost an additional R375 and yield approximately 1,200kg of maize meal. The consumer price (that is, replacement value) of an equivalent amount of shop-bought maize meal would be R1,815 (based on the price of maize meal at Tshiombo Co-operative: R121 for 80kg), thus providing the producer with an effective saving (gross profit) of R260.

TABLE 7.8
PRODUCTION COSTS FOR ONE PLOT OF CABBAGE (1.28 HA)

Item	Description	Price (R)
Ploughing	Government tractor	137
Discing	Government tractor	79
Seed	30,000 seedlings	1,350
Fertiliser (first application)	300 kg 2.3.2	354
Fertiliser (top dressing)	200kg urea	314
Agro-chemicals	10 litres Nuvacron	358
Total		2,592

A good harvest of cabbage could be expected to produce 20,000 mature plants, worth about R10,000 on the local market. This would generate a gross profit of over R7,000.

TABLE 7.9
PRODUCTION COSTS FOR ONE BED OF SWEET POTATOES (0.1 HA)

Item	Description	Price (R)
Ploughing	Private hire tractor	15
Harrowing	Hired donkeys	10
Seed	5 bags seedlings	100
Fertiliser (first application)	50kg Superphosphate	44
Fertiliser (top dressing)	–	–
Agro-chemicals	–	–
Total		169

A typical bed of sweet potatoes could be expected to yield approximately 500kg, which could be sold locally for about R250. This represents a gross profit of R71.

TABLE 7.10
PRODUCTION COSTS FOR ONE BED OF TOMATOES (0.1 HA)

Item	Description	Price (R)
Ploughing	Government tractor	12
Discing	Government tractor	8
Seed	200g	60
Fertiliser (first application)	50 kg 2.3.2	59
Fertiliser (top dressing)	25 kg KAN	27
Agro-chemicals	2 litres Bravo	60
	2 litres Nuvacron	76
Total		302

One bed of tomatoes might be expected to yield between 1,000 and 2,000 kg, with a farm-gate price of between R400 and R800. This would produce a gross profit of between R100 and R500.

As these examples show, costs of production varied considerably between crops (and between plot-holders), as did the return on investment. In order to arrive at an estimate of crop income which could be included in the analysis of total household income, direct costs were deducted from total crop income to produce a figure for each household which will be referred to as 'Net Crop Income' (see Chapter 8). In cases where plot-holders could not be precise about production costs, a figure equivalent to 40 per cent of gross income from that crop was assumed, the median figure for costs reported by plot-holders in the sample. Net crop income for households in the sample thus ranged between zero and R24,000 and averaged R2,805. Only seven households (8.4 per cent) had a net crop income of R5,000 or more.

7.7 CREDIT

The vast majority of farmers at Tshiombo, as elsewhere in the former home-lands, do not have access to formal credit facilities, either through state or commercial sources. The Agriven parastatal did provide short-term credit through the Tshiombo Co-operative in the 1980s and early 1990s, granting a total of 1,353 loans in 1988/89 of R256 on average [*Murray, Biesenbach and Badenhorst*, 1989: 7]. This facility was withdrawn in 1991/92, however, in the face of widespread default following the severe drought of that year and amidst reports of major financial problems within the parastatal. The last entry in the accounts of Tshiombo Co-operative showing a sale on credit was in May 1991. Agricultural Officers at Tshiombo were of the opinion that agricultural production had suffered badly since the withdrawal of credit facilities by Agriven, an opinion shared by many of the farmers within the survey. Management at the Tshiombo Co-operative also reported that sales had dropped substantially as a result of this change in policy.

No evidence could be found of informal credit systems – money-lenders, communal savings schemes, goods on credit from local shops or the like – playing any significant role within agriculture at Tshiombo or elsewhere in Venda. This is in marked contrast to the extensive informal credit networks described by Cross [1988: 269] for KwaZulu, and by Fenyes and Groenewald [1985: 407] for Lebowa, based on personal contacts, 'stokvels' (informal savings associations) and Tribal Authorities (see Chapter 2).

During 1994/95, a limited volume of funds was made available by the South African Agricultural Credit Board (ACB) for the provision of seasonal loans to small farmers in the former homelands. In Venda, this was available only through NTK and was taken up by 153 farmers, of whom 25 were plot-holders at Tshiombo (Interview with NTK Management, Shayandima, April 1995). Of the 83 survey respondents at Tshiombo, four (4.8 per cent) had received credit under the ACB scheme, for amounts ranging from R5,000 to R14,000. Credit was used mainly to pay for tractor ploughing, fertilisers and irrigation equip-ment. One woman reported that she had used the money thus saved to pay off the final instalments on an irrigation pump which she was installing on waste land adjacent to the Mutale River, while others used it to employ additional labour. All four plot-holders in receipt of credit under the ACB scheme held at least two plots on the irrigation scheme (one held five) and three had also acquired substantial areas of waste land (five to ten hectares) in recent years. All expressed themselves satisfied with the amounts received and the terms of repayment. Just one plot-holder in the survey had actually become a member of NTK, which cost him R800 and entitled him to a five per cent discount on purchases. Interestingly, he was not amongst the plot-holders in receipt of ACB/NTK credit. None of the other plot-holders in the survey said they had access to agricultural credit of any sort. Although a majority of survey respondents had availed of Agriven's credit scheme when it was available through the Tshiombo Co-operative, credit in general seemed to have negative connotations for many of them. One farmer said there was widespread antagonism towards Agriven because it continued providing loans even when harvests were failing because of drought and then demanded repayment when farmers were not in a position to pay. Furthermore, farmers at Tshiombo, and elsewhere in Venda, were being pressured to repay their debts, 'unlike the whites, who had all their debts crushed by the government', a reference to the widespread debt relief extended to white farmers during the 1980s and 1990s. Many respondents had not heard of the NTK/ACB credit scheme at the time of interview and some expressed interest in finding out more about it. Others felt that the R5,000 minimum on offer at NTK was beyond their needs and their ability to repay. For reasons that could not be established at the time, this credit programme was not continued beyond the first year.[8]

In 1993, and again in late 1995 (after the household survey had been completed), drought relief funds were made available to plot-holders at Tshiombo (and elsewhere in the Province) in the form of vouchers that could be redeemed at any of the co-operatives in the region. Farmers were granted R800 for each hectare of irrigated land, and less for dryland, but farmers at Tshiombo complained that waste land did not qualify for relief as it was not formally registered in their names. In just two months, February and March 1996, the Tshiombo Co-operative traded goods worth R70,390 for vouchers alone, more than double the total turnover (excluding fuel) for the same period in any of the previous four years. NTK at Shayandima also reported exceptional sales as a result of the voucher scheme. Although drought relief vouchers were intended for agricultural inputs only, it would appear that they were spent on a wide range of agricultural and domestic goods, including staple foods. Even large plot-holders found the drought relief payments 'very welcome' and said they allowed them to extend the area under cultivation and to apply more fertiliser than would otherwise have been the case.

7.8 AGRICULTURAL EXTENSION SERVICE

A sizeable field staff is employed by the state to support farmers at Tshiombo and maintain the irrigation system, including a scheme superintendent, twelve agricultural extension officers, water bailiffs, tractor-drivers and mechanics, office-cleaners, a clerk and various tradesmen and labourers. Agricultural Officers are mainly concerned with giving advice to farmers on aspects of crop production, both in their fields and through organised training sessions when specific topics – such as pest control, or use of fertiliser – are addressed. They are also responsible for organising government tractor services on their Blocks and for preparation of monthly crop reports. Individual Officers showed varying degrees of initiative in dealing with the problems faced by plot-holders and, in some cases, helping them to access new markets. In 1996, for example, one Officer was co-ordinating contacts with tomato-buyers in Durban (see below), while another was promoting a variety of sweet potato, for which there was said to be a strong demand from buyers at the new wholesale vegetable market in Pietersburg. Another had arranged for tractors to come from Mashamba (90 km away) to plough at Tshiombo and had even arranged temporary accommodation for the drivers.

Participants in the household survey were asked to evaluate the extension service, both in terms of its training and information functions and its effectiveness in solving problems they encountered. Opinions in this area, as might be expected, were highly varied, ranging from outright condemnation of the extension officers to considerable praise for their work. While many people were critical of aspects of the service, nearly all made use of it, and the official support services were widely seen as an essential part of agricultural life at Tshiombo. In speaking with plot-holders, it often proved impossible to differentiate between opinions regarding the extension service itself and opinions of the broader management and operation of the scheme, particularly when it came to the supply of irrigation water and the availability of tractors.

Overall, roughly two-thirds of plot-holders in the survey (67.5 per cent) pronounced themselves satisfied with the extension service and one-third (32.5 per cent) were dissatisfied. In a number of cases there appeared to be strong personal antagonisms between farmers and Officers and, in others, farmers claimed that the Officers were poorly trained or 'only fit for clerical duties'. Many older men felt that the Officers were of assistance to younger farmers and to women, but had little to offer more experienced farmers like themselves. The most common source of dissatisfaction, however, was that Agricultural Officers did not visit the plots on a regular basis, but as with other criticisms, this varied considerably from Block to Block (that is, from Officer to Officer).

The Agricultural Officers also had a number of criticisms regarding the management of the scheme and the conditions under which they had to work. All of them complained of a lack of working materials, such as basic stationery and information leaflets for farmers. The few publications and charts on display in the Block offices appeared to come mainly from commercial suppliers of agricultural inputs rather than from within the government service. Other common complaints concerned the lack of in-service training for Officers and information on recent developments in agriculture, as well as a lack of specialist expertise at head office upon which they could draw. One Officer said that he relied mainly on the magazine *Farmers' Weekly* to guide him in his work. Communications were also a problem on the scheme, as the only telephone available to Officers was in the superintendent's office and they lost a considerable amount of time travelling the length of the scheme by taxi in order to make reports.

Officers were provided with houses on the scheme, but they complained about the lack of running water and electricity and the poor repair of the houses. A number preferred to commute daily from outside Tshiombo, which resulted in frequent delays and absence from work. Officers also appeared to spend an inordinate amount of time away from the scheme for meetings at head office, with payment of salaries alone necessitating all the Officers spending at least one day a month (but often more) in Thohoyandou. Overall, the problems associated with the extension service at Tshiombo are very similar to those found by Bembridge [1988] in the mid-1980s for the service in Venda as a whole.

7.9 CROP SALES AND MARKETING

The great majority of plot-holders at Tshiombo sell some portion of their agricultural produce every year and, for most, it is well over half their total output (by value). Even the largest producers, however, said that their first priority was to meet their household food needs, and the proportion of crops sold tended to rise in line with total output. Households with relatively smaller holdings and lower output generally consumed some or all of every crop grown, but larger producers spoke of growing particular crops, such as green mealies, cabbage and chillies, specifically for sale.

Crop sales are overwhelmingly through what can be called informal (that is, unrecorded) channels, in the form of direct sales to the public in and around Tshiombo, and to traders who visit the plots and plot-holders' homes. Non-monetised transactions are rare, although payment of labourers with a share of the harvest was said to occur occasionally and three plot-holders in the survey reported bartering tomatoes and sweet potatoes for maize in the dryland areas north of Tshiombo. The most important destination for marketed produce from Tshiombo, and indeed from much of Venda, is the Sibasa-Thohoyandou complex, whether brought there by the producers themselves or by merchants. Smaller markets operate in surrounding villages and at taxi halts in places such as Makonde and Mutale, while individual stalls are to be found at the road-side at Tshiombo and at various points along the tar road in the direction of Donald Fraser Hospital.

A minority of plot-holders in the survey (15, or 18.1 per cent) reported that they had sold nothing at all over the previous twelve months, but this included three plot-holders who had not actually produced anything. Four stated that they generally produced only for domestic consumption, five reported that their crops had failed completely in the year in question (this may have been a slight exaggeration in some cases) and three said they had not sold anything because they had produced less than expected due to a shortage of irrigation water. Eleven out of this group of twelve were located on Blocks Three and Four, the dryer parts of the irrigation project, and none produced crops worth more than R1,000 over the year.

The most important crops marketed at Tshiombo (in terms of value and the number of households involved) are tomatoes, sweet potatoes, groundnuts, cabbage and china spinach. As noted above, the most commonly grown crop – summer maize – is largely intended for household consumption (mainly in the form of maize meal) although much of the winter maize harvest, and a smaller amount of the summer harvest, is sold as fresh cobs ('green mealies'). Less common crops grown largely for sale include onions, chilli peppers and beans.

Only a small minority of plot-holders (12 per cent) sold any produce via 'formal' channels during the year in question (1994/95). This involved selling tomatoes to the canning factory at Makhado or mangoes to achar (pickle) factories at Shayandima and Levubu, or, in just two cases, selling chilli peppers on the Johannesburg morning market (see below). For most of these households, the volumes sold via formal channels represented a relatively small part of total marketed produce, and all sold some produce through informal channels as well. A number of respondents mentioned selling maize to the NTK mill during the 1970s and 1980s, but none had done so in recent years. The remaining 58 plot-holders who sold produce did so through informal channels only, as shown in the following table.

The most important formal marketing channel used is the sale of tomatoes to the Giants canning factory at Makhado. Established in the early 1980s, Giants purchases most of its raw materials from large-scale (that is, white) farmers in the Louis Trichardt and Messina districts, but also buys considerable quantities from farmers in Venda. Its main products are tomato paste for the fish canning industry in Namibia and the Cape, tomato powder and a range of canned vegetables.

TABLE 7.11
MARKETING CHANNELS USED BY PLOT-HOLDERS

Marketing Channel	Number of Plot-holders	Percentage of Plot-holders
Nil	15	18.1
Informal only	58	69.9
Formal channels	10	12.0

Most white farmers supplying to the factory grow crops on contract, planting an agreed area and receiving an agreed price for every tonne delivered, but Giants also buys unsolicited produce at prevailing (wholesale) market prices. For 1995/96, the factory was paying R300 per tonne delivered for tomatoes.

Management at Giants reported that they had agreed contracts with farmers in Venda in the past, but ceased this practice due to difficulties in enforcing the contractual obligations within the former homeland. It was their opinion that farmers in Venda were liable to divert their produce to the open market if prices were higher there, and tended to use the factory only as 'a buyer of last resort'. For a number of years the factory supplied small farmers (including plot-holders at Tshiombo) with tomato seed on credit, in order to encourage production, but this was abandoned when it was found that many of the farmers concerned did not deliver any produce to the factory, and the cost of the seed could not therefore be recovered (Interview with the Director, Giants Canning (Pty) Ltd., May 1996).

Giants' management confirmed that transport was a problem for many smaller suppliers (see below), who were exploited by private operators, and suggested that Agriven or local co-operatives could perform a valuable service by providing group transport for farmers at cost price. The factory itself had only four eight-tonne trucks and was not in a position to serve all its suppliers. Moreover, the Director did not believe that tomato production was a viable commercial option for small-scale farmers, who, he said, tended to obtain yields of less than 20 tonnes per hectare, as compared to between 60 and 90 tonnes achieved by large-scale farmers outside Venda. Attempts were made by the company to interest local farmers and the Department of Agriculture in other high-value crops, such as gooseberries and green beans, but these were reported to have met with little success.

Plot-holders at Tshiombo had a number of complaints about the experience of selling to the canning factory, particularly the low prices paid. None of the farmers interviewed had grown produce on contract and many had been unaware of the prices being paid by the factory when they sent their produce there. Plot-holders were paying private truck-owners up to R100 per tonne for delivery, more than twice the rate charged by the factory-owned trucks, which severely eroded their earnings. Survey respondents were also highly critical of the system of payment, whereby they were paid only at the end of the season, by cheque, when many were in urgent need of cash and did not have bank accounts. Other complaints centred on what people saw as the unfair purchasing policy of the factory – in one instance, a large, shared, truckful of tomatoes was said to have been rejected by the factory because one farmer's produce was of poor quality. Overall, it was clear that many plot-holders did not fully understand the system used by the factory and felt cheated when they ended up with what they considered to be extremely small payments at the end of the year.

As an alternative, a group of Agricultural Officers at Tshiombo arranged for a canning plant in Durban to send trucks to Tshiombo for tomatoes, which is somewhat ironic considering that Durban is over 1000km away and Makhado is only 80km. This arrangement was said to have begun in 1992 and was much favoured by the producers, both because of the prices offered and the prompt method of payment. Tomatoes were purchased for R11 per 25 kg crate in May 1996 (R440 per tonne), with no transport costs to the producer. This compares with a net amount of between R200 and R270 per tonne obtainable from Giants (depending on the amount deducted for transport). Moreover, the buyers from Durban paid cash directly to the farmers at the time of purchase and the deal was completed in a single transaction, rather than leaving them waiting many months for a cheque. No further details could be obtained about these buyers, but over a quarter of plot-holders in the sample said they had sold tomatoes to them during the previous year.

Only six households in the survey reported selling mangoes to the Mango Man achar factory at Shayandima (Thohoyandou), although a number of others said they had done so in the recent past. The prices paid by the factory – R200 to R300 per tonne – made such sales unattractive to anyone without their own transport, and most producers preferred to sell their mango crop to hawkers or to consume it within the household. The only other formal marketing channel used by plot-holders at Tshiombo was to send produce to the Johannesburg Morning Market (at City Deep mine) via a commercial transport company based at Levubu. Only two households in the survey had used this method to sell chillies during the previous year, but others said they had tried it in the past for both chillies and cabbage. All were dissatisfied with the experience, as they had no knowledge of prevailing market prices and the actual prices obtained sometimes failed to cover even the cost of transportation.

Informal crop-marketing takes a number of forms. At its most basic, it involves carrying small volumes, on the head or in wheel-barrows, for sale at the roadside at Tshiombo. Moving up the scale somewhat, plot-holders with their own vehicle, or the means to hire one, may transport produce to neighbouring villages, or to larger markets in Thohoyandou and Sibasa, for sale to hawkers or directly to the public. Probably the most important form, however, is selling to merchants (wholesalers) or hawkers (small-scale retailers) in the fields. One farmer, located close to the main road, explained that he 'advertises' by word of mouth when his crops are ready, and hawkers who know him come to his plot for cabbage and tomatoes. Hawkers, generally women, buy as much produce as they can carry and take it to roadside stalls, to their home villages, or to Thohoyandou market for sale to the public. Larger dealers, from Thohoyandou and Giyani (Gazankulu), usually have their own van or truck, and may buy up to four tonnes of produce at a time, for sale to shops and hawkers over a wide area. The biggest dealers frequently buy an entire crop from a number of plot-holders.

Surprisingly few plot-holders were themselves engaged in the buying and selling of produce – just three survey respondents described themselves or members of their households as hawkers, or reported buying produce from other plot-holders for resale. In addition, one plot-holder said that he hired a vehicle two or three times a year to sell his own produce in Thohoyandou and Giyani, while another occasionally brought produce to Louis Trichardt or to Johannesburg in her son's taxi. Another woman reported that she sent produce for sale in Johannesburg every two months with a returning migrant worker.

Overall, producers attempt to combine these marketing methods as best they can, and those with their own means of transport are obviously in a stronger position to take advantage of the full range of market opportunities. While demand for produce at Tshiombo generally appeared to be good, a number of plot-holders, mainly on the upper reaches of the scheme (Blocks One and Two), furthest from the main road, reported problems with disposing of their produce, saying that the hawkers were unreliable and often failed to come as far as their plots. After the heavy rains of 1995/96 in particular, many plot-holders complained of a glut of tomatoes and cabbage on the scheme, and much of the crop was left to rot in the fields.

7.10 TRANSPORT

Various forms of transport are used to move goods to and from plots at Tshiombo. There is reasonable vehicular access to most plots, via dirt tracks, but a number of plots close to the Mutale are accessible only by foot during the wet season. The maximum distance from any plot to the main gravel road is about two kilometres and the distance to the nearest tar road, at Makonde, is between one and ten kilometres (see Map 3).

Plot-holders in the survey were asked to list the main forms of transport they used in connection with agriculture over the course of the year and the results are shown Table 7.12 (below).

Private hire of vehicles – typically a one-tonne *bakkie* (pick-up truck), and less commonly a four-tonne 'half-truck' – was the most common form of transport used. Over one-third of households (36.1 per cent) reported that they had hired a vehicle at some time during the previous twelve months, mostly to take produce to markets at Sibasa or Thohoyandou, or to take maize to the mill at Shayandima. Plot-holders also hired vehicles to bring produce from the fields to their homes, however, including some who did not actually sell any produce. The reported cost of hiring a one-tonne vehicle ranged between R20 and R40 for a single journey within Tshiombo and from R60 to R100 per journey to Sibasa or Thohoyandou. Transport was said to be a major problem by roughly a quarter of plot-holders (24.1 per cent), who either found it prohibitively expensive or experienced difficulties in obtaining a vehicle during periods of peak demand.

TABLE 7.12
PRINCIPAL FORM OF TRANSPORT USED BY PLOT-HOLDERS AT TSHIOMBO

Form of Transport	Number of Plot-Holders	Percentage of Plot-Holders
Foot/Barrow	26	31.3
Public Transport	1	1.2
Hired Vehicle	30	36.1
Own Vehicle	26	31.3
Total	83	100

Less than one-third (31.6 per cent) of plot-holders in the survey had regular access to a vehicle within their household. In many of these cases, the vehicles concerned were used by family members in other lines of work, or belonged to their employers, and were only available to plot-holders at weekends. Of the 26 plot-holders with access to a vehicle, only two reported hiring it to other plot-holders from time to time (charging R30 for a journey within Tshiombo) and one used his bakkie to sell vegetables in neighbouring villages.

Another substantial group of plot-holders (31.6 per cent) did not use any vehicle during the year. Most of these relied on hawkers to come and collect produce directly from their plots. Others transported produce on their head, or by wheel-barrow, to the gravel road for sale to the passing trade, or to their own homes for consumption. Only a single plot-holder reported using public transport (bus and taxi) to take produce to Thohoyandou for sale, although a steady stream of women hawkers come from Thohoyandou by mini-bus taxi in order to purchase produce.

Plot-holders with relatively high crop output tended to own their own vehicle and those who did not generally hired one as required. Smaller producers tended to rely more on hired vehicles, if they could afford them. Of those with the smallest holdings (that is, just one plot), less than a quarter owned their own vehicles, slightly more hired on occasions, but half did not use any form of vehicle throughout the course of the year. Access to a vehicle also tended to be correlated with the sex of plot-holders: 37.5 per cent of men had access to a vehicle within the household, compared to 22.9 per cent of women. None of the five households without an adult male member possessed their own vehicle.

7.11 AGRICULTURAL DIFFERENTIATION

No single factor, or set of factors, explains the wide differentials in the value of crop output found amongst households in the survey sample, although size of land-holding, choice (and area) of crops and the sex of plot-holders would all appear to play a part. Not surprisingly, larger land-holders tended to produce more than smaller ones, although there were important exceptions to this pattern, as will be shown. Plot-holders with relatively high output also tended to concentrate on higher-value crops, such as tomatoes and green maize, and to plant larger areas of each crop, typically from half a hectare upwards. Smaller producers, especially those with a relatively good supply of water, tended to produce just as wide a range of crops as larger ones, but usually limited production to one or two beds of each crop. They also gave more emphasis to crops with relatively low market value and low production costs, such as *muxe* and sweet potatoes, of which a relatively high proportion were consumed within the household.

Plot-holders with relatively high value of crop output tended to be men, usually in their fifties or sixties. The sex of plot-holders cannot, however, be separated from other factors, particularly the size of land-holdings: women plot-holders had, on average, only 70 per cent as much land as men and produced roughly half the value of crops. Men were also in a much stronger position with regard to their ability to command household labour. Virtually all the male plot-holders in the sample were able to draw on the labour of their wives and other women in their households, whereas most women plot-holders received only minimal assistance from their husband (if they had one) or other men in their households.

For larger producers, many of whom had relatively low off-farm income, agriculture was effectively self-financing, with the income from one year's production being invested in the next. Smaller producers tended to consume a higher proportion of their produce and, therefore, relied more on transfers from other income-generating activities to finance agricultural production. Larger producers (and larger land-holders) were also more likely to hire labour, although some near-average producers with relatively small holdings also hired labour. In these latter cases, hired labour was not used as a means of expanding the area under cultivation, as it appeared to be for the larger land-holders, but as a way in which plot-holders (particularly women) with access to regular wage income could generate some additional earnings and a supply of food for their household.

Considerable variation in marketing strategies was also evident between plot-holders in the sample. Larger producers were more likely to own their own vehicle and to make use of a range of formal and informal marketing opportunities over a wide geographical area. Smaller producers tended to have just one way of disposing of their produce, typically through selling to hawkers or to the passing trade at Tshiombo. With regard to one key factor of production, however, no difference could be found between large and small producers – both were overwhelmingly reliant on hired tractors for ploughing. It is possible that access to affordable tractor-ploughing by plot-holders, regardless of scale, has allowed many poorer households to sustain production under difficult circumstances, or to quit and re-commence agricultural production as resources allowed, and has thus kept the extent of differentiation between households below what might have been the case if tractors (or teams of draught animals) were in the hands of just a few. Indeed, relatively successful crop producers were found to be the biggest accumulators of livestock. Four out of the top six producers (below) owned at least ten head of cattle and two of these were also the largest owners of goats and chickens in the sample.

Some idea of the importance of these and other factors may be obtained by looking more closely at the top crop producers in the sample. Table 7.13 (below) summarises information on key aspects of agricultural production for the six plot-holders with crop output worth at least R10,000 for the year in question.

This group included the three largest land-holders in the sample (Nos.52, 55 and 81), each with between two and six plots on the irrigation scheme and between eight and ten hectares of waste land. These were also the biggest crop-producers, and Nos.52 and 81 each had almost double the output of any other plot-holder in the sample.

The land-holdings of the other three members of this group (Nos.5, 40 and 54) were far smaller: respondent No.5 had just one plot on the irrigation scheme, No.40 had two plots and No.54 had three.[11] None had any waste land.

Although they produced less (in value terms) than the other three in this group, their output per hectare was, in each case, substantially higher.

TABLE 7.13
TOP SIX CROP PRODUCERS

Respondent No.	05	40	52	54	55	81
Land Holding (Ha)	1.28	2.56	17.7	3.84	16.4	11.6
Age of Plot-holder	73	68	55	60	51	44
Off-farm Income (per month)[9]	430	430	860	0	430	4,000+
Household Size (persons)	5	13	16	6	14	8
Livestock Income (annual) (R)[10]	3,000	0	3,750	11,550	0	2,850
Labour Employed (no. of workers)	0	0	5	2	3	3
% of Land Used (annual)	100	100	80	100	75	70
Main Crops (by value)	Tomato Chilli Mango	Maize S. Potato Beans	Cabbage G.Nuts Maize	S.Potato Maize Tomato	Cabbage Maize Tomato	Cabbage Tomato Maize
Crop Income (annual) (R)	12,400	10,500	42,000	15,000	16,200	30,650
Crop Income per Hectare (R)	9,688	4,102	2,373	3,906	989	2642

This was particularly true of Respondent No.5, who had an income of almost R10,000 per hectare. This farmer made intensive use of his plot and obtained well above average yields across a range of crops, probably due in part to the position of his plot on Block One, close to the head of the irrigation channel. For the year 1994/95, he obtained 28 bakkie loads of tomatoes from six beds (with continuous harvesting over many months), which were sold to the canning factory at R230 per load – a total income of R6,440. Such a yield is far greater than those obtained by other plot-holders in the sample for the year in question, but is comparable to some of the figures reported for previous years. A further R2,280 was obtained from 'more than half a tonne' of chillies (from six beds), which were shipped to the Johannesburg morning market, and R2,400 from six bakkie loads of mangoes which were sold to the *achar* factor at Levubu. He also harvested 15 bags of maize from five beds (again well above the yields reported by other plot-holders), which were deposited at the NTK mill. Other crops grown were *muxe* (three beds) and sweet potatoes (also three beds), some of which were sold to hawkers directly from the field. Virtually all labour was supplied by the plot-holder himself, with occasional assistance from his wife and children. No hired labour was used.

All six of the plot-holders shown here concentrated on the production of either maize (summer and winter), tomatoes or cabbage, with smaller areas planted to sweet potatoes, groundnuts, chillies, beans and mangoes. None of the four largest land-holders grew less than half a hectare of any crop, with the largest areas (one to three hectares) being given over to maize, tomatoes, sweet potatoes and cabbage. Respondent No.54, for example, grew just four crops – maize, sweet potatoes, tomatoes and groundnuts – on his three irrigated plots (believing green vegetables to be a waste of time) and only ever planted whole plots (1.28 hectares) to a single crop. All of this group made exceptionally high use of their land over the course of the year, especially considering the location of most of them on the lower reaches of the irrigation scheme. The three smaller land-holders in the group (Nos.5, 40 and 54) used all of their land in both winter and summer seasons, while the larger land-holders used between 70 per cent and 80 per cent over the year.

All the plot-holders in this group were men and all but one (No.81) were effectively full-time farmers, although Nos.5 and 40 were in receipt of pensions. Two others (Nos.52 and 55) had pensioners (but no wage-earners) within their households, leaving Number 54 as the only member of this group with no source of off-farm income. Respondent No.81 was exceptional in a number of ways, including his age (at 44 he was considerably younger than the rest of this group) and the fact that he was in full-time (local) employment as a school-teacher. His wife was also a teacher and his mother was in receipt of a pension, making this the highest earning household in the sample in terms of off-farm income. Indeed, it is striking that the three biggest producers in the sample, who were also the three biggest landholders, were all relatively young men (aged between 44 and 55 years), men 'in their prime' who had been able to acquire additional land and expand agricultural production well above the norm.

Households in this group varied considerably in size, ranging from five to 16 persons, but size did not appear to relate directly to the scale of crop output. Probably of greater importance was the role of hired labour, which was employed by the four largest plot-holders in this group and by five of the seven largest land-holders in the sample (that is, those with holdings greater than four hectares). The largest land-holder in the sample (and the largest producer of crops, No.52) employed five full-time workers all the year around, while Nos.55 and 81 (with 16.4 and 11.6 hectares respectively) both employed up to three workers for various periods during the year. In the case of the two top producers (Nos.52 and 81), the majority of labour was supplied by hired workers, as opposed to household members, but this was not true for most other households using hired labour.

Households in this group did not differ from the rest of the sample with regard to their dependence on hired tractors for ploughing, with the exception of No.54, who was the only plot-holder in the sample with his own team of plough-oxen. With three irrigated plots on the scheme, this farmer ploughed continuously throughout the year, and stated that he had reached the limits of his productive capacity using this method.

In terms of forward and backward linkages to agricultural markets, this group differed from the majority of households in the sample in a number of important ways. All owned their own vehicles and all combined a range of strategies to dispose of their produce, including sales to hawkers, sales into formal channels and use of markets outside the immediate Tshiombo area. Respondent No.52, for example, sold groundnuts to hawkers at his home, used his own bakkie to carry chillies to Levubu (40 km away) for trucking to Johannesburg and shared in the hire of an 8-tonne truck to take tomatoes to the factory in Makhado. In addition, all used purchased seed, fertiliser and pesticides (in varying quantities) and travelled to specialist suppliers outside Venda for at least some of their seeds and seedlings. Respondent No.55, for example, purchased tomato seed direct from the canning factory and travelled to the 'white' farming area of Levubu for cabbage seedlings and sweet potato runners. Smaller producers, by contrast, tended to be more dependent on retained seed and whatever varieties were available through the Tshiombo Co-operative.

The example of these larger producers, and the rest of the findings presented in this chapter, provides some indication of the range of agricultural activities on the Tshiombo scheme. The next chapter examines the position of agriculture within overall household livelihoods and discusses how some of the constraints affecting plot-holders might be addressed at the level of public policy.

NOTES

1. As agricultural production is liable to be interrupted at any point in the cycle, for a variety of reasons, the effective definition of land use applied throughout was 'land ploughed and seeded', regardless of whether a crop was actually harvested.
2. Crop names are those used by Agricultural Officers at Tshiombo for reporting purposes, and in official publications relating to Venda [e.g., *DBSA*, 1991].
3. Yield estimates for maize and other crops have been standardised as kg/hectare (or tonnes/hectare), although many households planted considerably less than this, some as little as two beds (0.2 ha) in a year.
4. Differences in planting times, in the supply of irrigation water, and in the resistance of crops to stress from heat and drought are amongst the possible explanations for the very different performances between crops, and between plot-holders, within the same season.
5. Even for maize, the producer price for grain (on local, informal markets) was effectively the same as the consumer price for maize meal, once the cost of milling was taken into consideration.
6. 'Close' in this case meant within 25 per cent of the amount recommended by the Block Agricultural Officer for the crops concerned. I am indebted to the Officers at Tshiombo for assisting me in this regard.
7. The amounts recommended by the Agricultural Officers were well above the amounts used by

small-holders in other parts of the country [*Marais*, 1989: 360; *Cairns and Lea*, 1990: 89].

8. Watkinson [1996: 80] refers to a credit scheme called the Agricultural Financial Assistance Programme (AFAP), part of the national government's Broadening Access to Agriculture Thrust (BATAT), which was introduced in 1995 and withdrawn in 1996 after investigation by the Auditor General. It would appear that this was the scheme under which credit was offered to farmers in Venda by NTK.

9. The recurrence of the figure R430 (and multiples thereof) is due to the prevalence amongst this group of persons with state old-age pensions, which paid this amount per month. The figure of R4,000 for household No.81 is possibly an underestimate, as precise details of salaries could not be obtained (see below).

10. For the sake of consistency, annual crop and livestock incomes are shown gross, that is, without any deduction for costs.

11. No convincing reason could be found as to why three of these plot-holders were located in close proximity on Block Three. Although the supply of irrigation water is generally not very favourable on this Block (see above), the topography of the scheme means that relatively large areas of waste land are to be found on the lower reaches, sizeable tracts of which have been acquired in recent years by Nos.52 and 55 (as well as by No.81, adjacent to Block Four).

8

Household Livelihoods and the Prospects for Development at Tshiombo

Chapters 5, 6 and 7 (above) have presented an overview of the Tshiombo irrigation scheme and the main findings of the household survey. This chapter analyses those findings further and examines the prospects for the further development of the local economy. It starts by addressing the central question of this thesis, the position of agriculture within household livelihoods, and draws some conclusions based on the evidence from the household survey. This is followed by a summary of plot-holders' opinions of the Tshiombo scheme and their priorities for reform. These findings, supported by interviews with key local informants and government officials, and direct observations from the field, then provide the basis for an evaluation of the current state of agriculture at Tshiombo and recommendations for public action.

8.1 ANALYSIS OF HOUSEHOLD INCOME

As shown above, households at Tshiombo obtain their livelihoods from three main sources – off-farm wages (from both migrant and local employment), pensions (largely state old age pensions) and agriculture (in cash and kind, from both crops and livestock). In previous chapters, each of these sources has been discussed separately and problems of data collection and data accuracy for each have been noted. This section combines data on these main types of income to produce estimates of total income for households in the survey. This involves a considerable degree of supposition and the use of imputed figures to fill various gaps in the data, as outlined above, but the objective is to focus on broad patterns of income, and differentiation between households, rather than on precise numerical results. Income data are correlated with other household characteristics, such as size of land-holding, household size and sex of plot-holder, in an attempt to understand the processes by which households obtain a livelihood and to explain the wide differences between households revealed by the survey.

Total household income was calculated by aggregating off-farm income (as discussed in section 6.3, above), net livestock income (section 6.8) and net crop income (section 7.6). Average household income (in cash and kind) for the survey sample was thus estimated at R13,825 per year, or R1,152 per month. A breakdown of this figure is shown in the following table.

TABLE 8.1
AVERAGE MONTHLY HOUSEHOLD INCOME AT TSHIOMBO

Source	Amount (R)	Percentage
Wages	443	38.4
Pensions	409	35.5
Crops	234	20.3
Livestock	46	4.0
Other	20	1.7
Total	1,152	100

Over a third of all income (38.4 per cent) came from wages (migrant and local) and slightly less (35.5 per cent) from pensions. Other non-agricultural income (craftwork, hawking and remittances from non-household members) accounted for a negligible 1.7 per cent of the total. Agricultural income made up the remaining quarter (24.3 per cent) of household income, of which about one sixth came from livestock and the balance from crops.

Per capita income for the sample was R1,804 per year (or R150 per month), which is somewhat below that found in some recent large-scale studies in South Africa. The Human Sciences Research Council's estimate of annual per capita income for Africans in South Africa in 1993 was R2,717, while the Bureau of Market Research put it at R2,415 for 1995 (both cited in SAIRR [1996: 279]. SALDRU [1994: 314] estimated annual income for Africans in the Northern Transvaal (Northern Province) to be R1,620 in 1993/94, and income for all rural Africans in South Africa to be R1,920. The relatively low figures for Tshiombo would appear to support the widely-held view that households in the Northern Province are significantly poorer than in other parts of the country, and that household income tends to be lower in rural than in urban areas (see Chapter 3).

In order to investigate the distribution of income between households in the sample, households were ranked in order of income and divided into quintiles (fifths), with the first quintile being composed of the highest earners and the fifth quintile composed of the lowest (Table 8.2). Each quintile was then analysed in terms of various characteristics, including household size, land-holding, sex of plot-holders and the relative contribution of agricultural income. Note that, in the discussion that follows, the category *Agricultural Income* is the sum of *Net Crop Income* and *Net Livestock Income* and the

Proportion of Income from Agriculture represents total agricultural income for the quintile expressed as a percentage of all income for that quintile.

TABLE 8.2
ANNUAL HOUSEHOLD INCOME AT TSHIOMBO, BY QUINTILES

Quintile	1st (n=17)	2nd (n=16)	3rd (n=17)	4th (n=16)	5th (n=17)	Total (n=83)
Average Income (R)	24,319	16,219	13,934	9,761	4,792	13,825
Average Off-farm Income (R)	18,064	12,772	11,322	7,328	2,781	10,463
Average Net Crop Income (R)	4,659	3,262	2,365	1,950	1,765	2,805
Av. Net Livestock Income (R)	1,596	184	247	484	246	557
Av. Agricultural Income (R)	6,255	3,446	2,611	2,434	2,011	3,361
Average Land-holding (ha)	3.4	3.0	2.1	1.8	2.5	2.6
Av. Household Size (Persons)	10.8	6.8	7.4	7.4	5.9	7.7
Ratio of M/F Plot-holders	100: 54	100: 77	100:89	100:100	100:54	100:73
Average Age of Plot-holders	57.8	62.8	62.5	52.5	55.0	58.1
Proportion of Income from(%) Agriculture	25.7	21.2	18.7	24.9	42.0	24.3

The distribution of income between households in the sample was found to be highly unequal. The top 20 per cent of households, with an average income of R24,319 per year, received 36 per cent of total income for the sample, while the bottom 20 per cent, with an average income of only R4,792 per year, received just 7.1 per cent. When differences in household size are taken into consideration, members of households in the top quintile still enjoyed a per capita income nearly three times greater than those in the bottom quintile.

Agricultural income contributed approximately a quarter (24.3 per cent) of total income for the sample, but analysis by income quintiles revealed that it was of much greater importance to the poorest households. While the top four quintiles obtained broadly similar proportions of their income from agriculture (18.7 to 25.7 per cent), the bottom (fifth) quintile obtained 42 per cent of its income from agriculture.[1] Better-off households still tended to obtain more income from agriculture than poorer ones in absolute terms, but in relative terms, agriculture was considerably more important as a source of livelihood for those with lowest income.

Male and female plot-holders (as discussed in section 6.4) were distributed relatively evenly between income quintiles. Thus, while it was argued above that women plot-holders tend to have less land, less livestock and less agricultural income than men, their households tend to be no poorer than those with a male plot-holder once all forms of income are taken into account.

It is clear from these figures that relative poverty equates with a lack of off-farm income. Of the 17 households in the bottom income quintile, none had a member in paid employment and only eight contained a pensioner. Five had a member engaged in some form of petty commodity production outside agriculture, or were in receipt of remittances from a non-household member (see 'Other Income', above), but this still left eight households with no source of off-farm income. All but three households in the bottom quintile obtained some income from agriculture but only one managed to earn as much as the average agricultural income for the sample as a whole. Of particular concern must be the five poorest households in the sample, each with an annual income of less than R3,000. All had a permanently-resident male plot-holder and none had any source of off-farm income. Despite being close to the sample average in terms of landholding and household size, the most any of these earned from agriculture was R2,600 over the year. There can be little doubt that such households lead a precarious hand-to-mouth existence and depend heavily on the support of family and neighbours.

Relative affluence, on the other hand, was associated with high levels of off-farm income but also, in a number of cases, with high agricultural income. Of the 17 households in the top quintile, 15 contained at least one man in paid employment (migrant or local) and five had a woman in paid employment as well. Pensions were another significant source of income: eight out of the 17 households contained two pensioners, seven contained one, and just two households in this quintile had no pension income. One household had a pensioner and no wage income, leaving just one household without any source of off-farm income.

The top quintile contained three of the four highest agricultural earners in the sample (Nos.52, 54 and 81), all with net agricultural income above R15,000, but also had nine households which earned less than R2,000, and agriculture did not contribute a high proportion of total household income in most cases. Twelve households obtained less than a quarter of their income from agriculture (including one with no agricultural income) and only two households obtained the majority of their income (73 per cent and 100 per cent, respectively) from agriculture. Although 11 of the plot-holders in the quintile were men, only two of them (Nos.52 and 54) were full-time farmers of working age (that is, between the ages of 21 and 64).

Agricultural Income

As shown above, agriculture contributed a relatively minor share of total income, 24.3 per cent over the entire sample, albeit with wide variations between households. In absolute terms, agricultural income ranged from zero to nearly R27,000 and averaged R3,361 per household. In relative terms, agriculture contributed anywhere between zero and 100 per cent of total household income and only 15 households (18.1 per cent of the total) obtained half or more of their income from agriculture.

In order to examine the distribution of agricultural income, households in the sample were ranked in order of agricultural income and again divided into quintiles, as shown Table 8.3 (below). It should be noted that the quintiles shown here represent very different groupings from those in Table 8.2 (above), although there is some overlap between the two (as discussed below).

As the following table shows, the distribution of agricultural income between households was highly skewed, even more severely than total income. The top 20 per cent of agricultural earners received over half (52.2 per cent) of all agricultural income for the sample, while the bottom 20 per cent received only 3.4 per cent.

TABLE 8.3
ANNUAL AGRICULTURAL INCOME AT TSHIOMBO, BY QUINTILES

Quintile	1st (n=17)	2nd (n=16)	3rd (n=17)	4th (n=16)	5th (n=17)	Total (n=83)
Average Agricultural Income (R)	8,565	3,668	2,491	1,422	566	3,361
Average off-farm Income (R)	7,687	12,300	11,612	9,495	11,273	10,463
Average Land-holding (Ha)	4.9	2.4	2.2	1.8	1.5	2.6
Average Net Crop Income (R)	6,529	3,300	2,294	1,312	529	2,805
Av. Net Livestock Income (R)	2,036	366	197	109	36	557
Average Total Income (R)	16,252	15,966	14,103	10,917	11,838	13,825
Av. Household Size (Persons)	8.8	8.3	7.6	7.3	6.3	7.7
Ratio of M/F Plot-holders	100:21	100:60	100:113	100:60	100:183	100:73
Average Age of Plot-holders	57.6	58.2	55.8	55.0	64.0	58.1
Proportion of Income from (%) Agriculture	52.7	23.0	17.7	13.0	4.8	24.3

It may also be seen that agricultural income does not show any direct correlation with off-farm income at the quintile level. This is most apparent for the bottom four quintiles, which show a sharp decline in agricultural income alongside a relatively even distribution of off-farm income. The exception to this pattern is the top (first) quintile, which shows the highest agricultural income and the lowest off-farm income. This is suggestive of some trade-off between agricultural and non-agricultural earnings, at least amongst the top group of producers, which may be related to the role of men in generating both agricultural and non-agricultural income. Despite the prevalence of extended family structures, most households contained only one man of working age (that is, 21–64). Having this individual engaged in paid employment tended to boost off-farm income considerably but depress agricultural income. Conversely, having him working full-time in agriculture tended to depress off-farm income and boost agricultural income. The returns from agriculture, however, were generally less than those from wage employment. Thus, for men to opt for a career as a farmer would appear to imply some drop in overall household income and it is not surprising that those who described themselves as full-time farmers tended to be over 50 years of age – that is, towards the end of their formal working life or in receipt of a pension. The great majority of men in their twenties, thirties and forties in the sample were in, or seeking, paid employment (see Chapter 6).

The relatively even distribution of off-farm income between quintiles means that disparities in agricultural income do not translate into wide differences in overall income. Indeed, the fifth quintile shown here has nearly three-quarters (72.8 per cent) as much income as the first quintile when all sources of income are taken into consideration. Once again, this is suggestive of some trade-off between agricultural and non-agricultural income. While a certain amount of off-farm income would appear to be necessary (in most cases) for households to achieve moderate (that is, average) levels of agricultural output, greater off-farm income does not necessarily translate into greater agricultural income. In other words, high agricultural income does not necessarily require high levels of off-farm income and the trade-off involved (in terms of loss of off-farm income) means that households with high agricultural income are not especially well-off. Thus, the average income for households in the top quintile in Table 8.3 (those with highest agricultural income) is substantially below that of households in the top quintile in Table 8.2 (those with highest overall income).

The importance of off-farm income to the ranking of households in Table 8.2, and of agricultural income to Table 8.3, means that the composition of both sets of quintiles was very different but there was some continuity between the two. Six households were in the top quintile in both tables, which meant they had relatively high agricultural income and sufficient off-farm income to give them a high overall income. At the opposite extreme, five households were in the bottom quintile in both tables, which meant they had very low agricultural income and little or no off-farm income, and were effectively destitute. Other households, with low off-farm income and relatively high agricultural income, moved from the lower quintiles in Table 8.2 to the higher quintiles in Table 8.3, and households with high off-farm income and low agricultural income moved the opposite way.

The composition of agricultural income also changed considerably between the quintiles shown in Table 8.3. The top quintile obtained 23.8 per cent of its agricultural income from livestock, and the balance from crops, but none of the other four quintiles obtained more than ten per cent from livestock. Thus we can say that households with high agricultural income achieved this largely due to their greater crop income but also because they were particularly dominant in terms of livestock. In fact, three-quarters of all livestock income (74.9 per cent) accrued to the top quintile shown, as compared to a negligible 1.3 per cent to the bottom quintile.

The disparities in agricultural income between male and female plot-holders, discussed above, are again apparent from the quintile distribution (Table 8.3). Women were concentrated in the lower quintiles, especially the very bottom group, while the top quintile was heavily dominated by men. The average age of plot-holders differed little amongst the top four quintiles (from 55 to 58 years), but was substantially higher in the bottom quintile (64 years). While older plot-holders would appear to earn less from agriculture than younger ones, the importance of pensions and other source of off-farm income means that (relative) poverty is not a problem of the elderly in particular. This is also apparent from Table 8.2, where the two bottom quintiles (those households with the lowest overall income) had the lowest average age of plot-holder. Finally, agricultural income would appear to be weakly correlated with household size, which tends to support the earlier suggestion that high agricultural output is more likely to be achieved through the use of hired labour than by the presence of a large household.

Overall, it is clear that there are wide differences in income between the households in the sample and this is largely due to differential access to off-farm income (wages and pensions). The distribution of agricultural income is also highly uneven, but does not correlate with off-farm income and so does not greatly exacerbate income differentials between households. On the basis of this analysis, it is possible to identify two distinct groups for which agriculture has particular significance – very poor households, who depend heavily on agriculture (due to a lack of off-farm income), and the most successful farmers, who combine high agricultural earnings with below-average off-farm income to achieve relatively high income overall.

8.2 PRIORITIES FOR REFORM AT TSHIOMBO

Essential to any evaluation of agriculture at Tshiombo, or discussion of the prospects for reform, are the views of plot-holders themselves. This section presents one final set of survey findings which have not previously been discussed, concerning plot-holders' perceptions of the scheme and their opinions on how the local agricultural economy should be developed. These findings provide a basis for the discussion of the possibilities and problems of reform that follows.

Survey respondents were asked to identify the three main problems they faced in trying to gain a livelihood from agriculture. Of the 83 plot-holders in the sample, six stated that they did not have any problems, or did not wish to answer this question, 43 provided only one or two responses, while 34 were able to name three issues of concern to them. Responses to this question were dominated by two issues: the supply of water for irrigation and the state of the government tractor service. An array of other issues came far behind, the most common being the high cost of agricultural inputs, matters relating to land tenure and availability and the limited local market for agricultural produce. The following table shows the frequency with which these issues were raised, broken down by respondents' location on the irrigation scheme.

TABLE 8.4
MAIN PROBLEMS EXPERIENCED BY PLOT-HOLDERS AT TSHIOMBO, BY BLOCK

	Block 1 (n=20)	Block 2 (n=19)	Block 3 (n=18)	Block 4 (n=26)	Total (n=83)	% of Respondents
Irrigation Water	11	13	18	26	68	81.9
Tractor Service	12	13	12	20	57	68.7
Cost of Inputs	4	4	1	2	11	13.3
Land	2	0	3	2	7	8.4
Local Market	1	3	1	1	6	7.2

The supply of water for irrigation was clearly the issue of greatest concern to plot-holders across the sample but was more frequently mentioned by plot-holders on the lower reaches of the irrigation system. On the upper half of the scheme (that is, Blocks 1 and 2), less than two thirds of respondents (61.5 per cent) mentioned the irrigation system as a problem, while on the lower half (Blocks 3 and 4) all respondents mentioned it.

Various explanations were offered for the poor water supply, including the design of the irrigation system itself, the recurring drought of recent years, the ineffectiveness of the water bailiffs in controlling water usage, and the reduction in the flow of the Mutale following the damming of the Tshirovha River (a tributary of the Mutale, upstream from Tshiombo). Plot-holders on the lower reaches of the scheme made the additional complaint that plot-holders closer to the water source were making unauthorised use of irrigation water and thus depriving others further down the canal.

Problems regarding the hire of tractors for ploughing were the second most common cause of complaint, being mentioned by over two-thirds (68.7 per cent) of survey respondents. Complaints centred on the near-collapse of the state service and the high prices charged by private operators (see Chapter 7), but the main problem appeared to be that there were not enough tractors available, from all sources, to service the scheme adequately.

The question of the high price of agricultural inputs was frequently raised during the study and 13.3 per cent of respondents included this amongst their top problems. Most believed that the solution to this problem lay with the government supplying inputs – particularly fertiliser – at reduced prices. A relatively small number of respondents (8.4 per cent) included issues relating to the availability, or quality, of land amongst their most pressing concerns. Two plot-holders stated that a more secure form of individual tenure was required on arable land in order to encourage people to make improvements to the land and to prevent accumulation of land by people close to the traditional leaders. Three respondents were of the opinion that land should be taken from those who were not fully utilising it and given to more 'progressive' farmers, while another felt that it should be taken from people with multiple plots and redistributed to those without land. Finally, one respondent reported that her land was of such poor quality that she could grow nothing on it and wanted to exchange it for another plot elsewhere on the scheme.

The only other issue raised with any frequency was the lack of a local market place. This was mentioned by six survey respondents (7.2 per cent), who complained of the unreliability of hawkers and the lack of big buyers in the vicinity. They were of the opinion that the construction of a permanent market site would boost demand for their produce by attracting larger buyers and more of the general public to Tshiombo.

The discussion of current conditions on the scheme elicited a range of opinions on the general level of satisfaction with the Tshiombo irrigation project. Survey respondents were virtually unanimous that conditions for agricultural production on the scheme were less favourable than at any time in their memory, even though demand for agricultural produce was said to be better than ever. The general feeling amongst those interviewed at Tshiombo was that the 1970s had been the high point of the scheme, when water was plentiful and the government services were efficiently run, and that conditions, and incomes, had declined throughout the 1980s and 1990s. Perhaps the most telling criticism, heard many times during the course of the study, was that 'this is not really an irrigation project at all', stated by numerous plot-holders on the lower reaches of the scheme (particularly Block Four) who were effectively practising rain-fed agriculture on their plots.

While it is possible that plot-holders at Tshiombo had a somewhat nostalgic view of the past, there can be little doubt that both the climatic and the political events of recent years have given them plenty of grounds for dissatisfaction (see Chapters 3 and 4). The severe droughts of the early 1980s and early 1990s were compounded by ongoing problems within the local administration during and after 'independence', the most notable examples of which were the withdrawal of farmer credit facilities in 1992, and the total (if temporary) collapse of the tractor service in 1995. These events would appear to have contributed to a widespread fatalism, with many plot-holders saying they were no longer willing to invest in agriculture due to the increasing difficulty of obtaining a reasonable return. Many people were of the opinion that the progress that had been made in the early years of the scheme – both in terms of upgrading facilities in the villages and the development of the irrigation scheme itself – was now being undone through official neglect. People who had come to Tshiombo with high hopes of gaining a living from agriculture were clearly frustrated by the direction the scheme had taken in recent years, and many made unfavourable comparisons between standards of living at Tshiombo and those enjoyed by town-dwellers in Thohoyandou.

In terms of individual achievements, the picture was somewhat more positive. Many respondents, including some who were highly critical of the current state of the scheme, stated they had done well from agriculture, citing evidence of houses built, children educated and vehicles purchased on the strength of farming at Tshiombo. One plot-holder declared he had made a fine living in the 1970s and built a modern, six-room house 'all from two plots', but was of the opinion that agriculture had been in decline since the mid-1980s and that many plot-holders were now barely surviving. There was widespread pessimism about the future of agriculture in the area, with many plot-holders stating their belief that 'the youth' were not interested in farming. While respondents were more optimistic about the new political dispensation in the country, most felt that it was unlikely to make much difference to them as farmers.

8.3 THE PROSPECTS FOR DEVELOPMENT AT TSHIOMBO

The above sections have analysed the position of agriculture within household livelihoods and outlined what plot-holders themselves see as the main problems facing them. This section uses these findings in order to draw some conclusions about the current status of Tshiombo as a development project and make recommendations for reform. Discussion focuses on the five priority issues raised by plot-holders, all of them central to the future of the irrigation project and the development of the local agricultural economy, namely the irrigation system itself, state services to farmers, the supply of agricultural inputs, land reform and crop marketing.

The Irrigation System

The irrigation system lies at the heart of agriculture at Tshiombo, but throughout the main period of fieldwork virtually everyone encountered at Tshiombo was agreed that it was inadequate to the needs of plot-holders and constituted a serious limitation to agricultural production.[2] Problems relating to the irrigation system can be divided into three inter-connected areas: the overall supply of water to the system, the design and maintenance of the irrigation infrastructure and the management and use of water. All are worth considering in some detail.

The general feeling amongst plot-holders and officials on the scheme was that the supply of water had been sufficient in the early years of the scheme but had deteriorated dramatically during the 1980s and 1990s. Plot-holders on Blocks 1 and 2, those closest to the head of the canal, still received enough water to produce two crops in most years but supply deteriorated steadily further downstream, and on much of Block 4 farmers reported that they could grow crops only during the rainy season. Officially, water was available once a week during May 1995, for a period of six hours, which plot-holders described as sufficient to irrigate two beds (0.2 ha) per plot, and only once a fortnight in winter. Crops such as maize and tomatoes could survive if they were watered once a month but others, such as cabbage, required irrigation every week.

The most obvious explanation for the deterioration in water availability is the prolonged drought which affected the region since the early 1980s and the dramatic decline in the flow of the Mutale River. A number of informants attributed the decline not to the weather, however, but to the damming of the Tshirovha River, which joins the Mutale upstream from Tshiombo. This dam was constructed in the mid-1980s to supply the Sapekoe tea estate at Mukumbani, on the south slopes of the Soutpansberg (see Chapter 4). Other explanations offered by plot-holders were the greater number of people using their plots in recent years, a greater intensity of production on individual plots, and less effective supervision by the authorities. One plot-holder on Block 4A reported that there were 36 'very active' plot-holders ahead of her on the same secondary canal and as a result water rarely reached as far as her plot. At times, she said, she had no choice but to fetch water from the 'ground dam' (reservoir) by bucket.

Most informants believed that, with the exception of the most severe drought years, there was sufficient water in the Mutale River to supply the scheme if it could be stored and its use properly regulated, a view echoed in a report by the engineering consultants Murray Biesenbach and Badenhorst [1987: 30]. Regardless of the overall availability of water, however, it would appear that the infrastructure at Tshiombo is not adequate to supply the required volume of water to all plots, and the situation would appear to have deteriorated over the years due to poor maintenance of the canals and associated works. Murray Biesenbach and Badenhorst [1987: 30] found that 'in its present form, the canal does not fulfil the water requirements for 1,150 ha of irrigation, since the flow rate at the beginning of the canal is only 510 *l/s* [litres per second] and approximately 780 *l/s* is needed. The latter figure . . . will be sufficient [only] if the buffer storage dams are repaired and enlarged.'

Plot-holders and local officials were virtually unanimous in their demands that the irrigation system be improved, something they believed had long been under consideration by various official bodies, including the Development Bank of Southern Africa. Apart from the construction of a main dam, plot-holders suggested that the canals and control mechanisms be covered in and made secure, both in order to reduce water loss by evaporation and to prevent unauthorised use, and that sprinklers be introduced on all the plots. For inspiration in this regard, plot-holders at Tshiombo have the adjacent Agriven scheme at Makonde, where diesel-powered central-pivot sprinkler systems operate virtually around the clock.

Changes to the infrastructure would improve the irrigation system only if some means were found to regulate the use of water more effectively. Observations on the scheme suggested that unauthorised use of water was rife, especially amongst plot-holders on the upper parts of the scheme, some of whom appeared to be irrigating on a daily basis. Conflict between farmers on different parts of the scheme over water use was said to be a growing problem, with reports of some plot-holders blocking the main canal, and others draining the ground dams in revenge, leading to occasional fights. 'People here are chopping each other with axes over water', said one water bailiff. While the bailiffs made some effort to regulate water usage, it was clear that they did not have the full co-operation or the respect of all the plot-holders, and were incapable of imposing effective sanctions on known abusers. Bailiffs were not helped in their task by the design of the mechanical controls on the scheme, especially the 'DBs', which could be operated by anyone, to obtain water for an arable plot or for domestic (or even malicious) purposes and were frequently left open after use.

What was perhaps most surprising with regard to the management of the irrigation system was the absence of any effective organisation among plot-holders themselves. The design of the scheme means that Blocks are effectively in competition for the available water supply and plot-holders are at the mercy of all those above them on the main canal. This would suggest that close co-operation between users would be essential for the regulation of the water supply and for preventing unauthorised use but in practice there were no effective mechanisms for co-operation between users or for resolving disputes. Disputes between users on the same Block could be referred to the village headman, but there were no such remedies for disputes between the six village on the scheme. Individual headmen generally support their own villagers, and are not inclined to negotiate with headmen from other villages. Chief Tshivhase and the Tshivhase Tribal Authority, with a large territory and population under their jurisdiction, have no direct involvement in the operation of the scheme, while the emerging local government structures have not yet become involved in such matters and appear unlikely to do so. Many survey respondents were pessimistic about the ability of plot-holders to regulate their own affairs, and called for firmer action by the authorities: 'the government must be strict', said one.

Overall, the technology employed at Tshiombo could be said to be highly 'appropriate', as it is relatively robust and reliable and can largely be controlled and maintained by the users themselves and local officials. Being entirely gravity-fed, there are few 'moving parts' (for example, pumps) to break down, and plot-holders (or the appropriate authority) are spared the recurring costs of fuel, spare-parts and specialised maintenance staff associated with more advanced technologies. The down-side for such 'low-tech' furrow irrigation systems, however, is that they tend to be relatively inefficient in their use of water, compared to sprinklers, for example, and extremely labour-intensive at the point of application [*Booher*, 1974: 111]. An unknown quantity of water is lost at Tshiombo due to leaks in the canals and the DBs, evaporation from the open canals and excessive seepage in the earthen furrows. The distribution of water within plots also tends to be uneven, leading to water-logging in places. The amount of labour required to open and close the earthen furrows at the time of irrigation, and ensure an even flow of water between the ridges, means that even when water is plentiful few plot-holders at Tshiombo attempt to irrigate more than two or three beds at a time.

The absence of any substantial water-storage capacity means that the system does not maximise the supply of irrigation water during the natural dry season, which would allow for true year-round production. Supplementary (pro-cyclical) irrigation does, however, make a major contribution to cultivation by prolonging the effective wet season, and providing continuity of water supply. This is essential to obtain the full benefits of 'improved' agricultural technologies such as chemical fertiliser and hybrid seed varieties [*Moris and Thom*, 1990: 17]. The growing season at Tshiombo starts earlier and ends later than on comparable rainfed lands, thereby boosting output considerably and allowing at least some plot-holders to produce two crops in the year.

In terms of reform, there can be little doubt that both the irrigation infrastructure and the way in which the water supply is managed are in need of major over-haul. Tshiombo has already been the site of considerable invest-

LIVELIHOODS AND DEVELOPMENT AT TSHIOMBO 243

ment by the state and it would be difficult to make a case for major new spending while farmers in many other parts of Venda (and the other former homelands) remain without support services of any kind. Arguments for or against the construction of a dam on the Mutale go beyond the scope of this study, but discussion with officials at various levels of government suggest that this is not a likelihood anyway.

The two consultancy reports by Murray Biesenbach and Badenhorst [1987, 1989], however, provide a number of relatively low-cost means by which the supply of water could be improved, such as replacing the main canal with a subterranean pipe line from the confluence of the Tshirovha and Mutale rivers, raising and repairing the side of the main canal, lowering some of the overflow structures, increasing the capacity of the seven buffer dams and raising the level of the existing weir on the Mutale, but all of these have implications for downstream water users and the riverine ecology. Past decisions on water use in the Mutale Valley, such as the construction of the Tshirovha dam, have tended to be made in a largely non-transparent and unaccountable fashion, with little obvious concern for the mass of water users or for the long-term protection of water resources. Any further developments in the area should begin with the creation of a statutory Catchment Authority for the Mutale River, composed of representatives of all water users and local authorities, with the power to regulate water use and protect the environment.

Any improvement in the functioning of the irrigation system will also require a greater degree of participation by plot-holders at block and scheme levels, and more effective regulation of water usage, but it is far from clear where the initiative for such changes could come from. Attempts were being made by the Department of Agriculture during 1996 to facilitate the formation of a new plot-holders' organisation, but this met with considerable resistance from many plot-holders who felt it was not sufficiently independent of the state and was likely to be dominated by the biggest land-holders on the scheme (see Chapter 4).

State Services

The state has played, and continues to play, a central role in the development of agriculture in the homelands, as outlined in Chapter 2. At Tshiombo, apart from the overall management of the irrigation system, the main services provided by the state are agricultural extension and tractor ploughing. Officials of the Department of Agriculture District Office in Thohoyandou were of the opinion that the Department was providing an effective service in terms of extension but accepted that there were problems with water supply and tractors. This they blamed on the Department of Works and argued that all state services at Tshiombo should be brought under the control of the Department of Agriculture. The generally poor performance of government services revealed by this study certainly points to the need for a unified and decentralised management structure with a full-time supervisor based on site.

The weaknesses of the state tractor service at Tshiombo have been discussed at length above. While part of the problem would appear to be the short supply of tractors, perhaps more important was the inability to keep the existing machinery operating, whether due to inefficiency or financial constraints, or a combination of the two. The remnants of at least eight government tractors were visible outside the Tshiombo Co-operative but no more than three were actually operating at any point during fieldwork in 1995 or 1996. For much of 1995, none was in service due to the lack of diesel fuel. As noted in Chapter 7, routine maintenance and repairs frequently kept tractors out of service for lengthy periods – weeks and months, rather than days – despite the presence of government mechanics at Tshiombo. Even something as straight forward as mending a puncture could involve waiting many days for a government bakkie to come to Tshiombo to take the wheel to Thohoyandou where it would be fixed and eventually returned to Tshiombo, during which time the tractor would remain idle.

Survey respondents praised many aspects of the state tractor service, particularly the power of the tractors, the range of implements and the skill of the drivers and mechanics. These positive attributes, and the importance attached to them by plot-holders, clearly makes the reform of the state tractor service an urgent priority. Other methods of tillage, such as animal draught or hand-hoeing, were not acceptable to the vast majority of plot-holders and would not appear to represent viable alternatives given the lack of suitable livestock and what would appear to be a severe labour constraint in most households.

The solution advocated by most plot-holders in the survey was for the government to provide more tractors but, as with water for irrigation, it is clear that increasing the supply could have little long-term benefit unless ways were found to use existing resources more effectively. In terms of repairs and maintenance, this would require a well-managed and well-equipped mechanic's station at Tshiombo, with the means to carry out maintenance and repairs of tractors and implements in a timely and cost-efficient fashion, as well as access to more specialised services for major repairs. The problem with fuel supplies in 1995 was largely a result of the general financial chaos of the homeland administration before and immediately after reincorporation and appeared to have been resolved, at least temporarily, by 1996. A review of fuel storage capacity at Tshiombo, however, and the setting-up of a standing agreement with one of the commercial fuel merchants within reach of Tshiombo to provide diesel during interruptions in the states' own supply, would certainly be worthwhile.

Short-falls in the state ploughing service were being filled, at least in part, by private tractor owners, although plot-holders were critical of their higher charges and poor quality of service. The initiative shown by the private owners does, however, suggest a number of ways in which the state could intervene in order to improve the range of services available to plot-holders. One relatively low-cost option would be to offer training to private drivers to bring their skills up to the standard of the government operatives. Another would be to open up state maintenance services to private owners, possibly on a cost-price basis, as part of an overhaul of the state's own facilities. One private owner told of waiting six months to obtain spare parts for the 20-year-old tractor he had bought from a white farmer in Louis Trichardt.

Serious consideration also needs to be given to assisting local entrepreneurs (including plot-holders themselves) to invest in more powerful tractors and adequate implements. A number of plot-holders outside the survey sample, and the management of the Tshiombo Co-operative, reported that they had been offered credit by Agriven to buy tractors but were reluctant to take on such a large financial obligation. The leading concern of those spoken to was that sooner or later the tractors would break down and they would not be able to afford the necessary repairs. Then, with their machines out of service they would be faced with mounting debts and no means of generating income. Clearly, if public bodies are considering such approaches they must find ways of reducing the risk to would-be buyers. One solution would be for the state to lease machines to private operators for a set period, perhaps with an option to buy at the end, while retaining responsibility for major repairs. It is unlikely that private tractors will replace the state service in the foreseeable future, but it is important that the state, and others concerned with rural development, explore a range of options in order to ensure that plot-holders at Tshiombo obtain the service they require in a timely and affordable manner.

Apart from irrigation and the tractor service, the most important service provided by the government at Tshiombo is the agricultural extension service, even though much of its work is concerned with managing linkages between farmers and the broader agricultural economy rather than the more usual focus on production. Agricultural Officers are involved in almost every aspect of day-to-day life on the scheme, and play a key role in the co-ordination of government services, negotiating with buyers and transporters, and advising the Tshiombo Co-operative on stock purchasing. As indicated in Chapter 7, the service suffers from a wide range of constraints, and it is difficult to say just how effective it is in meeting its primary goals of agricultural training and advice.

A number of reforms are urgently needed within the extension service at Tshiombo. While the office buildings were generally adequate, Agricultural Officers were highly critical of the state of living accommodation, and this would have to be greatly improved if all the officers were to live permanently on the scheme. Working materials, such as stationery and information leaflets, were also in extremely short supply. There is a pressing need for basic information sheets in *Luvenda* and English, suitable for a semi-literate audience, on topics such as seed selection, fertiliser application and pest control. Field officers also need more timely access to crop specialists and other support services at head office in order to solve specific problems encountered in their work.

The appropriateness of the advice given by the Agricultural Officers, and the training and direction they receive, must also be questioned. Advice to plot-holders at Tshiombo was based on relatively expensive purchased technologies and showed little appreciation of the resource constraints they faced or any awareness of more traditional (and accessible) solutions. Thus, advice on fertiliser was based almost entirely on commercial products, with little or no reference to the use of organic materials such as compost or animal manure. Indeed, the idea of any integration between arable and livestock farming would appear to have been ignored by officialdom since the beginnings of the scheme, although hostility to livestock farming was said to have abated somewhat in recent years. Similarly, advice on pest control was based entirely on the use of expensive chemical products, which were beyond the means of many plot-holders, and present particular problems for non-literate users. Alternative techniques of improving fertility and controlling pests, such as inter-cropping, were neglected or actively discouraged. This should not be seen as a criticism of the officers concerned, but as a reflection of the training and general ethos of the agricultural extension service within the former homelands.

Valuable back-up to the official extension service is provided by the water bailiffs, whose official responsibility is limited to the supervision of water use on the scheme. Discussions with plot-holders and direct observations in the field revealed that bailiffs provided advice not only on practical aspects of irrigation but on many other areas of agriculture as well. A number of plot-holders, particularly older women, stated that they found this informal 'extension' more useful than the advice they received from the Agricultural Officers. A possible explanation for this may be that the bailiffs tended to be older and less educated than the Agricultural Officers, and lived permanently within the local community, and therefore tended to be more socially compatible with the plot-holders. There may be scope for an enhanced role for water bailiffs in support of the Agricultural Officers, which would require some additional training.

Finally, systems of management and communication within the public service were in need of urgent review, although once again such matters go beyond the scope of this study. As noted above, Agricultural Officers spend considerable time at the Regional Office in Thohoyandou for meetings and other duties. A decentralised management structure, with a senior manager based permanently on the scheme, would be an essential starting point for any improvement in this area. Reporting systems also need to be reformed. Officers spend much of their time compiling reports on their activities and on agricultural production on their blocks, with little or no feed-back to plot-holders. The forms used are largely in Afrikaans, and probably pre-date Venda's 'independence'. Agricultural Officers might be more usefully employed in assisting plot-holders to keep their own records in a simple format, thereby allowing plot-holders to monitor their performance and develop their own strategies for improving productivity. Such records could be stored at the Block Office, and a summary prepared periodically by the officers in order to meet the internal reporting requirements of the Department.

Agricultural Inputs

The use of purchased agricultural inputs was generally well established, if somewhat uneven, at Tshiombo. Artificial fertilisers were used by the great majority of plot-holders in the survey but application rates varied considerably from plot to plot, and from year to year, depending on individual ability to purchase. Recommendations from the extension officers as to types and quantities of fertiliser tended to be quite general, and could be no more specific in the absence of regular soil analysis and local agricultural research. The use of certified seed was also widespread, especially for tomatoes and cabbage, but for maize and other crops it tended to be mixed with retained seed, if used at all. Agro-chemicals, for control of insect and bacterial pests, were less widely used and once again the level of application tended to vary considerably in accordance with individual ability to purchase, and knowledge of, these products.

The main suppliers of agricultural inputs for plot-holders at Tshiombo were the Tshiombo Co-operative, the NTK store at Shayandima (Thohoyandou) and the Agriven store at Makonde. Both NTK and Agriven offer competitive retail pricing, but no special terms for small farmers, and neither is particularly accessible for households without their own vehicle. Agriven's main concern is with 'emergent' commercial farmers and it is under increasing political pressure to show a profit on its operations. It is therefore unlikely to have much to offer relatively small-scale (and poor) farmers such as the great majority of plot-holders at Tshiombo. NTK, although a co-operative in name, is also effectively a retail supplier within Venda, and most plot-holders are unlikely to be able to afford the membership fee of R800 which might give them access to membership benefits such as credit facilities, annual dividends and specialist technical services.

By contrast, the Tshiombo Co-operative would appear to be well-suited to meeting the needs of plot-holders but suffers from a number of disadvantages relative to its competitors. According to its manager, the Co-operative received a discount of seven per cent on all fertiliser from the manufacturers, compared to 17 per cent obtained by Agriven, and was charged VAT on all purchases which, he believed, was not the case with either Agriven or NTK. Unlike other outlets, Tshiombo Co-operative paid cash on delivery to all suppliers, with the exception of the NTK roller mill which offered 30 days' credit on mealie meal. An audit by the South African Registrar of Co-operatives in January 1995 found that the Co-operative was in a sound financial position but was receiving less than favourable treatment from its bank (First National Bank), which was charging it over R1,000 a year in bank charges, despite it having more than R50,000 on deposit over the period [*Registrar of Co-operatives*, 1995].[3] Government agencies have also been less than supportive of the small black-run co-operatives. Of particular concern to the Tshiombo Co-operative management committee in 1995 was the South African Agricultural Credit Board's small farmer credit scheme. In Venda, these funds were available only through NTK (see Chapter 7) and the Co-operative committee members feared that this would encourage some of their larger customers to transfer their custom to NTK. The Northern Province's Drought Relief funds of 1996 were available to all co-operatives in the area, however, and both Tshiombo and NTK reported sizeable increases in turnover as a result.

Apart from occasional drought relief, it is very unlikely that the state is going to provide the solution sought by many plot-holders at Tshiombo, which is to supply agricultural inputs at reduced prices. It is therefore important that plot-holders combine their purchasing power through appropriate non-profit institutions, such as the Tshiombo Co-operative, which could address the specific needs of small-scale farmers. In order to provide competitive prices and other benefits to members, however, and to overcome the many structural obstacles and discriminatory practices of the apartheid era, these organisations must be able to obtain competitive terms from their suppliers and equitable treatment from state bodies.

A good start has been made by the office of the Registrar of Co-operatives, which has provided staff training and assistance with book-keeping to the Tshiombo Co-operative, but a lot more remains to be done if the few relatively effective co-operatives in the former homelands are to survive. For example,

Agriven, which is effectively in competition with the independent co-operatives at present, could work more closely with them, perhaps acting as a guarantor in dealings between them and their suppliers. Other public bodies, such as the Agricultural Credit Board, could find ways of channelling funds through the small black co-operatives rather than effectively discriminating against them as they have done recently. Public pressure could also be brought to bear on private sector companies, such as fertiliser manufacturers and the commercial banks, to offer more favourable terms to the black co-operatives, possibly as part of their contribution to the RDP. NTK, itself the beneficiary of generous state support in the past, and now in a dominant position within agri-business in Venda, should be encouraged to be more supportive of small black co-operatives, rather than supplanting them as it is currently doing through its take-over of failed co-op premises. Finally, the provision of direct state support to the Tshiombo Co-operative – perhaps in the form of financing to lease a truck, or a line of credit to enable it to hold more stock – would be a highly effective means of indirectly assisting the great majority of plot-holders at Tshiombo, especially the very poorest households which depend most on their local co-operative.

Agricultural Markets

Problems related to the marketing of crops or livestock were not the most pressing priorities for plot-holders at Tshiombo but were mentioned repeatedly throughout the survey. Indeed, from a project planning point of view marketing has been the most neglected aspect of the Tshiombo scheme, highlighting the limited vision and contradictory objectives of 'development' policy in the region over the years.

Marketing opportunities were said to have been virtually non-existent in the early years of the scheme but have undoubtedly improved over time with the growth in population, especially in towns and 'closer (that is, landless) settlements', improvements in transport and gradually rising purchasing power amongst a portion of the population. Local producers do not have a monopoly on these markets, however, and larger markets such as Thohoyandou were reported to be dominated by white farmers who could provide more consistent supply and better quality than their black counterparts.

Crop marketing at Tshiombo remains piece-meal and largely unorganised and producers are heavily dependent on relatively small-scale, informal buyers coming to their fields. Although demand is generally good, it is not always reliable and hawkers have been know not to show up when required. Crops were reported to have rotted in the fields during periods of exceptionally high yield. Some remoter parts of the scheme, such as Block One, up to 12 kilometres from the tar road, are particularly poorly served by buyers. Formal marketing channels, both within and outside Venda, for crops such as tomatoes, mangoes and maize, hold little attraction for small farmers at Tshiombo due to the relatively low prices on offer and high cost of transportation (see Chapter 7). Inadequate price information presents a further disincentive to those contemplating sending produce to more distant markets such as Johannesburg.

Options for reform of marketing at Tshiombo are very limited, due to the relatively small scale of production, the limited market within Venda and the Northern Province, and the relatively well-established commercial networks (formal and informal) already in place. The conventional solution to the problem might be the introduction of large-scale agro-processing facilities but this would be unlikely to meet the needs of the majority of plot-holders, as clearly shown by the examples of the NTK maize mill and the Giants tomato canning plant (Chapter 7). The prices offered by large-scale processors in the region are determined by conditions in the white-dominated modern sector of the agricultural economy, where cost structures, scales of production and productivity tend to be very different from those in small-scale 'homeland' agriculture.

The most common solution proposed by plot-holders in the survey, the construction of a central (wholesale) market place at Tshiombo, would not in itself overcome these obstacles but would certainly make life more comfortable for sellers, and perhaps give plot-holders from different parts of the scheme more equal access to buyers. A concentration of sellers would also have the potential to attract new buyers who did not wish to seek out individual producers in their fields or their homes. More importantly, perhaps, it would provide the possibility for producers to act collectively, possibly pooling their produce in order to attract bigger buyers or to obtain more favourable terms. With professional management, this could provide the basis for more formal marketing arrangements and the sale of tomatoes to Durban-based processors in recent years has shown that such an approach is possible. This form of sale was greatly favoured by plot-holders because transport was provided and cash was paid at the time of sale. The central role of the Agricultural Officers in setting up and mediating these transactions must be acknowledged and the appointment of one Officer or other individual to promote arrangements of this sort should be given serious consideration by the relevant authorities.

Central to any marketing reform at Tshiombo is the question of transport. As already noted, most plot-holders did not have access to a vehicle within their household, and the cost of hiring one was prohibitively expensive for many. Attempts have been made by Agricultural Officers to arrange group transport with private companies, especially to the tomato-canning factory at

Makhado, but most users found this too expensive relative to the prices obtained for their produce. There would appear to be a compelling case for such a critical service to be provided by a state (or parastatal) agency, ideally at cost price, either directly, through a commercial sub-contractor or in collaboration with the Tshiombo Co-operative. The experience of the tractor service at Tshiombo, however, would suggest that the state may not be in the best position to provide transport services.

The combination of a central market place and bulk transport could provide access to more distant markets not currently used by producers at Tshiombo, such as the newly established (1995) fresh produce market adjacent to Pietersburg airport. It could also provide a link to established long-distance trucking companies that operate between the 'white' farming areas of Levubu and Tshipise and the Johannesburg morning market. Existing local transporters could, perhaps, concentrate on carrying goods between plots and the central market place, or to other local markets such as Thohoyandou.

Finally, the comparative advantage of the Tshiombo producers would appear to lie in sales of fresh produce to local markets over a relatively long season and this is where reforms should be concentrated. By removing some of the more obvious obstacles facing producers, such as a lack of transport and price information, and providing professional marketing advice, it might be hoped that producers would be able to gradually increase production and tailor it more closely to the demands of a variety of markets. New market outlets, however, will have to be appropriate to the scale of the producers, be clearly comprehensible to them and be willing to pay suppliers cash on delivery.

Land

Issues relating to land-holding – including tenure, the system of land allocation, and redistribution – did not feature largely in the Tshiombo survey, despite their prominence in broader political debates of recent years [*Bernstein*, 1992; *Levin and Weiner*, 1996]. Some possible reasons for this have been outlined, including the relative success of plot-holders at Tshiombo in accumulating land, a low incidence (by homeland standards) of forced removals amongst the survey sample and widespread support for the principle of communal tenure (although not necessarily for the chiefs and headmen who administer it). To this might be added the lack of any obvious 'target' for redistribution – the nearest 'white' farms are at Levubu, 40 km away, and plot-holders at Tshiombo are unlikely to be the first in line if land outside the former homelands were to be made available to black farmers under a reform programme.

A minority of survey respondents stated that they would be interested in obtaining more land (see Chapter 6) and nearly all aspired to this within the existing system of communal tenure. The strengths of the communal tenure system, as far as plot-holders at Tshiombo are concerned, are that land can be obtained (virtually) free of charge, access to land is relatively egalitarian (all households having, in theory, a right to some land), and 'the community' (in the person of the Chief and the Tribal Authority), rather than the occupant, retains ultimate 'ownership' (control) of all land. As with other areas of the former homelands, however, there is insufficient arable land available at Tshiombo to accommodate all those with formal rights, and the system of land allocation is open to patronage and corruption on the part of the 'traditional leaders'. The result is that a minority of households at Tshiombo has been able to acquire substantial holdings (for example, upwards of five hectares) while a growing number of households (possibly as high as 40 per cent of all households at Tshiombo) are without arable land. Access to land for housing is considerably more contentious, and has emerged as the leading point of conflict between 'tribal' and 'democratic' factions in the area since 1994 [*Lahiff*, 1997: 103].

To date, the reforms introduced by the new ANC-led government have had no direct impact on the system of land-holding at Tshiombo, and it is difficult to see what the current reform programme has to offer households deep within the former homelands. This programme, as outlined in the 1996 Green Paper on Land [*Department of Land Affairs*, 1996: 3] is made up of three distinct components – redistribution, restitution, and tenure reform:

> Redistribution is a broad based programme which aims to provide the disadvantaged and the poor with land for residential and productive purposes. Its scope includes the urban and rural very poor, labour tenants, farm workers as well as new entrants to agriculture.

> Land Restitution covers cases of forced removals which originate since 1913. They are being dealt with by a Land Claims Court and Commission, established under the Restitution of Land Rights Act, 1994.

> Land tenure reform is being addressed through a review of present land policy, administration and legislation to improve the tenure security of all South Africans and to accommodate more diverse forms of land tenure, including types of communal tenure.

Of these, restitution has least relevance to people at Tshiombo who do not, by and large, constitute a displaced people as envisaged by the Green Paper. There are, however, many displaced communities in Venda (such as the Manenzhe and the Ratombo peoples), who have strong claims to 'white' land adjoining the former homeland, and many former labour tenants now living in closer settlements throughout Vuwani and Dzanai districts may also have claims for restitution. Reform of land tenure may become an issue for some larger farmers seeking a more 'individual' form of private property rights but did not appear to be a priority for plot-holders at Tshiombo at this time. There would probably be support for more efficiency and openness in the way that plots on the irrigation scheme are allocated, and perhaps even for some increase in the annual charges, but this would only be acceptable to the majority of plot-holders as part of a general improvement in the services on offer.

Of much greater potential significance for people throughout Venda is the possibility that sizeable areas of 'white' farmland would be made available under a state-assisted programme of land redistribution. This could give selected farmers, or those wishing to become farmers, the possibility of expanding their holdings and reduce pressure on land in more populous areas. For most households at Tshiombo (and elsewhere in Venda), however, whose principal investment is their homestead, there is considerable resistance to moving away from their home and their community. None the less, a small minority of larger landholders, with their own transport and capital to invest, expressed an interest in acquiring land away from Tshiombo and relocating if necessary. Indeed, 'commuter farming' is already well established in Venda, with many larger plot-holders on irrigation schemes such as Nwanedi and Sanari living upwards of 50 km from their lands.

As yet, land reform has not emerged as a major political issue within the Northern Province, and the manner in which the programme has been implemented to date raises questions over the provincial administration's commitment to land reform in general and to meeting the needs of the rural poor in particular. In discussion with senior members of the administration in Thohoyandou and Pietersburg, 'land reform' was nearly always interpreted as meaning the creation of larger farming units for a relatively small number of 'progressive' farmers, whom it was generally assumed would be strongly commercially-oriented, full-time, and male. Little or no support could be found for agricultural or land reform as a means of alleviating poverty, or as part of a livelihood strategy that would include non-agricultural employment. One District Controller in the former Venda Department of Agriculture, speaking of Tshiombo, went so far as to say that it was now time to take land from poorer households and redistribute it to more 'progressive' farmers: 'We must push these grannies off the land, and give it to people who can really farm it.'

Overall, while land reform is widely seen as key to the post-apartheid transformation of the South African countryside, current policy does little to address the needs of people in the 'deep rural' areas of the former homelands.

Reforms that would make a difference to people at Tshiombo include separating control of residential land from control of arable land and, more specifically, shifting responsibility for residential land from the chiefs to the elected local councils. It may also be possible to involve elected representatives in the allocation of arable land within the system of 'communal' tenure, although this would be strongly resisted by the 'tribal' leaders. Perhaps the most important, and most immediate issue, however, is the status of the many large areas of (currently) uninhabited land under the direct control of the state, including land used (or intended) for state agricultural projects, and land acquired by the former Venda government for allocation to its own senior members and supporters. While most if not all of this land may become the subject of land claims by previously displaced communities, it is nonetheless of great importance because of its strategic location (within Venda), the generally high quality of the land involved and the fact that much of it is currently lying unused. The process by which Agriven, in particular, has 'privatised' many of its projects during the final years of apartheid was carried out with little public scrutiny or accountability and, as far as could be ascertained, did not consider alternative models of land use and tenure. While redressing the great racial imbalance in land-holding in the country is clearly a priority at the national level, if land reform is to mean anything to people in the former homelands in the shorter term it will require equitable access to unused land and the large holdings of the former homeland elite, in ways which break with the clientilism and the bias towards 'economic' farming which have long characterised the struggle for land in these areas.

8.4 CONCLUSION

Plot-holders at Tshiombo have shown the ability to sustain irrigated agriculture over many decades, often under very difficult circumstances, and thereby generate a substantial contribution to household incomes. In the absence of effective private-sector or collective institutions, however, plot-holders remain heavily dependent on the state and it is therefore essential that the state plays a role in any reform of the local agricultural economy. Given the concentration of state resources up to now on projects such as Tshiombo and the ineffectiveness of much of the state service within the former homelands, further spending may not be feasible and may not in itself offer a solution to the area's problems. Rather, ways need to be found of involving plot-holders themselves in the management of the scheme, and involving other collective organisations or private-sector agents in the supply of agricultural services.

The irrigation system is clearly an area where greater involvement by plot-holders has potential but this would require a willingness on the part of the state to delegate responsibility to representative local structures, and to provide the necessary training and support to make them effective. While there will certainly continue to be a role for the state in the provision of tractor services, the evidence of recent years suggests that this might be achieved more effectively through partnerships with private owners and farmers themselves, possibly organised through the Tshiombo Co-operative. Likewise, the supply of agricultural inputs and the marketing of crops lend themselves to more collective forms of organisation amongst plot-holders, but will again require specialist advice and ongoing support in areas such as negotiating with suppliers and buyers, the hiring of transport, and the development of more professional and varied marketing strategies.

At the same time, there is an urgent need for the state to review those activities which actively discriminate against small farmers, including much of the work of the Agricultural Development Corporations (such as Agriven) and the Agricultural Credit Board, and monopolistic practices by large white-run co-operatives and manufacturers. While none of this can be expected to transform the agricultural economy at Tshiombo, there is undoubtedly scope for greatly improving the general economic conditions facing those who depend on agriculture for some or all of their livelihood.

NOTES

1. In a recent study of Mamone village in Lebowa, Baber [1996: 301] found a similar pattern, whereby 10.3 per cent of total household income was obtained from agriculture, rising to 25 per cent for the poorest third of households. Similarly, May [1989: 9] found that, in rural KwaZulu, poorer households tended to be more dependent on agriculture than richer ones.
2. By the second period of field work (April 1996), the supply of irrigation water had greatly improved throughout the scheme due to the exceptionally high rainfall in the summer of 1995/96.
3. I am grateful to the Venda Registrar of Co-operatives for making a copy of this report available to me.

9

Conclusion

9.1 SIGNIFICANCE OF THE STUDY

This study set out to investigate the condition of small-scale agriculture in the homelands, its contribution to livelihoods and the prospects for its further development. What it found at Tshiombo was, by homeland standards, a thriving agricultural sector, which despite severe shortages of working capital, poorly-developed markets and often inefficient support services, makes a significant contribution to household incomes. This chapter summarises the main findings of the study and assesses their implications for wider issues of rural development and agricultural reform in South Africa.

The first half of this study attempts to draw together the limited information on land and agriculture in the homelands in a way that has not been done before. Although up to one million households in the homelands may be engaged in some form of agriculture, no substantial study of the subject has yet been written and few of the local studies cited attempt any inter-homeland comparisons. In the case of Venda, no substantial study, other than 'official' publications, has been made of the history, society, economy or politics of this highly distinctive area and very little has been written on the agricultural sector. This study draws on all available works (published and unpublished) to create an overview of conditions in Venda, past and present, and a context for the Tshiombo case study.

The case study itself provides an in-depth socio-economic analysis of small-holders on the Tshiombo irrigation scheme, covering household history and demography, occupations and sources of income, patterns of land-holding, agricultural production and plot-holders' own perceptions of the scheme. It also examines the role of the state and other institutions in the local agricultural economy and identifies a number of areas suitable for reform. The emphasis throughout is on the opportunities and constraints facing households in their pursuit of livelihoods and the variety of ways in which households deal with them.

The study suffers from a number of limitations. The methodology employed relied heavily on the oral accounts of plot-holders themselves, which meant that certain issues, such as the functioning of local informal markets, the system of land allocation, relations between plot-holders and hired labourers and the experience of landless households, may not have been adequately covered. This approach also gave rise to problems of measurement and verification on subjects such as the value of migrant remittances and crop yields, where some further 'triangulation' or independent measurement may have been appropriate. In addition, the desire to include as representative, and thus as large, a sample of plot-holders as possible meant that many issues were not investigated as thoroughly as they might have been. A sample of half the size, with proportionally more time spent with each household, might have provided greater understanding of the processes underlying household livelihood strategies. Finally, the focus on just one agricultural year means that the study lacks an adequate longitudinal dimension, which might have revealed more about the changing fortunes of households over time. None the less, this study represents by far the most comprehensive study of any community in Venda to date, and hopefully will contribute to the understanding of this much neglected area at the formal end of apartheid.

9.2 THE LESSONS FROM TSHIOMBO

As a development project, Tshiombo is a survivor from a bygone age, before the direct involvement of the state in agricultural production or the emergence of a class of large-scale 'commercial' farmers within the homelands. Yet in many ways it is in keeping with contemporary thinking in terms of its relatively small individually-managed holdings, the combination of agriculture with a range of other income-generating activities within households and the 'appropriateness' of the gravity-fed furrow irrigation system to the resource-levels of users. Nearly 40 years after its construction, the irrigation system continues to deliver water to most parts of the scheme in most years and over 600 farming households manage to produce at least one crop a year, whether for sale or for domestic consumption. The resilience of plot-holders over the decades shows a high level of skill and commitment under difficult conditions, not only in meeting their own food needs but also in supplying disparate markets and expanding production beyond the formal limits of the scheme.

The clear strengths of the project are the low recurring costs of the irrigation system (excluding the excessive staff component), the relatively secure tenure (evidenced by the low turnover of plots), access to land for the majority of householders at Tshiombo, including many woman, and the substantial crop yields that are achieved in most years. Its most obvious weaknesses are the poor regulation of water usage, reflecting a tradition of top-down management and a lack of organisation amongst users, reliance on an inefficient state ploughing service and an inflexible (and often inappropriate) agricultural extension service that emphasises production to the neglect of broader issues such as transportation and marketing.

Underlying these characteristics is enormous expenditure by the state, probably the defining characteristic of the Tshiombo project. No cost-benefit analysis of the project was attempted, and it may not be relevant (or even possible) at this stage in its development, but the fact remains that Tshiombo receives levels of state support far in excess of most other parts of Venda or the rest of the homelands, which would be difficult to justify economically or politically. It is also clear that the way in which public resources have been managed – in terms of personnel, agricultural services and capital assets – has been extremely inefficient, and much of the benefit has not been passed on to the plot-holders. At the same time, the state has been less than effective in recovering costs from service users, and there can be little doubt that most plot-holders could afford to pay substantially more than the purely nominal irrigation fee of R12 per year. It is certainly possible, on the evidence of this study, to envisage much more being achieved in terms of development with the same or even reduced levels of public expenditure, given more effective management by the government agencies concerned and greater involvement by the plot-holders themselves.

The exceptional level of state support for the scheme over the years has not been matched by the development of other complementary institutions among plot-holders or in the private sector. Particularly striking is the absence of any effective organisational structures for crop marketing or the regulation of water-use on the irrigation scheme. The most notable exception to this is the Tshiombo Co-operative, which plays a key role in the supply of agricultural inputs but struggles to contend with continuing neglect by state and private sector organisations and increasing competition from the much larger 'white' co-operatives. Private-sector operators have recently begun to provide ploughing services on the scheme but are more heavily involved in transportation and crop marketing, the areas most neglected by the state. Professional marketing advice is probably the area with greatest potential for boosting agricultural incomes on the scheme, but would need to be accompanied by improvements in bulk transport and marketing facilities at Tshiombo.

The impact of the Tshiombo project on household livelihoods has certainly been substantial, allowing plot-holders to extend the growing season and increase crop yields relative to neighbouring (rainfed) areas and, in many cases, to specialise in the production of higher-value crops such as tomatoes, cabbage and green maize. Despite the poorly-developed state of local markets, over 80 per cent of total crop output (by value) at Tshiombo for the year in question was sold and the great majority of households in the sample sold at least half their output. Production for the market has not been at the expense of household food needs, however, which all the plot-holders in the survey considered a high priority. It is significant that the main crop (by area), summer maize, is almost entirely intended for domestic consumption, although many other crops are grown specifically for sale.

Plot-holders at Tshiombo are severely constrained in their ability to work their land and, on average, cultivated little more than half of all available land in 1994/95. Probably the most important constraints were a shortage of household labour, which especially affected those without a permanently resident man of working age, followed by shortages of cash for tractors, fertilisers and hired labour. More widespread problems, such as a lack of irrigation water, delays in the government ploughing service or limited access to markets also constituted constraints on agriculture but plot-holders in the study displayed wide disparities in their ability to overcome them.

Livestock farming has effectively been excluded from project planning at Tshiombo, which is somewhat surprising given its potential contribution to ploughing and supply of manure. Only a quarter of households in the sample kept cattle, and far fewer kept donkeys or goats, but for the households concerned they made a substantial contribution to income in both cash and kind.

Despite the relative strength of the agricultural sector at Tshiombo, households were heavily dependent on non-farm sources of income, of which the most important was wages, with slightly less coming from pensions. The distribution of income from all sources was highly unequal, with households in the top income quintile earning five times as much as those in the bottom quintile. These disparities were largely a question of differential access to wages and the very poorest households were those without access to any non-farm sources of income.

Agriculture accounted for approximately a quarter of household income on average, but tended to be relatively more important for poorer households. Survey participants reported that agricultural income for the year in question (1994/95) was approximately half that which could be achieved in very good years, suggesting that agriculture might, under very favourable circumstances, account for up to 40 per cent of total household income. Furthermore, the study probably underestimated the value of fresh produce consumed within households, especially amongst poorer households which tended to consume a high proportion of their crops.

Clearly, not everyone living at Tshiombo has benefited from the irrigation scheme. A substantial minority of households did not have access to arable plots, and some of their members worked on other people's plots for very low rates of pay. In addition, a number of households with land obtained little or no income from agriculture due to illness, old age or other unspecified reasons.

Differences between households in terms of agricultural output reflected considerable disparities in land-holding but choice of crops, proportion of land used, access to a vehicle, use of hired labour and the sex of plot-holders also had an influence on the value of crops produced. Approximately half of all plot-holders in the survey had acquired land in excess of the standard irrigated plot (1.28 hectares), either on the scheme proper or on so-called waste land, much of which had been brought under irrigation by farmers themselves. This 'colonisation' of riverine land by farmers with access to capital for irrigation equipment extended along the length of the Mutale River and appeared to be a feature of the last ten years [*Lahiff*, 1997: 88].

Some access to off-farm income, in the form of wages or pensions, was generally needed for households to expand production beyond the norm but no evidence could be found that the value of agricultural output rose in line with the value of off-farm income. Indeed, there appeared to be a considerable trade-off between wage income and agricultural output among households in the survey. Households with full-time male farmers tended to have more land, more livestock and more agricultural income than households where all the men were in wage employment (and the few households without men) but tended to be no better-off overall due to the loss of wage income this entailed. Not surprisingly, men at Tshiombo demonstrated a strong preference for wage employment in their twenties, thirties and forties, when their financial responsibilities (to wives, children and parents) tended to be at their highest, and were more likely to take up full-time farming in their fifties and sixties as their prospects of (and enthusiasm for) migrant employment diminished. The biggest farmers in the sample, in terms of land-holding, crop output and live-stock ownership, were all male and full-time resident at Tshiombo. Most were in their fifties or sixties, owned their own vehicles and made use of both household and hired labour. Female plot-holders tended to have less land, less livestock and less agricultural income than male plot-holders but, as most had husbands or sons in wage employment, their households did not tend to be any worse-off in terms of overall income.

Detailed comparisons of income between this and other studies were not attempted, but the available evidence would suggest that average household incomes at Tshiombo are marginally below those for the homelands generally. The proportion (and probably the amount) of income obtained from agri-culture, however, is exceptionally high. Of all the sources cited in Chapter 2, only Cobbett's (1984) study of sugar-cane growers in Noodsberg (KwaZulu) and the studies of the Farmer Support Programmes in KaNgwane and Lebowa [*Singini and van Rooyen*, 1995] reported higher average proportions of income from agriculture.

Concomitant with a high contribution from agricultural is a relatively low contribution from wages, but what is most striking is the source of wage income. Approximately two-thirds of household wage income, on average, came from local (that is, resident or non-migrant) employment and one-third from migrant remittances, a clear reversal of past patterns in the homelands. All the studies cited in Chapter 2 dating from the 1980s [e.g., *P. Moll*, 1988: 316; *Nattrass and Nattrass*, 1990: 526] show levels of income from migrant remittances well in excess of local wage income, but more recent studies from throughout the homelands [e.g., *Weiner, Chimere-Dan and Levin*, 1994: 43; *Ardington and Lund*, 1995: 565] show the opposite. This can be related to contraction within many traditional employers of migrant labour (notably mining) since the mid-1980s, a rise in daily commuting and an expansion of public sector employment in the homelands, pointing to fundamental changes in the nature of the household economy in recent years [*Murray*, 1994: 32]. The total number of pensioners in the study was also exceptionally high, compared to other homeland studies, suggestive of an ageing but well-established population. Pensions are a vital source of cash income and an important source of investment in agriculture for many households. Overall, the irrigation scheme does not appear to have made participating households richer than those elsewhere in the homelands, but it seems likely that it has offered them an important foothold in the countryside and a supplementary source of income that has allowed them to survive and expand.

9.3   WIDER IMPLICATIONS OF THE STUDY

The formal end of apartheid clearly has not brought about a transformation of the agricultural economy in the homelands. The problems faced by black farmers in Tshiombo and elsewhere are deeply rooted in decades of exclusion from the advanced sectors of the economy and chronic lack of investment in the homelands, and can only be overcome through long-term structural change in the society and economy of South Africa. As this study has shown, however, there is considerable potential for the development of small-scale agriculture in the homelands but this will require a more differentiated view of rural development than has been applied to date and a radical re-evaluation of the role of the state and other institutions.

Meeting the needs of small-scale, poor and part-time farmers in the homelands will require considerable retraining and reorganisation in areas such as agricultural extension, but also the introduction of new services such as marketing advice and small-scale credit. Given the weakness of local organisations, only the state is in a position at present to lead such a process, although current policy direction is towards reducing the direct involvement of the state in the agricultural economy. Moreover, the capacity of the state to deliver services within the homelands is extremely weak. Therefore, attention must be paid to creating new forms of partnerships between the state and local entrepreneurs, co-operatives and individual farmers, with farmers themselves increasingly playing a leading role. Ploughing, transportation and the supply of agricultural inputs are areas where it may not be appropriate for the state to be directly involved in the longer term, but there will remain a need for training, credit and other forms of support to build the organisations and services required by farmers in the homelands. At the broader level, it will be necessary for public policy to re-evaluate the role of state agencies such as the Land Bank and the Agricultural Credit Board which continue to neglect small black farmers and their organisations.

This and other recent studies have identified strong demand for land within the homelands, for both residential and agricultural purposes, even though such demands have yet to be effectively articulated at the national political level. There are also signs of growing opposition to the role of the chiefs in the allocation of land, expressed through the emerging 'civics' and the recently-elected local government structures, although there would appear to be considerable support for retaining some form of communal tenure which provides access to land other than through the market.

As yet, the reform policies of the new government have had very limited impact in the 'deep rural' areas of the homelands. Government, at both the national and provincial levels, has shown great reluctance to throw its weight behind major changes in property rights or to confront the vested interests of white farmers and 'tribal' chiefs. Other, more broadly-based programmes, generally under the banner of the RDP, have begun to have some impact, particularly in the areas of public works and the supply of electricity and water to rural villages. The most important contribution to rural livelihoods, however, is likely to remain access to paid employment, although expansion in this area is likely to be very limited given current restrictions on public sector employment and the broader shift away from a low-skill labour-intensive economy.

Ultimately, neither the state nor any other body can hope to overcome the extremely peripheral status of the homelands, which will undoubtedly remain heavily dependent on the urban-industrial centres for the foreseeable future. While most rural households have some involvement in the urban economy at some stage, it is clear that many people want to live in the rural areas for at least part of their lives, to raise their children there and, ultimately, to retire there and enjoy the company of extended networks of family and friends in familiar surroundings.

The ability to do so, however, depends on access to land for residential and agricultural purposes, not as a principal source of income but as one part of a wider livelihood strategy. Given the present state of agriculture in the (former) homelands, and the relative poverty of much of the rural population, it is inappropriate to view land reform and support for small black farmers simply in terms of macro-economic development or the creation of a class of 'full-time commercial' farmers. The focus on full-time farming in much of the literature displays an inadequate understanding of agriculture within the homelands, which, in the great majority of cases, represents part of a household livelihood strategy that includes wage work, migrant remittances, pensions and various forms of petty commodity production. Even at a very small scale, agriculture can provide a valuable source of fresh foods that may not be available through the market and a vital safety-net during periods of unemployment, retirement, illness or other changes in the household's ability to generate income. Farmers such as those at Tshiombo, the majority of them 'part-time', have shown the ability to provide their households and the local area with a steady supply of fresh produce and a substantial contribution to income over many decades. There can be little doubt that with a more favourable policy environment they can continue to do so on an even greater scale.

APPENDICES

Organisations Consulted during the Study

African National Congress, Johannesburg
Agriven, Thohoyandou
Akanani Rural Development Association, Elim Hospital
Department of Land Affairs (RSA), Pretoria
Department of Water Affairs and Forestry (RSA), Tzaneen
Development Bank of Southern Africa, Midrand
Easy Farm Irrigation, Thohoyandou
Environmental Development Agency, Johannesburg
Giants Foods (Pty.) Ltd., Makhado
Greater Thohoyandou Urban Council
Independent Development Trust, Thohoyandou
Institute for Soil, Climate and Water, Pretoria
Land and Agriculture Policy Centre, Johannesburg
Lawyers for Human Rights, Pietersburg
Levubu Co-operative, Levubu
Makuya Tribal Authority, Ha-Makuya
Mashamba Co-operative, Mashamba
Mphaphuli Tribal Authority, Makwarela
Mulima Co-operative, Mulima
Murray Biesenbach and Badenhorst Inc., Pretoria
Mvlua Trust, Pietersburg
National African Farmers' Union (NAFU), Pietersburg
National Land Committee, Johannesburg
Nkuzi Development Association, Pietersburg
Northern Province Commission on Traditional Authorities, Pietersburg
Northern Province Department of Agriculture, Pietersburg and Thohoyandou
Northern Province Department of Land, Housing and Local Government, Thohoyandou
Northern Province Department of Tourism and Environment, Thohoyandou
Northern Transvaal Land Research Group, Elim Hospital
NTK Roller Mills, Shayandima
NTK Stores, Louis Trichardt
Rand Afrikaans University, Johannesburg
South African Weather Bureau, Pretoria

Tshiombo Co-operative, Tshiombo
Transvaal Rural Action Committee (TRAC), Johannesburg
University of the North, Turfloop
University of Venda (Univen), Thohoyandou
Venda Farmers' Supply Store (NTK), Shayandima
Venda Farmers' Union, Makhado
Venda Registrar of Co-operatives

Household Questionnaire, Version 2 (Tshiombo)

INTERVIEW NUMBER	PLOT NUMBER	DATE

NOTES

NAME OF PLOT-HOLDER   M/F

OBSERVATIONS – Location, land, services, general appearance, special status

1.1 How long have you or your family lived in this place; where did you live before and why did you move?

1.2 How much land do you have on the irrigation project, and what other land do members of your household have access to? When and how did you obtain it?

SECTION TWO: HOUSEHOLD COMPOSITION, OCCUPATIONS AND
SOURCES OF INCOME

2.1 Who lives in this household, some or all of the time, and what do they do?

TOTAL ADULTS:			TOTAL CHILDREN:
M/F	AGE	MARITAL STATUS	OCCUPATION AND INCOME/REMITTANCE
1.			
2.			
3.			
4.			
5.			
6.			
7.			
8.			
9.			
10.			
11.			
12.			
13.			
14.			
15.			
OTHERS			

2.2 What are the main sources of income for this household, and do you receive support from anyone outside the household?

SECTION THREE: CROPS

3.1 Outline how you have used your land over the past twelve months – crops planted, crops harvested .

MONTH	CROPS/AREAS PLANTED	CROPS/AREAS HARVESTED
April		
May		
June		
July		
August		
September		
October		
November		
December		
January		
February		
March		

3.2 What happened to the crops you harvested this year - how much of each was sold, and at what price; how much was consumed within the household?

CROP	VOLUME HARVESTED	VOLUME CONSUMED	VOLUME SOLD, AND WHERE	INCOME
1.				
2.				
3.				
4.				
5.				
6.				
7.				
8.				
OTHERS				

3.3 How many fruit trees do you have on your plot, or elsewhere? What type are they?

3.4 How much fruit did you harvest this year, and what did you do with it?

3.5 How do you market your crops?

3.6 What method of transport do you use to bring your goods to market, and how much does this cost you? Do you own, or have the use of, any vehicle?

3.7 How many of your household work on your land, and what tasks do they do?

3.8 Do you employ anyone from outside the household to work on your land? How often do they work, what tasks to they do and how much do you pay them?

SECTION FOUR - CROP INPUTS

4.1 How did you plough your land this year, and how much did it cost?

4.2 What other inputs have you used for your crops in the last year, and how much did they cost (3 main crops only)?

CROP/AREA	SEED	FERTILISER	CHEMICALS	OTHER
1.				
2.				
3.				
NOTES				

4.3 Where do you obtain your agricultural inputs?

4.4 Do you obtain goods on credit - amount, frequency, terms, repayments?

4.5 Do you use kraal manure on your land - where from, and how much does it cost?

SECTION FIVE - LIVESTOCK

5.1 What animals do you/your household own?

CATTLE	GOATS	DONKEYS	PIGS	FOWL

5.2 How has this changed much over the years, if at all?

5.3 What grazing do you use - location, quality of grass, fencing, water supply?

5.4 What animals and animal products have you consumed, sold or given away in the last year – when, why, income?

	CONSUMED	SOLD/GIVEN AWAY	INCOME/NOTES
CATTLE			
SHEEP/GOATS			
FOWL			
PIGS			
DONKEYS			
OTHER PRODUCE – Milk, eggs, etc.			

5.5 Have you bought any new stock this year – where, how many, at what prices?

5.6 What other expenses are involved in livestock production – dips, salts, feeds, medicines?

5.7 Have you lost any livestock due to drought, disease or theft in the past year?

SECTION SIX – GENERAL

6.1 Do you assist any other plot-holders with labour, ploughing, loan of animals or machinery, transport, seeds, or does anybody else assist you? What payment do you receive/make?

6.2 Are you a member of any farmers' associations, co-operatives, savings clubs, etc. – what benefits do they provide?

6.3 What assistance/advice/training do you receive from the agricultural officers on the scheme? Are you satisfied with the service they provide?

6.4 Does your household have as much land as it needs? Could you work more land than you have at present?

6.5 What are main problem facing farmers at Tshiombo today? – *list three*

1.	
2.	
3.	

6.6 What do you think the government (national, provincial or local) should be doing to help people in this area?

6.7 Do you think this area/scheme has changed much over the years you have been here – in what ways?

FINAL OBSERVATIONS

Agricultural Officers' Questionnaire, Tshiombo

Block Number	Name of Agricultural Officer	Date
Notes, observations		

1. How many plots are there on this Block – give plot reference numbers.

2. How many plot-holders are there on this Block – men, women?

3. How would you describe the supply of water on this Block – now and in general?

4. Do you think anything needs to be done to improve the supply of water?

5. What are the main sources of income for people on this Block?

6. Who are the biggest/best farmers on this Block?

7. How do they differ from the others, and how can you explain this?

8. How do plot-holders plough their land?

9. Where and how do plot-holders market their produce?

10. What would you estimate to be the average income per irrigated plot?

11. What would be the highest possible earnings?

12. What labour do people use (hired, household etc.)?

13. How are the plots on this Block allocated?

14. Is there much turn-over amongst plot-holders? When was the last time a plot on this Block changed hands?

15. Are there landless people trying to obtain land on this Block?

16. How many government officials/workers are employed on this block, and what do they do?

17. Do you feel you are able to provide a useful service to plot-holders?

18. What are the main problems you experience as an extension officer?

19. Do you consider the Tshiombo Scheme to be a success, and why?

20. What could be done (by government or others) to improve the prospects for agriculture in this area?

Bibliography

Acocks, J.P.H., 1988, *Veld Types of South Africa*, Pretoria: Botanical Research Institute.

African National Congress (ANC), 1994, *The Reconstruction and Development Programme: A Policy Framework*, Johannesburg: African National Congress.

Agriven, 1988, *Annual Report 1987–1988*, Thohoyandou: Agriven.

Amin, Nick and Henry Bernstein, 1996, *The Role of Agricultural Co-operatives in Agricultural and Rural Development*, Johannesburg: Land and Agricultural Policy Centre.

Ardington, E.M., 1984, *Poverty and Development in a Rural Community in KwaZulu*, Durban: Development Studies Unit, University of Natal.

Ardington, Elisabeth and Frances Lund, 1995, 'Pensions and Development: Social Security as Complementary to Programmes of Reconstruction and Development', *Development Southern Africa*, Vol.12, No.4.

Baber, Rupert, 1996, 'Current Livelihoods in Semi-Arid Rural Areas of South Africa', in M. Lipton, F. Ellis and M. Lipton (eds.), *Land, Labour and Livelihoods in Rural South Africa; Volume Two: KwaZulu-Natal and Northern Province*, Indicator Press: Durban.

Beinart, William, 1982, *The Political Economy of Pondoland 1860 to 1980*, Johannesburg: Ravan Press.

Beinart, William, 1992, 'Transkeian Smallholders and Agrarian Reform', *Journal of Contemporary African Studies*, Vol.11, No.2.

Beinart, William, 1994, *Twentieth-Century South Africa*, Oxford: Oxford University Press.

Beinart, William, and Colin Bundy, 1987, *Hidden Struggles in Rural South Africa*, London: James Currey.

Beinart, William, Delius, Peter and Stanley Trapido (eds.), 1986, *Putting a Plough to the Ground: Accumulation and Dispossession in Rural South Africa 1850–1930*, Johannesburg: Ravan Press.

Bembridge, T.J., 1985, 'Agriculture and Rural Development in LDCs, With Special Reference to South Africa', *Development Southern Africa*, Vol.2, No.3.

Bembridge, T.J., 1986, 'An Overview of Irrigation Development in Some Less Developed Countries of Africa', *Journal of Contemporary African Studies*, Vol. 5, No.1/2.

Bembridge, T.J., 1987, 'Successful Irrigation: Requirements for Successful Irrigation Projects with Special Reference to the Tyefu Irrigation Scheme', *Ciskei Agricultural Journal*, Vol.2, No.5.

Bembridge, T.J., 1988, *An Evaluation of the Venda Agricultural Extension Service*, Thohoyandou: Department of Agriculture and Forestry, Republic of Venda.

Bembridge, T.J., 1990, 'Agricultural Development in the Developing Areas of Southern Africa', *Africa Insight*, Vol.20, No.1.

Bennett, T.W., 1995, *Human Rights and African Customary Law Under the South African Constitution*, Cape Town: Juta.

BENSO (1979), *The Independent Venda*, Pretoria: Bureau for Economic Research: Co-Operation and Development; Johannesburg: Institute for Development Studies, Rand Afrikaans University.

Bernstein, Henry, 1992, 'Agrarian Reform in South Africa: Who? What? How?', paper to the tenth Ruth First Memorial Colloquium, University of the Western Cape.

Bernstein, Henry, 1996, 'South Africa's Agrarian Question: Extreme and Exceptional?', *The Journal of Peasant Studies*, Vol.23, Nos.2/3, Special Issue on 'The Agrarian Question in South Africa', edited by H. Bernstein.

Bernstein, Henry, 1996b, 'How White Agriculture (Re)Positioned Itself for a "New South Africa"', *Critical Sociology*, Vol.22, No.3.

Bonner, Philip, 1983, *Kings, Commoners and Concessionaires: The Evolution and Dissolution of the Nineteenth Century Swazi State*, Johannesburg: Ravan Press.

Booher, L.J., 1974, *Surface Irrigation*, Rome: Food and Agricultural Organisation.

Bradford, Helen, 1987, *A Taste of Freedom: The ICU in Rural South Africa, 1924–1930*, New Haven, CT and London: Yale University Press.

Bromberger, Norman, 1988, 'Cash-cropping, Subsistence, and Grazing: Prospect for Land Tenure in KwaZulu', in Cross and Haines (eds.) [1988].

Bromberger, Norman and Francis Antonie, 1993, 'Black Small Farmers in the Homelands: Economic Prospects and Policies', in M. Lipton and C. Simkins (eds.), *State and Market in Post Apartheid South Africa*, Oxford: Westview Press.

Brown, Barbara B., 1983, 'The Impact of Male Labour Migration on Women in Botswana', *African Affairs*, Vol.82, No.328.

Budlender, Geoff and Johan Latsky, 1991, 'Unravelling Rights to Land in Rural Race Zones', in M. de Klerk (ed.), *A Harvest of Discontent: The Land Question in South Africa*, Cape Town: Institute for a Democratic South Africa.

Bulpin, T.V., 1965, *Lost Trails of the Transvaal*, Cape Town: Books of Africa.

Bundy, Colin, 1979, *The Rise and Fall of the South African Peasantry*, London: Heinemann.

Burke, E.E. (ed.), 1969, *The Journals of Carl Mauch: His travels in the Transvaal and Rhodesia 1869–72*, Salisbury: National Archives of Rhodesia.

Butler, Jeffrey, Rotberg, Robert I. and John Adams, 1977, *The Black Homelands of South Africa: The Political and Economic Development of Bophuthatswana and KwaZulu*, Berkeley, CA: University of California Press.

Cadman, Vicki, 1986, 'Venda: A One Party State of Affairs', in *Indicator SA*, Vol.4, No.2.

Cairns, R.I. and Lea, J.D., 1990, 'An Agricultural Survey of Subsistence Farmers in the Nkandla District of KwaZulu', *Development Southern Africa*, Vol.7, No.1.

Callinicos, Luli, 1993, *A Place in the City: The Rand on the Eve of Apartheid. A*

People's History of South Africa, Volume 3, Johannesburg: Ravan Press.

Cartwright, A.P., 1974, *By the Waters of the Letaba: A History of the Transvaal Lowveld,* Cape Town: Purnell.

Casley, D.J. and D.A. Lury, 1987, *Data Collection in Developing Countries,* Oxford: Clarendon Press.

Cell, John, W., 1982, *The Highest Stage of White Supremacy: The Origins of Segregation in South Africa and the American South,* Cambridge: Cambridge University Press.

Chambers, Robert, 1992, *Rural Appraisal: Rapid, Relaxed and Participatory,* Brighton: Institute of Development Studies.

Charton, Nancy (ed.), 1980, *Ciskei: Economics and Politics of Dependence in a South African Homeland,* London: Croom Helm.

Cobbett, Matthew J., 1982, 'Agricultural and Social Change in KwaZulu South Africa: The Impact of Sugarcane Farming in the Noodsberg Sub-Region', Ph.D. thesis, London School of Economics.

Cobbett, Matthew, 1984, 'Sugarcane farming in KwaZulu: Two Communities Investigated', *Development Southern Africa,* Vol.1, Nos.3/4.

Cobbett, M., 1987, 'The Land Question in South Africa: A Preliminary Assessment', *The South African Journal of Economics,* Vol.55, No.1.

Cobbett, William and Robin Cohen (eds.), 1988, *Popular Struggles in South Africa,* London: Review of African Political Economy, James Currey.

Colvin, Paul M., 1985, 'Cattle Sales in KwaZulu: A Systems-Based Approach to an Improved Marketing Strategy', *Development Southern Africa,* Vol.2, No.3.

Cooper, David, 1988, 'Ownership and Control of Agriculture in South Africa', in J. Suckling and L. White (eds.), *After Apartheid: Renewal of the South African Economy,* London: James Curry.

Cooper, David, 1991, 'Agriculture in the Bantustans: Towards Development Policies', in M. De Klerk (ed.), *A Harvest of Discontent: The Land Question in South Africa,* Cape Town: Institute for a Democratic Alternative for South Africa.

Cooper, David, 1992, 'Apartheid in South African Agriculture', in A. Seidman, K. Wa Chimika Na Mwanza, N. Simeland and D. Weiner (eds.), *Transforming Southern African Agriculture,* Trenton NJ: Africa World Press.

Cousins, Ben, 1996, 'Livestock Production and Common Property Struggles in South Africa's Agrarian Reform', *The Journal of Peasant Studies,* Vol.23, Nos.2/3.

Cross, C.R., 1988, 'Credit, Mortgage, and Savings: What Does Rural Agriculture Need to Succeed?', in Cross and Haines (eds.) [1988].

Cross, Catherine and Richard J. Haines (eds.), 1988, *Towards Freehold: Options for Land and Development in South Africa's Black Rural Areas,* Cape Town: Juta.

Cross, Catherine and Peter Rutsch, 1995, 'Losing the Land: Securing Tenure in Tribal Areas', *Indicator SA,* Vol.12, No.2.

Crush, Jonathan, Jeeves, Alan and David Yudelman, 1991, *South Africa's Labour Empire: A History of Black Migrancy to the Gold Mines,* Oxford: Westview Press.

Das Neves, D. Fernandes, 1987, *A Hunting Expedition to the Transvaal,* Pretoria: State Library (originally published London: George Bell & Sons, 1879).

Davidson, Jean (ed.), 1988, *Agriculture, Women and Land: The African Experience*, London: Westview Press.

Davidson, J.H. and Stacey, G.D., 1988, 'A Potato a Day from the Pensioner's Pay? Hawking at Pension Payout Points', *Development Southern Africa*, Vol.5, No.2.

DBSA, 1986, *Venda Information File*, Midrand: Development Bank of Southern Africa.

DBSA, 1987, *Statistical Abstracts: SATBVC Countries*, Sandton: Development Bank of Southern Africa.

DBSA, 1989, *Economic and Social Memorandum Region G*, Halfway House: Development Bank of Southern Africa.

DBSA, 1991, *Development Information: Region G; 6.1 Agriculture and Forestry*, Midrand: Development Bank of Southern Africa.

DBSA, 1993a, *Statistics on Living Standards and Development Regional Poverty Profile: Eastern and Northern Transvaal*, Halfway House: Development Bank of Southern Africa.

DBSA, 1993b, *Venda Development Perspective* (draft), Midrand: Development Bank of Southern Africa.

DBSA, 1994, *South Africa's Nine Provinces: A Human Development Profile*, Halfway House: Development Bank of Southern Africa.

Dederen, J.M., 1992, *An Evaluation of the FSP in Venda: Interim Report*, Thohoyandou: University of Venda.

Dederen, J.M., 1993, *Supplementary Report: FSP Venda*, Thohoyandou: University of Venda.

de Klerk, Michael, 1984, 'Seasons That Will Never Return: The Impact of Farm Mechanisation on Employment, Incomes and Population Distribution in the Western Transvaal', *Journal of South African Studies*, Vol.11, No.1.

de Klerk, Michael, 1991, 'The Accumulation Crisis in Agriculture', in S. Gelb (ed.), *South Africa's Economic Crisis*, Cape Town: David Philip; London: Zed Books.

de Vaus, D.A., 1986, *Surveys in Social Research*, London: George Allen & Unwin.

de Wet, Chris, 1995, *Moving Together Drifting Apart: Betterment Planning and Villagisation in a South African Homeland*, Johannesburg: Witwatersrand University Press.

de Wet, Chris J. and P.A. McAllister, 1983, *Rural Communities in Transition: A Study of the Socio-Economic and Agricultural Implications of Agricultural Betterment and Development*, Grahamstown: Institute of Social and Economic Research (Development Studies Working Paper No.16).

Delius, Peter, 1980, 'Migrant Labour and the Pedi, 1840–80', in S. Marks and A. Atmore (eds.), *Economy and Society in Pre-Industrial South Africa*, London: Longman.

Delius, Peter 1983, *The Land Belongs to Us: The Pedi Polity, the Boers and the British in the Nineteenth Century Transvaal*, Johannesburg: Ravan Press.

Delius, Peter, 1993, 'Migrant Organisation, the Communist Party, the ANC and the Sekhukhuneland Revolt 1940–1958', in P. Bonner, P. Delius and D. Posel (eds.),

Apartheid's Genesis, 1935–1962, Johannesburg: Ravan and Witwatersrand University Press.

Delius, Peter, 1996, *A Lion Amongst the Cattle: Reconstruction and Resistance in the Northern Transvaal*, Johannesburg: Ravan Press.

Department of Land Affairs (South Africa), 1996, *Our Land: Green Paper on South African Land Policy*, Pretoria: Department of Land Affairs.

Department of Water Affairs and Forestry (South Africa), Unpublished streamflow reports for the Mutale River, Tzaneen.

Desmond, Cosmas, 1971, *The Discarded People: An Account of African Resettlement*, London: Penguin.

Drew, Allison, 1996, 'The Theory and Practice of the Agrarian Question in South African Socialism, 1928–60', *The Journal of Peasant Studies*, Vol.23, No.2/3.

Dubow, Saul, 1989, *Racial Segregation and the Origins of Apartheid in South Africa 1919–36*, Oxford: Macmillan, in association with St. Antony's College, Oxford.

Dzivhani, S.M., 1940, 'The Chiefs of Venda', in N.J. van Warmelo, *The Copper Miners of Musina and the Early History of the Zoutpansberg*, Pretoria: Department of Native Affairs.

Eales, K.A., 1993, *Administrative Requirements: Homelands*, Johannesburg: Land and Agricultural Policy Centre.

Elphick, Richard, 1977, *Kraal and Cattle: Khoikhoi and the Founding of White South Africa*, London: Yale University Press.

Fenyes, T.I. and J.A. Groenewald, 1985, 'Aspects of Agricultural Marketing in Lebowa', *Development Southern Africa*, Vol.2, No.3.

Ferguson, James, 1994, *The Anti-Politics Machine: 'Development', Depoliticisation and Bureaucratic Power in Lesotho*, Minneapolis, MN: University of Minnesota Press.

Fischer, A., 1987, 'Land Tenure in Mhala: Official Wisdom "Locked Up" in Tradition and People "Locked Up" in Development', *Development Southern Africa*, Vol.4, No.3.

Fouché, Leo (ed.), 1937, *Mapungubwe: Ancient Bantu Civilisation on the Limpopo*, Cambridge: Cambridge University Press.

Fraser, G.C.G., 1994, 'Provision of Accessible Marketing and Extension Services in Less-Developed Agriculture', *Development Southern Africa*, Vol.11, No.1.

Fredrickson, George, M., 1981, *White Supremacy: A Comparative Study in American and South African History*, Oxford: Oxford University Press.

Gaigher, M.J., van Rensburg, H.C.J. and A.N.J. Bester, 1995, 'Health and Development: The Venda Care Group Organisation', *Development Southern Africa*, Vol.12, No.2.

Greenberg, Stanley, 1980, *Race and Class in Capitalist Development: Comparative Perspectives*, New Haven, CT: Yale University Press.

Haines, Richard and C.R. Cross, 1988, 'An Historical Overview of Land Policy and Tenure in South Africa's Black Areas', in Cross and Haines (eds.) [1988].

Haines, Richard and C.P.G. Tapscott, 1988, 'The Silence of Poverty: Tribal

Administration and Development in Rural Transkei', in Cross and Haines (eds.) [1988].

Hall, Martin, 1990, *Farmers, Kings and Traders: The People of Southern Africa 200–1860*, Chicago, IL: University of Chicago Press.

Harries, Patrick, 1987, '"A Forgotten Corner of the Transvaal": Reconstructing the History of a Relocated Community through Oral Testimony and Song', in B. Bozzoli (ed.), *Class, Community and Conflict*, Johannesburg: Ravan.

Harries, Patrick, 1989, 'Exclusion, Classification and Internal Colonialism: The Emergence of Ethnicity Amongst the Tsonga-speakers of South Africa', in Leroy Vail (ed.), *The Creation of Tribalism in Southern Africa*, London: James Currey.

Hendricks, Fred T., 1990, *The Pillars of Apartheid: Land Tenure, Rural Planning and the Chieftaincy*, Uppsala: University of Uppsala.

Heron, G.S., 1991, 'The Household, Economic Differentiation and Agricultural Production in Shixini, Transkei', *Development Southern Africa*, Vol.8, No.1.

Hill, Christopher R., 1964, *Bantustans: The Fragmentation of South Africa*, London: Institute of Race Relations and Oxford University Press.

Hirson, Baruch, 1989, *Yours for the Union: Class and Community Struggles in South Africa, 1930–1947*, London: Zed Books.

Horrell, Muriel, 1973, *The African Homelands of South Africa*, Johannesburg: South African Institute of Race Relations.

Houghton, D. Hobart, 1973, *The South African Economy*, London: Oxford University Press.

Huffman, Thomas N. and Edwin O. Hanisch, 1987, 'Settlement Hierarchies in the Northern Transvaal: Zimbabwe Ruins and Venda History', *African Studies*, Vol.46, No.1.

Indicator SA (no author), 1994, 'Election Results', *Indicator South Africa*, Vol.11, No.3.

ISCW, 1996, *Land Type Map 2230 Messina* and Accompanying *Memoir*, Pretoria: Institute of Soil Climate and Water.

James, Deborah, 1985, 'Family and Household in a Lebowa Village', *African Studies*, Vol.44, No.2.

Jaques, A.A., 1931, 'Notes on the Lemba Tribe of the Northern Transvaal', *Anthropos*, Vol.25.

Jeannerat, Caroline, 1997, 'Invoking the Female *Vusha* Ceremony and the Struggle for Identity in Tshiendeulu, Venda', *Journal of Contemporary African Studies*, Vol.15, No.1.

Jeeves, Alan H., 1985, *Migrant Labour in South Africa's Mining Economy: The Struggle for the Gold Mines' Labour Supply, 1890–1920*, Kingston Ontario: McGill-Queen's University Press.

Keegan, Timothy, J., 1986, *Rural Transformations in Industrialising South Africa: The Southern Highveld to 1914*, Johannesburg: Ravan Press.

Keenan, Jeremy and Mike Sarakinsky, 1987, 'Reaping the Benefits: Working Condition in Agriculture and the Bantustans', in G. Moss and I Obery (eds.), *South*

African Review 4, Johannesburg: Ravan Press.

Kirsten, J.F., Sartorius von Bach, H.J. and van J. Zyl, 1995. 'The Farmer Support Programme in Venda', in R. Singini and J. van Rooyen (eds.), *Serving Small Farmers: An Evaluation of the DBSA's Farmer Support Programmes*, Halfway House: Development Bank of Southern Africa.

Klu, Johnson, 1994, 'Agricor and Rural Development in Bophuthatswana', in Levin and Weiner (eds.) [1994].

Knight, J.B. and G. Lenta, 1980, 'Has Capitalism Underdeveloped the Labour Reserves of South Africa?', *Oxford Bulletin of Economics and Statistics*, Vol.452, No.3.

Koch, Eddie and Ritchken, Edwin, 1988, 'General Strike in Venda: "The Boys are Doing a Good Job"', *South African Labour Bulletin*, Vol.13, No.7.

Krige, E. Jensen and J.D. Krige, 1943, *The Realm of the Rain-Queen: A Study of the Pattern of Lovedu Society*, London: Oxford University Press.

Kuper, Adam, 1982, *Wives for Cattle: Bridewealth and Marriage in Southern Africa*, London: Routledge & Kegan Paul.

Lacey, Marian, 1981, *Working for Boroko: The Origins of a Coercive Labour System in South Africa*, Johannesburg: Ravan Press.

Lahiff, Edward, 1997, *Land, Water and Local Governance in South Africa: A Case Study of the Mutale River Valley*, Manchester: Institute for Development Policy and Management.

Land and Agricultural Policy Centre, 1995, *Provincial Overview: Northern Transvaal*, Johannesburg: Land and Agricultural Policy Centre. Working Paper 24.

Land Research Group, 1995, *Land Reform Research Programme: District Report, Far North*, Elim: Northern Transvaal Land Research Group.

Lestrade, G.P., 1932, 'Some Notes on the Ethnic History of the VhaVenda and Their Rhodesian Affinities', in N.J. van Warmelo (ed.), *Contributions Towards Venda History, Religion and Tribal Ritual*, Pretoria: Department of Native Affairs.

Letsoalo, Essy M., 1987, *Land Reform in South Africa: A Black Perspective*, Johannesburg: Skotaville.

Levin, Richard and Sam Mkhabel, 1994, 'The Chieftaincy, Land Allocation and Democracy in the Central Lowveld', in Levin and Weiner (eds.) [1994].

Levin, Richard, Russon, Ray and Daniel Weiner, 1994, 'Social Differentiation in South Africa's Bantustans: Class, Gender and the Politics of Agrarian Transition', in Levin and Weiner (eds.) [1994].

Levin, Richard and Daniel Weiner, 1991, 'The Agrarian Question and the Emergence of Conflicting Agricultural Strategies in South Africa', in S. Matlhape and A. Munz (eds.), *Towards a New Agrarian Democratic Order*, Amsterdam: SAERT.

Levin, Richard and Daniel Weiner, 1994, 'Towards the Development of a Participatory Rural Land Reform Programme in a Democratic South Africa', in Levin and Weiner (eds.) [1994].

Levin, Richard and Daniel Weiner, 1996 'The Politics of Land Reform in South Africa after Apartheid: Perspectives, Problems, Prospects', *The Journal of Peasant Studies*, Vol.23, Nos.2/3.

Levin, Richard and Daniel Weiner (eds.), 1994, *Community Perspectives on Land and*

Agrarian Reform in South Africa (Report to the John D. and Catherine T. MacArthur Foundation, Chicago).

Levin, Richard and Daniel Weiner, 1997, 'From Apartheid to Development', in R. Levin and D. Weiner (eds.), *No More Tears: Struggles for Land in Mpumalanga, South Africa*, Trenton, NJ: Africa World Press.

Lipton, Merle, 1977, 'South Africa: Two Agricultures?' in F. Wilson, A. Kooy and D. Hendrie (eds.), *Farm Labour in South Africa*, Cape Town: David Philip.

Lipton, Merle, 1986, *Capitalism and Apartheid: South Africa 1910–1986*, Aldershot: Wildwood House.

Lodge, Tom, 1983, *Black Politics in South Africa since 1945*, Harlow: Longman

Lyne, M.C. and W.L. Nieuwoudt, 1991, 'Inefficient Land Use in KwaZulu: Causes and Remedies', *Development Southern Africa*, Vol.8, No.2.

Lyster, David Mark, 1990, 'Agricultural Marketing in KwaZulu: A Farm-Household Perspective', MSc. thesis, Department of Agricultural Economics, University of Natal Pietermaritzburg.

Maize Board, 1992, *Annual Report 1991/92*, Pretoria: The Maize Board.

Maize Board, 1994, *Annual Report 1993/94*, Pretoria: The Maize Board.

Makhanya, Edward, 1994, 'The Economics of Small-holder Sugar Cane Production in Natal', in Levin and Weiner (eds.) [1994].

Maliba, A.M., 1981, 'The Conditions of the Venda People', pamphlet issued by the Johannesburg District Committee of the Communist Party, Dec. 1939 (Reprinted in *South African Communists Speak: Documents from the History of the South African Communist Party 1915–1980*), London: Inkululeko Publications.

Maloka, Tshidiso, 1996, 'Populism and the Politics of Chieftaincy and Nation-Building in the New South Africa', *Journal of Contemporary African Studies*, Vol.14, No.2.

Marais, J.N., 1989, 'Sequential Maize Planting: A Cropping Strategy for the Small Farmer', *Development Southern Africa*, Vol.6, No.3.

Marcus, Tessa, 1989, *Modernising Super-Exploitation: Restructuring South African Agriculture*, London: Zed Books.

Marcus, Tessa, Eales, Kathy and Adele Wildschut, 1996, *Down to Earth: Land Demand in the New South Africa*, Johannesburg: Land and Agricultural Policy Centre; Durban: Indicator Press.

Marks, Shula, 1975, 'Southern Africa and Madagascar', in R. Gray (ed.), *The Cambridge History of Africa, Volume 4*, Cambridge: Cambridge University Press.

Marks, S. and S. Trapido, 1981, 'Lord Milner and the South African State', in P. Bonner (ed.), *Working Papers in Southern African Studies, Volume 2*, Johannesburg: Ravan.

Martin, William G. and Mark Beittel, 1987, 'The Hidden Abode of Reproduction: Conceptualising Households in Southern Africa', *Development and Change*, Vol.18, No.2.

May, Julian, 1989, 'Differentiation and Inequality in the Bantustans: Evidence from KwaZulu', *Social Dynamics*, Vol.13, No.2.

Mbeki, Govan, 1984, *South Africa: The Peasants' Revolt*, London: International Defence and Aid Fund for Southern Africa. (originally published by Penguin, 1964).

McAllister, P.A., 1989, 'Resistance to "Betterment" in the Transkei: A Case Study from Willowvale District', *Journal of Southern African Studies*, Vol.15, No.2.

McCaul, C., 1987, *Satellite in Revolt: KwaNdebele, an Economic and Political Profile*, Johannesburg: South African Institute of Race Relations.

McCracken, J., Pretty, N. and G. Conway, 1988, *An Introduction to Rapid Rural Appraisal for Agricultural Development*, London: International Institute for Environment and Development.

McIntosh, Alastair, 1995, 'The Rural Local Government Question in South Africa: Prospects for Locally Based Development', *Development Southern Africa*, Vol.12, No.3.

McIntosh, Alastair and Anne Vaughan, 1995, 'State-centred commercial smallholder development: Haves and have-nots in KaNgwane', *Development Southern Africa*, Vol.12, No.1.

Mfono, Z.N., 1989, 'Women In Rural Development in Venda, *Development Southern Africa*, Vol.6, No.4.

Moll, Peter, 1988, 'Transition to Freehold in the Reserves', in Cross and Haines (eds.) [1988].

Moll, Terence, 1988, *No Blade of Grass: Rural Production and State Intervention in Transkei, 1925–1960*, Cambridge: African Studies Centre.

Moodie, T. Dunbar (with Vivienne Ndatshe), 1994, *Going for Gold: Men, Mines and Migration*, Berkeley, CA: University of California Press.

Moody, Elize and Christina Golino, 1984, *Area Study on Venda*, Second Carnegie Inquiry into Poverty and Development in Southern Africa, Paper No.251. Cape Town: SALDRU.

Moris, Jon R. and Thom, Derrick J., 1990, *Irrigation Development in Africa: Lessons of Experience*, Boulder, CO and London: Westview Press.

Morris, M.L., 1976, 'The Development of Capitalism in South African Agriculture: Class Struggle in the Countryside', *Economy and Society*, Vol.5, No.3.

Mpanza, Zamakhosi and Jill Nattrass, 1987, *Poverty, Migration and Unemployment in Dumisa: A Rural Area of KwaZulu*, Durban: Development Studies Unit, University of Natal.

Murray, Colin G., 1981, *Families Divided: The Impact of Migrant Labour in Lesotho*, Cambridge: Cambridge University Press.

Murray, Colin, 1987, 'Displaced Urbanisation: South Africa's Rural Slums', *African Affairs*, Vol.86, No.344.

Murray, Colin, 1992, *Black Mountain: Land, Class and Power in the Eastern Orange Free State, 1880s to 1980s*, Edinburgh: Edinburgh University Press.

Murray, Colin and Gavin William, 1994, 'Land and Freedom in South Africa'. *Review of African Political Economy*, No.61.

Murray, Martin J., 1994, *Revolution Deferred: The Painful Birth of Post-Apartheid South Africa*, London: Verso.

Murray, Martin, 1995, ' "Blackbirding" at "Crooks' Corner": Illicit Labour Recruiting in the Northeastern Transvaal, 1910–1940', *Journal of Southern African Studies*, Vol.21, No.3.

Murray Biesenbach and Badenhorst, 1987, *Report on the Upgrading of the Tshiombo and Rambuda Irrigation Scheme*, Tzaneen: Murray Biesenbach & Badenhorst Inc.

Murray Biesenbach and Badenhorst, 1989, *Venda Farmer Support Programme: Tshiombo and Rambuda Farmer Support Projects*, Pretoria: Murray, Biesenbach & Badenhorst Inc.

Mutshekwane, M., 1993, 'Settlement Patterns in Thohoyandou Magisterial District, Venda', M.A. thesis, University of Venda.

Naledzani, A.T., 1992, 'The Farmer Support Programme and Agricultural Development in Venda', Ph.D. thesis, Department of Agricultural Economics, University of Pretoria.

National Land Committee, 1990, *The Bantustans in Crisis*, Johannesburg: National Land Committee.

Nattrass, Jill, 1988, *The South African Economy: Its Growth and Change*, Cape Town: Oxford University Press.

Nattrass, Jill and Julian May, 1986, 'Migration and Dependency: Sources and Levels of Income in KwaZulu', *Development Southern Africa*, Vol.3, No.4.

Nattrass, Nicoli and Jill Nattrass, 1990, 'South Africa, the Homelands and Rural Development', *Development Southern Africa*, Vol.7, No.4.

Nemudzivhadi, M., 1985, *When and What: An introduction to the Evolution of the History of Venda*, Thohoyandou: Office of the President.

Nieuwenhuysen, J.P., 1964, 'Economic Policy in the Reserves since the Tomlinson Report', *South African Journal of Economics*, Vol.32, No.1.

Northern Province, 1996, *Report of the Commission of Inquiry into Witchcraft Violence and Ritual Murders in the Northern Province of the Republic of South Africa*, Pietersburg: Government of the Northern Province.

O'Keeffe, J.H., Uys, M. and M.N. Bruton, 1992, 'Freshwater Systems', in R.F. Fuggle and M.A. Rabie (eds.), *Environmental Management in South Africa*, Cape Town: Juta.

Peil, Margaret (with R. Mitchell and D. Rimmer), 1982, *Social Science Research Methods: An African Handbook*, London: Hodder & Stoughton.

Platzky, L. and C. Walker, (for the Surplus People Project), 1985, *The Surplus People: Forced Removals in South Africa*, Johannesburg: Ravan Press.

Pretorius, 1994, 'A Socio-Economic Analysis of the Communal Land Tenure System in Venda', M.Sc. thesis, Department of Agricultural Economics, Extension and Rural Development, University of Pretoria.

Ralushai, V.N.M.V., 1977, 'Conflicting Accounts of Venda History with Particular Reference to the Role of *Mutupo* in Social Organisation', Ph.D. thesis, Queens University, Belfast.

Ramphele, Mamphela, 1995, *A Life*, Cape Town: David Philip.

RAU, 1979, *Planning Proposals for Venda, Vol.1*, Johannesburg: Institute of Development Studies, Rand Afrikaans University.

Registrar of Co-operatives, 1995, 'Tshiombo Co-operative Limited: Visit Report', unpublished paper, Office of the Registrar of Co-operatives, Pretoria.

Republic of Venda, 1993a, *Statistical Report No.1 of 1993: Population Census, 1991,*

Thohoyandou: Republic of Venda, Statistics Division.

Republic of Venda, 1993b, Unpublished Census Data: Population Census, 1991, Thohoyandou: Republic of Venda, Statistics Division.

Robertson, Michael, 1989, 'Dividing the Land: An Introduction to Apartheid Land Law', in C. Murray and C. O'Regan (eds.), *No Place to Rest: Forced Removals and the Law in South Africa*, Cape Town: Oxford University Press.

Rogers, Barbara, 1976, *Divide and Rule: South Africa's Bantustans*, London: International Defence and Aid Fund for Southern Africa.

Roodt, M.J., 1988, 'Bophuthatswana's State Farming Projects: Is Failure Inevitable?', in Cross and Haines (eds.) [1988].

SAIRR, 1994, *Race Relations Survey 1993/94*, Johannesburg: South African Institute of Race Relations.

SAIRR, 1996, *South Africa Survey 1995/96*, Johannesburg: South African Institute of Race Relations.

SALDRU, 1994, *South Africans Rich and Poor: Baseline Household Statistics*, Cape Town: SALDRU, University of Cape Town.

Schmidt, M.I., 1992, 'The Relationship between Cattle and Savings: A Cattle-Owner Perspective', *Development Southern Africa*, Vol.9, No.4.

Schutte, A.G., 1984, *Poverty and Rural Deterioration: Two Case Studies from Post-'Independence' Venda*, Second Carnegie Inquiry into Poverty and Development in Southern Africa, Paper No.64. Cape Town: SALDRU.

Sender, John and Deborah Johnston, 1995, *A Fuzzy Snapshot of Some Poor and Invisible Women: Farm Labourers in South Africa*, Department of Economics Working Paper No.56. London: School of Oriental and African Studies.

Shackleton, C.M., 1993, 'Are the Communal Grazing Lands in Need of Saving?', *Development Southern Africa*, Vol.10, No.1.

Sharp, John and Andrew Spiegel, 1990, 'Women and Wages: Gender and the Control of Income in Farm and Bantustan Households', *Journal of Southern African Studies*, Vol.16, No.3.

Shuma, 1988, 'Aid Programme for Farmers'. *Journal of the Venda Development Corporation Ltd. and the Venda Agricultural Corporation Ltd.*, Thohoyandou.

Simkins, Charles, 1981, 'Agricultural Production in the African Reserves of South Africa, 1918–1969', *Journal of Southern African Studies*, Vol.7, No.2.

Simkins, Charles, 1984, *What has been Happening to Income Distribution and Poverty in the Homelands?* Second Carnegie Inquiry into Poverty and Development in Southern Africa, Paper No.7, Cape Town: SALDRU.

Singini, Richard and Johan van Rooyen (eds.), 1995, *Serving Small-Scale Farmers: An Evaluation of the DBSA's Farmer Support Programmes*, Halfway House: Development Bank of Southern Africa.

Sonntag, Christoph (no date), *My Friend Maleboch, Chief of the Blue Mountains: An Eye-Witness Account of the Maleboch War of 1894 from the Diary of Christoph Sonntag* (adapted and translated from the German by K. Sonntag), Pretoria: K.C.G. Sonntag.

South African Weather Bureau, Various unpublished reports from meteorological stations in the northern Transvaal, Pretoria.

Southall, Roger, 1982, *South Africa's Transkei: The Political Economy of an 'Independent' Bantustan*, London: Heinemann.

Spiegel, Andrew D., 1980, 'Changing Patterns of Migrant Labour and Rural Differentiation in Lesotho', *Social Dynamics*, Vol.6, No.2.

Spiegel, Andrew D., 1986, 'The Fluidity of Household Composition in Matatiele, Transkei: A Methodological Problem', *African Studies*, Vol.45, No.1.

Spiegel, Andrew D., 1988, 'The Ambiguities of Betterment: A Transkei Case Study', *African Studies*, Vol.47, No.2.

Standing, Guy, Sender, John and John Weeks, 1996, *Restructuring the Labour Market: The South African Challenge*, Geneva: International Labour Office.

Starkey, Paul, 1995, *Animal Traction in South Africa: Empowering Rural Communities*, Halfway House: Development Bank of Southern Africa.

Stayt, Hugh A., 1968, *The Bavenda*, London: Frank Cass (originally published by Oxford University Press, 1931).

Steenkamp, H.A., 1989, *Regional Population Estimates for 1989*, Pretoria: Bureau of Market Research.

Stewart, D.A. and M.C. Lyne, 1988, 'Socio-Economic Characteristics of the Rural Population in Gcumisa Ward, KwaZulu', *Development Southern Africa*, Vol.5, No.2.

Steyn, G.J. 1988, 'A Farming Systems Study of Two Rural Areas in the Peddie District of Ciskei'. D.Sc. thesis, Faculty of Agriculture, University of Fort Hare.

Surplus People Project, 1983, *Forced Removals in South Africa: Volume 5, The Transvaal*, Cape Town: Surplus People Project.

Tapson, D.R., 1990, 'Rural Development and the Homelands', *Development Southern Africa*, Vol.7, No.4.

Thompson, Leonard, 1969, 'The High Veld', in M. Wilson and L. Thompson (eds.), *The Oxford History of South Africa, Volume 1*, London: Oxford University Press.

Thompson, Leonard, 1971, 'The Subjection of the African Chiefdoms: 1870–1898', in M. Wilson and L. Thompson (eds.), *The Oxford History of South Africa, Volume 2*, London: Oxford University Press.

Thompson, Leonard, 1995, *A History of South Africa*, New Haven, CT: Yale University Press.

Thormeyer, Thilo, 1989, 'Socio-Economic Criteria for the Assessment of Smallholder Agricultural Schemes in South African Homelands', M.Sc. thesis, Department of Agricultural Economics, University of Natal, Pietermaritzberg.

Todaro, Michael P., 1989, *Economic Development in the Third World*, Fourth Edition, Harlow: Longman.

Trapido, S., 1971, 'South Africa in a Comparative Study of Industrialisation', *The Journal of Development Studies*, Vol.7, No.3.

TURP (Trade Union Research Project), 1994, *A User's Guide to the South African Economy*, Durban: Y Press.

Turrell, Robert, 1987, *Capital and Labour on the Kimberley Diamond Fields 1871–1890*, Cambridge: Cambridge University Press.

Union of South Africa, 1932, *Report of the Native Economic Commission 1930–1932* (U.G. 22/1932), Pretoria: The Government Printer.

Union of South Africa, 1955, *Summary of the Report of the Commission for the Socio-Economic Development of the Bantu Areas within the Union of South Africa* (UG 61/1955). [The Tomlinson Report] Pretoria: The Government Printer.

van der Berg, Servaas, 1985, 'An Overview of Development in the Homelands', in H. Gillomee and L. Schlemmer (eds.), *Up Against the Fences: Poverty, Passes and Privilege in South Africa*, Cape Town: David Philip.

van der Waal, C S, 1991, 'District Development and Closer Settlement Economy in Gazankulu', *Development Southern Africa*, Vol.8, No.3.

van der Waal, C.S., 1996, 'Rural Children and Residential Instability in the Northern Province of South Africa', *Social Dynamics*, Vol.22, No.1.

van Kessel, Ineke, 1993, ' "From Confusion to Lusaka": The Youth Revolt in Sekhukhuneland', *Journal of Southern African Studies*, Vol.19, No.4.

van Nieuwenhuizen, E.F.J., 1984, *A Socio-economic Survey in Tzikundamalema (Venda): An Interim Report*, Second Carnegie Inquiry into Poverty and Development in Southern Africa, Paper No.63. Cape Town: SALDRU.

van Rooyen, C.J, Vink, N. and N.T. Christodoulou, 1987, 'Access to the Agricultural Market for Small Farmers in Southern Africa: The Farmer Support Programme', *Development Southern Africa*, Vol.4, No.2.

van Vuuren, C.J., 1988, 'Community Gardens as Food Producing Units', *Development Southern Africa*, Vol.5, No.1.

van Warmelo, N.J., 1940, *The Copper Miners of Musina and the Early History of the Zoutpansberg*, Pretoria: Union of South Africa, Department of Native Affairs.

van Zyl, Johan and Johan van Rooyen, 1991, 'Agricultural Production in South Africa', in M. de Klerk (ed.), *A Harvest of Discontent: The Land Question in South Africa*, Cape Town: Institute for a Democratic Alternative for South Africa.

Vaughan, Anne, 1991, 'Cane, Class and Credit: Small Growers in the Glendale Area', *Antipode*, Vol.23, No.1.

Vink, Nicholas, 1986, 'An Institutional Approach to Livestock Development in Southern Africa', Ph.D. thesis, University of Stellenbosch.

Vink, N. and W.E. Kassie, 1987, 'The "Tragedy of the Commons" and Livestock Farming in Southern Africa', *South African Journal of Economics*, Vol.55, No.2.

Wagner, Roger, 1980, 'Zoutpansberg: The Dynamics of a Hunting Frontier, 1848–67', in S. Marks and A. Atmore (eds.), *Economy and Society in Pre-Industrial South Africa*, London: Longman.

Watkinson, Eric, 1996, 'Enforced Agricultural Change in South Africa: The Emergence of a Small Class of Commercial African Farmers', Master's thesis, Development Studies, University of Natal.

Weiner, Daniel, Chimere-Dan, O. and Richard Levin, 1994, 'Results of the CPLAR Bantustan Socio-Economic Survey', in Levin and Weiner (eds.) [1994].

Welsh, David, 1971, *The Roots of Segregation: Native Policy in Colonial Natal, 1845–1910*, London: Oxford University Press.

Wessmann, R., 1908, *The Bawenda of the Spelonken (Transvaal): A Contribution towards the Psychology and Folk-lore of African Peoples*, London: The African World.

Westaway, Ashley, 1995, *Land and Local Government: Policy Paper 27*, Johannesburg: Land and Agricultural Policy Centre.

Whiteford, Andrew and Michael McGrat, 1994, *The Distribution of Income in South Africa*, Pretoria: Human Sciences Research Council.

Wilson, Francis, 1971, 'Farming, 1866–1966', in M. Wilson and L. Thompson (eds.), *The Oxford History of South Africa, Volume 2*, Oxford: Oxford University Press.

Wilson, Francis, 1972, *Migrant Labour*, Johannesburg: South African Council of Churches and SPRO-CAS.

Wilson, Francis and Mamphela Ramphele, 1989, *Uprooting Poverty: The South African Challenge*, Report for the Second Carnegie Inquiry into Poverty and Development in Southern Africa. Cape Town: David Philip.

Wilson, Monica, 1969, 'The Sotho, Venda and Tsonga', in M. Wilson and L. Thompson (eds.), *The Oxford History of South Africa, Volume 1*, London: Oxford University Press.

Wolpe, Harold, 1972, 'Capitalism and Cheap Labour-Power in South Africa: From Segregation to Apartheid', *Economy and Society*, Vol.1, No.4.

Worger, William H., 1987, *South Africa's City of Diamonds: Mine Workers and Monopoly Capitalism in Kimberley, 1867–1895*, New Haven, CT: Yale University Press.

World Bank, 1994, *South African Agriculture: Structure, Performance and Options for the Future*, Washington, DC: World Bank.

Yawitch, Joanne, 1981. *Betterment: The Myth of Homeland Agriculture*, Johannesburg: South African Institute of Race Relations.

Yudelman, David, 1983, *The Emergence of Modern South Africa: State, Capital and the Incorporation of Organised Labour on the South African Gold Fields, 1902–1939*, Westport, CT: Greenwood Press.

Index

Printed in the United States
by Baker & Taylor Publisher Services